ANYA SETON

A Writing Life

LUCINDA H. MacKETHAN

CHICAGO
REVIEW
PRESS

In memory of Pamela Cottier Forcey
beloved daughter, mother, sister, editor, friend
November 3, 1925–April 26, 2019

Copyright © 2020 by Lucinda H. MacKethan
All rights reserved
Published by Chicago Review Press Incorporated
814 North Franklin Street
Chicago, Illinois 60610
ISBN 978-1-64160-086-6

Library of Congress Cataloging-in-Publication Data

Names: MacKethan, Lucinda Hardwick, author.
Title: Anya Seton : a writing life / Lucinda H. MacKethan.
Description: Chicago, Illinois : Chicago Review Press, [2020] | Includes
   bibliographical references and index. | Summary: "The first book-length
   biography of bestselling author Anya Seton, the top historical novelist
   of her era and still widely beloved today. With the support of Seton's
   daughters and her personal journal entries and letters, Lucinda H.
   MacKethan explores the hidden depths of not only this writer's beloved
   works but also her renowned research process and a life full of inner
   turmoil"— Provided by publisher.
Identifiers: LCCN 2020017267 (print) | LCCN 2020017268 (ebook) | ISBN
   9781641600866 (cloth) | ISBN 9781641600873 (Adobe PDF) | ISBN
   9781641600897 (ePub) | ISBN 9781641600880 (kindle edition)
Subjects: LCSH: Seton, Anya. | Authors, American—20th century—Biography.
   | Women authors, American—20th century—Biography.
Classification: LCC PS3537.E787 Z76 2020 (print) | LCC PS3537.E787
   (ebook) | DDC 813/.54—dc23
LC record available at https://lccn.loc.gov/2020017267
LC ebook record available at https://lccn.loc.gov/2020017268

———

*Unless otherwise indicated, all photos are from Anya Seton Papers, courtesy of
Library & Archives at Greenwich Historical Society*

Typesetting: Nord Compo

Printed in the United States of America
5 4 3 2 1

CONTENTS

AUTHOR'S NOTE

BEGINNING WITH HER FIRST BOOK, *My Theodosia* (1941), Anya Seton included an author's note, preface, or afterword in almost all her novels. She wanted everyone to know, as she said in her first note, that "I have tried to be historically accurate in every detail."[1] It was crucially, some would say obsessively, important to her that historical accuracy be the cornerstone of her fiction, although she recognized that her "slavish following of fact" might work against some of her readers' expectations.[2] After finishing *The Winthrop Woman* (1957), she wrote her publicist that "I suppose the reason I care so much to have the research recognized is that I have no illusion about my writing. It is swift, competent, pictorial, emotional, and I'm a story teller. I'm not very original and have no subtleties of style."[3] No matter how we might regard that self-assessment, it is true that Anya's attention to historical authenticity has always been the most highly praised feature of her novels.

In the following pages, I hope to present accurately the story of the writing life of one of the twentieth century's most popular historical novelists. The task has helped me to understand why author's notes were such a necessary indulgence for Anya Seton because I too feel the need to emphasize, as she did, where all the "facts" of this story have come from. And there's the rub. Anya Seton was the daughter of two writers who together with her constitute a family of prodigious talent, great passion, enormous charm, and fierce egotism. The Setons—Ernest Thompson, Grace Gallatin, and Anya—left a print record of themselves not only in their books (over forty for Ernest, seven for Grace, and thirteen for Anya) but in letters, journals, magazine pieces, and newspaper articles. In the author's note to *My Theodosia*, Anya spoke of the "vast amount of Burr material" that she had to absorb.[4] As her biographer, I sympathize. The story of her writing family extends from Ernest Thompson's first story, "Lobo, King of the Currumpaw" (1894) to Anya's last novel, *Smouldering Fires*

(1975). Then it extends far beyond to include the scholars, critics, and reviewers as well as the generations of readers who have continued to treasure Seton books, especially Anya's, long after their deaths.

As far as biographical or critical studies, the story is different. There are no book-length biographies of Anya or Grace, while there are three of Ernest Thompson Seton. As for Anya Seton, few who have studied the fate of popular women authors writing during the mid-twentieth century find the lack of scholarly attention surprising. Despite or because of her presence on the New York bestseller lists for over thirty years, she never had much chance for literary scrutiny. With the tags "Money Writer" and "Historical Romancer" all but stamped on her forehead, she easily disappeared from critical view, especially because she wrote during a time when women writers were often consigned to the categories of romance or "bodice rippers" or, at best, fiction targeted for the light entertainment of housewives. From the 1940s to the 1970s, the period when Anya had a wide readership, women writers of great popular appeal generally encountered the disdain of highbrow reviewers and academic arbiters of literary taste.

The climate has changed. One of the interesting things about many currently well-regarded historical novelists (Alison Weir, Philippa Gregory, Florence King, Sharon Kay Penman, and Mary Higgins Clark, to name a few) is how enthusiastically they cite Anya Seton as a formative influence. A look online shows that readers are often sharing their joy at discovering, or rediscovering, her adult novels. Those ten remain available in several editions and languages.

For me, the saga of critical reception is not what is most important to address, except as Anya herself expressed her feelings about it. So little is known about her actual life, especially what she called her "writing life," and so much material about that life has been made available to me, that tracing its history has become my calling.

Thanks to the generosity of Anya's daughters, Pamela Cottier Forcey and Clemency Chase Coggins, the Greenwich Historical Society contains enough Anya Seton files to make a researcher feel that no one in the family ever threw away anything. If it related to their writing, their interchanges with one another, their finances, or their publicity, they saved it, and most of it came down to Anya's and then her daughters' keeping.

There are also collections at the National Archives of Canada, the American Museum of Natural History in New York, and the Ernest Thompson Seton

Library at the Philmont Scout Ranch in Cimarron, New Mexico. Important additional materials for Grace Gallatin Seton are available at the Schlesinger Library of the Radcliffe Institute for Advanced Study. The valuable files pertaining to Anya and her publishers are housed in the Houghton Mifflin records in the Houghton Library at Harvard. I have been to all these places, an adventure that for me has echoes of the journey that Grace recorded in the subtitle to one of her travel narratives: "A half-year in the wilds of Mato Grosso and the Paraguayan forest, over the Andes to Peru," except that Grace had better scenery, and her trek took her only half a year, while mine has taken many years more.

All the collections contain rich evidence of how the Setons lived, wrote, and related to one another. One of my greatest difficulties has been the problem of how to keep Ann, then Anya, at the center of focus when her parents' accomplishments keep clamoring to be included. I have not given them the space that many might wish. I can blame the mountains of sources, but also remind myself of what Ann wrote when she had barely begun to be interested in writing—she wanted to be recognized *for herself* and aimed even more audaciously to be more popular than her parents.[5] That's her story, and I'm trying to stick to it while also presenting her very close relationships to her parents and their influence on her personally and professionally.

Next came the question of how best to capture the different sides of what Anya called her "bifurcated, trifurcated life," one in which, as she put it, "I try to ride too many horses."[6] My decision has been influenced by the place from which we hear Anya's own voice most clearly—from what might be called her own autobiography. At age seventeen she started writing what she called her personal "little book," what would eventually become over three thousand handwritten pages of journals, most of them filling ten three-hundred-page, leather-bound, red-spined, eight-by-eleven-inch, lined "ledger" notebooks.

I have only recently been able to study these in full and at length, again thanks to the generosity and trust of Anya's daughters, who have loaned them to me and given me permission to cite them however I choose. They have placed no restrictions on my use of any materials. I hope to give as full an accounting as time and space allow to answer the question of how Anya Seton created not only her novels, but also herself, as daughter, wife, mother, friend, and writer.

Ernest Thompson Seton might have been a model for teenager Ann's journaling through his own inveterate habit. His second wife described his massive output: "fifty-odd fat journals of his natural history observations, begun in 1879 and continued day by day until two weeks before the end of his life in 1946."[7] Explaining his intentions, he wrote that journals should capture "the simple fact, bald, untooled, perhaps incomplete, but honestly given as it was found. . . . It is always useful to have a record of one's doings," he added, "but, more important, writing a fact makes one observe it better."[8]

Unlike her father, Ann and then Anya Seton had no intention of just jotting down brief daily observations. Over the years, sometimes her musings, reflections, longing, lists of desires, descriptions of family rituals, love affairs, and illnesses went on for several pages. Ernest said that journal observations should be "honestly given." How do we know that Anya is speaking honestly, or accurately? What might she have intended? The accuracy of most of her facts is corroborated in letters written to or from her (she saved copies of many of her letters) and by information in articles about her or from interviews with her family. Sometimes she admitted that she was trying out the style of the autobiographies or diaries of writers she admired, from Katherine Mansfield to Ellen Glasgow and even Arnold Bennett.

What is so appealing, and sometimes sad, is that Anya was much more likely to be self-critical or doubting than self-promoting in her journals. Most of the time, what a reader experiences is the sense of listening to Anya talking to herself. Could she lie to herself? Certainly. Yet she was much more likely to vacillate between choices about how to think or what to do. She was usually serious, sometimes sentimental, often very funny or sarcastic. She could be brutally honest, and she could go on far too long about domestic dramas, her health, her psychoses, her fears. Yet she is never incoherent, and her handwriting is remarkably crisp and readable. Amazingly, she never crossed out words except to correct a fact.

Often over the years, Anya would go back to earlier journals and write comments in the margins, talking to or correcting an earlier version of herself. Her dominant and most tiresome subject was one she seemed driven to inspect far too intimately on paper—her long and volatile relationship with her second husband, Hamilton (Chan) Chase. Beyond that overdoing there are great rewards, from a biographer's view. Her journals afford startling self-perceptions and wisdom, touching expressions of sympathy and excitement, and most of all, engagement with writing and with her vision of herself as a writer.

As I begin her story with an author's note, Anya should have the last say, in part because her objective is mine as well. "My forte is story, and a peculiarly meticulous (fearful, yes) desire to weave historical fact into story. Make history come alive and as exciting as the past is to me."[9]

PREFACE
I WAS BORN

IN THE EARLY FALL OF 1957, Anya Seton wrote an autobiographical sketch of herself, undated, to her friend, Dell editor-in-chief Frank Taylor. He had agreed to her request to provide a "bio" in connection with *The Winthrop Woman*. Taylor was not associated with Anya's publishers, Houghton Mifflin, but as one of the book world's biggest names, sometimes he agreed to write publicity for the important book venues, such as book club editions. He had been an executive at various presses by this time and had worked with Vladimir Nabokov, Lillian Smith, Alfred Kazin, and Arthur Miller. To Anya he was primarily a longtime friend who had become a neighbor when she and her husband Hamilton "Chan" Chase had built their house, Sea Rune, on Long Island Sound in Old Greenwich in the early fifties.

Anya was moving in high literary society by 1957, having published six adult novels, all bestsellers. The most recent one, *Katherine* (1954), received almost universal admiration, even from some of her most negative New York critics. She knew Frank Taylor not only professionally, but also as a frequent visitor to Sea Rune, which was her small but enviable residence with its own private beach and boat dock. Frank would come over with his four young sons to swim and enjoy other water sports. For many other friends and neighbors as well, Sea Rune was a popular gathering spot because of both its waterside location and the parties that Anya and Chan frequently hosted. Through generous entertaining, they had access to an exclusive set of Greenwich society that included financiers, millionaires, writers, artists, actors, editors, and the town's prominent "Old Families." Anya, whose famous father had come to Greenwich in 1900 and built three homes in the area, was generally counted acceptable, even though the Chases had not acquired quite the same wealth as those who surrounded them.

The tone of Anya's letter to Frank Taylor was relaxed and conversational, even though she began by saying, "I shrink from too much personal detail given to the public, always feel that the Writer should be separate from the Woman as much as possible."[1] Although Anya had been in the public eye since the publication of her first novel in 1941, she could still be somewhat shy and wary with the press, especially when being interviewed or giving speeches. With Frank, she was at ease, also almost completely honest, not always the case when she was publicly asked about her life. The opening comment of her letter to Frank immediately identified the split she had always felt between being a "Writer" and being a "Woman." For her, being a "woman" meant her roles as wife, mother, daughter, homemaker, and civic citizen. Especially during the 1950s, she was, like most of her middle-class female readers, trying hard to live up to the period's expectations, which promoted stable marriages, nuclear families, proper femininity, and impeccable housekeeping skills.

Anya's autobiographical letter, written to a friend who was "in the business" as was she, provides us with a unique statement of how she chose to be seen as "Writer," not just "Woman." In the process, she makes a bow to both her parents, who a generation earlier had been well-known writers and celebrities themselves. She also, in passing, shows credentials to prove that she was providing adequate attention to wifely and mothering obligations. The space in her letter that is granted her father is not surprising, given that he cast a very long shadow over her life. By the time her career ended, she had accomplished the feat of making more money from writing than he did. Yet some of his books, like hers, have lived on in multiple editions, among new generations of loyal fans.

By the time she wrote her letter, Anya's *The Winthrop Woman* was in its final marketing stages, so she naturally wanted to put the novel in the forefront of her remarks. In this endeavor, she made an important link between her own artistic credo and her father's, a connection that meant a great deal to her. Also important was her insistence on marking out her exclusive distinctions as a popular historical novelist. Like most autobiographers, however, she started simply, with the form's common opening, "I was born."

To Frank Taylor:

I was born in NYC, only because the event was in January and mother was in town for the winter. I was brought back to Cos Cob, Connecticut, age 3 months, and have had a home in Greenwich township all my life, Cos Cob twice, Greenwich proper for years, and now O.G. (Old Greenwich). My early childhood was spent on the big place Wyndygoul—at Cos Cob, which was built by my father Ernest Thompson Seton, in his usual mixture of romantic English Tudor memories (manorial estate, 160 acres); Zoo (Daddy kept foxes, skunks, peacocks, possums, etc. etc.) and Indian woodcraft and camping. It was here that Daddy started the Woodcraft League and founded the Boy Scouts and held Indian Council Rings. My father was English born, of Scottish ancestry, and he never ceased to love the "motherland," though as I say he managed to reconcile these romantic ancestral memories with a passion for the American Indian and finally with a move to Santa Fe, New Mexico, where he died.

These interests I inherited and they explain, perhaps, some of my wish to write The Winthrop Woman, combining as it does the English roots and the old way of life there, with the pioneering here, and a treatment of our local Indians, the 17th century ones, the Sinoways, who lived once in Greenwich.

I have a very strong sense of closeness to the land which in Winthrop Woman enabled me to write of the places I love best—England, Massachusetts, and my own hometown of Greenwich. My life has included much travel, and about seven years (not consecutive) in England—satisfying that nostalgic half of my bloodstream, but my mother Grace Gallatin Seton is of Yankee stock, and in this book, it has amused me to write of some of her actual ancestors. Mother, by the way, originally a California girl, has written eleven books of poetry and travel (I don't have to mention Daddy's output, surely?). At any rate, with two author parents (I was the only child) I naturally disdained the idea of writing for years. The life held no glamour whatsoever, and I saw what hard work it was. My father was an extremely careful naturalist, fieldworker, and scientist. Though he popularized and fictionalized Natural History to some extent, it was never inaccurate. I think I have inherited his methods of writing and in my field of HUMAN history, try to do the same thing.

I thought through all my teens that I would be a doctor. I loved medicine and hospital work (and have kept up this interest with volunteer hospital jobs) but I never got very far, married at 18 instead, and went to live in England for two years. Then there were three children, now grown, and it was not until the youngest went away to nursery school that I one day conceived the idea of writing about Theodosia Burr. This fictionalized biography My Theodosia started me off on the work I like best. Katherine and this Winthrop Woman are of the same genre. Dragonwyck, The Turquoise, The Hearth and Eagle were more fiction, though I try always to ground my work on careful research. All my books by the way have simultaneous English publication and have done very well there, all have from six to nine foreign translations, and they've all been bestsellers. But I don't think we should say that.

My work habits, you must know pretty well??? I work every morning, until the last big push of about six months on Winthrop Woman when I work all day; see nobody I can help, and for days on end never leave the house. My husband is patient at these times, but very glad when the book is finished, and I return to circulation for a while. I love to cook, play bridge, and go to parties when I'm not in the creative treadmill. I also enjoy being a trustee of the Greenwich Historical Society. And doing little civic jobs. Our house (Sea Rune) is on the water, you know as well as anyone, and I hope (you know) my beloved green study with its shelves of books which represent my particular interests. It amuses me to think of them and see how faithfully they do just that: all the Dictionaries and Encyclopedias of Reference; the historical English section and historical American section; the one exclusively concerned with writers and writing; and the mystical shelves, from Vedanta to William James, to Zen and Evelyn Underhill, and C.S. Lewis etc. etc. This is a strong interest for me and certainly comes through in my books.

Not unallied with it is my spirit of "festival" and family gatherings which you know. The Christmas parties—the little customs and ceremonies—stemming partly perhaps from my fervent respect for and fascination by—the Past. But the Past must always be brought into the Present, invited and made to contribute, it is not static, and that is a strong theme in my books.

So, Francois my dear—this is the general idea as it trickles through my fevered little brain, and I hope may be helpful.

Yours, Anya

The "life" that Anya presented to Frank Taylor of course left out a great deal and contained at least two intentional inaccuracies, her age when first married and the number of books published by her mother. There was much more to come, including very shortly the triumph of *The Winthrop Woman*'s reception, which would constitute the apex of her career. In her letter she importantly defined in clear terms the niche she had established as a writer of her own time—one that she still claims close to fifty years after her last book was published. She revered the past, respected every detail of it that she could find as she wrote her books, but also brought it into the present, and into her own personal, private present perhaps most of all.

1 | THE STARVING ARTIST, THE HEIRESS, AND THE PRINCESS

THE SETONS' CAREER AS A WRITING FAMILY had two possible starting points. In the fall of 1893, a thirty-three-year-old British Canadian decided on a whim to pause from his budding career as a nature artist so that he could take on the challenge of bounty hunting wolves in New Mexico. He had learned how to trap wild animals in Manitoba while homesteading with his older brothers, and wolves were a specialty, both as a species and a subject for his drawings. While his deepest desire since he had been a boy on a farm was to draw and paint wildlife, he had been frustrated in his many attempts to make a living through his art. Now, however, just as he was beginning to be paid well from commissions as an illustrator, the opportunity to be among real wolves again emerged. Earlier that year, he met the father of a fellow art student he had known in Paris and learned that the wealthy businessman owned a cattle ranch in the Southwest. Soon Lewis Fitz Randolph was inviting his daughter's eccentric friend to go out and "show the boys some ways of combating the big cattle-killing wolves."[1] It would not have been in Ernest Thompson Seton's nature to turn down such an opportunity.

The trip might have looked spontaneous, but it also provided Ernest with needed relief from the serious eyestrain that he was to suffer all his life, the cost of his passion for studying, writing, observing wildlife, and drawing. In one of those fateful coincidences that Ernest manufactured, the invitation came just after his doctor had told him that "unless you wish to go totally blind, you will quit all desk and easel work and go for a long holiday in the wild."[2] From October 1893 to February 1894, he lived on the L Cross F Ranch. In New

Mexico, out in the wide-open range, he was soon successful as a wolf killer, although in his autobiography he talked mostly of the wild cowboys and drifters he encountered. His most important killing was of a particularly dangerous wolf he named Lobo, whom he lured by capturing his mate, Bianca. When he returned to Toronto, he managed to finish and sell a stirring melodrama based on the majestic specimen. "Lobo: King of the Currumpaw" came out in *Scribner's*, a leading American literary magazine, in November 1894. Its success began the fiction writing career that would bring Ernest more fame and wealth than all his other skills put together.

If he had known how popular such a tale would turn out to be, Ernest might not have taken another step that could also be considered a starting point for the Seton family of writers. After his return to Toronto and New York from his wolf hunting, and with his usual impulsiveness, Ernest found himself not stepping but leaping from a dock onto a departing ship. The vessel in question was the SS *Spaarndam*, leaving the port of Jersey City for France on July 7, 1894. Ernest later noted in his journal that "the entire course of my history would have been changed" if he had not made the jump just as the ship began to pull away from the dock.[3] With his eyesight greatly improved and with new energy, he was ready again to try to find fame as an artist in Paris.

During the Atlantic crossing, Ernest met an attractive fellow passenger named Grace Gallatin. She too was headed to Paris, with plans to advance a career in journalism. She had already tried her hand at travel writing and had been abroad several times with her mother. Ernest was almost, but not quite, a confirmed bachelor of thirty-four. Grace, still chaperoned by her mother Clemenzie (always known as Nemie), was twenty-two. Despite the age difference, Ernest Seton-Thompson (a name he had chosen years earlier to replace his birth name of Ernest Evan Thompson) quickly caught Grace's eye. The embodiment of tall, dark, and handsome, he looked much younger than his years. He was also the picture of rugged good health, and while he dressed casually, he carried himself with easygoing self-assurance.

For his part, Ernest just as quickly found much to admire in Grace Gallatin, a petite, vivacious, blue-eyed blonde who dressed expensively and enjoyed lively conversations. While she had a socialite's manners, she was evidently never too stiff or formal, because by the time the *Spaarndam* reached port in France, the two were moving toward a romance. Their affair was fueled not only by attractiveness and charm but by their mutual interests in writing, art, and travel. Another similarity that was eventually to prove more problematic was their ambition. They were both confident, willful, and absolutely determined to achieve individual goals at whatever cost. In addition, they both had a sense, in part due to a shared mystical bent, that they were destined for greatness, which meant that they would be not only competitive but also combative about getting what they were sure they deserved.

While in temperament, talent, and focus, Ernest and Grace had much in common, their backgrounds were a very different matter. Ernest Evan Thompson was born in 1860 in the port town of South Shields in northeastern England. He would change his surname several times in his life as he forged new identities and shrugged off old ones. His immediate forebears had mostly made their living by the sea. His father and both grandfathers owned small shipping fleets, but by 1866, father Joseph Thompson had experienced a run of bad luck in a business that he already disliked.

Like so many others, Joseph's solution was to pack up his large family (Ernest was the eighth of ten sons, with one sister) and move them across the Atlantic, in his case to what was then frontier Ontario, where he planned to reinvent himself as a gentleman farmer. Four years later he gave up on that idea and moved to Toronto, where he fared better as an accountant. Yet his second to youngest son had found the environment he would always love best as he explored the open spaces near the first family farm. In Toronto, Ernest sought out natural habitats beyond the city and sketched all the wildlife, particularly birds, that he encountered. When he reached the age of sixteen, his penny-pinching father was impressed enough with his artistic talent to permit him to become an apprentice to a local painter.[4]

Money was always a sticking point between father and son. Joseph's habitual stinginess led him to bill Ernest, when he reached the age of twenty-one, for everything he had spent on the boy's upbringing, including the doctor's charges at his birth. Ernest was infuriated, and although he supposedly did pay up, he scorned his father for the rest of his life. In 1879, when he was nineteen, he did manage to get Joseph to loan him money for a trip in steerage to London, where with little money left for food or lodgings, he earned a scholarship to study at the Royal Academy of Arts. There was no question that he was unusually talented, but he also worked incredibly hard, with almost no money for necessities. While not quite starving, he did not eat or live well while he studied. Although he stayed in England only until 1881, when ill health forced him to go back home to Toronto, he still learned enough to set the course of his life.

Perhaps the most important lesson that Ernest learned while at the Royal Academy was that he didn't belong there. His first love was animal anatomy, hardly valued as a useful niche by his classicist instructors. Their prizewinning scholarship student spent much of his time at the British Museum, where for several hours at a time he took notes and made sketches from hundreds of plant and animal life studies. He later said that he had learned more at the London Zoo than in his academy classes. Back home in Toronto, he camped out in his old bedroom, increasingly angry with his father, who considered him a dilettante and a failure. When Joseph wanted his loan repaid and told Ernest it was time to move on, his son did just that. Over the next close to ten years, the geographical and occupational range of his explorations was astonishing. He farmed, hunted, and trapped animals in Manitoba, made friends with the western Canadian Cree Indians, sold skins and other animal specimens to museums, established markets for his bird illustrations, and created lasting connections with the leaders of the Smithsonian and the American Museum of Natural History.

In 1890, having been told that he lacked the essential academic training to be an animal scientist, Ernest decided that fame would have to come from an artistic career, so he decided to give painting one more try. This time he went to the true artist's mecca, the city of Paris, where he studied with other Canadian expatriates at the Académie Julian. Within a year he was rewarded by having one of his paintings chosen for an exhibition at the Grande Salon. The painting, perhaps prophetically, was of a sleeping wolf. According to Seton scholar David Witt, this work was "probably the finest he produced in his entire career."[5] But his next year's offering was rejected, and again he returned to Toronto, where he established a prosperous enough business as an illustrator operating between Toronto and New York. Then he went off to deal with real wolves in New Mexico before boarding the *Spaarndam* for a second adventure in art in Paris.

Grace Gallatin had a very different start to her life, but she was like Ernest in two important respects—she was very much a vagabond by nature as well as circumstance, and she had decided on a career involving both art and books. Grace was born into upper class comfort in Sacramento, California, in 1872. She was the daughter of Clemenzie Rhodes, originally from Michigan, and

Albert Gallatin, distantly related to the more famous Albert Gallatin, United States treasurer under President Thomas Jefferson. Albert and Nemie met when he left his family's homestead in western New York and showed up in her frontier town in Michigan, where he started a hardware store. In 1860, not long after their courtship began, he decided at age twenty-five to head for California, both to avoid becoming swept up in the coming Civil War and to try his hand at gold mining. As one biographer reported, "He soon learned that it was more profitable to mine the miners."[6] Returning to a home base in Sacramento, Albert became a lowly store clerk for Huntington Hopkins, the largest hardware outfitters on the Pacific coast.

At the end of the Civil War, when travel was safe, Albert asked Nemie to join him in California, and the two were married in Sacramento in April 1866. With his wife's help, Albert Gallatin soon had a name to be reckoned with. His fortune was assured when he became a leading advocate for Huntington Hopkins's involvement in the construction of the Central Pacific Railroad. Before his third child, daughter Grace, was born, he had made himself into one of the richest men in California. Nemie proved her mettle when she traveled alone on a months-long journey to marry him. The trip had taken her from Chicago to New Orleans, across the Panama Isthmus and then up the California coast. Once there, she became an essential partner in Albert's financial rise, appointed trade director for one of his businesses and assisting him in the formation of the Sacramento chamber of commerce.

Through her parents' successes, little Grace enjoyed a privileged existence. At age five, she was living in her family's palatial Italianate mansion. When it was completed in 1877, it was an imposing structure with a gaslight tower that proclaimed its owner's social and financial prominence. Gallatin sold his gaudy, three-story showplace in 1888, coincidentally to the parents of Ernest's future close friend, the writer Lincoln Steffens. A few years later, in 1903, the mansion was sold again, this time to the state of California, where it became for sixty-some years the governor's mansion.

Young Grace, however, had been taken away from her palace years before the sale to the Steffens family. Her fairy tale life ended in 1881 when her parents divorced, their sensational split precipitated by her father's interest in an eighteen-year-old neighbor, Malvena Robbins, whom he married a year after the divorce was finalized. First wife Nemie, not afraid of scandal or independence, initiated the proceedings and abruptly moved out of her husband's home. Of her three children, she retained custody only of nine-year-old Grace. Sister Jane, thirteen, and brother Albert, eleven, stayed with their father. It would not be until after Grace and Ernest married that she reconnected with her siblings.

Nemie's course of action after leaving Albert was courageous and unconventional, but also inevitable. Staying in Sacramento was impossible, given Victorian prescriptions against divorce and her husband's influence in the city. She and her youngest child began a years-long odyssey, living as homeless but hardly hapless wanderers. During cross-country travels they stayed with family and friends or took suites in good hotels. Nemie had received a large settlement but still had to be careful with expenses. When Grace was a young wife, she investigated making a legal claim for child support against a father she had hardly seen since the divorce. Albert's death in 1905 ended that possibility, but along with her siblings, she did receive a $10,000 bequest. In the 1890s, mother and daughter settled long enough in New York City for Grace to study at the Packer Collegiate Institute in Brooklyn, but like Ernest, she was never to earn any recorded college degree. By the summer of 1894, she had published a few travel pieces, but she also wanted to study art, so mother and daughter booked passage on the *Spaardam*, planning to do some touring and then settle for a while in Paris.

Once Grace arrived there, she and Ernest saw one another frequently. As a couple, they might have come across as stereotypes of the heiress and the starving artist. She was sophisticated and perfectly "turned out" while he enjoyed presenting himself as a combination Rough Rider and Daniel Boone (several sources, including his daughter, hinted that this persona included a lifelong disdain for personal hygiene). Ernest had begun to achieve some important notice for his illustrations and magazine pieces, such as his tour de force story about Lobo, but he was hardly economically secure. For Grace, his knowledge of the art world of Paris mattered much more than his finances. For Ernest, Grace's stock increased not primarily because she was "socially well placed" as he later put it,[7] but because she was happy to help him with his numerous book projects.

An important turning point in the affair came when Grace took on an indispensable role in the design and production details for Ernest's ambitious new project. It was to be a groundbreaking zoological reference work that he entitled *Art Anatomy of Animals*. Adorned with his skilled drawings of both domestic and wild species, from elephants and tigers to horses, dogs, and birds, the book filled a much-needed niche in the publishing world. The result attracted both scientific and general audiences. When *Art Anatomy* came out to enthusiastic reviews in the spring of 1896, it gave a strong boost to Ernest's reputation and the pair's romance. Shortly after it was published, they returned with Nemie to the States, where she soon announced her daughter's upcoming marriage. Somewhere along the way, Nemie herself had picked up a second husband and was now "Mrs. Craig." She was much more economically secure and would be able to help "the children" establish themselves comfortably. Seton was not an American citizen, but he was engaged to a beautiful American woman who like him had big dreams and talent. It seemed a perfect match. One mysterious note is that the wedding took place not in October, as originally announced, but instead four months earlier. Some family speculations have included the possibility of a pregnancy and miscarriage.

Grace and Ernest were married in New York City on June 1, 1896. The next four years realized dreams that both had been confident they could achieve. They first set up housekeeping on a large but rundown colonial estate in rural New Jersey, the rent paid by the indulgent and image-conscious Nemie Craig. Despite Ernest's pleasure in the rustic surroundings at Sloat Hall, the newlywed Setons were drawn to the much more stimulating artistic and social advantages of New York City. Before long they established themselves, again with Nemie's assistance, in the upper floors of a fashionable building at 144 Fifth Avenue, where they rented a spacious apartment complete with an art studio. An article about Ernest and his studio, appearing with photographs in the *New York Times Saturday Review of Books and Art* for August 3, 1901, illustrates the Seton legend that was beginning to form. Fellow nature artist and reviewer William Whitelock wrote, almost worshipfully, that "there is an intangible something in the dwelling that carries one in spirit to the wide stretches of the West, to the uninvaded domain of the wolf and eagle and mountain lion."[8] The studio contained animal skins hanging over Japanese screens, deer antlers and tree boughs decorating walls along with Persian rugs, while one of Seton's wolf paintings had a prominent place over the mantel in the dining area.

Grace had much to do with building the Setons' status as a fashionable couple, including her tolerance of living quarters that were more than a little eccentric. A letter from her mother congratulates the new wife on how she had been able to "bring Seton out."[9] Prominent members of New York's intelligentsia such as Frank Chapman, William Hornaday, Lincoln Steffens, and Hamlin

Garland had already befriended Seton, but Grace worked hard to make sure he fit in with an expanding group of influential friends. Grace's granddaughter Pamela Cottier Forcey has written that "when Ernest and Grace were married in 1896, he thought she was a socialite, interested mainly in receptions and parties." However, as Forcey notes, "He changed his mind about her" in many respects. In the first years of their marriage, in fact, "they were a team."[10] For twenty years, Grace advised her husband on the design of his books, choosing and arranging all the graphic elements. She was also his publicist, especially in the early years when he was finding his audience.

In later years Ernest would complain that Grace was primarily a status seeker, but the label applied as much if not more so to him. He was motivated partly by his lifelong bitterness over what he saw as his father's failures. Not only did Joseph Thompson refuse to support him adequately and fail at several of his own businesses, but he also ignored his forebears' tenuous links to a Scottish peerage through a sixteenth-century earl (Lord Seton, the Earl of Winton). The old Scottish Winton names of Ernest's two grand houses in the Greenwich area, Wyndygoul and De Winton, illustrate the son's interest in the lineage that the father cared nothing about.

Ernest's frequent changes of surname also reflect his attempt to claim the aristocratic ancestor whose high rank, he believed, was his birthright. To the confusion of publishers, readers, and biographers, he went from being Ernest Evan Thompson to Ernest Seton Thompson, then to Ernest Seton-Thompson when he and Grace were first married. Soon there was another switch, to Ernest Thompson-Seton, before finally, in 1901, the couple became legally the unhyphenated Ernest and Grace Thompson Seton. Thereafter Ernest often signed letters and referred to himself as "ETS." His wife, addressing him in letters, referred to him consistently as "Dear Boy." To his daughter, he was always "Daddy," and she, for him, was usually simply "Baby."

With Ernest's first American book of fiction, published in 1898 by the esteemed house of Scribner, he was close to transforming himself into the famous figure he had set out to be. *Wild Animals I Have Known* was a collection of animal stories including the already popular "Lobo." "Silverspot the Crow," "Bingo the Dog," the "Pacing Mustang," and the "Springfield Fox" used Ernest's encyclopedic understanding of animal traits and habits but added personalities and feelings with wit and sympathy that captured all but the most cynical and scientific purists. There were also two hundred of his own whimsical drawings. The author included a preface that may have later given his daughter her idea of what she should emphasize in her own introductory remarks. "These Stories are true," he declared in his first sentence. Although he was willing to admit that "I have left the strict line of historical truth in many places," he nonetheless insisted that the animals "were all real characters" and, most important, "They lived as I have depicted.[11]

Wild Animals I Have Known remains a widely revered example of animal character fiction, a genre Seton perfected, one in which animals are given names and personalities to go with realistic habits and habitats. He followed it, over the years, with at least a dozen more original collections, all reprinted as well. The first collection's combination of fact and imagination placed its handsome outdoorsman-illustrator-raconteur in an elite group of writers who could make a good living through book and magazine article sales. The book's author was at this time still "Ernest Seton Thompson," and his wife Grace, whom he thanked for her contributions in his opening, was Grace Seton Thompson. She was also the person named "Jim" to whom the author dedicated the book, although few would have known her by that private nickname. By 1900 the soon to be Ernest and Grace Thompson Seton had added three more animal folklore volumes to their list, and together they went on the first of many lucrative lecture tours. In this momentous opening year of a new century, Grace and Nemie also arranged a well-publicized New York showing of Ernest's paintings that brought numerous offers of work as an illustrator, and publishers began to compete to provide profitable venues for his short stories.

Hamlin Garland, already a well-recognized author of several books of non-fiction and story collections, estimated that by this time, his friend Ernest had amassed "a small fortune of $200,000.00."[12] ETS was forty years old, married to a lovely, supportive wife of solid social credentials, and had created for himself an enviable position in American literary society. He had managed what he predicted for himself when he was a penniless, untrained artist back in Canada: his transformation into a new breed of baronial entrepreneur as well as a famous writer, complete with a name that reflected his lineage. All he needed now was an address, a "place" of rock, mortar, and scenic views that would properly announce his place in the world. The House of Seton that Ernest was looking for would also need to be a working headquarters for what was now the couple's industry, a business base where they could write, edit, and entertain for profit and prove to one and all that they had arrived.

By 1904, with his lucrative triple careers as writer, artist-illustrator, and naturalist, Ernest had found that place, a home for himself, his wife, and the addition of an infant daughter. His search for the perfect setting had begun in 1898, as he explored a frontier located only thirty-five miles from his Manhattan apartment. With his close friend Lincoln Steffens, Ernest roamed the countryside of rural southern Connecticut. He narrowed his search to backcountry near Cos Cob, hardly more than a fishing village on Long Island Sound, near the fashionable "New York suburb" of Greenwich. In his 1931 autobiography, Steffens described their jaunts: "Real estate men and the natives could not understand what he [Seton] saw in tangled swamps and hopeless woods. They preferred land that had at least been cleared." What Seton would answer, Steffens reported, was "How deer would love that."[13] Both writers were already acquainted with the area through their membership in a loosely organized village artist colony that included John Henry Twachtman and Childe Hassam, who were soon to be recognized as America's leading impressionist painters.

It took Ernest two years, but in 1900 he finally pieced together six abandoned farmsteads that he was able to buy for an inexpensive purchase price of around six dollars an acre. The package made him the owner of some 120 acres that combined deep forests, pastures, swamps, and boulder-strewn hills. His land, as he described it, was a "naturalist's paradise," with "rocky hills, sloping green banks, noble trees, birds in abundance, squirrels in the woods, fish and turtles in the pond." He added with pride, "and all was mine."[14]

With skills developed by years of hiking and building shelters in wilderness settings, he proceeded to turn the rugged landscape into a grand country estate into which he introduced exotic flora and fauna, dozens of species of mammals, and birds from wrens to peacocks. His crowning effort, besides the house built in what became known as his unique Tudor Indian style, was the twelve-acre lake that he created by damming a brook on the property. The location was ideal as a space that had all the picturesque scenery of a park, where he could indulge his love of nature while remaining within easy commuting distance of the social and business contacts that he and Grace cultivated in the big city.

The manor and formal grounds that ETS designed and built himself proved that, in addition to his other skills, he was a master architect, a landscaper and horticulturalist, and an engineer. His estate was named Wyndygoul, after the Scots Winton family castle that, like the surname Seton, tied Ernest to his lost patrimony. To stress that name, he built stone pillars topped with griffins at the entranceway which held up iron gates bearing, on brass plates, the large letter *S*. The manor itself was set on the crest of the highest hill on the property, with a long drive leading uphill to a promontory of sweeping views. Beyond and below this pinnacle was a parterre encircled with rustic stone walls.

In a 1903 article entitled "The Home of a Naturalist," appearing in *Country Life in America*, enraptured reporter and fellow nature writer Charles Roberts extravagantly praised the design and workmanship that had gone into Wyndygoul, connecting the picturesque qualities of Seton's nature preserve to his trademark as a writer:

> It is the same blending, with the addition of an admirable literary form, which has differentiated Mr. Seton's books from all their predecessors, and made him the founder of the new school of nature-study, a school which, while yielding nothing to the old-school naturalists in the matter of exact observation, goes much beyond them, in that it seeks for the motives underlying the conscious acts of sentient beings.[15]

Seton was to write many popular books from his summer dreamhouse, where his upper story windows commanded a view of Long Island Sound and, he claimed, even Teddy Roosevelt's Oyster Bay. But he also raised skunks not only to perform genetics experiments on them but also to sell their pelts. Ever curious and imaginative, he fashioned a hollow fake tree at the edge of his lake that allowed him, after climbing interior steps, to photograph birds and other wildlife perched on its branches. What a paradise this might be for any offspring lucky enough to grow up there. The child who did spend her first eight years in this paradise later wrote that the lesson she learned best from the father who took her for long walks through his domain was to be the closest possible observer of the world around her.

Ann Seton was born early in the morning of January 23, 1904, not at Wyndygoul but in her parents' fashionable studio apartment in the Beaux Arts Apartments, 80 West Fortieth Street, where they were living in the winter of 1903–04. Grace recorded in Ann's baby book that the Setons took their first family trip to the Connecticut house on May 4, remarking that Ann "appeared to notice the difference in the motion of the railroad cars."[16] The house was not completed—in fact it would never be to Ernest's satisfaction—but by late spring it was comfortable enough for a family stay. Greenwich had already become such an important commuter community that the Setons, with baby Ann, would have boarded one of over twenty trains that now linked New York with central Greenwich. Two years before her birth, a trolley line had been built that could now transport them from Greenwich to Cos Cob, where some kind of coach could take them up the hilly roads and long driveway to Wyndygoul.

In Hamlin Garland's celebratory birth poem, he saluted Ann as a "pink little bud of a famous Tree," foretelling her entrance to "the gardens of Wyndygoul" where "black-throat swans with trumpet call" would "herald thy coming to 'Seton's Hall.'"[17] From the very start, her identity was marked by her parents' growing fame. In July 1904, among a large group who came up to the new estate for her christening were high society and intelligentsia from New York City as well as locals from Cos Cob. One might have thought that Ernest and Grace were ready to settle down to enjoy being doting parents for a while. Ernest's delight in his baby girl's birth had been reported in the *New York World*: "the arrival of little Ann has made him look more like the happy bridegroom of a year than the sedate married man of eight years, forty-four years old and for the first time a father."[18]

The word "sedate," however, was never going to apply to Ernest Thompson Seton. In the two years before Ann's birth, Ernest's property in Cos Cob had become much more than a country retreat on which to raise a daughter. As the story has often been told, during the three years that he was building Wyndygoul, Ernest was increasingly provoked by a group of rowdy boys who vandalized the grounds during his absences. Instead of charging them with trespassing, Ernest invited them to come out to camp on his premises. The first group, who arrived on Good Friday, 1902, had no idea that the manor lord's plan was to mesmerize them into good behavior through theatrical storytelling and rituals. Drumming, hiking, swimming, and cooking outdoors were accompanied by lessons on how to work and play like American Indians, promoted as nature's peacekeepers, at one with the forest primeval. Most enthralling was Ernest's own mastery of the outdoors and his ability to transmit his enthusiasm to any audience. He could howl, dance, chant, and build a fire in seconds with his rubbing sticks. His lessons did the trick.[19]

With his new tribes at Wyndygoul, and even before, Ernest had begun promoting Native American culture as a corrective to modern white civilization's militarism and materialism. His enormously popular *Two Little Savages, Being the Adventures of Two Boys Who Lived as Indians and What They Learned*, was published in 1903, a year before Anya was born. Although the autobiographical novel provides a consistently white, usually stereotypical point of view on the Native peoples the boys imitate, it also shows that very early in his life, Ernest respected Native life, though he also romanticized it. As his biographer David Witt has written, "However high the Seton Indians may be on today's political incorrectness scale, at the time there was nothing else like it" to "connect young people to nature, the outdoors, and even the customs of another race."[20] *The Birch Bark Rolls*, which codified so many of the practices that Ernest was adapting to his Woodcraft organization, were published during Anya's years at Wyndygoul. Native chiefs often appeared, from local but also Canadian and Southwestern tribes, and the grounds were dotted with teepees of the Great Plains tribes and the wigwams from the Southwest.

When Ann's christening took place, she was greeted not only by New York literati, but also by a swarm of boys in costume. The *New York Times* reported that after the ceremony, "a large number of boy Indians did war dances on the lawn."[21] Ann's fate from that time was linked with theirs. The press loved the connection, seeing stories about Seton's baby girl as a means to give a new slant to her father's fascinating enterprise. Two weeks after Ann was born, the tabloid *New York World* emphasized how her birth would affect her father's role as a leader of boys. Included were pictures of Wyndygoul and local youngsters dressed in their garb. In an accompanying interview, the proud father prophesied that his little girl would be "an outdoor child," "barefoot" and "bareheaded" like the Woodcraft Indians. He insisted that Wyndygoul was the family's permanent home, where "we are trying to get as near the primeval life of the forest as possible."[22] Another paper responded to this prediction sarcastically: "Such a healthy, vigorous outdoor life will do wonders for the child, and think of all the nice copy it will make for Papa Seton."[23] Yet another proclaimed, "Ernest Thompson Seton has at last been blessed with a daughter! Now he can have a chance of putting into practice his theories of 'Wild Animals He Has Known.'"[24]

By the time Ann was four years old, there were weekly camps at Wyndygoul every summer, with her father, now called "the Chief" or "Black Wolf," holding forth in American Indian garb. His estate became a scenic theme park where canoes and teepees dotted the lake and grounds. The entire compound was stocked with many native wild mammal and bird species. None of these attractions, however, meant much for Ann. In 1938, newly embarked on her own writing career and self-renamed Anya, she asserted that the predictions of her father and the tabloids were inaccurate. In this first of many private reminiscences about her childhood, she remarked that her participation in outdoor activities at Wyndygoul was surprisingly minimal: "I never played with any little boys. This in spite of the fact that the property was overrun with Daddy's woodcraft indians [sic]. I was often referred to as little Princess Ann."[25]

On the grounds of her castle, young Ann might take comfort in the fact that while she could not be a Woodcraft Indian, she was certainly royalty. Her father was worshiped by his warriors and visited by a growing number of curious writers, naturalists, and outdoors activists. The Chief's youth camping movement was one of the earliest and most successful incarnations of a new national craze known as "boy-building." Always an entrepreneur, he began to set up well-run tribes throughout the country, bringing leaders back to train at Wyndygoul. The nation's most prominent naturalist at the time, John Burroughs, wrote after coming out to see the program at Cos Cob: "Seton has got hold of a big thing in his boys' Indian camp. All the boy's wild energy and love of deviltry are turned to new channels, and he is taught woodcraft and natural history and Indian lore in a most fascinating way."[26] The many accolades helped Ernest to grow his income and establish what became an international reputation.

As had been the case in her husband's publishing ventures, Grace was also deeply involved in Woodcraft. She took charge of designing costumes, organizing new chapters, and managing long weekend meetings with leaders, campers, and sometimes chiefs who arrived from the far West and Canada. As Leonard Clark, one of the early campers, wrote, "You can't give Mr. Seton all the glory. Mrs. Seton was a wonderful, wonderful woman. She used to come over to the camp fire. I remember very distinctly when Mrs. Seton brought a baby over and said, 'This is our new baby, and she's a new papoose,' and that was Anya Seton."[27] Part of the mystique of Wyndygoul and some of her husband's popularity were owed to Grace's gifts. She seemed effortlessly to combine enviable touches of high style with a healthy appreciation of nature. Her beauty was also a magnet. As one newspaper account put it, "Mrs. Seton is one of the most beautiful women in New York; her beauty is of a wholesome order that suggests splendid health and is refreshing as well as interesting."[28]

Motherhood, Woodcraft, and home fashioning were not the only occupations to involve Grace in the new century. In 1898, during the second year of their marriage, she joined Ernest on a two-month paid excursion to the wilds of Yellowstone and North Dakota. There she learned how to be an expert at "roughing it" while Ernest studied wildlife and became an even more reverent disciple of the practices of the Plains Indians he met. When they returned, and with Ernest's blessing, Grace turned their trip into an important literary event for 1900, a travel narrative that she coyly titled *A Woman Tenderfoot in the Rockies*. In the foreword, she announced that "the author" hoped to convince "some going-to-Europe-in-the-summer woman" to go "Out West" instead. She named herself "Woman-who-goes-hunting-with-her-husband," and then, in a breezily informal style, demonstrated how she accommodated herself to the Wild West. She included detailed illustrations to show her women readers a high-fashion riding costume of her own design, one with a split skirt made so that a woman could seem to be "riding side saddle on both sides" when she was really riding "astride."[29] When Grace described how she used a frying pan to kill a rattlesnake, she was wittily demonstrating her own heroic reformation of domesticity.[30]

In *A Woman Tenderfoot*, Grace portrayed herself as someone who could be a lady without having always to act like one. After Ann was born, Grace traced the 1899 travels she had taken with Ernest to the High Sierras of eastern California in a *Tenderfoot* sequel called *Nimrod's Wife* (with Seton as Nimrod), which was published in 1907. It was dedicated "To the Baby."[31] That year, Ernest left home for a two-thousand-mile canoe trip into the far northwestern territories of Canada, remembering his daughter enough to name his canoe the *Ann Seton*. The resulting work, called *The Arctic Prairies*, was published to scientific acclaim in 1911. The little girl back home did not see her father for the more than seven months that his trip took, nor very often thereafter. Ernest was also gone for months during the "off season" of her Wyndygoul years, touring Woodcraft camps around the country and giving lectures throughout the United States and abroad.

By the time she was three years old, Ann's identity was established as the offspring of two parents for whom writing, traveling, and adventure were staple ingredients. Wyndygoul's tranquil beauty, at least during the months when not mobbed with Woodcraft Indians, made it the envy of many visitors, but neither Ernest nor Grace chose to be there for any length of time. Sometimes Ann was taken along on travels that carried her parents together or separately throughout the United States, Canada, and most of the countries of Europe. At other times, as the adult Anya remembered, governesses were her "constant companions," either in the Setons' Manhattan apartment or out at Wyndygoul.[32]

When she was five years old, one of these companions came to stay and never left. Johanna (Hanna) Engstrom "came to Mother," author Anya later wrote, "as lady's maid and seamstress" and became her "Classic Nanny." Hanna was "a confidante, and above all, she was ever dependable, the steady background behind constantly changing circumstances."[33] When Hanna was critically ill soon after her preparatory school graduation, Ann voiced her deep concern in a 1921 journal entry: "After all," she said, "Hanna raised me."[34] After Ann's marriage, Hanna remained with Grace as her steady companion, cook, and housekeeper. When Ann, with her second husband, moved into another ETS-built house with Grace during the Depression, Hanna became companion, cook, and confidante for Ann's three children as well.

Until she was eight years old, Ann's life revolved around her parents' big city and country residences and their many trips away from them. In some ways her upbringing might not have differed from that of other rich children. As Anya wrote in her "Childhood" notes of 1938, "There was a great deal of Lord of the Manor feeling out at Wyndygoul."[35] Although the estate offered stunning vistas of nature, most photographs of little Ann pose her on porches or in the house, wearing lace and ruffled dresses hardly fit for romping, and never barefoot. In one portrait, she stands rather sad-faced next to a somber Ernest, with a pretty puppy between them. The father-daughter expressions might have reflected the fact that as Anya later recounted, her father refused to allow any domestic pets at Wyndygoul. His interest in animals was not at all personal, only professional. The photographed dog's idyllic days there were probably numbered, as any pups or kitties brought to Wyndygoul simply disappeared.

Author Anya later wrote that she could read by the age of four and at naptime "used to carry on a continued story to myself." "I always knew I was intelligent," she commented. "My parents used to boast of it." She clearly remembered her first foray into authorship. At age five or six, she took her parents a "sketch about a mouse which I thought was excruciatingly funny. Felt frightfully clever and humorous."[36] In her private recollections, Anya Seton later projected an image of herself as a precocious child, the progeny of remarkably accomplished parents who gave her a legacy of talent and social privilege. What Anya Seton also later believed was that she did not receive from her father the essentials of attention and encouragement.

During the years of Ann's childhood, Ernest's schedule became increasingly frenetic, divided between lecture tours, Woodcraft meetings, and expeditions to remote destinations from Wyoming to Norway. Between 1904 and 1912, the years when the family lived most often at Wyndygoul, ETS published no fewer than fourteen book-length publications and scores of articles. Grace was certainly more often the one who stayed "home" with Ann, but she managed to keep herself in the limelight as well. A 1912 interview with Grace Seton at Wyndygoul, published in *Good Housekeeping*, did not even mention that she had a daughter, while it lavished praise on Grace the homemaker. The piece, entitled "The Feminine Charms of the Woman Militant," set out to paint a flattering portrait of a carefully chosen group of suffragettes. The stress on "their personal attractiveness and housewifely attainments," as the subheading announced, seems to have been intended to provide positive propaganda for a group who were often accused of unladylike behavior.[37]

Grace Thompson Seton had been vice president of the Connecticut Women's Suffrage Association for two years when she was interviewed for *Good Housekeeping*, and she would soon take over as president. The article began by describing her "bearing in the drawing room," which, readers were told, "gives one the impression of a sheltered, beautifully groomed hostess and seems to contradict her adventurous spirit." However, the reporter could also see "in her sparkling blue eyes . . . the mischief-loving, determined, highly intelligent being" who "loves danger and deliberately courts it." After going back in time to talk of Grace's adventures in the West, the reporter still felt it necessary to conclude, reassuringly, that "with all her talents Mrs. Seton is perhaps most proud of her ability to invent new dishes and design new gowns." It was not mentioned that one of those "gowns" was the riding outfit that Grace designed for her "Cowgirl" days.[38] The skills of mothering evidently were not considered relevant, to the reporter or her interviewee.

Domesticity and social polish came easily to Grace, but as she later proved, she was far more than simply a model of the domestic virtues. She entertained, founded and participated actively in many women's clubs, and also took a close interest in her daughter's education with a series of governesses. With Ernest's backing, she also became a leader of the Camp Fire Girls movement in 1911, along with the Setons' friends Luther and Charlotte Gulick.[39] At the start of his Woodcraft programs at Wyndygoul, Ernest wrote nothing to indicate that girls could not join in its activities, and a few did. Ann was never involved in the Campfire Girls but was sometimes pressed into Woodcraft service later, as a teen wearing a dress made by Grace and leading a Woodcraft League–designed snake dance. In 1910, however, as Grace was turning to the suffragette cause, Ernest was being pulled away from support for both women and America's Native peoples. Caucasian boys were soon to become his main preoccupation.

Since 1902, Seton had been writing articles on Woodcraft creeds and practices for the *Ladies' Home Journal*, which in 1906 he gathered into a book—part manual, part philosophy—called *The Birch Bark Roll*. The ultimate result of its yearly editions was a meeting in London in 1906 between Seton and Robert Baden-Powell, the British Boer War hero who had been planning his own boys' organization, which he called Scouting. Baden-Powell produced his Boy Scouts in 1908, and in 1910, the Boy Scouts of America was founded. Other boys' movement activists were involved in the BSA, but it was Ernest Thompson Seton who was honored with the title Chief Scout.[40] In 1910 he hastily created a compilation of guidelines, the *Official Handbook of the Boy Scouts of America*, which was based largely on his *Birch Bark Roll*. It became one of the most important but also most controversial books he wrote.

The controversies over Ernest's leadership of the BSA, still sometimes heated one hundred years later, boiled down to factors that included his colleagues' disapproval of Grace's growing notoriety as a leading suffragette. Other issues proved even more controversial at the time, since Grace's style of activism was considered sufficiently ladylike. Seton was not an American citizen and stubbornly retained his British citizenship until finally becoming an American in 1931, but even this problem might have been overlooked, given his celebrity status. However, with war raging in Europe by 1914, loyalty to country was a patriotic imperative. In this nationalistic climate, the Chief Scout faced increasingly strong opposition because of his vocal criticism of Baden-Powell's militaristic scouting model. The Scouts, with mentor Teddy Roosevelt and Boy Scout cofounder James West, felt that they had a sacred duty to introduce drilling, marching, and combat readiness into Scouting.

Teddy also joined others who opposed the Chief Scout when he insisted on promoting the "Indian way." Seton's absolute commitment to what he saw as the American Indian's superior worldview was viewed with dismay, even disgust, in many quarters. The Chief Scout's touting of a "primitive" race was made much worse by the fact that he unashamedly called himself a non-Christian and preached his "Gospel of the Red Man." By 1915, when he was either fired or resigned from the BSA, depending on one's source, all the firm beliefs that Seton poured into the first Boy Scout Handbook had been expunged. His reaction was to reclaim many of his original band of followers for what he now marketed as the Woodcraft League. Daughter Ann, who had virtually nothing to do with the Scouts, had, at Wyndygoul, been a witness to her father's colorful, carefully researched use of Native American practices and rituals, and she would be again as a teenager when he resurrected Woodcraft in a new Greenwich location. As Anya Seton, she returned to his Indian gospels, which became part of the lore she included in many of her novels.

Grace, meanwhile, was faring much better with her women's causes. She was popular as a leader with the Connecticut League of Suffragettes, and in 1916, just as Ernest faced galling humiliation, she was quite literally leading the parade. An official history of the suffrage movement recounted how in 1916, in Chicago, "the Connecticut League . . . marched under the leadership of Mrs. Grace Thompson Seton in the great parade of the National Suffrage Association that braved the wind and rain on the way to the Coliseum, where the cause of women's suffrage was presented to the resolutions committee of the Republican National convention."[41] In the many photographs taken of her group, suffragette Grace is shown to be a commanding, self-assured, and always impeccably dressed figure.

The question that anyone might have asked during these years became, where was home for the Seton family? They were so seldom at Wyndygoul that they clearly did not need the forest estate where Ann was princess of her father's domain. Its 1912 sale was announced in the *New York Times*, which commented dramatically, "That Mr. Seton should be content to part with his place, upon which he has spent a small fortune and over ten years' work to bring it into a state of wild natural beauty, was a decided surprise to his friends."[42] News accounts also made much of the fact that Seton had sold his naturalist's paradise for a record amount, the impressive sum of $250,000. The purchasers were also celebrities—Maurice Wertheim, a millionaire financier and supporter of Jewish causes, and his independently wealthy wife Alma Morgenthau Wertheim, parents of Barbara Tuchman. In later years, this daughter wrote her Pulitzer Prize–winning *The Guns of August* (1962) in a small house she built on the Wyndygoul estate, and she became a friend of Old Greenwich neighbor Anya Seton.

Ann was eight years old when her parents sold Wyndygoul, around the same age Grace had been when she and Clemenzie left Albert Gallatin's elegant mansion in Sacramento in 1881. Perhaps this congruence helps to explain the things that Grace did or didn't feel were important for her daughter when she reached this age. After Wyndygoul was sold, Ann, much like her mother when a child, had no fixed home. There is something poignant, and perhaps also prophetic, about a letter Grace's friend Isabel Proctor Lord wrote to her after the Wyndygoul sale, in which she asked, "What alarms me is whether you included Ann in the sale? You remember you told me one was as likely to be sold as the other?"[43]

When Ann turned nine, the ex-princess of Wyndygoul became one of the privileged young ladies who attended Manhattan's Spence School. Grace had inquired about their curriculum in 1912, wanting to know whether at age eight, Ann could begin advanced instruction in French, English grammar, and geography. The headmistress replied tactfully that at this age, "the main thing is to have her get a good foundation in the elementary work of Reading, Spelling, Writing, and Arithmetic."[44] This answer kept Ann with governesses for one more year, but in 1913, she was enrolled at Spence, located not far from the Setons' Manhattan apartment. The school's founder and headmistress, Clara Spence, would make sure that Ann's experiences there were anything but dull, even if she might have to suffer through some basics first.

Grace Seton and Miss Spence were both passionate suffragettes, so young Ann was a close witness to partisan battles for women's rights both at home and at school. Clara B. Spence had founded her school with her partner, Charlotte Baker, in 1892.[45] Spence and Baker, two "spinsters," not only lived together openly in what was then called a "Boston marriage," but they also adopted four children together. They were so committed to promoting same-sex couple adoptions that they founded their own agency, which is still in existence. They lived with their children in an apartment on the fifth floor of the school, where they often invited students as well as famous guests, such as Booker T.

Washington and Aldous Huxley, to dine with them. Spence brought in Isadora Duncan, who was both bisexual and a Communist, to teach interpretive dance, a class Ann particularly enjoyed. The school, the headmistress said, was to be "a place not of mechanical instruction but a school of character where the common requisites for all have been human feeling, a sense of humor, and the spirit of intellectual and moral adventure."[46] These were brave goals, and time would tell if Ann Seton could make them her own.

2 | HOUSES DIVIDED

ANN SETON ATTENDED SPENCE SCHOOL OFF AND ON from 1913 to 1921, receiving opportunities there on a par with those that came with being the daughter of two remarkable parents. There was no way to escape the influence of Grace Thompson Seton and Ernest Thompson Seton—the vivid impressions that they made on those around them, the elite company they kept, or the pace they kept. Still, at Spence, Ann could take a few steps toward making a separate circle for herself. She was, however, quite often not in attendance. For Grace and Ernest, with their unstructured educational backgrounds, formal schooling for Ann was not a high priority. She was taken out of school to travel with her parents whenever it was convenient for them, so she was not exaggerating when she later said that she had made "eight Atlantic crossings" as a child.[1] Ann could not count on being in her "real" school any more than she would be able to count on a home that she could feel was her own, something that eluded her for decades.

The sale of Wyndygoul left the Setons without a house, but not without Connecticut property. Before the deal to sell the Cos Cob estate was closed, Ernest and Grace had purchased prime land on which to build an even grander estate. The extensive wooded property was on Lake Avenue, a sparsely settled but highly valued neighborhood stretching beyond Greenwich Township proper. They probably didn't suspect at the time of purchase that their new estate would function even less as a permanent home than Wyndygoul had been. The husband's and wife's very different causes had been creating an ever-widening gap in their relationship, and by 1918 the

22

worldwide war moved them further apart. When the 1920s roared in and the Great War ended, they began to turn their weapons on one another in their new Lake Avenue arena.

When Ernest left the Boy Scouts, he attempted to reclaim his Woodcraft movement. He was determined to recast his original organization as a counter-force against those who had tried to humiliate him personally and to belittle the beliefs closest to his heart. By 1916 he began taking Woodcraft boys and their leaders out to his new Greenwich property, where there would be no suitably grand house for two more years. The land was all Ernest really needed, and he had found a spectacular property. The estate named DeWinton featured low sloping hills and rippling streams, along which he built a curving drive and stone bridges that carried vehicles over two Seton-built lakes. When completed, the main house sat on a rise that overlooked the lakes. Until it was finished, guests, and sometimes Ann and Grace, could live in a rustic two-story bungalow that Ernest built first, called Fern Lodge. Friends were often pressed into service as carpenters and masons for the much larger mansion. Hamlin Garland, who was often there, told of helping Ernest to build a bedroom suite for Ann, which they "jokingly referred to as the 'Ann-ex.'"[2] Not far from the new house, Seton took special advantage of a large rock that jutted out dramatically over the flat space below, to make a perfect "council ring." More than a hundred campers could gather under the rock for colorful ceremonies and storytelling.

DeWinton itself was ready for occupancy by the fall of 1918. Ernest had to oversee many of the decisions related to furnishing and decorating its interior because in the months before the opening of the grand Seton residence, Grace was not available. When the United States finally entered World War I, she became leader of a group of New York City clubwomen who raised funds to purchase several transport trucks for use by the Allies in France. The drivers of the unit, named *Le Bien-être du blessé* ("For the Welfare of the Wounded"), were all young women, emphasizing Grace's belief that gender should not restrict any kind of service. By June 1918, forty-six-year-old Grace joined her drivers in France, determined to see action abroad herself. She was back home barely in time to join Ernest as the first lady of DeWinton.

For her volunteer work in France, Grace won three medals of honor from the French government. In 1914 Ernest had asked the Canadian government to assign him some role in the war, but he received no commission. It must have been hard for a man so familiar with the limelight to find himself upstaged by an increasingly independent spouse. In his autobiography, Ernest later credited Grace's war work as "paramount service," adding simply that "I had little part in the Great War, although I offered my services at Washington, Ottawa, and London; but my age (fifty-four) ruled me out."[3] The signing of the armistice in November 1918 did give husband and wife some time together at home in their fine new house, working hard to resurrect what was now called the Woodcraft League. They also traveled together to several western states on lecture circuits for which ETS was still a draw. His performances brought in much needed funds but also stirred Ernest's growing distaste for East Coast culture.

While Grace had gone off to become a war hero and Ernest was hosting campers at DeWinton, Ann was more regularly studying at Spence. However, as soon as the war was over, early in 1919, Grace took her daughter with her on another trip across the Atlantic, where they toured postwar hospitals springing up throughout France and Germany. Fifteen-year-old Ann was even allowed to have some training in nursing, at a time when the Spanish flu pandemic was finally subsiding. Her experiences greatly inspired her. In later biographical sketches she insisted that her first vocational choice was to be a doctor. Although she never pursued any formal schooling toward that goal, volunteer hospital work became an interest that she kept up for much of her adult life. Several of the male characters in her fiction are doctors, and many women characters are called on for their nursing skills.

Mother and daughter returned to the United States in time for Grace to help with the last push to get the Nineteenth Amendment ratified, which finally occurred on August 18, 1920. It was also time to get Ann back to Spence so that she could graduate with her class. Grace's mother, the indomitable and generous Clemenzie Gallatin Craig, had joined the family at DeWinton too, but she died there in June 1920. An amazingly independent woman until almost the very end of her life, she had lived on a ranch in Missouri with a beloved male companion named "Duffy" for many of her later years. Hanna Engstrom was also in residence, able to provide the one element of continuity that Ann retained no matter where she lived. Ann wrote in 1921 of Hanna that "she is just like a member of the family to me and I think next to my parents I love her better than any other."[4] Ann must have found stability hard to come by during her last two years of school.

Visitors, seeing the Setons living in their beautiful new house in another large, scenic park, likely thought that affection and harmony reigned. Under the surface, however, as the 1920s began, Ernest was not happy with Grace's increasingly frequent absences from home. Her travels were getting very expensive at a time when DeWinton was costing him both more time and money. In addition, she was not available to assist him with a monumental animal study that he was trying to advance, nor with the administrative chores connected to the Woodcraft League. It was clear that she had taken the women's rights movement personally, increasingly choosing her own prerogatives over her husband's. In the spring of 1921, after her graduation from Spence, seventeen-year-old Ann Seton went home to DeWinton to enjoy its advantages but also to witness her parents' friction.

The motto Spence had promoted was "Not for school but for life we learn," and Ann was ready. She and her parents had ruled out one obvious course that some of her classmates had chosen. Without any college degrees, Ernest and Grace were leading lights intellectually and socially, so Ann was confident that she was more than ordinarily prepared for the world beyond academia. As she thought about her future, her goal was not a humble one. As she wrote in a diary that she began in June 1921, she wished "to be very popular, to have power, to be beloved and universally admired." She also wanted something else that tells a great deal about some of her own and perhaps even her mother's feelings. As she put it, "I want to be someone myself—not to shine by reflected glory [of] my father."[5] Ann called her diary her "little book." Her father had written faithfully in his journal from boyhood on, which might have partly inspired her. But as she declared on her own page one, her book would be not just a record of daily doings but would express the "matters" that interested her deeply, or "*au fond*," as she put it in her well-practiced French. On the title page, she insisted that what she wrote in her book would include "*especiale-ment* the passions, the emotions, the ecstasies *de mon coeur.*"[6]

As the book's pages began to fill, Ann sometimes found herself being "too introspective," but she excused herself by saying, "No book can be as interesting as one's life (to oneself), for each day is a surprise." With great seriousness, she also declared, "I could write, I know, but the trouble is that I want to *live* vivid exciting things, not write them for imaginary creatures."[7] Her assurance that she could become a successful author, *if* she so desired, was not a naive boast. With parents who all her life had been writing to live, or living to write, that occupation was in the air she breathed. Thirty years after her early journal entry on the subject and by then a bestselling novelist, the author, self-renamed

Anya, would explain her distaste for her parents' work. Their example had made her "thoroughly aware of the seamy side of the profession—the drudgery, the essential loneliness, and the tough hide needed to persevere through discouragement and misunderstandings."[8] What she really wanted at seventeen was a life that would be just as exciting as any fiction that she could imagine, without any of the "drudgery" that gave writing a "seamy" side.

During her first summer at home, Ann seldom made comments of any substance about her parents' activities. She did note that Ernest had "a fiendish temper" but that unlike her friends' fathers, he was at least always glad to give her money for shopping or entertainments. Mostly, however, the sentiment that became most familiar in her journal was boredom. She had enjoyed all the usual "gay times" as she called them—meeting her parents' well-heeled visitors, vacationing with friends in Maine, participating in a daily round of afternoon teas and evening dances in Greenwich. Yet as she told her journal, "even when I have a wonderful time . . . I always want something more."[9] Voice lessons and "social services work" at a local hospital gave her some useful distractions. Still, taking stock of her "many talents," she feared she might simply be a "Jack of all trades. . . . I sing a little, dance more, write a little, drive a little, and am a linguist, yet in none of these am I really proficient," she complained.[10]

Ann had begun her last year at Spence just after women had secured the ratification of the Nineteenth Amendment in August 1920. There were few external limitations to hinder her from striking out as she pleased. She had her parents' wealth and liberal views about strong women as well as her own beauty, intelligence, and extensive, if somewhat haphazard, education to encourage her. Doors were opening in many directions: 1921 was the year that Amelia Earhart took her first flying lessons and Margaret Sanger founded the American Birth Control League. Many upper-class young women were opting for more years of schooling in colleges and universities that began to accept them into professional programs. Yet Ann, after toying briefly with the exalted vocations of doctor or opera singer, began instead to chart a course that would turn out to be totally traditional.

Coming of age at the beginning of the Roaring Twenties, Ann was part of a new generation of young women who, after their mothers had won them the vote, were lured into much more self-centered kinds of activism. They chose to make daring gestures about style, trying out bold fashion statements, a new, racy vocabulary, and liberating social codes. Some found their way into well-paying careers. But after these experiments, according to the popular ladies' magazines of the day that Ann absorbed, a proper and fortunate girl was expected to get on with the time-honored business of finding a husband and becoming a mother. Thus 1921 was a year of mixed messages for white, well-bred young women of Ann Seton's class. Amelia Earhart and Margaret Sanger were set against Clara Bow and Fanny Brice, who debuted in June 1921 with the Ziegfeld Follies singing what became her trademark song, "My Man."

As a girl of the twenties, Ann had many new notions to consider about the opposite sex, and especially how one of their number might alter her future. Ernest had even asked Grace if it wasn't about time for their daughter to be getting on with finding a husband. As if to answer him, Ann's "little book" began to fill with assessments of possible admirers. In the entries of the first few months, disappointment was the chief result of "coming out." Ann felt far more mature than the "sapling" types she had met, who were interested in her only because she was "a good dancer, pretty," and, she added pointedly, "the daughter of Ernest Thompson Seton."[11]

As the closely supervised product of a girls' school, Ann had limited experience with "spooning," as she called dating. She wrote primly in her journal that she knew she belonged to what "the papers" labeled "the decadent generation." Most girls, she concluded, were "promiscuous," while boys "expect all girls to give themselves from the waist up." Appalled by these low standards, she vowed that "the next man who tries to kiss me will be told that I will not kiss anyone except when there is true and mutual love," although admittedly, it would be "hard to resist passion."[12] Writing more on the subject several days later, she complained about how many of the "boys" she knew simply loved "goo-goo eyes" and noted that "I always have gotten on better with older men."[13]

Taking stock of her assets, Ann recorded her vital statistics for posterity: height 5 feet, 6 inches; weight 128 pounds; measurements 34-25-37, eyes hazel. Photographs from these years show a strikingly beautiful girl who had her father's thick, black curls and flashing eyes and her mother's finely shaped nose and chin. In her wish list of characteristics that would make an "Ideal Me," she created headings that included "Looks, Charms, Qualities, and Abilities." In "Looks," among other attributes, she wanted to be "willowy and hold a graceful carriage." In terms of "Charm," she hoped for a "musical and caressing" voice and to be "humorous" but "unsarcastic." Some of the ideal "Qualities" to possess would be "tact, pep, intensity, and enthusiasm," and some of the abilities to cultivate were "singing, dancing, languages, and knowledge," in fact "good knowledge of any subject." Following this analysis was the comment that she would also like to be more knowledgeable about "current events" because, she admitted, "my life is very self-absorbed."[14] In this confession, she was very much a girl of her time.

By October 1921 Ann's assets had attracted "three lovers," according to her journal, although she added, "I don't love any of them—yet."[15] Of the three, it was Hamilton Cottier, a Princeton student of literature four years her senior, whose courtship began to dominate her drama. Hamilton fit nicely into Ann's vow that she would kiss no one who had not shown true and honorable love. He was shy and courtly, sober and scholarly. He was handsome too, in a somewhat delicate way, not at all like the rugged he-man that Ernest typified. Hamilton and Ann met at one of those boring garden parties in September 1921, an occasion that they had been forced by their mothers to attend. They talked for hours that afternoon, mostly about poetry. He could claim a solid enough family lineage, even though it had come to him through adoption. His stepfather, Alonzo Cottier, married his mother, Blanche Busey, after she had divorced her alcoholic husband, John Russell Kelso, on the grounds of adultery when Hamilton was two years old. For Ann, Hamilton's chief attraction was that he loved literature and took her seriously. He might have been just a little too bookish, but she was sure she could broaden his horizons through her family's connections.

Ann found her scholarly Princeton beau to be perfectly compatible, but the two lovers' families were another matter. Ann's comments concerning Hamilton's parents were reserved for letters to him, and these made clear that Hamilton's father did not like Ann or her parents. Ernest was like Alonzo Cottier only in being a self-made millionaire who was also listed in the New York Social Register. Alonzo was an astute, conservative businessman and a dour Presbyterian whose wife had been trained to be a beautiful, silent ornament by his side. To him, the Setons were more bohemian than aristocratic, and Ann was too brash and demonstrative with his son. For her part, Ann was disdainful, writing to Hamilton, "If I may be permitted to be so conceited, I think we three [she and her parents] have achieved enough to make their opinions of value, even in opposition to your parent's."[16]

Ann's romance was not to Grace's liking either, so she decided to take her daughter with her on an already planned research trip to Egypt, adding some touring in Italy and France. Grace believed that Ann had too little experience to handle a serious relationship, so she hoped to give her some different interests to consider. During the trip, while in Egypt, Ann met King Faud's wife, Queen Nafir, and the writer H. G. Wells, but she was not impressed. She spent most of her time writing sometimes twenty-page letters to Hamilton. In one she reported that "Mr. Wells, like all Englishmen of note, is a frightfully boring, beefy, ultra british [sic] old flirt." At eighteen, she found nothing to admire and was bold enough to comment that she saw in Mr. Wells "no indication of the brain which wrote the 'Outline of History.'"[17]

The long letters, thirty-two in all, that Ann wrote to Hamilton during her "tour" seem as painfully naive as they are frank. In one she advised, "Be assertive, and especially in managing me, a woman loves to be gently bossed."[18] In some letters she asked him if he was sure of his love, urging him to "always tell the truth," as it was the only "basis for a perfect marriage." In the same letter, she told her own truth: "I adore books as much as you, but they are not life. I'm going to make you *live* a good half the time."[19] Several of the heroines that Anya Seton later created for her books illustrate this contradiction. They want a dominating lover who will "manage" them, but they also chafe at restrictions on their own will. On this tour with her mother, what Ann wanted most was to pin down her future, which she now defined exclusively as marriage, as soon as possible.

Grace had made careful preparations for her trip to Egypt months before she decided to take Ann along. Her idea had been to gather materials for a new book, her first attempt in fourteen years. When the book came out in 1923, she gave it the title *A Woman Tenderfoot in Egypt* to capitalize on the fame she had achieved with her 1900 western adventure. Anya later pointed out, in her own copy of her mother's book, that she was never mentioned in it.[20] Pamela Forcey, noting this omission, speculated that Grace left out her daughter "probably" because she "wanted to give a picture of herself, in her book, that she thought would be diluted by the presence of a grown daughter."[21] In this as in all her later books, Grace was a one-woman show, intent that her readers be completely engrossed in her drama and message. Ann must have been aware, while tagging along on her mother's visits, that she was in many ways already on her own. The actions of both parents offered no assurance that they wanted to include her in their very separate lives.

In the note to her readers that Grace placed at the beginning of *A Woman Tenderfoot in Egypt* dated "Greenwich, 1922," she describes herself waving good-bye to the Statue of Liberty from the deck of the SS *Adriatic*, not mentioning that Ann was alongside her. Grace was savoring the realization that she was not, as she put it, "permanently stuck on a granite base, but could follow the will o' the wisp of the true traveler."[22] Her message to the world, including her daughter and husband, was not only that she had come "unstuck," but also that she was outward bound on a solo course. In future years, Grace would become Ann's closest companion, her chief source of both emotional and monetary support. But in the time before her daughter's marriage, after their trip to Egypt, Grace almost completely disappeared, for reasons related to Ernest's wandering attentions as well as her own new vow to be a "true traveler." She was in China for much of the year before Ann's wedding, and shortly afterward, she set off for India.

As for Ernest, Ann had seldom been able to depend on him for support or companionship. Growing up, she had watched him blow in like a hurricane, bringing frantic rounds of excitement, before he just as suddenly took off again, often for months at a time. As a child, she had sometimes traveled with him and Grace on lecture tours, but during these trips he was usually busy enjoying his larger-than-life celebrity and hardly interested in his background daughter. In a 1966 "Childhood Memories" typescript, Anya wrote that "Daddy is the idol of thousands of children," but "it bored him to take me anywhere."[23] The famous leader of boys must have always seemed inaccessible to his young daughter. Still, in their letters back and forth, she always sought his approval and spoke affectionately. Their most memorable times together were trips that took them throughout the American Southwest. On the first of these, which began in August 1915, Grace also went along. For Ann, the journey was the beginning of a lifelong attraction to the West and to Native American culture, while the family stayed in Santa Fe and toured nearby pueblos and reservations. In January 1923, while Grace was in China, Ann again accompanied Ernest on a trip west, this time to Arizona and California. In two novels, Anya Seton later mined her memories of these territories, carefully reconstructing the worlds that had been opened to her through these rare times with her father.

For Ernest, the 1923 western trip was motivated in part by his need to recruit Woodcraft League members in new areas. Beginning in the early twenties, he was mostly home on the DeWinton estate. However, he had already become disenchanted with the showplace that he had poured so much time and energy into creating. Money was almost certainly the main reason that he decided to build yet another home, a much smaller one, on a back portion of the DeWinton property. He would not admit it, but his ultimate aim was to sell the grand house. At the same time, he was also trying to keep his Woodcraft organization afloat by marketing it to more campers. His most compelling pursuit, however, was his work on what he hoped would be his most significant scientific study of animal life. If he could not beat the Boy Scouts at their game, he was still determined to prove wrong everyone who had doubted his right to be recognized as a bona fide animal scientist.

To assist him in this goal and have someone assume the Woodcraft business that no longer interested Grace, Ernest hired a secretary, almost thirty years his junior, to take on a variety of tasks. Julia Moss Buttree, a married woman with Hunter College degrees in classical languages and drama, would later write about the first time she met the Chief at a lecture on Woodcraft: "When we first touched hands in a casual introduction, we knew."[24] She had felt a "thrill" simply listening to him, the kind of admiration that Grace had not provided in a long time.

When Grace took Ann away on the SS *Adriatic* in January 1922, she perhaps had some inkling of what Ernest might do back home. A letter that Ann wrote to Hamilton in late April 1922, as she and Grace were returning by ship to the United States, spelled out the serious trouble. The mother-daughter excursion was going to end ahead of schedule because Grace had received a letter warning that Ernest was now openly showing his enchantment with a "fair charmer."[25] Publicly, no word was said, and no stories printed, but anyone close to the family had to be aware of the facts. Ernest had constructed a "studio" to live in, hoped to find long-term renters for DeWinton, and would soon finish a bungalow on the estate for Julia and her husband Ted. He had even set up Ted Buttree as manager of a tea room that he opened on the main Greenwich thoroughfare, the Old Post Road. Called the Black Bear, the tea room supposedly featured a large bear kept in a cage on the premises, until animal rights advocates succeeded in getting it removed.[26] Julie, as Ernest called her, reminisced later that when he first met her in 1918, he had commented, "My, but we could have a lot of fun together."[27] With a tearoom, a studio, an ambitious scientific book project, and a smart young woman eager to help, he was indeed having fun.

Ernest was never happier than when he was designing and building houses, and this was the other fun that occupied him during Grace's absence. He began thinking about the house he called "Little Peequo" when DeWinton was barely two years completed. This also "Tudor Indian" style house included a lake that would feed into the lower one at DeWinton. It also featured a lush formal garden dotted with pools and fountains. The stucco siding was decorated with his usual symbols, sayings, and even a silhouette of one of his famous animal characters, Johnny Bear. Inside, however, and especially when compared to the big house, Little Peequo would have felt cramped and dark, a situation somewhat remedied when he added a larger wing a few years later.

In the summer of 1922, back from her trip with Ann to Egypt and Europe, Grace went off to Onteora, a Catskills resort in Tannersville, New York, to finish her book on Egypt. She refused to enter her husband's new architectural fancy, which she called a "rotten little cottage."[28] For the next four years, it became her pattern to go to Tannersville to finish whatever book she was writing. In 1924, Ernest wrote her that he would always provide her with "a comfortable place" to live, adding disingenuously that while "of course, your room [in Little Peequo] is here awaiting you," he suspected that work on her own book, this one based on her trip to India, would "impose on you very nearly the same routine as that of last summer."[29]

A Woman Tenderfoot in Egypt contained Grace's interviews with several upper-class Egyptian women who were becoming leaders in government and social causes, often against their husbands' wishes. Grace's words in her preface, announcing her newfound freedom to travel solo, might have reflected what she was bound to have recognized about her failing relationship with her husband. In any case, she was planning another trip that would also promote the dual themes of the Egyptian one: women's rights and the author's bold encounters with foreign people and places. Completing her Egypt manuscript in record time, she was off to China by the fall of 1922.

From the summer of her return from Egypt until her marriage, Ann did not have her mother nearby for any sustained time. Ann lived mainly at Little Peequo with Hanna while Ernest spent most of his time working in his studio. In a letter to Hamilton, studying at Princeton, she wrote that "Father is crusty because he hasn't enough booze over here and he can't get his Daphne on the phone."[30] There was no question for her what was happening to her parents' marriage or that they did not see her as a primary concern. In January 1923, when Ann had traveled west with "Daddy," she stayed much of the time with California friends or her Gallatin relatives, while Ernest arranged to move Woodcraft's headquarters to Los Angeles. The Chief, with his Julie, also met with Native American activists fighting for political rights. From this time forward, he was much more vocal in advocating that the government end their mistreatment.

When Ann was in residence back in Greenwich, Hamilton Cottier often visited, and when he was at Princeton, she wrote letters to him that were intimate and desperate. All her letters, she admitted, served the same purpose as her journal entries. Just as intensely introspective and self-analytical, they gave her the added pleasure of a responsive audience whom she could also enjoy analyzing. Viewed with hindsight, her correspondence demonstrates how little she understood her lover or herself. First, while she was touring Europe with Grace, she began to question Hamilton's single-minded focus on his studies. Her love of poetry had created a bond with him, but she was not seriously interested in its finer points. Hamilton, on the other hand, was at the time working intently on a master's degree at Princeton and looking forward to a year of postgraduate study in Oxford, England. What was he to make of the letter in which Ann declared, "I *don't* approve of the professorship for you as I have said before"?[31] Her father denigrated stuffy academics who had often sniffed at his superior credentials in animal studies. Both he and Grace were acclaimed by general readers for their firsthand experiences with their subjects, and Ann absorbed that value.

Clearly proud of the advantages her parents had provided, at least in her letters to Hamilton, Ann told her soon-to-be fiancé that after he joined "our world," he would enjoy broader horizons: "I don't think I have ever met at home or with my parents, anyone who is not very prominent, famous, or a success, in their particular line." Even more bluntly, she voiced her doubt that Hamilton had "the teacher's personality." He could be "much more."[32] Her opinion could not have been more mistaken, at least from her suitor's point of view. Never in his lifetime did Hamilton consider any nonacademic vocation.

The other area in which Ann completely misread Hamilton was in the matter of sex. Her letters became increasingly frank on this subject. By the fall of 1922, she had come a long way from the prudish girl who bemoaned the decadence of her generation. One letter in particular revealed a great deal about her parents' sex lives as well as her own change of views. First she reviewed for

Hamilton what Ernest told her while Grace was in China. She quotes Ernest's very explicit words, dramatic enough to have come from a novel: "Ann, during all these twenty-six years, your mother has never spent a night with me in my bed, or voluntarily lived with me, she's been cold, cold to me and it is almost impossible for such a man as I to bear that. It means so much."[33]

Whatever Ann might have thought of this confession, Ernest conveyed one message above all that she wanted to press upon Hamilton: "Oh, how important sex is," she exclaimed. "If there is any need for adjustments between us for God's sake let's be frank and put that before all else till it is perfect."[34] Her openness on this front did not scare Hamilton away from the altar, although perhaps it should have. Alonzo Cottier was a remote, stern, and stuffily upright father, the kind of man who would make it very difficult for a son to admit asexual, much less homosexual, tendencies. Anya's journals contain no mention of any similar ardor on Hamilton's part, but by early 1923 she was convinced enough of his feelings to engineer an engagement and a wedding date for the coming June.

Grace returned from China in late April 1923 only to supervise Ann's wedding plans. She had been forced to accept the reality that her daughter was going to marry sooner rather than later. She also knew that Ernest was not going back to DeWinton. From thousands of miles away, she had begged him not to rent out their home again. In one letter, dated December 8, 1922, she pleaded, "De Winton is Ann's Patrimony and I am awfully fond of it,"[35] ignoring the fact that she had frequently chosen to be as far away from it as she could get. Other letters were even more plaintive. She wrote that she was homeless "while aliens occupy our treasured abode."[36] Ernest's last word on the subject, dated March 14, 1923, not long before her return, was abrupt: "Have rented De Winton," and "The China trip is all paid for and I have paid two months' rent besides and am taking care of Ann and Hanna and myself for the present so you ought to be pleased."[37] In three months, the popular Ernest and Grace Thompson Seton would put on a spectacular wedding at DeWinton, which they had to rent back from their renters for the occasion. The event was one that befitted their well-documented social status but was a sham in terms of their private lives.

Ann's wedding took place on June 30, 1923, in Christ Episcopal Church, Greenwich. It was attended by many of the most prominent members of New York society: industrialists such as Cyrus McCormack, publishers such as

Edward Bok, suffragettes from Grace's retinue, and Ernest's writer and artist friends. One of the most interesting news stories about the wedding was a glowing article that appeared in a posh magazine called the *Spur*. Throughout the 1920s its pages targeted wealthy New Yorkers with news about fashion, gardens, travel, horses, and other accessories of high society. Naturally the magazine sent a reporter to cover Ann's nuptials, one of the most newsworthy society events of the summer season. Clearly, the reporter was most entranced by the location of the reception, attended by some "1000 guests."[38] He provided a little information about the bride and her Princeton groom, even less about the well-known mother of the bride, but a great deal about the natural wonderland designed by the bride's father, the noted master of the estate.

DeWinton, the unsigned reporter told his readers, was "a fit setting" for Ernest Thompson Seton's Woodcraft organization. He gave an admiring picture of its lakes, a lodge, extensive trails, and council rings, affirming that Seton's new estate "outshone Wyndygoul." DeWinton had a more "magisterial" central house set in surroundings that "seem more like the Adirondack wilderness . . . than suburban NY," a term Greenwich locals despised. The house featured several rooms of enormous size "designed for extravagant entertaining" and various bedroom suites that could accommodate "any number of houseguests." The effect of the whole, he concluded, was "rugged in character within and without." Ironically, this most extensive public description of DeWinton did not appear until the family no longer lived there. Not much later, Ernest posted a FOR SALE advertisement for DeWinton that included a similar description.

The *Spur*'s reporter did not know, or at least did not mention, that none of the Setons had for any sustained period lived or entertained at DeWinton from the time it was built or that the house would soon be on the market. The bride's mother, several months after the wedding, had stiff words for reporters as she boarded a ship headed for India: "Having subordinated everything to bringing up my daughter . . . I now feel free to travel and achieve the results to which hitherto I have given secondary consideration."[39] The father of the bride simply wrote in his journal for June 30, 1923, on the wedding day, "The end of a Big Chapter in our Lives."[40]

3 | DEAREST AMBITIONS

ANN'S MARRIAGE TO HAMILTON COTTIER IN JUNE 1923 launched seven years of turmoil for all the Setons. Living almost completely separated after their daughter's wedding, both Grace and Ernest reached the pinnacle of their writing careers. By 1930 Grace had traveled the world and published four books about her journeys to some of the most exotic places on three continents. Then she was right back where she had started, living in Little Peequo, the only house left for her as well as the one that was so completely unsuitable, she believed. Ernest at first hunkered down at Little Peequo to write his magnum opus, the four-volume *Lives of Game Animals*, with Julia Buttree by his side. But by 1927 he too had begun to wander, in his case to the American Southwest again, where he had long ago found the frontier that turned him, through the great wolf Lobo, into a famous writer.

Daughter Ann, at nineteen, began married life with Hamilton as he began his studies at Oxford. In this very British university town she was far away from the tumult she had seen coming back in Greenwich. A long, typed letter from Ernest to Ann, dated December 21, 1923, reveals as much about her parents' situation by what it does not say as by what it does. The letter began, "I suppose you and Mother are together now, talking it over. There's a lot of water running under the bridge these days." He did not elaborate on the "it"—his involvement with Julia Buttree—but instead moved on quickly to ask Ann to give "Mother" some news about Woodcraft business, since she would be in Oxford with Ann for Christmas. He also described his landscaping work on Little Peequo, "a beautiful thing," he added, as though he were making a real estate pitch. News of all his holiday dinners and the magical visit of a red fox finished up his letter, to which he added a handwritten note and his sprawling ETS signature. The letter was also signed, at the bottom, by Julia Buttree, who wrote, "Merry merry Christmas."[1]

Reading that signature and looking between the lines of the letter, it takes little guesswork to surmise that Ernest's secretary was at least a partial editor of what the letter told and did not tell. Grace had spent her first of four summers, that of 1923, in the Catskills resort of Onteora, which had become a popular retreat especially for single women artists and writers. Here she worked to complete *Chinese Lanterns*, the book about her trip to China taken in the months before Ann's wedding. Ernest had continued during those months to refuse to return to DeWinton, telling her disingenuously both before and after the wedding only that she would always be welcome at Little Peequo. After spending Christmas 1923 with the newlywed Cottiers in Oxford, early in 1924 Grace left for the other side of the world, the Indian subcontinent, to gather material for her next travel narrative. *Chinese Lanterns*, published around the same time as this departure, had provided the opening she needed to achieve new stature on her own. The cost, however, was clearly going to be her position as Ernest Thompson Seton's wife, something that by this time she must have known.

In Oxford during the summer of 1923, Ann had stepped into a life that could not have been more different from everything she had known before. In some ways, she was upbeat about her change of circumstances, relishing the heady academic atmosphere and the comfortable, Old World pace of Oxford life and enjoying forays into homemaking. Her marriage, however, left her confused and filled with what she called "cowlike apathy." This was her self-diagnosis, written on the first page of the diary that she began keeping in 1924, almost a year after her wedding day the previous June. Her explanation for not writing earlier was that "marriage is awfully intimate. I don't feel entirely myself anymore, it seems as though I'd lost some of my identity." As though she had said something wrong, she went on quickly to claim, "I love to have Hamilton around," and also that "when I AM alone, I don't feel so—because my whole existence is shared." She did not say whether this was good or bad, but did add, "I wish I could get quite away from Ham for a while—though I'd miss him awfully." Her one hasty attempt to hide what was more than just ambivalence did not hold up. As she said, with deep disappointment in this first entry, Hamilton was "darling, sweet, and affectionate," but there was no "grande passion." "Perhaps I'm not developed enough," she worried, "though I fear he hasn't it in him." All her dreams were still on hold, and as she vowed, "I haven't 'lived,' and I want to—I will."[2]

Ann followed this startling, sad confession of how expected marital bliss had turned into "emotional torpor" with a description of someone else's courtship, one that she was witnessing at close hand. The Cottiers' little three-room rented flat was owned by Mrs. Amy Trew, a landlady whom Ann described as "semi-cultivated" and "dishonest." Trew had a daughter Christine, whom Ann described in equally unflattering terms as "hideous, awkward, ultra clever." Whatever her drawbacks, Christine was being honored by "a real Irish Earl," who was "paying court." It might have been comforting for Ann to add, "Poor Lord Longford. I don't think he's actually half-witted but very nearly. Fat, pink, and cold with a cackling laugh!"[3] Was she perhaps a bit jealous? If so, she would have been more so later if she ever knew that once married, Christine, as Lady Longford with her Irish lord, became the wealthy sustainer of the Gate Theatre Company in Dublin, for which she wrote plays, including an adaptation of Ann's beloved *Pride and Prejudice*.

In Ann's next diary entry, there was no more talk of the Trews or of Hamilton's failures in lovemaking. Thanks to more of Grace's financial help, the couple was able to have a cycle car, a "baby Morgan" named "Grace" that "coughs if you request her to go under 20 in high gear." At this "terribly speedy" rate, they happily explored the countryside.[4] In a response to a description of some of the houses she had seen on their travels, written by Ann to Ernest, he replied that he noted "with satisfaction that you are learning to love the English Tudor." He also assumed that she had visited South Shields and seen the house where he had been born, "#4 Wellington Terrace," where supposedly, the Boy Scouts had placed "a plaque on the wall."[5] "Daddy" was always, it seems, self-promoting.

Occasionally the young Cottiers were invited to dinners and house parties. Describing one of these weekends at "Lady Henry's," her parents' friend Lady Tanksersly, Ann did drop broad hints at the state of her marriage while describing a perhaps typical evening among the British upper class. The first night there, she said, was "just awful," partly because she was forced to play bridge with an older couple when she wanted to "dance and flirt." While Hamilton took to brooding or playing bridge without her, Ann found herself being admired by more than one of the other male guests. A rather unattractive "Spaniard" who was nevertheless someday "going to be a Duke" told her point blank that "anyone could tell I wasn't happily married." Writing about his attentions, she didn't disagree. She also wrote that while at first, she had felt very uncomfortable and bored, on the second night, when "I had a little liquor, things got better and better."[6] A marriage that was not visibly happy to onlookers and the comfort that liquor provided might have seemed inconsequential in a twenty-year old's commentary, but in Ann's case, these were both warnings of great trouble to come.

Whatever the young Cottiers' problems, Hamilton did have a brief burst of libido early in the new year, with the result that, by March 1925, Ann was pregnant. Her husband was undoubtedly trying to live up not only to Ann's expectations but also his father's. Alonzo Cottier wanted an heir, and it is possible that even monetary support was tied to this demand. Hamilton's cold and self-righteous adoptive father had, in his own past, a scandalous secret that made the continuation of his line a very sore point. As a younger man, he had been married and sired a daughter in what was a very unhappy union. His wife left him, taking their young child, claiming when she was found that he had been abusive to both. She refused to tell Alonzo, the police, or even a trial judge the whereabouts of the little girl and served time in prison as a penalty for her silence. After their widely publicized divorce in 1896, Alonzo searched for his child for many years, but she was never found.[7]

The older, even wealthier Alonzo Cottier, now married to beautiful Blanche, could not have been a comfortable father figure. Hamilton adored Blanche Busey (Kelso), the mother who had taken him away from his birth father, John Russell Kelso IV, whom he was too young to remember. She had bravely supported her son entirely on her own before marrying her wealthy employer. There is little question that Hamilton's life as adopted son and heir left him badly scarred and resentful, but also generally unassertive. After more than a year in Oxford, he failed to receive the necessary approval for work he was doing for his master's degree back at Princeton. Alonzo himself was surely partly to blame. He had never approved of Hamilton's choice of an academic career over a position in the business world, so it was almost a self-fulfilling prophecy that his son would fail. With their own child on the way and no prospects at Oxford, the young Cottiers returned to the United States, settling by the fall near the university in Princeton. Hamilton's alma mater offered a part-time teaching appointment, so for the time being the couple found both family and financial difficulties eased. Ann went to New York and stayed with her mother as her delivery time came closer, since both wanted the baby to be born at Fifth Avenue Hospital. Hamilton made it there for the birth of their daughter, Pamela, on November 3, 1925.

In an ironic parallel, throughout the time that Ann and Hamilton were uneasily establishing life together as a married couple with an infant daughter, Grace and Ernest were navigating a separation that would take ten years to finalize. While publicly there was no official word of trouble, all who knew them well had to be aware that Grace had been supplanted by Julia, both as Ernest's romantic interest and as his editorial and Woodcraft business assistant. The Woodcraft movement went on as usual, even with headquarters now on the West Coast. The great acclaim ETS was granted, including the Burroughs Medal and the Elliot Medal, for his stellar work on his *Lives of Game Animals*, was proof that Ernest had been working extremely hard to produce this masterpiece. With this achievement, there seemed to be little for anyone to say about his private life. Grace remained a harder subject even than Ernest for the gossip columns because she became such a moving target. Returning from India, she again went to the Catskills resort to write. *Yes, Lady Saheb* was published to good reviews in 1925 and was one of her most fascinating narratives, including an important interview with Mahatma Gandhi.

After Pamela was born in November 1925, Ann, as a Princeton scholar's wife, was able to enjoy being both a mother and a daughter. Considering that she was only twenty-one when Pamela was born, and that she had the help of a full-time nanny, it isn't surprising that she was also frequently bored. By the spring of 1927, she was seriously thinking about what she wanted to do to relieve her restlessness and longings. In a May 27 journal entry, she wrote out a list of "dearest ambitions." Number 6 was "to have published the work of my pen," followed in Number 7 by a significant addition, "to have my name at least as famous as my parents." Just as she had in 1921, she saw her ability to be a writer as a strong possibility and also saw herself in competition with her parents. Yet the first ambition on the list, which also colored several other "ambitions," was her desire to experience "the ecstasy of sexual passion" (Number 1) followed by "being completely in love" (Number 2). She wanted to have "at least two satisfying extramarital liaisons" (Number 3) and to have "ten more men in love with me" (Number 15).[8]

If these wishes seem fantastical and immature coming from a married woman with a toddler daughter, Ann had some reason. When she wrote her list in 1927, she was barely twenty-three, yet as a wife had never enjoyed any kind of fulfilling physical relationship with her husband of four years. Two other items, "to have at least one more baby" (Number 4) and "for the child to be a boy" (Number 5), demonstrate that the younger Cottiers were able, sometimes, to "cohabit." To be a writer, to have lovers, to be a mother—these were the tangled web of possibilities that Ann contemplated. Number 4 was accomplished first. By September of 1927, the Cottiers were expecting again. Alonzo wanted a grandson, and Hamilton and Ann wanted Pamela to have a sibling. With her pregnancy, Ann temporarily put away the other ambitions on her list.

During the year after Pamela was born, Grace often visited with her daughter and granddaughter, but in 1926, not long after *Yes, Lady Saheb* was published, she was asked to take the position of historian for an expedition to South America sponsored by the Field Museum of Chicago. The venture would allow her to explore more unknown territory as well as to be in the company of some noteworthy companions. After only six weeks, however, Grace left the expedition in Brazil, partly because Evelyn Field, the flamboyant, independently wealthy wife of Marshall Field III and the expedition's financier, had come along on the trip and proved to be too irritating for Grace to tolerate. She continued to explore on her own, through Paraguay, Chile, Bolivia, Peru, and Panama. Two years later, she made a second brief trip to Brazil and combined the two journeys to write her fourth book in five years. Her South American adventures were published in 1932 in London as *Log of the Look-See* and in the United States, in 1933, as *Magic Waters*, but she wrote the accounts in record time. Life back home was, however, harder than battling the creatures of the Amazon. In letters and during infrequent meetings in the late 1920s, she and Ernest had gone back and forth with varying degrees of civility concerning finances and the dwindling possibility of ever living together again.

After completing *Lives of Game Animals* Ernest spent no time resting on his laurels. While keeping Grace at bay with some cordial communications and visits, he began to move forward to fulfill the dream that he had been considering for some time, a permanent exodus from the East Coast. The Woodcraft movement, in its established, mostly northeastern venues, had stagnated. Rugged outdoor life, especially as the Natives practiced it, was much less popular in the increasingly urban areas where Seton's program had first flourished. Sixty-seven-year-old Ernest had achieved great and deserved celebrity by 1927—as an artist, a naturalist, a writer, a leader of the Boy Scouts, and a literary entertainer. As he aged, however, he looked toward two causes that would find little support in the East: land conservation and American Indian rights. Also, he wanted to recover some of the sense of adventure, out in the wild, that had stimulated his earlier life, just at the time that Grace seemed ready to give up her own remarkable treks into the unknown.

Beginning in 1927 and for the next two years, Ernest made his priorities clear. He and Julia took six trips to New Mexico to find the perfect home for a last great encounter with the Native people and the Wild West that had started his climb to fame. By 1928, after completing her South American story, Grace was finally back, although only intermittently, in Greenwich. Due to Ernest's long absences, and probably to financial considerations as well, she at last took up residence in the hated Little Peequo, now enlarged and embellished. Ted Buttree, Julia's long-suffering or possibly indifferent spouse, remained there as well in his own cottage on the grounds. Still, clearly determined to do what brought her the most joy and acclaim, Grace took little time in designing her most daring and also whirlwind adventure, the trip to Indochina which she began in late 1928 and completed by February 1929. This time she traveled first into Vietnam's northern and least known interior jungles, then to Bangkok, Siam, on to the Philippine mountains, and finally to the sunny isle of Bali. All her accounts of these sites were accompanied by her own photographs and detailed maps. She too was claiming new ground, established imaginatively through her own vibrant voice and vision. But while she was in Bali, she also spent three weeks in a hospital recovering from a debilitating bout of bacterial dysentery—an experience she does not describe but one that would leave her with ongoing serious health problems.

While Grace had been in her jungles, Ernest and Julia were deciding that their future belonged to New Mexico. They began in 1929 to focus on a large undeveloped property, known as the De Vargas tract, close to two thousand acres of land, some level, but with canyons, arroyos, and granite outcroppings. This rare expanse was located six miles south of Santa Fe. It was a magnificent territory of natural and spiritual beauty, a worthy successor to the scenic masterpieces that Seton had developed in Greenwich. Looking toward this last frontier, Ernest was crossing an irreversible geographical as well as emotional divide that increasingly blocked out his wife and daughter. That Grace, in Bali, felt the chilling wind coming can be seen in her description of her last day in that island paradise. In the last paragraph of the book she was to write about her time in Southeast Asia, she looked ahead to what she knew she was going to find when she returned to the country she had so often fled. First, she listed what she had witnessed on her final transcontinental adventure, "the dark and sinister picture of Indo China's decaying peoples," the modernity of "opulent" Siam, and Bali's "happy people." Then she added, "I leave them for the hysteria of Western civilization—for home."[9]

Ann, in Princeton, was during these times chronicling the equally momentous changes in her life. April 9, 1928, brought the arrival of a son, given Ann's maiden name Seton. It was, of course, also the chosen surname of his westward migrating grandfather, a choice that could not have pleased his paternal grandsire Alonzo. By this time, however, Ann hardly cared what her hostile father-in-law thought. Only three months after Seton was born, in a diary entry dated July 27, 1928, she wrote a long meditation analyzing her experience of marriage. Clearly the young Cottiers, despite their shared delight as parents of two small children, were in other essential respects living as emotionally apart as were her parents.

Ann began her extraordinary late July diary entry by noting that her life thus far could be divided into two parts—two years of "love and aching passion for Hamilton—five years of domesticity and maternity." Seton, the second child and longed-for boy, had brought no real improvement to the marriage. While "we are certainly as happy as most couples," she wrote, "he [Hamilton] touches my inner life not at all." That life, she added, "which is symbolized by these diaries, has been submerged." Any hope of "real love," something beyond simple "affection," had died on her "wedding night," she now confessed, when Hamilton had shown that the sex act with his eager bride was repugnant to him. What was left of their relationship five years later was "a community of interest, love for our children, and some affection." Yet, "life is not entirely worth living for me without sex," she wrote, adding her determination to have "a lover or many lovers, and success from writing." At the end of her long entry, she concludes, "Check off matrimony, check off virginal palpitations, check off maternity, check off domesticity, check off travel (but not permanently), I am ready for more. I want universal popularity, a lover, success in making money, presumably by writing. Above all I want sex."[10] On New Year's Day

1929, not six months later, she looked back to the "Ambition List" she had written in 1927, writing in her diary, "It gives me a thrill to put down that the lover came, and three more ambitions were satisfied by him. I'm in a hell of a mess, but I do not regret it. Better this than nothingness."[11]

When Ann Cottier, not long before her twenty-fifth birthday, wrote that her lover had come, she began a new kind of journaling, intensely dramatic and self-centered. In her long entry of July 27, 1928, she had begun shaping her dilemma into the popular romantic mold of a beautiful girl's search for passionate love and self-fulfillment, as though her life might itself resemble a story from one of the pulps that she and so many women were reading in the 1920s. At this point, she resembled some of her own later novels' young heroines, by turns ambitious, self-pitying, determined, guilt-ridden, and above all, swept away by desire. In the seven years since her graduation from Spence School, she had grown from a restless, sheltered, somewhat shy girl into an equally restless twenty-four year old "matron," the mother of two young children unhappily settled into the role of a not-quite faculty member's wife, with too much time on her hands and only one major preoccupation, the lack of any sexual pleasure in her marriage.

By choosing marriage at nineteen, Ann was motivated largely by the need to escape from her disintegrating family. She had little experience with romance, much less love, and no idea who Hamilton Cottier really was, a young man trapped, much like her, in a family situation that made him miserable. Ann's parents were completely self-absorbed throughout most of the 1920s, and they had made no effective provisions for their daughter's future. Ann herself was not a risk-taker, in spite or perhaps because of her parents' experiences as young people without stable homes and then as self-willed individualists in the spheres they chose for themselves. They had raised a bright, talented daughter and perhaps assumed that she, like them, would make her own way successfully as they had done. She would eventually follow in their footsteps in terms of a career, but not until she had tried to find a different path. Writing was always in the back of her mind.

Ann Seton did inherit her parents' drive and determination, as her "Ambition List" showed. In 1927 she had staked out her territory with her list, which included motherhood, writing to make money in a way that would outdo her parents, and a satisfying love life. By the start of 1929, she had the son and the lover, and writing was still in the picture. In her long earlier diary entry of July 27, 1928, she had written that she wanted just "two things," a "love affair" and "success at writing." She was bored, "waiting and restless," she said, "waking up each morning with a flat loathing for life and a feeling of unrealized possibilities." She honestly admitted that her unhappiness was fueled by the fact that she had "not enough to do," since both of the Cottier children's grandmothers were willing to provide plenty of "service" for the family. She also understood that "I expect too much," and "I am too much preoccupied with myself."[12] Ann could see herself very clearly sometimes but also lacked self-confidence, meaning that the preoccupations reflected in her diaries were full of doubt as well as willfulness.

By early August 1928, in a rather astonishing case of wish fulfillment, Ann had found the man who would put an end to her boredom and yearnings. Her lover was a tall, ruggedly handsome, twenty-five-year old bachelor. In a startling coincidence, he was another Hamilton, Hamilton Mercer Chase. He had grown up in Silverton, Colorado, where his father was a mining engineer, and had graduated from the University of Colorado in Boulder, but he had no interest in a career in the mining industry. Instead, he came east to Harvard Business School, leaving after one year when he ran out of money. Like so many others in the 1920s, he was impatient to make his way in New York City. By the time he met Ann, he had secured a starting position as an investment counselor with the New York City office of the prestigious Boston firm Scudder Stevens and Clark.

The lover's name was matched by another coincidence—Ann met both her husbands through her mother. Hamilton Cottier and Ann had met in 1921 at a garden party that both had begrudgingly attended with their mothers. Ann met Hamilton Chase when he came out to Little Peequo in Greenwich at Grace's invitation. Many years earlier, Grace and this second Hamilton's grandmother, Ann Sanborn Hamilton, had been active together in the League of American Pen Women. It was a natural thing for Mrs. Hamilton to secure an invitation for her grandson to visit Grace, as he was newly arrived and by himself in the big city. Beyond these parallels, Hamilton the lover and Hamilton the husband could not have been more different, especially in their ability to provide Ann "the ecstasy of sexual passion," which she had listed as her first ambition back in 1927.

Ann met Hamilton the Second when she was visiting Little Peequo in the summer of 1928 with husband "Ham," three-year-old Pamela, and three-month-old Seton. Ernest was also there, briefly returned to Greenwich from Santa Fe. During the visit, as Pamela Cottier was often told in a story she liked to repeat, she fell into a small goldfish pool located in the middle of the garden. While everyone else stood frozen, Ernest "reacted like lightning," according to Pamela's version, and pulled her out.[13] The afternoon had a more momentous consequence. The fact that Ann was married and the mother of two young children did not keep bachelor Hamilton from finding her temptingly attractive, and she evidently did not discourage him. By Saturday, September 8, 1928, she was recording that she "had fixed a rendezvous" with "Chan" for the following Monday.[14] Already he was responding to this differentiating nickname, which the pair had chosen because for some reason they were using the name "Mr. and Mrs. Channing" when they registered for brief hotel trysts. It wasn't long before Ann was considering the step of joining Chan in Manhattan for an extended stay. She wrote in her January 1, 1929, diary that when she and her husband talked about this shocking plan, Hamilton told her that she could "Go," adding that "I must expect no more sex from him at all," whether she stayed or went.[15]

The first week of February found the lovers together for a five-week interlude in an apartment whose address Ann listed as 358 Lexington Avenue. Diary entries written during her stay bore witness to the relationship that was developing. "We electrify each other," she said, so much so that "no matter what happens I will at least have known sexual bliss, and great love."[16] Ann had a great deal of time to write during these weeks, and she used her skill to create a fairly explicit drama of passion, intensified with what she conceived as desperate choices. She feared going against "convention," acknowledging some lingering feelings for Hamilton, who at least represented security and expectations that she knew how to navigate. Mixed in were concerns for Pamela and Seton, but not as many as might have been expected. Ann knew a great deal about what it was like to be mostly in the care of nannies, so she seems to have assumed that her very young children could be well enough nurtured with a similar situation. At ages three and not quite one, however, they would hardly have understood much about their mother's disappearance, which was bound to have caused considerable anxiety. Pamela and Seton would battle ambivalence towards their often emotionally absent mother for the rest of their lives.

A week before Ann was preparing to go back to Princeton, Hamilton met her at Penn Station to talk about the future. She reported about the meeting on

March 4, 1929, that she was undecided about a divorce, while he was willing to grant one. Still, he "thinks the children need a mother," she wrote, although he said that his emotions toward her were "dead." She added bitterly that he told her he was willing "to try mildly to make me happy. 'Nothing physical' hastily added." All that Ann took away from this interchange was that "I must see my babies again. Perhaps that will help decide."[17] Back in Princeton for not quite two weeks, Ann found no relief or resolution. She poured out her misery in her diary pages. Not only did she miss Chan more than she had expected, she found herself disgusted when Hamilton told her that he was having his own affair with a faculty wife named Mary. It is doubtful that he entertained much if any interest in this woman, and whatever his intention in telling Ann about her, the result was that she became more resolute about leaving him.[18]

Ann's first response to her husband's stilted attitude was to call her mother, recently returned from her Southeast Asia sojourn, who soon arrived in Princeton for "frank" discussions about divorce. As Ann reported on March 16, 1929, Hamilton did not see "why we can't be friendly, good parents, and each have physical relations on the side."[19] Not surprisingly, Ann did not find this solution acceptable. With Grace as go-between, an agreement was reached whereby Ann agreed to stay with him through his fall 1929 semester of teaching, since he was also trying to finish the thesis he had started in Oxford. This arrangement did not preclude her seeing Chan. By April 8, 1929, she had agreed to marry him, writing that when she said, "Yes," "this time I meant it with my whole heart." Now, she felt, Chan was completely her "mate." "We like the same things, we laugh continually, and we seem to share every mental and physical reaction. I admire his looks and his character. I am never bored by or with him." Hamilton, who was "cold" and so often made her feel "inferior," could not compete.[20]

Ann and Chan were together frequently in the summer of 1929 and once went out to Little Peequo when Ernest was there for another of his brief visits. This time he had returned from Santa Fe with Julia in order to preside over the annual Woodcraft meetings and ceremonies traditionally held at Little Peequo. During this visit, Ernest and Grace met with lawyers in New York City, where they wrangled mainly over financial obligations connected to their failed marriage. Soon Ernest was on his way back to New Mexico to resume land-hunting with Julia, leaving Ann on the verge of making her own escape from an unhappy home in Princeton.

An assessment of Ann's troubled life with Hamilton Cottier over their six-year marriage needs to include the chilling effects of her father-in-law Alonzo. A letter from Alonzo to Hamilton in September 1929 says a great deal about the father's personality and attitudes. Alonzo was responding to a letter from his son containing news that he had been withholding for months—the fact of what he called "strained relations" with Ann. He also voiced his need for additional help financially to pay the children's caretakers during his wife's absences. In Alonzo's response, he pointed out immediately that he had received the news and request for money with "ill humor." Now that Hamilton was being honest about his marriage and need for funds, his father self-righteously proclaimed that he held to "the possibly out of date view that a married woman's home should be the scene of her greatest activities."[21] Alonzo was a very wealthy man but he had shown before, when his son had just begun married life, that monetary assistance would always be granted grudgingly, with sermons and strings attached.

Without expressing any sympathy over Ham's situation, Alonzo responded by launching into a tirade concerning the one time that he and Blanche had stayed overnight in Hamilton's Princeton's home. He reminded his son that on the "only occasion" that "your mother" had visited, poor Blanche was expected "to get up, dress, and go out to a restaurant for her breakfast" because the young Cottiers' house servants were themselves in an "ill humor." It was an affront Alonzo could not forgive, something that "no woman should have had to endure."[22] Recounting this unforgivable insult to Blanche, it was as if nothing going on in Hamilton's marriage could compare to how the lady had suffered that morning. Stiff, demanding, and hypercritical, Alonzo was a real-life villain who, if nothing else, gave his daughter-in-law a model for one kind of cruel father character who would appear in some of her novels.

Although Alonzo berated both Hamilton and Ann in his diatribe, he did begin to provide some assistance by October 1929, if only because by that time Ann had left Princeton for good. Little Seton, six months old, remained with his father, but relations between Ann and the Cottiers were so strained that there was little point in Ann staying. She took Pamela with her to Reno, Nevada, where she booked rooms in an upscale apartment hotel. Here she would wait out the several-week separation period that allowed one to end a marriage quickly in this famous divorce capital. As she put it in her diary entry for November 19, 1929, "Well, I'm in Reno like a million other dissatisfied wives."[23] A New York tabloid that got wind of her proceedings enjoyed sensationalizing her situation with inaccurate but tantalizing information: "Prof. Hamilton Cottier, brilliant young Princeton savant, was too erudite for domestic bliss, Mrs. Cottier, a vivacious young matron of 26, charged in her divorce plight." The news clipping's headline read, No. 1 Too Highbrow, She'll Try Lawyer as Husband No. 2.[24]

Throughout 1929, Grace must have been exhausted with all the legal negotiations that swirled around her, since she was involved in both her own and Ann's separation negotiations. The peace that she had found so recently in Bali was bound to feel very far away as she also tried to work on the manuscript that would eventually become *Poison Arrows* while still trying to sell a book about her adventures in South America. Living back in Little Peequo, she became a fierce fighter for her own marital rights as well as those of her daughter. She joined Ann in Reno at Christmastime, a holiday during which Pamela had to have her tonsils removed. A settlement had been reached with the Cottiers, mostly concerning custody of the children, for whom Ann would be primary caretaker. Their father would have them for long vacation periods and pay an equal share of expenses for nannies, schooling, and various other necessities. With these terms decided, on February 10, 1930, Ann's Reno divorce was finalized. She became Mrs. Hamilton Mercer Chase scarcely two weeks later, on February 25, with Grace in attendance for a brief New York civil ceremony. Ernest had declined the invitation to join them, sending instead a telegram of congratulations from Santa Fe, where he was scouting several nearby wilderness properties that were for sale.

During the first months of 1930, all the Setons were beginning to reckon with the Depression, but they continued their various personal missions. In a book about her life with Ernest, Julia later described a "memorable evening" in February 1930, when she and her Chief went out to look over their recent purchase of the huge De Vargas tract south of Santa Fe, where they watched a "sunset of unspeakable light."[25] Ernest's heart and as much of his money as he could control belonged from this time forward to the place that would soon be known by two names: Seton Village and the College of Indian Wisdom. He would also be working to put together a way to belong legally with the woman who was eagerly taking over his life in the new homeplace.

Ernest came back to Greenwich in July 1930 on a Woodcraft business trip that included a visit with Ann, Chan, and Grace. Whether or not he spoke to

Grace at this point about a divorce, he was doing everything his lawyers advised to move ahead on that front. One sign of his intent was that he began the process of becoming a naturalized American citizen, something he had always resisted. Making his move now, when he had lived in the United States since his marriage to Grace in 1896, was partly a marital and partly a political decision. If he hoped to have a stronger voice in his new cause, promoting American Indian rights and land conservation, he needed to have a legitimate political identity as a concerned American citizen. His other reason was more pressing. According to his lawyers, he would look more sympathetic to the judges handling any divorce petition if he, like Grace, was a citizen. On November 6, 1931, the British born and Canadian bred ETS became an American.

With Seton's purchase of his Village in 1930, there was now no question, for Grace or Ann, that they had lost the head of their family. Beyond the matter of sheer pride in being the wife and daughter of a greatly admired celebrity, they had received little support, emotional or financial, for a good while. For Grace, the seven years of self-exile that followed Ann's marriage had sent her on journeys through many of the most distant, remote parts of the world. Those remarkable trips resulted in five books and international recognition that freed her from being identified only as the wife of an illustrious spouse. That she had tried to hang on to her marriage through those years shows not so much any deep affection but a stubborn will to retain the status that she had achieved as his partner. By 1930, she was at least able to make Little Peequo her own headquarters even though her husband was still its owner. Hanna was in attendance, with her services supplemented, as they had usually been, by those of another maid, a gardener, and a chauffeur, who had their own lodgings on the estate.

With this adequate retinue, Grace had time not only to work on her last travel narrative, but to make an independent mark in other ways. She served as president of the National League of American Pen Women from 1926 to 1928 and again from 1930 to 1932, traveling throughout the country to open new branches. At the time of the 1933 World's Fair in Chicago, she took on the monumental task of assembling a Women's International Books Exhibit to be on display there. It was made up of books and musical scores from more than thirty-four countries. During the same year, her book on India, *Yes, Lady Saheb*, was chosen by the Century of Progress Exposition as one of the best one hundred books by an American woman in the preceding century.

While Grace was launching herself into different orbits after Ernest permanently left Greenwich in 1930, Ann and Chan Chase (whose friends continued to call him Ham) were struggling just to make ends meet as a married couple with two children. They were able to rent houses in Greenwich, first on River Road and then on Strickland Road, but by 1932 they were forced to move into Little Peequo with Grace. She was happy to have the company and the slight supplement that Chan's salary could provide. Before he decamped for good, Ernest had built a large wing on one side of Little Peequo, providing a spacious living area and a bedroom suite upstairs, so it was no longer just a cottage. When the Chases moved in, Grace and Hanna took over the newer upstairs portion, while the others made do with much more cramped upstairs space on the older side. In the next few years, two more bedrooms and a playroom were carved out, with more downstairs bedroom space for a live-in maid. The Chases had arrived at a good address where they and the children could thrive, even with a national depression going on around them.

In November 1932, Ann wrote long descriptions of her mother and her nanny at this time in all their lives. Forty-four-year-old Hanna, she said, was "faithful and amiable, and untidy. An expert needlewoman and good cook, she is the backbone of the household, knows all about us, and has never let us down. She has gorgeous, silk blond hair that she bundles up anyhow. She would have made a fine wife." About her mother, she wrote, "She looks about 48, she is actually 60. She is very pretty, blue eyes and lovely smile and dyed light-brown hair. Dominant and positive, often irritable and impatient, sometimes unreasonable; nevertheless, she has sweetness and great understanding." The warmth that she felt for the mainstay of her life continued: "In large issues she is tolerant, she has a fine sense of humour and is good company. Above all she has unbounded energy and driving force. . . . Her faults are all superficial, or so it seems to me." The two would have many quarrels over the coming years, but these would cause no lasting bitterness. As Ann said, her mother might be "miserly and fearful with small things," but she was "generous with [anything] large."[26] Having two mothers, Grace and Hanna, in the same house with her, as well as her husband, no doubt reduced Ann's sense of responsibility and agency, but the situation also gave her great freedom.

Although Grace's household might have looked wealthy, the Seton-Chases still had plenty of monetary problems. The fact that Grace's employees were given housing made it possible to pay very low wages. Chan's salary at Scudder

Stevens and Clark was greatly diminished, and he was even laid off briefly, causing Ann to turn more seriously to writing, with only money in mind. The market she chose was short fiction for the pulp women's romance magazines, since payment was much more important at this point than literary merit. She had to note, in November 1932, that "my writing has slumped. I sent out "Blizzard" to Harper's. They fired it back. Since then have done nothing. Conditions in the magazine world are impossible. Neither Daddy nor mother seems able to land."[27] Misery had plenty of company, in terms of publishing opportunities and money. "Poor Daddy," Ann wrote the next March. "He sounds pathetic. We must be calm. He can't send money to mother or me."[28] Out at Seton Village, Ernest was scraping by, mostly trying to create housing for himself and students for his nascent College of Indian Wisdom. As for making some income of her own, Ann could only report a month later that "my writing does not progress." While she wondered why, she did admit that "all my creative powers run into the easiest channel."[29]

Grace was more focused than her daughter or husband in looking for publishers. A Bridgeport, Connecticut, news article announced in December 1932 that she had a new book coming out soon. This was *Log of the Look-See*, in its first, British edition; it would appear the next year in an American edition entitled *Magic Waters*. The Bridgeport paper, close to her hometown and undoubtedly with her help, put the most positive spin possible on her marriage. Its headline gave Grace some gratifying publicity both as a writer and as Mrs. Seton. The headline read: MRS. SETON ADDS TO BOOKS; HUSBAND RESTS ON RANCH. GREENWICH WOMAN OF AMAZING ENERGY PLANS ANOTHER VOLUME WHILE ONE IS BEING PRINTED. WIFE OF MR. SETON? SHE DISAVOWS REFLECTED GLORY.[30] Two years later, the question of the identity of the wife of Mr. Seton would have to be answered with a different name.

Traveling with Ernest to Juarez in the fall of 1934, Julia Buttree secured a Mexican divorce from husband Ted, who was back at Seton Village with a girlfriend, working as general handyman. While in Juarez, Ernest set wheels in motion for his own Mexican divorce. Although Grace resisted the procedure he went ahead, but then returned immediately to Santa Fe to get a more legally acceptable American divorce, which was finalized on January 22, 1935. This time Grace agreed, since somehow her steadfast lawyers had been able on short notice to negotiate an acceptable settlement. Grace was granted all the royalties from Seton's books published before *Lives of Game Animals* as well as a cash and stock settlement that could not have been easy for Ernest to manage. Finally, she also became sole owner of Little Peequo with its remaining seventeen acres of land, outbuildings, and picturesque lake. On January 23, 1935, the day after Ernest and Grace's thirty-eight-year marriage ended, the Chief, age seventy-five, and Julia Moss Buttree, age forty-five, were married in Santa Fe. Ann Seton Chase turned thirty-one on the day of her father's marriage. The day after what was very likely a subdued celebration, she wrote in her journal for January 24, 1935, only that "Daddy married the Buttree."[31]

For Grace, the ex-wife now ensconced in her last Greenwich home, life went on pretty much as usual. She continued her heavy schedule of traveling, both for her literary efforts and her increasing involvement in Indian mysticism, and for winter vacations. At least for a good portion of each year, Little Peequo was left to the five Chases, the family increased by the addition of a second daughter, Clemency (soon nicknamed Zizi), born on June 12, 1934. When Grace was in residence, Hanna did all her cooking but also helped with child care and housekeeping.

Granddaughter Pamela remembered that Grace insisted that her grandchildren call her Lotus, which they turned into Loti, and that every morning they could hear her "ring-ring-ring a bell" that signaled Hanna to bring her breakfast up to her bed.[32] What Pam mainly enjoyed was being able to chauffeur Grace around Greenwich when she was old enough to drive, since her grandmother, like Ernest, never learned the skill.

This now was Ann's world, with a sympathetic but also imperious mother, a husband getting on with a solid financial career in nearby Manhattan, and children who had others to call on when their mother was busying herself with other things. The myth of the housewife who turned to writing in order to hold her family together would become a staple of Anya Seton's career story, yet she hardly felt the usual drudgeries of that role. She did continue to worry about money and to write through the mid-thirties, but the result was always rejection slips for products that she herself branded as "tripe." It was easy to turn to other goals that were much less trying to her ego. She continued to gloat over "undisputed culinary gifts" that she had described in 1932, a skill that allowed her to create "epicurean masterpieces" for which "the applause is instant."[33] At twenty-eight, when beginning her relatively sheltered, privileged life at Little Peequo, she had worked hard on her appearance, obsessing about her weight and writing to famous New York charm school consultant Alma Archer, who replied that her hair was her most glorious asset and that she should strive for "subtle fashion choices."[34]

By 1934 Pam and Seton, ages nine and six, were in private school all day, and Ann had substantial help with baby Zizi. Still, her interest in making writing into a lucrative career was again put aside for most of the next year. Her dominant interests were "spiritual delving, baby care and tending children, writing, cooking, on a lesser scale beautifying, dieting, bridge, music." She added, "Just a housewife at heart."[35] Ernest, Grace, and Ann were all in a kind of stall at this time, as far as their careers as writers were involved. Grace's publication of the American and British versions of her South American odyssey (*Magic Waters* and *Log of the Look-See*, respectively) were met with only middling reviews and little money. Her last book, *Poison Arrows*, despite its enticing subtitle, "Strange Journey with an Opium Dreamer: Annam, Cambodia, Siam, and the Lotos Isle of Bali," was not published until 1938, and disappeared after hardly any notice. This was a shame, since her study of matriarchal tribes and her time in many uncharted South Asian territories constituted her most important work.

In December 1935, Ernest visited Greenwich with new wife Julia, and a "reconciliation and harmony were established" between father and daughter, although not between ex-husband and first wife. Not long afterward, assessing her "muddlehead" philosophy of life, Ann wrote that more than anything else, she wanted "to be loved,"[36] which for her partly explained why she was happier when she was not trying to publish anything. The continual rejection slips were a hard blow to her self-esteem. Perhaps too, her desire since childhood to be loved by a mercurial and usually unavailable father subconsciously fueled her obsessive yearnings for approval and her fear of rejection.

Not long after Ernest's visit, at the start of 1936, Ann was gleeful that she and Chan were close to paying off their debts and could begin saving. She asserted, "How can I doubt now that the things one wants if one demands them often and hard enough one gets."[37] Still, a month later she concluded that there was no point in trying to write, since she simply had "no guts" for rejection slips.[38] The urge to write would return later that year, but it would take longer for her to regain the confidence to go with it. In one 1936 journal entry, after describing several social events, she commented that "all this has nothing to do with my real ambition, Writing. I feel as though I were whistling in the dark." The solution, she added, was to "Just be strong and courageous and persist. Ha!"[39] She would finally find her way out of the dark when she discovered the narrative possibilities involving a father-daughter relationship drawn from early American history. What stirred her was the well-known drama of charismatic Aaron Burr and his adoring daughter, Theodosia. Courage and persistence, aided perhaps by a strong intuition that she had some experiences in common, allowed her to feel much more certain about her "real" ambition. With determination and destiny combined, she was going to get what she most wanted.

4 | FROM ANN TO ANYA

FOR THE FIRST FIVE YEARS OF HER SECOND MARRIAGE, Mrs. Ann Seton Chase talked as much about *not* writing as she did about her efforts to write. Content after Zizi's birth in 1934 to be "just a housewife," she also worried about both her ability and the market she was trying to corner. "I am beginning to doubt that I shall ever be an authoress," she said. "My will not to write is too strong, and I know I am weak on plots—popular plots. I think they're silly—they bore me to read so why try to write them." This assessment was written two days after her thirty-first birthday in 1935, and Ann followed it up with two lists, one enumerating her character "weak points" and a second her "positive virtues." She was "sloppy," often irritable with her children and Chan, and said "mean things" to or about others. Another flaw was one that she battled throughout her career as a writer. "I take most criticism badly," she admitted. There were not nearly as many virtues for her to list. She was "thrifty," as she would indeed always be, and "appreciative"; she "didn't cry over spilt milk," and she "could see both sides" of issues. A significant perception for her later life was that she could "control my lusts when I wish to."[1] At this point, her two lusts were eating too much, which she could control by dieting, and smoking, which she was able to quit, although never permanently.

Motherhood was generally a fulfilling occupation during this time, in spite of irritating moments. Ann even thought of writing a spiritual book for children or of making a collection of "Great Books" for children, since she worried that "we are surfeited with trash."[2] She loved reading to her own children. On Sunday afternoons, daughters Pam and Zizi remember, their mother often gathered the children in bed with her to listen to her read, mostly poems that she loved, including Poe's "The Raven" and "Ride a Cock-Horse." Pam, Seton, and later Zizi attended Greenwich's private Edgewood School, which, like Ann's Spence School, was both a progressive and a prestigious place of learning. Edgewood was built on the idyllic estate that was once the home of Marjorie Meriwether Post, and Ann's children could take pride in the fact that their grandfather ETS had been commissioned to build one of his iconic council rings on the school grounds.

Ann had to rely on Hamilton Cottier and Grace to pay the tuition at Edgewood, but generally the Chases had no trouble moving socially in the best circles even though their wealth hardly matched their neighbors'. They made lifelong friends with couples who lived nearby, the Eustace Seligmans, the Stanford Whites, and Bob and Nina Quinby. By 1936, Chan's position at Scudder Stevens and Clark was improving along with some portions of the nation's economy. A "$50.00 raise" was "cause for rejoicing," although there were still "some horrid debts."[3] Ann did part-time secretarial work at nearby Blythewood Sanitarium through Grace's friendship with its director, Anna Wiley. It was work that she enjoyed, as she could socialize with the doctors and study the patients, who piqued her interest in mental disorders.

With more freedom from childcare as well as lingering economic insecurity, Ann decided to try one more time to write for the romance magazine market. That summer, the Chases rented a cottage at Lordship Beach, farther north on the Connecticut coast, for the months of July and August. There, on August 5, 1936, Ann wrote, "I have been WRITING again. Stories, stories, and more hope than I've ever had. The writing urge did not descend until July 7th."[4] In October, after receiving word that Grace would soon be home from a long trip to Yugoslavia, Ann insisted that the family's living quarters upstairs in Little Peequo be renovated to give her a better place to work. Trying to keep peace in the family, Chan designed an alcove, what Ann called her "nook," using part of their bedroom as well as some of son Seton's. It provided just enough space to fit her large writing desk, and there, on October 5, she wrote "I have just dedicated this little nook, the first spot in this house that I have been able to call my very own."[5]

The demand for this tiny room of her own was connected to Ann's decision to invest money for professional writing help. She did not at first try to get advice on how to write but was willing to pay for some insider influence on how to sell. Her journal for October 5 announced that with the completion of the small renovation, she now had to "prove myself by WRITING," adding that she had already taken "four stories to Jane Hardy, agent in NY. She kept two to send out which encouraged me no end." Then Ann added a rhyme: "I know full well that I shall sell."[6] Going to an agent was a big step, particularly because it was going to cost money. But Ann was full of confidence, at least for a little while.

Jane Hardy was a good choice to get Ann set more firmly in the direction of writing to sell. She and her husband, Robert Thomas Hardy, ran a successful New York literary agency that catered mostly to those who wanted to write for money. Yet by November 12, 1936, Ann still had no success in that line, as she reported, "the writing is not going as I wish it to. I did do a pretty good love pulp 'Bride of Ice' which the agents took and liked but it apparently has not landed yet. I get discouraged. Oh for just a little success. I'm not WILLING right." As the new year 1937 began, and Ann celebrated another birthday, her thirty-third, on January 23, she had received no word about three stories that were still with the Hardys. She felt as though she were "crying in the wilderness" but was stubbornly persisting, commenting "It is necessary for my happiness that I sell stories." Then she asked a question that brought her genetic inheritance and her determination together: "Others not half so naturally well-endowed as I, can do it. Why not I?"[7]

By that fall of 1937, Ann was using some parental name-dropping to market herself. To the editor of *Household* magazine, she wrote, in a letter sent with some stories, "My parents, Ernest Thompson Seton and Grace Thompson Seton, are both writers, so that inheritance at least should prevent me from spending the rest of my life as a hopeless amateur."[8] Earlier that summer, she decided to make a different kind of investment in "what I want most." On June 13, 1937, she noted, "Am sick of floundering around. Have established tenuous contact with Tom Uzzell. Perhaps he can help me. Hope to see him Tuesday."[9] It is possible that Jane Hardy had recommended "Tom" Uzzell, although Ann might have been responding to one of the notices he placed regularly in journals targeting writers, many of them "would-be," that she read assiduously. In small squares on the back pages of such nationally prominent journals as *Writer's Digest* and *Bookman*, Thomas H. Uzzell offered practical instructions for those who were *serious*, he emphasized, about selling short fiction. He was no charlatan, but a writer, editor, and teacher with impressive credentials. In the 1920s he had been fiction editor for the well-regarded national weekly magazine *Colliers*, and he also served on the writing faculty of New York University. In 1934, he published a book of advice for writers that became one of the most important of that genre. *Narrative Technique* was known for decades to come as one of the best guidebooks on how to write for publication and went through three editions.

The subtitle of Uzzell's book, "A Practical Course in Literary Psychology," highlighted his approach. Uzzell was practical more than formulaic although he did like informal charts and diagrams. Writers needed to aim for emotional impact on the reader psychologically by making their story lines "interesting."[10] Plotting meant taking whatever was going to happen and manipulating it through pacing and dramatic highlighting. Uzzell emphasized how to move a story through organizing events in a way that built suspense and surprise. His diagram visualized how plotting could be worked out effectively, and he provided literary examples from successful stories published in the 1920s. Plotting, as Ann knew, was her weakest point, so Uzzell, she assumed, would have much to show her.

On June 22, 1937, Ann recorded meeting Thomas Uzzell at his New York office. "Last Tuesday," she wrote, "I had a personal interview with Uzzell in his anteroom. He is an attractive man. I was impressed and enrolled in his 'course.' 100 Bucks! Have since then bombarded him with the material he requested. Hope it comes to something. I was pleased with the stuff I sent, anyway."[11] In September, she provided her journal with a long description of her interactions with her mentor, which generally took place by correspondence. "Sent to Uzzell the 1st love pulp I have done under orders, i.e. he gave me the plot, 'Just Sally.' Don't think it's any good, but a triumph for me as it's the first time I've written direct on typewriter without any preliminary draft. It took me three days of pretty steady work. About 6–7 hours a day." This "hunt and peck" draft writing would serve her for her entire career, which she always followed up with professional copying. As for feedback, Ann added in her entry that "so far Uzzell's comments on everything have been 'trite stock characters' (except a couple he said were well written but did not quite click)."[12]

So far the student didn't seem to mind the teacher's criticism, but Ann's last entry describing their collaboration, written on October 28, 1937, shows some irritation. "Still working frantically with Uzzell, he makes me mad, I think he's pig-headed but I'm getting my money's worth." She noted that she had sent two stories to *Household* magazine, and while the editor had not accepted them, he had at least written, as she quoted, that "These stories have merit, but would not please our readers." So Ann could add, "Am getting somewhere with the Love Pulps. No sales but they will come."[13] The pattern of hope turning to despair and back again was another lifetime habit.

The hope offered by an editor telling her that her stories were worth something was short lived. By January 1938, something made Ann give up all effort. That month, she experienced the first prolonged bout of a "mysterious illness" that incapacitated her completely for over a month and lingered for several more. Her doctors came up with a variety of physical diagnoses, from "grippe" to allergies. However, a letter from Thomas Uzzell, dated January 11, 1938, was at least partly the cause, as Ann herself intimated. The letter was sent not to Ann, but to "Mr. Chase." In it, Uzzell made a request that neither Ann nor Chan would have found appropriate. What seems likely is that no matter to whom Uzzell addressed the letter, Ann read it, either instead of Chan or with him. Its contents, given her independence in terms of how she pursued her career, could not have been more insulting, or devastating.

Uzzell's purpose, he said, was to get "Mr. Chase" to help with "problems" connected to his wife's "literary ambitions." Her great needs required a husband's "assistance," specifically, Chan's permission to "let" Ann attend Uzzell's "Foundation of Fiction Writing" course, which would meet once a week at New York University beginning in February. Uzzell said, "I know she is interested in it, but I gather that she hesitates attending only because she does not want to sacrifice this one night a week." The "sacrifice," presumably, would be the time spent away from her husband. So, Uzzell explained, "I am asking you to encourage her." The class would cost only twenty dollars, he added, so there was certainly no "financial angle" involved for himself.[14] Uzzell spoke as one patriarch to another, envisioning that to reach Ann effectively, he could most profitably go through her husband. The idea that Chan would need to give Ann "permission" or even "encouragement" indicates how little Uzzell understood about their marriage. Ann might have led him to his assumption, using the made-up excuse of her husband's reluctance to mask her own decision not to join Uzzell's class. However, she would hardly have expected him to go "above" her.

What was much worse than his request for Mr. Chase's aid was the analysis that Uzzell provided of Ann's prospects. His wife's efforts, the teacher told

Chan, "are seriously handicapped by reason of her sheer lack of information about the fiction game," something he, of course, could remedy. The most damaging sentence in the letter came next, as Uzzell wrote that "She gropes and is tormented constantly over her struggling with problems which beginners should understand." She was, he stressed, "an amateur, and she must be professionalized." Uzzell ended by saying that he had planned to tell "Mrs. Chase" these things "at her convenience," but that "I have said in this letter to you what I had in mind to tell her." In his own handwriting, he did add, "Mrs. Chase has talent—much neglected."[15] Uzzell's letter was an extraordinary example of "literary psychology," one that boomeranged.

Ann's illness, which she began to suffer not long after Uzzell's letter was dated, included vertigo so violent that she could not leave her bed. Whatever the consulting doctors thought, she was honestly certain that a "psychological block" about her writing "had something to do with it." In her February 5, 1938, journal entry, written when the worst of the affliction had passed, she asked herself, "Someday, will I look back on my writing unhappiness as something trivial and unreal?" Yet she followed this dim hope with a self-diagnosis of her health problems that included Uzzell: "It's all bound up with the writing, the fear of failure. I've lost confidence in myself, and my brain is dry of ideas, because any that I have, I at once think bad, Uzzell would say so, etc."[16] His voice in her head paralyzed her. Eventually she would learn to fight harder against the self-doubts that almost any criticism could ignite, but fear of failure would always be the result of any criticism, sending her into dramatic tailspins.

Whatever was behind Uzzell's letter or Ann's reaction, he never appeared in her journals again. He did, however, make one more known contact with her four years later, after she had achieved success as the newly named Anya Seton. In 1942, he wrote a letter to congratulate the woman he still addressed as "Mrs. Chase." In it he had the audacity to praise a story that she had published, on her own, in the *Ladies' Home Journal*, one of the most lucrative markets for short fiction. In passing Uzzell mentioned the novel she had recently published "about Aaron Burr" (*My Theodosia*), which had come out to good reviews in March 1941. It is telling that while he admitted *not* reading the novel, and he did not name its title, he assumed it was about the father, the famous man, and not his daughter, Theodosia Burr Alston.

Uzzell did give Mrs. Chase high marks for her *story*, however, and told her that "I always knew you were the student most likely to succeed, if you gave yourself a chance." Then he rehashed all the help he had given her, mentioning how "restive" she had become at the expense involved in his class and adding that he had gone so far as to "invite her to attend without charge." He also indicated that she had not accepted this generous offer. Finally, he invited her to write a "testimonial" for him, which would be included with the praise of four or five of "my" other "most successful writers" in an advertisement he planned to place in *Writer's Digest*.[17] There are no other later letters to or from Uzzell in any available Seton records. He also received no nod of gratitude from Mrs. Chase in any of the dozens of interviews and publicity bios that Anya Seton wrote over the years to explain how she came to be one of those "most likely to succeed" writers.

Although Ann was through with Thomas Uzzell by the beginning of 1938, she remained ill, both physically and mentally, through February, causing Grace to call in a nurse for her care. The symptoms included breathing problems, vertigo, terrible headaches, nausea, and panic. For the rest of her life, these bouts would plague her, always linked to fear of rejection, which she always acknowledged but could not exorcise.

By springtime, Ann roused herself and began doggedly, again, to write and send out stories. She did not record these efforts until a July 1, 1938, journal entry in which she described the spring as "a time of shadows." The vertigo, in particular, continued to plague her, to the point that she feared a brain tumor. Reassured by doctors, she again confessed that her problem was "neurotic," and sprang from "the writing trouble . . . the fear of failure—frustration."[18] The same entry, however, recorded that she had sent out three stories since April.

By late July, from her rented vacation cottage at Lordship Beach, she was calling her disorder "a full-fledged anxiety neurosis" that "darkened all my prospects." The writing, she noted, was "a mess—part of the trouble," but a new and slightly amorous doctor, whom she called "Chunky," diagnosed her as simply being "bored with life—forced into a middle-class mold, and yearning for greater expression," in her words.[19] Ann was also thinking about her drinking as a possible cause or a possible cure. The doctors did not "proscribe liquor," she said. In fact, it helped so much that she began "having a couple of Scotch highballs every evening," so that soon she created a habit. "What would I have done without the release of liquor?" she asked and then provided a rationale to answer the question. One of her doctors, unidentified, had told her, "When you feel desperate take a drink. Much better than a sedative."

She reports that she had asked him, "But aren't you afraid I'll end up in the alcoholic ward?" and the reply was, "No—you're not the type."[20] Whether she had heard him correctly or not, in her journal she was happy to agree.

Whatever was causing or healing Ann's neurosis, on August 5, 1938, she announced momentous news, "my joy in my first sale," an event that should have provided great relief. On that day she received word that her story, "Two Husbands," had "sold to *Romantic Story* for $80.00!!!!!" Her response was "wild joy. . . . I nearly fainted when I got the letter," she added. The sum would be worth almost $1,500 in today's terms and was the going rate for top magazines during this time. As Ann celebrated, she was not shy about giving the credit to her own indomitable will to succeed, but she was already thinking ahead, as she vowed, "I must go on to much higher achievement."[21] At age thirty-four, she had finally received the validation she had sought as early as her "Dearest Ambition" list written ten years earlier. Her tumultuous summer was nearly over, and it seemed she was at last truly on her way.

In the August 24, 1938, entry that recorded her doctor's advice to use alcohol medicinally, Ann noted her health's improvement, perhaps due more to the wonderful letter from *Romantic Story* than her nightly highballs. She remarked on that day that "I am almost well now, and the panic, depression, and suffering are hazy." Grace had joined her at Lordship Beach on August 18, and "my darling, beautiful, understanding mother" also made her feel "much better." Yet the same entry disclosed another piece of the puzzle of the summer's "valley of shadows," events that had occurred back in June that Ann had not mentioned before. There were, in fact, no entries in her journal at all for the month of June 1938, and the reason why was disclosed in the August 24 journal. Ann wrote, "I think I uncovered the hidden fear that was eating me" in the early summer. "It had to do with Daddy." For the first time in her life, she expressed feelings that she had suppressed before. "Resentment toward Daddy. God knows he's let me down. Hatred."[22] Whatever unhappiness Ernest had caused in Ann's life up to this point, being the daughter of the charismatic Ernest Thompson Seton formed the bedrock of her identity. What he and Julia set in motion in June 1938 permanently damaged that foundation.

A year earlier, in July 1937, Ann and Chan had enjoyed a visit to Seton Castle, part of a "glorious trip" that they took out west that summer. Ann seems to have been working especially hard on this trip to mend fences following her parents' divorce. After that visit, back home in Little Peequo, she reported that "the visit to Santa Fe with Daddy and Julie was unexpectedly pleasant. We were closer than we have been in ages, and at last I can see why he did it. They have a kinship of spirit."[23] What Ann did not know then was that her father and his wife of two years would soon be taking steps to replace Ann with a child of their own. By February 1938 Julia had found a pregnant young woman willing to stay with them at Seton Castle until her child was born and to allow them to adopt the baby. Julia, forty-eight, and Ernest, seventy-eight, were moving ahead to create their own exclusive dynasty.

On June 6, 1938, Beulah Seton was born, named by her adoptive parents for the pet label, "Beulah land," which they had created for their property. For a few days, Ernest hinted to curious reporters that he had fathered this daughter, provoking a minor media frenzy. While a few of the details about the adoption were eventually aired, the facts of parentage were never widely known. In all their interviews, Ernest and Julia emphasized how young they felt and what a blessing it was to have this child, who began to accompany them on lecture tours when she was barely two months old. As Anya wrote in her late August entry, "'Beulah.' That poor baby. What is it? Surely not the legitimate and normal offspring of these two—*ne pas possible*."[24] She and Grace wrote to Santa Fe friends to find out more about the baby's identity, and the truth did come out, reluctantly provided, in snippets, by her parents. For Ann and Grace, the whole affair was an embarrassing scandal.

The Chases had returned from their vacation in Lordship Beach to Greenwich by September 1938, and Ann was still feeling "better," in spite of her father's behavior and other species of chaos churning around her family and the world. Her September 28 entry began with notice of "the horrible threat of war in Europe." Ann asked, "How could we go through all that again so soon?" Next came a New England hurricane, with "frightful flood here." Then Pam and Seton were back from their long summer visit with father Hamilton, who was "wrought up" over their son, who had taken to "lying and stealing." With what must have been relief, Hamilton turned over his children so that they could return to school, while he looked forward to his second marriage, which took place on November 7, 1938. His new wife was Janet Frantz, a woman whom Ann liked, "after the first shock," but still she had to deal with daughter Pam, who was "very much upset."[25] Janet and Hamilton remained married until his death in 1979, living quietly together in Princeton, where Pam soon became reconciled to the new wife.

Settled into the usual fall routine in Greenwich, Ann in her October 25, 1938, journal entry looked back at a summer that had been "hellish." She made no mention of her one great victory, the sale of a story to one of the nation's most important women's magazines, nor did she allude to any attempts to follow up on that success. She did, however, mention a purchase that clearly made an impact in that area. While in New York, she noted, "I bought a remarkable book on writing by one Brenda Ueland. Was so moved by it that I wrote her a fan letter."[26] The most important aspect of Ueland's slim book, which was entitled *If You Want to Write*, was its total rejection of the kind of advice that Thomas Uzzell gave to his students. Ueland wrote the book using her experiences in teaching women writers at a YWCA program in Minneapolis. Its subtitle, *A Book About Art, Independence, and Spirit* announced her pep talk slant, and its chapter headings offered therapy much more than technical pointers on writing. Following her months-long struggle with depression, caused in part by Thomas Uzzell's voice telling her that she was "no good," Ann could take heart when reading Ueland's chapter 1, "Everybody Is Talented, Original, and Has Something Important to Say," or chapter 7, "Be Careless! Reckless! Be a Lion! Be a Pirate! When You Write!," and of course, chapter 8, the answer to Uzzell: "Why You Are Not to Be Discouraged. Annihilated by Rejection Slips."[27]

There was also a chapter to show Ann that the journaling habit begun when she was seventeen had been not at all in vain. Chapter 14 was entitled, "Keep a Slovenly, Headlong, Impulsive, Honest Diary." It is little wonder that Ann wrote Brenda Ueland a fan letter.

In the same October diary entry, shortly after quoting Ueland's advice to "Live Now," Ann announced that "I've spent a great deal of thought on a new front name. I hate Ann, no one fond of me has ever called me that [for] long." As she played with different possibilities, she listed various nicknames that she had been called along with other names she liked, which included "Annie—Annice—Annis—Cherry—Anna—Baby [always her father's name for her]—Amanda—Angela." After trying out "Andreya" for two weeks, she decided "Anya seems the best."[28] Ann did not act on this choice for a while, but if she were both talented and original, as Ueland said, then an original name was certainly one way to start carving out a new identity, which Ann increasingly felt she needed.

The imperative Ann felt for a break with the past was reinforced when Ernest's lecture tour brought him finally to Greenwich, with wife and daughter in tow, on November 17, 1938. Ann described the day of their arrival at Little Peequo, "with an Indian nurse!," in her journal entry for November 21. She reported that Ernest and Julie still claimed the baby, whom Ann called "it," "as their own actual child," but a note in the entry page's margin added later that "they were forced into admission that Beulah was adopted." The pair "were pleasant," and "the interview passed off well," although for her it resulted in "a slight neurotic recurrence perhaps definitely attributable to the Daddy business."[29] A snapshot showed Ernest posing happily with his three grandchildren, but if he demonstrated any special affection for them, Ann did not report it. Grace was not in residence.

Ernest and Julia made it clear to the world that Beulah was the sole member who mattered in an entirely new family unit. Just after their visit to Little Peequo, the *New York World Telegram*, on November 19, 1938, quoted the pair as saying that they "had" Beulah because "someone has to carry on, and we want our own child to do it. Beulah will be saturated with our work." The headline for the article played up the drama: IT ISN'T AT ALL REMARKABLE THAT HE'S A FATHER AT 78, SAYS ERNEST THOMPSON SETON. Julia helped to muddy the waters of Beulah's parentage by commenting that she "looks just like her father. She has his black eyes and curly hair."[30] Ann could only feel bitter abandonment to know that her father saw no place for her, or even for the grandson named for him, in his plans for the future. Eight years later, in a will written shortly before his death in 1946, Ernest left all his assets and belongings to Julia and Beulah. To make his feelings cruelly clear, he stated that Ann was well able to provide for her family. The wound that this caused Anya was so deep that none of her journals mention the disinheritance at all.

In her journals, Ann did not mention her father, nor did she talk seriously about her writing, until well into the next year, 1939. In April, after trips with Pam and her mother to New Orleans and with Pam and Seton to Bermuda, she wrote that she had again "lost faith in myself." More stories had been turned down, and "I haven't the real impulse to write," she stated, "or have I?" The statement followed by the question moved her on to ask another, "Am I kidding myself?" What "I must face," she answered, is that "writing is not a spontaneous, imperative urge. There is a cleavage, my real life on one hand, writing on the other. They don't coalesce well for me." At the root, however, was one overriding, determining factor: if she did not write, she firmly believed, "life has no serious purpose." She had children, a home, and a husband, all "terribly important," but "I must be me too," she claimed, and followed up with the motto she took from Brenda Ueland, "Live Now."[31] A June postcard from the McClure syndicate, accepting her "short-short" story, "China Mascot," was an "insignificant but very nice" bit of news that at least proved "life isn't static."[32]

Summer came and went with no journal entries until August 28. Ann did not write while she and Chan traveled out west for much of July and August. They stopped in Silverton to visit the Chase family and took Chan's younger brother Charles along for an excursion to Mexico. On their return, they stopped in Santa Fe for what Ann described, with no elaboration, as a "very harmonious visit to Daddy, bless him." Almost exactly a year earlier, she had voiced, for her journal, her "hatred" of the father who had so completely "let me down." Now she was no longer suffering from the deep depression of that time, instead seeming as determined as ever to keep some bond with him. Her entry included the information that she had sold another story for eighty-five dollars, proving that "it isn't impossible after all."[33] As another autumn season in Greenwich was set to begin, there seemed to be good reason to feel upbeat.

Unfortunately for the world, there were overriding reasons for panic and gloom. Ann announced Hitler's invasion of Poland on the first page of her September 1, 1939, journal entry, and three days later described how she and Chan had listened to the voice of a "tired old man" announcing on the radio that England had gone to war with Germany. Upheaval and new challenges were now coming for everyone. Anya worried about how the war would affect her family and her country. She opposed any suggestion that the United States should join the conflict, in this respect sounding very much like Ernest, who so ardently spoke out against World War I. Ann distrusted the pro-war propaganda stirring in the United States. "Why in God's name," she asked, "should we who cannot be in danger bog down in hysteria and idealism again?" Hers was a common sentiment for most Americans at the time, who like her worried about its impact at home. "How is it to affect my work, my budding literary career," as well as "Chan's business," she had to ask, but also understood: "We feel the relentless flood sweeping us along. I feel it. This terrific thing makes everything else unimportant."[34]

Ann's mention of her "budding literary ambitions" on September 4, 1939, was not a reference to her usual goal of making story sales to the romance market. She was, in fact, following up on an idea that had "seized her" on August 31. That day she made "a discovery" that turned out to mark the beginning of Anya Seton the novelist's career, although Ann Chase was not looking so far ahead. On September 1, 1939, she wrote that a day earlier, "I was seized with an idea that thrills me. Have always toyed with the thought of writing a novel about Dolley Madison, but she has been done to death. Suddenly discovered Theodosia Burr. I think she'd make a swell novel. 29 years of exciting life dominated by her father." Ann even had a title, "The Passionate Daughter," and whether this "thrilling" conception was going to amount to anything or not, she added, "Am doing research anyway."[35] The future proved that she did not give up on this plan.

September moved into October, with constant stress created by the news in Europe but few outward signs nationally of "any relentless flood" for Ann to trace. Home at Little Peequo, however, she did note a "wild upheaval" on October 14, 1939.[36] Once again she was making the fuss by demanding more space. The result was the very quick construction of a small "cabin" behind Little Peequo, called Casanya, where Anya could work on writing something big. The reason for demanding more space to write this time was the discovery she had made on August 28. The kernel of a novel plot that she recorded that day had almost miraculously enticed the interest of a major publisher. Someone from Houghton Mifflin was going to come out to talk with her, even though Ann had not yet begun to write this possibly "swell novel" about a young woman whose "exciting life" was "dominated" by her father. Autobiographically, however, Ann knew by heart the story of a similar situation, one whose ending she could, in her own life, try to change.

While she had not started to write "Passionate Daughter," Ann did now have ready the name that would identify her authorially for the career to come. "Anya" had continued to suit her for her front name, from the time she had taken it to the top of her brainstorming list a year earlier. The choice of a last name was more fated. "Seton" was the surname that Ernest Evan Thompson had chosen for himself soon after he began to be successful in publishing the animal stories that led to his fame and fortune. Choosing to use her maiden name gave Ann a re-association with her famous sire that was important to her psychologically, a way to remind her father and the world that she was irrevocably his daughter. The connection, of course, could also help her in the marketplace, where Ernest Thompson Seton was revered even though he was seldom publishing at this time.

While Ann seemed to be giving herself a new persona through the name Anya, it wasn't long before she concocted a myth concerning its inception that would also tie her closely to her American Indian–loving father. For interviewers and publicity releases beginning in the early 1940s, Anya Seton created one of her most popular fictional narratives. "Anya," she said, was the name attached to her when she was a toddler at Wyndygoul, where her father, universally called Chief or Black Wolf, inaugurated his Woodcraft movement. In her story, a visiting Native chief christened her "Anutika," a name meaning "grey" or "stormy" eyes, even though her eyes were hazel. Before very long, she explained, the name had been shortened to Anya, which people had been calling her for many years.

Reporters and reviewers loved the author's explanation for her somewhat exotic name and never questioned its accuracy. It was accepted as truth throughout Anya's life in reviews, interviews, as well as biographical sketches down to the present time. There exists no archival evidence that Ann was ever known as Anya before she considered the name in 1938—not from the prolific records of her parents and friends, nor in any of her own letters or journals. Anya created a "historical" fantasy that served her well throughout her life. She had a public, professional identity, a writing "self," to market beginning in 1939, and the passionate daughter brought one of her father's best skills to bear on the task, starting with her name.

5 | PASSIONATE DAUGHTER

IN 1957, ANYA WROTE A LETTER to Houghton Mifflin's publicist to be used for marketing her novels. In it, she suggested a theory about what had made her into a popular novelist. By this time, she had published six best-sellers over a sixteen-year career. Her novel *Katherine* had been published to great acclaim and phenomenal sales in 1954. Soon *The Winthrop Woman* (1958) would achieve almost equal success. So, it is somewhat surprising that she would still be looking back to her famous father, Ernest Thompson Seton, to explain her talent. "Though he popularized Natural History to some extent," she wrote, "it was never inaccurate. I think I have inherited his method of writing, and in my field of HUMAN history, tried to do the same thing."[1] It is likely that by this time, Anya could believe that her success as a popular writer was coming close to matching her father's. Yet she was also demonstrating how central to her writer's psyche the connection to him would always be.

Anya's competition with her father began with her jottings about a possible first novel, which she was calling "Passionate Daughter" or "Daughter of Such a Man." In 1939, Chan told two old college friends that his wife was trying to write a fictional biography based on Theodosia, the daughter of Aaron Burr. Anya was more nervous than grateful when one of these friends, Hardwick Moseley, asked to come out to Greenwich to chat about what she had in mind. Hardwick had been Chan's classmate at the University of Colorado, and the two graduates, like two Jay Gatsbys of the same 1920s era, had "come east" together to make their fortunes. Both had done well, Chan in investment counseling and

Moseley as head New York sales manager with the top tier Boston publishing house of Houghton Mifflin.

On October 7, 1939, Hardwick appeared at Little Peequo to take a look at Anya's preliminary notes for her "Theo." The result, she fretted, was that while "Mr. Moseley" was "enthusiastic about Theo" and "wants to publish it," this was not necessarily good news. As she said, "But I haven't written it! Or scratched the surface of research."[2] As it turned out, Hardwick Moseley was not just a sales manager. As Houghton Mifflin executive editor Paul Brooks wrote in a memoir, Moseley also "brought us several successful writers," explaining that "the salesmen became friends with booksellers all over the country, and through them, with local authors."[3] Chan and Hardwick and their wives became lifelong friends, with Hardwick often serving as one of Anya's most forthright critics.

"Theo," the novel that did get written, went through the publishing process at a rapid pace. Anya's journal reveals how quickly Houghton Mifflin moved her along. She remarked on November 1: "Lee Barker—Houghton Mifflin's New York man is coming to see me Saturday morning—and I'm apprehensive. Not ready for him, feel so inadequate. Style, research, everything."[4] On November 18, she summarized the result: "Lee Barker—H. Miff man did come and was wildly enthusiastic about my 'Passionate Daughter.' I am trying to whip stuff together to submit to them, and he practically guaranteed contract and advance."[5] Barker, who soon became known as Lee, had quickly gained Anya's trust, while he just as quickly saw in her the makings of a writer who would do well in the mass market arena that his company was cultivating. What he read out at Little Peequo could not have been much more than the early draft of a few chapters and also a scenario sketch of the plot, which was what Anya always felt she needed to generate before she went very far in creating any chapter. In her November 18, 1939 journal, she also indicated that she had been doing research in New York, so the novel was in its earliest stage.

Barker might be impressed with Anya's love of history and her dedication to research, but as an editor he also had to have strong faith in any writer's technical skills and marketability if he were going to recommend a contract. Whatever Anya showed him, he proved that he had enough confidence by December 19, 1939, although his new find didn't share it. On that day Anya reported that "I've got my contract and advance—500 bucks—from Houghton Mifflin, and for two days it was wildly exciting. Now it no longer is. I have horrible fears of not being able to deliver the goods. My poor Theo is being pinned down on the board, and I am engrossed in all the titanic struggles."[6] The deadline for delivery was June 30, 1940. A woman writer who had begun getting acceptance notices from love pulp magazines only a year earlier now had six months to produce a novel. Her journal entries would demonstrate that 1940 was going to be an intense year. Just before the new year began, she called writing the novel her "business," which "rather appalls me. How I've got to work. Glory be."[7]

Lee Barker and Anya formed a bond, as she did with Hardwick Moseley, that was both professional and personal. In Barker's case, the friendship lasted much longer than his tenure with her publishers. He held the post of New York editor only until 1943, when he moved to Doubleday, a change that Anya mourned. As Arthur Hailey, one of his most successful Doubleday fiction writers, later commented, Lee Barker "had an uncanny instinct for what would and would not work in terms of fiction," and more important, for the historical novelist that Anya was to become, Hailey added, "with him history was both an art and a profession."[8] Barker was the first of several editors at Houghton Mifflin, who, like those at other major publishers of the time, established close relationships with their authors. As Paul Brooks, who would become Anya's editor by 1944, wrote in his memoir, "The early nineteen thirties through the sixties" was "a time when book publishing was as much a profession as a business, with the personal relationship between writer and editor at its core."[9] Sharing Anya's great respect for history perhaps was the spark that ignited editor Barker's long friendship with this writer.

In her journals, Anya always used January 1 to take stock of her family and to review the past year. For the first day of 1940, she supplied a gloomy introduction: "Impossible to enter a New Year and a new decade without feelings of excitement, sadness, and portentousness." Almost, she said, she had chosen the word "doom," primarily because of Germany's advances in Europe during the fall of 1939, after Hitler had been joined by the Soviets. In Anya's journal, the war received first but only cursory mention. What followed was a familiar affirmation of the "family feeling" that December holidays always triggered. As usual, she had in her own terms gone "all out" to make Christmas 1939 a festive family occasion. On New Year's Day, she was also in a rare good mood about living at Little Peequo. Casanya, the small cabin that was supposed to have been "my retreat, my compromise, my ivory tower, my self-expression" had almost immediately been found unsuitable. Anya decided that she preferred her crowded house to this other potential sanctuary. With Grace and Hanna headed for their winter headquarters in Florida, she could use her mother's room for writing, as she had done in the past. Anya also confessed in her New Year's journal that she did not really like being removed from the family's daily, noisy "bustle and confusion which I think I hate."[10]

Anya's change of heart about Casanya and Little Peequo was matched in the new year by ambivalence about her relationship with Chan. This too was not an unusual preoccupation. Over time Chan had certainly been a consistently ardent lover, according to her journals. In them Anya had early on created two shorthand ways to indicate the times when she felt amorous with her husband or even with other men. One was a symbol, the letter *X* inside a circle. The other was her use of the French term *etreinte*, which for her meant any kind of foreplay hinting at possible sexual pleasure. The word and the symbol meant lovemaking, which did not, for Anya and others of the era, necessarily mean having sex. Like her two codes, a mention of lovemaking could suggest anything from flirting to petting, or beyond. Writing on January 1, 1940, about some "abeyance" of *etreinte*, Anya berated herself for her "hungry hunting for sex.... Want to be made love to," she wrote, "Ego needs building up all the time.... Don't want an affair," she added, "just the [x inside a circle] excitement."[11]

Preoccupations about house and husband disappeared soon after New Year's Day. Almost immediately Anya went south on her first source-hunting adventure. The two-week research trip to South Carolina and Washington, DC, was "glorious fun." On February 8, she described in glowing terms how she had fared: "I felt alive, vital, competent, sexy." Son Seton, now almost twelve years old, had traveled with her only for the first few days, after which she left him with her mother and Hanna, who were also traveling south and stayed a few days with her in Charleston. Once on her own, she was in her element, "accomplishing so much" and basking in "the nostalgic sweetness of the Waccamaw Neck and Theodosia lore."[12] Her journal left the details of her research activities with little more than that generalization. She did mention that in Charleston she had "my first interview," which duly appeared in an article titled "Writing a Biography of Theodosia Burr." "Anya Seton Chase," the article reported, "is doing general research on the atmosphere of Charleston during the early 1800s that Theodosia Burr and her husband visited." The new author was also going to "spend several days in Georgetown before returning to Greenwich to complete the final version of her book."[13]

The rest of Anya's February 8, 1940 summary of her trip was devoted primarily to a description of the male flattery she received. As she put it, she had "picked up" three men during her travels. Two of these, Forest Knowles and Victor Stanley, evidently were her escorts around Charleston and the low country plantations. The third, George Auxier, a young scholar who became her guide and assistant at the Library of Congress in Washington, DC, offered an opportunity for a bit more than flirting. Anya reported that they had lunched together, once at his apartment where "he kissed me on the neck," she exclaimed, but she added that there had been no further actions.[14] Both the research and the flirtations that enlivened Anya's first career-related journey would become the pattern for the many working trips to come. When and wherever she went, she felt free of the distractions of home, she had a fixed purpose that she relished, and she charmed attractive or at least interesting men who eagerly joined her cause. In this respect, she resembled Grace Gallatin Seton, who on her exotic tours also found willing guides to accompany her.

Returning to Little Peequo meant resuming the roles of mother and house-wife. On March 22, 1940, she had to admit that "work on Theo is slow as may be imagined."[15] In an "impulse" to record "details, minutiae" instead of "evanescent" emotions in her journal, Anya wrote a long entry for April 10, 1940, in which she described the daily life to which she had returned. There were astute analyses of three active children to whom she paid often critical attention. Pamela, now fourteen, was "too fat," somewhat "lethargic," and "not social enough," but was "completely reliable" and still, "perhaps the nearest to me." Seton, at twelve, could often "move me to fury" with his "mean little tricks" and a recent period of "petty thievery." She complained that her son "hates study" and "can't spell," but that he was also "sensitive" and possessed "real charm." Five-year-old Zizi was "enterprising and sociable and passion-ate and naughty." Chan, she admitted, she could not see "objectively," and so "I can't write of him now," she concluded, although she added some of the habits that bothered her, including some "thickness" and lack of any hobbies. For the record, Anya even described the faithful, live-in "little Polish maid" Stella who had been with the family for almost seven years, off and on. She was "plump as a quail," also "industrious and efficient, childish and moody and untidy."[16] Her entry showed Anya did not skimp on involvement with her children, although she could count on two live-in, paid helpers—Hanna and Stella (or a substitute), as well as Chan, who at least drove the older children to school on his way to catch the train to his office in Manhattan.

The Chases, during the spring of 1940, were becoming much more social, even while Anya was trying to work on "Theo." She and Chan began a ritual of Sunday afternoon cocktail parties, with Anya noting that "I do think we mix people better than most." Their attendees, as she noted in her April 10 entry, showed how she was acclimating to a circle that increasingly included a literary element. Lee Barker was one her journal described, but also John and Adelaide Marquand, good friends whom Anya liked especially because they never behaved like celebrities. Also attending on this occasion was Tom Chubb, whose study of the colorful sixteenth century Italian satirist Pietro Aretino had just been published. Anya felt "pleasantly lion-huntressy with the 2 authors" in attendance. It was, she boasted, "Salon stuff."[17]

As for "Theo," Anya reported that the novel "crawled along" in March but by April 1 was going better. "I simply don't know whether I'm doing a good job or not," she complained, worrying that her novel might be all "amateurish and childish."[18] War news made it especially hard to concentrate after Hitler's forces moved to take Norway and Denmark. Anya admitted that along with being "terrifying," the reports from Europe also sparked in her an "immediate selfish reaction." What would happen to the stock market that her family depended on for much of its income or to a book that no one might want to read?

Anxiety was diminished when Lee Barker came out to check on her progress and was "delighted" with her first four chapters. His only criticism was one with which she ruefully agreed. He said, she reported, that "I over-write." She interpreted this criticism to mean that she was guilty of sentimental exaggeration, and she was quick to agree, blaming "partly pulp training and partly my own emotionalism."[19] From this time on, she would often use Barker's term "over-writing" or her own favorite, "mawkishness," to describe the tendency toward melodrama that she feared would take over her plots.

In her response to Barker's early criticism, Anya showed one of the qualities that those who worked with her generally admired. She was honest about herself, her writing, and her own character traits, sometimes to a fault. With those she trusted as friends and mentors, she was straightforward and often very funny. It was not her nature to be coy or phony, a trait that some interviewers over the years noted appreciatively. Beginning with her first years at Houghton

Mifflin, her editorial team (and their wives), including Lee Barker, Hardwick Moseley, Lovell Thompson, and Paul Brooks, became her good friends. They recognized Anya's talent and also appreciated her lively, frank conversation. She did not attempt any "amours" with these men, whom she regarded as fellow professionals in the writing business. From them she craved not just attention but relationships based on intellectual stimulation and candor.

Anya worked hard to finish "Theo," sometimes, she reported, "grinding out 2000 words a day, as best I can" while recognizing that she would need another year to make it "a superb book."[20] Hardwick Moseley and Lee Barker, however, had from the start seen her potential as a creator of popular bestsellers, not literary fiction. The gulf between these two categories was increasing in critical parlance in the 1930s, with the lead book reviewers of venues such as the *New York Times* and *New Yorker* beginning automatically to associate big moneymaking novels with mediocrity. Not very surprisingly, these mostly male reviewers, like the male literature faculty at elite universities, were also designating most women writers of any genre, but particularly historical novels, as mediocre too, with very few exceptions. Anya often named Willa Cather and Jane Austen, two women who escaped censure, as her favorite models.

For her entire career, Anya would wish for more time, as well as more editorial assistance, to make her novels better and to earn the respect of the mostly male reviewers who had the power to establish the literary canon of the day. Being a woman was one strike against her, and being a historical novelist was another. Houghton Mifflin's own emphasis on moneymakers, added to her gender and her chosen genre, was going to mean that she could seldom break free from the stereotypes that the critics designed for her. Working on her first novel, Anya was understandably naive about the political realities of publishing, and in 1940, in any case, she needed money more than praise, so she did not complain.

Money was tight for all Americans during this time, and Chan was so discouraged about the prospects of investment counseling in a volatile pre-wartime economy that he very briefly took over as director of Blythewood Sanitarium in Greenwich where Anya had worked as a secretary soon after their marriage. The sanitarium, well-known among psychiatrists and their elite, wealthy patrons, had been started by Boss Tweed on his lavish Greenwich estate in 1905. Its purpose was to cater to socialites with a great variety of mental problems who valued and could afford the privacy and accoutrements of the estate's five hundred acres and well-appointed accommodations. Grace Seton's friendship with Blythewood's director, Anna Wiley, seems to have led to the invitation for Chan to take on the enterprise of directing the place. However, it was as risky a venture at the time as the stock market: Blythewood had been recently involved in sensationalized events including a fire and the death of patients due to leaking fumigation gas. Chan lasted there only three weeks, after which Scudder gladly took him back and gave him a raise. He was to stay with Scudder Stevens and Clark into the 1970s, for the rest of his working life.

The Blythewood episode was one of many that kept Chan as the main subject of Anya's journal. As she began to think more confidently of her own career, she tended increasingly to be more restless in her marriage and more critical of her husband. She knew, she wrote, that Chan "isn't getting what he should from life," and she was willing to blame herself for much of his unhappiness.[21] What contributed to the unhappiness of both was that they were drinking heavily. The Chases' long 1940 summer vacation, again in a rented house at Lordship Beach, up the Connecticut coast from Greenwich, was a case in point. The sojourn started off well enough, with Anya happy to be released from Little Peequo. As usual during the summer months, Pam and Seton were spending vacation time with their father, but Zizi was with her mother, enjoying the ocean and her summer friends under a housekeeper's care. Anya was free to write and to socialize with a constant parade of visitors, which meant all-day drinking. Chan could commute to New York when necessary but be back to participate in evening festivities. It was the summer routine for many suburban New Yorkers of their set, and the Chases were an entertaining magnet.

Writing in her journal at Lordship on August 5, 1940, Anya described a conversation in which she and Chan agreed to try not drinking at all, although she commented, "Still I do love my highballs after the day's work is done." The couple made it dry from Tuesday until Saturday. That night, with the weekend's "big party" in full swing, Chan slapped Anya "on the ear, enough to make it ring" when she berated him for coming home very late. Writing about it, Anya admitted that she could not remember what she had said, "partly" because of "my own 2 highballs in p.m." It was a "degrading scene" for which she quickly took some of the blame. "I know he has a rare but lightning temper, and I suppose I said hateful things," she wrote. Sorting out how either one of them had really acted, when her own actions were so blurred, did not happen, but the fight had been, she knew, "liquor-born, like all this type of mess." The solution was available, but as Anya added, "Don't know the exact method to handle it. To go completely on the wagon seems so dull and unjoyous. Social drinking is fun. But it [the wagon] may be necessary."[22]

Even at Lordship amid marital turmoil and hangovers, Anya was somehow able to keep working on "Theo" enough so that Lee Barker appeared in June to read through a first draft. Anya thought the draft was "awful, and who's going to care anyway." Lee, however, was very "encouraging," as usual.[23] Good friend Sara Lynn Anderson, and "of course Hardwick," she wrote in August, "read the 1st 4 chapters of Theodosia and were very enthusiastic," even though, as she said, "there is so much drinking around us."[24] The autumn return to Greenwich provided an atmosphere more conducive to writing, so that on September 20, 1940, Anya delivered her completed manuscript to Houghton Mifflin. Lee and other members of the Houghton team helped her to celebrate "a wonderful, exhilarating day," but then the publication process seemed to stall, leaving Anya, as she put it, in a "mental slump."[25] The letdown after months of work made her feel by November that "nothing pleasant has happened in months. No comeback on novel or stories out, and no title for Theo. Can't think of a new idea for a plot etc."[26]

Anya turned to writing and selling more short stories, which had become a lucrative outlet for her, but the November 1940 gloom did not lift. Politically, she despaired after Franklin D. Roosevelt won the presidential election over her favorite, Wendell Wilkie. "Nothing ahead for us but War, Taxes, Class Hatred, and Insecurity," she predicted.[27] Her agent Edith Haggard had not been able to get "Theo" landed as a magazine serial, nor had anyone taken a film option on the novel. Still Anya comforted herself by remembering that two years earlier, she "was wildly happy over a five-dollar check from McClure syndicate." Now, she said, she had made $900 in one year, the moral being, "One gets what one wants in this life if one wants it hard enough."[28]

Shortly after she voiced this consolation, Houghton Mifflin began giving the novel, finally titled simply *My Theodosia*, a "fine build-up." Anya had publicity shots taken by a well-known professional photographer, Ed Lewis, who not surprisingly made some *etreinte* advances. With her novel ready to go, she was willing to admit on December 31 that 1940 had, "on the whole," been "a good year."[29] She had to wait impatiently until the actual "coming out" of *My Theodosia*, which took place on March 4, 1941, at which point she was happy to announce that it was heralded with "an excellent press" and "swell reviews. . . . Have been quite the little lioness in Greenwich," she added, which was "nice but unimportant."[30]

Anya's aside about her hometown lionizing reflected her realistic attitude toward smaller town benefits, although any accolades for a first novelist must have been gratifying. Anya Seton Chase (as she now liked to be known beyond the publishing world) had accomplished a remarkable feat for a housewife with no college degree and very little formal training in writing as a creative art. Her first attempt at producing a novel made the *New York Tribune* bestseller list, even if only for one week, and her publishers were "pleased enough" with a sale of six thousand copies.[31] The *Greenwich Press* called the book "brilliant, arresting, moving" while the *New York Herald Tribune* said that "readers will be grateful to Miss Seton" for telling such a compelling story."[32]

For the rest of her career, there were few reviews of "Miss Seton" that did *not* mention her deft handling of stories taken from historical events. Yet while Anya always greatly respected history and insisted on accurately depicting it, she eventually sought to differentiate at least some of her work from the genre of historical fiction. *My Theodosia* was the first of what Anya later called biographical, instead of historical, novels. For her, it was a crucial distinction. She drew on the lives of specific people, and especially women, for her plots, and all her novels would involve careful, extensive research into places and times. Still, she was even more intent on making *My Theodosia*, *Katherine*, and *The Winthrop Woman* portraits of individuals. Like these two later, more popular works, her first novel begins with the picture of a young woman whose outlines come from history but whose character has not yet been formulated by internal desires or by events around her. As Theodosia takes shape, her inner and emotional development is consistently foregrounded, superseding the documented dimensions of her known life.

The real Theodosia Burr (Alston) was indeed the passionate daughter of a well-known, fascinating historical figure whose interests dominated her life— from her girlhood, where Anya's story begins, through her marriage, until her mysterious disappearance on a ship bound for New York City in 1813. For most, the one fact that made Theodosia interesting was the unsolved mystery of her disappearance and death. She was generally presumed to have been lost at sea on the schooner *Patriot* headed north, where she planned to reunite with her long-exiled father. Beyond dramatizing her own poignant theory of

Theodosia's end, Anya utilizes the historical record to involve readers in the underpinnings of a character who was always extraordinary. Theodosia Burr was a precocious, motherless girl whose father energetically, even obsessively, worked to ensure that she would turn into a beautiful, brilliant, and above all, dutiful daughter. We meet Anya's Theo at age seventeen, when Aaron Burr is the vice president of the United States, having narrowly lost the presidency to his hated rival Thomas Jefferson. To please her father, Theo consents unhappily to a politically advantageous marriage to Joseph Alston, a rising political figure in South Carolina politics. It is a time when Burr needs southern alliances, so his daughter is sacrificed to a bumbling boor of a man, in Anya's rendering, the scion of an insufferably snobbish slave-owning family.

Following her father through years of both fame and shame, Theo interacts with a well-drawn cast of figures from the early nation's history, two of whom were Anya's favorites: the author Washington Irving and Dolley Madison, future president James Madison's wife. Burr's duel with Alexander Hamilton occurs off-stage in Anya's story, supplanted, in terms of drama, by the one great passion that Anya provides her heroine—a love affair, never quite consummated, with another historical figure, the transcontinental expedition coleader Meriwether Lewis. This attachment was almost, although not quite, without historical validity. A few shadowy references, however, allowed Anya to include him so as to fulfill another requirement of all her fiction: a romantic engagement in forbidden, or at least tumult-filled, love.

While Meriwether Lewis comes into Theodosia's life only briefly at the time of her marriage (he disappears for much of the novel to complete his long search for a Northwest Passage with William Clark), Theodosia is left to become a more mature but also increasingly unhappy southern wife. It becomes her lot primarily to agree to her father's endless schemes for enhancing himself and to try only halfheartedly to adjust to her husband's attempts to squeeze her into his family's southern ideal of prestige and womanliness. Some critics objected to *My Theodosia*'s fanciful use of Meriwether Lewis as romantic love interest, while others questioned her interpretation of Theodosia and Joseph Alston's marriage as loveless and strained. South Carolinians, for example, were deeply offended by her interpretation of one of their political heroes. The real Joseph was, after all, an Alston, bred from one of the state's wealthiest rice planter families no less, as well as speaker of the state house of representatives and governor during the War of 1812. To this regional audience,

Anya Seton had done nothing but put "A Splash of Mud" on the "Theodosia Legend." Her "literary license," one reviewer huffed, "is as ill-mannered as it is abysmal bad taste."[33]

As for Anya's take on Aaron Burr, what is most notable is her ability to make her readers understand and even sympathize with this traitor's demons and demands. In later novels, too, Anya molded potentially one-dimensional villains into characters who while terribly flawed are also compellingly human. As far back as her time at Spence School, Anya had been a curious student of psychology, a subject perhaps related to her interest in medicine. Her library contained books ranging from clinical diagnoses of psychopathic symptoms to popular theories about personality disorders. Freud and Jung had many popularizers, and the 1920s and 30s abounded with books by pop psycho-analysts, which Ann read avidly. From the mid-1930s on, Anya could also draw on her extensive experience with the therapists she visited for treatment of her own difficult neuroses.

The male triangle that is constructed in *My Theodosia*, attaching father Aaron, husband Joseph Alston, and lover Meriwether Lewis, dominates the psychological landscape of Anya's first drama. Their obsessions create an emotional prison for Theodosia, pushing her from one angle to another until her tragic death. Many of Anya's later novels continued to fashion these three-sided male entrapments. In later cases, Anya sometimes merged two of her male characters so that a young heroine is attracted to and dominated not by a biological father but by a father-figure who then becomes a husband or lover. In some of the notes that Anya made for her therapists, she explored her "father fixation" from multiple perspectives that included the possibility of incestuous longings. An Electra complex was not unlikely for someone craving and denied a male parent's affection, but Anya went so far as to wonder if her deep disappointment with her father and her first husband might explain why she often felt so frustrated and unsympathetic with son Seton.

For Anya's Theodosia, beyond the triangle of male power figures are peripheral family groups that close in around her. We watch her first in her own tightly bound home with Aaron, then smothered within the formidable Alston clan, and finally struggling to maintain her little nuclear family with Joseph and son Aaron. During her short life, she grows painfully from daughter to wife, and briefly at last to matriarch. As Anya's first heroine, Theodosia is sadly marked by her isolation from healthy female interactions, allowed only the bonds that might form between a mistress and her dependents or servants (but never the enslaved women with whom she is surrounded, whom she detests). In each successive novel, Anya slowly began to change the dominant male triangle of her plots to include and eventually emphasize structures connecting mothers with daughters who might become themselves loving and forceful mothers. In *My Theodosia*, however, the unusually intelligent but psychologically stunted main character is never allowed by history to benefit from the resources of a healthy family, bound as she is by almost total dependence on her father's will.

My Theodosia made its way successfully in the marketplace not as a family drama but as a historical romance. Despite her later stress on the biographical nature of her fiction, Anya, for this first novel, allowed herself to be placed into the history niche. The novel opens with an author's preface through which she displayed the wealth of sources that had provided the basis for her plot. In this way, she pushed her readers to expect that she saw historical drama as her natural territory. Her 1957 letter to her publicist compared her mission of enlivening "human history" to her father's well-deserved recognition as a gifted natural historian. Her later linkage demonstrates not only how this daughter never outgrew her need to claim her paternity, but also how often Anya Seton the writer revised her narrative of self-assessment.

The consequence for the many analyses of Anya's novels has been that, while there is every reason to praise her ability within the historical genre she claimed, her accomplishment in a broader arena has been shortchanged. What Anya personally knew about and wrote about best were the dynamics of family. She focused closely on how families come into being and how easily they can fracture. In this first narrative, all that is left is tragedy for a loving woman and her small family. Not surprisingly, the novel's jacket called attention to Anya's own family. The biography of the author on the flap began, "The daughter of two writers, Ernest Thompson Seton and Grace Gallatin Seton, the author of 'My Theodosia' grew up in a literary household."[34] The title that she had steadfastly preferred for her novel came from a letter that the actual Theodosia wrote to her father, in which she declared, "You appear to me so superior, so elevated above other men. I had rather not live than not be the daughter of such a man." Anya quoted the letter on a prefatory page to *My Theodosia*.[35]

Ernest Thompson Seton was a shadow that Anya had all her life wanted to get out from under, but he was also a valuable link to a literary heritage that she both needed and wanted to claim. Undoubtedly, too, the Chief's charismatic ability to charm any audience had cast a spell over his young daughter, but it was a charm that had often been darkened by his terrible temper, his lack of attention, and ultimately his rejection of Anya and her mother. Her lifelong ambivalence about ETS is reflected not just in her letters and journals but also in many of her novels. What she envisioned in terms of Aaron Burr's personality and motives was striking in its blunt portrait of him as a man dominated not only by arrogance and self-interest but also by charm and eloquence.

As for Anya's own family, in the fall of 1940 there was one sharp irony relating to her absent father. On November 12, 1940, Ernest Thompson Seton's book, the autobiography *Trail of an Artist-Naturalist*, was published by Scribner's "to good reviews," as Anya noted in her November 26 journal. She listed it without further comment there, also recording that Hemingway's *For Whom the Bell Tolls* was the "big leader."[36] The great majority of *Trail of an Artist-Naturalist*, edited by the famous Maxwell Perkins for Scribner's, was designed to deal exclusively with ETS's early boyhood through young manhood. Only the last sixty pages of over three hundred total followed his life after 1896, the year he married Grace Gallatin. Ernest's reflections on Lord Baden-Powell had been deemed, by both wife Julia and his editors, as far too unbecoming for inclusion, so there was no mention in the book of the scandalous details connected to the Chief's time with the Boy Scouts of America. Seton's marriage to Grace Gallatin does not appear until page 343. Anya knew her father's book was coming a year before its publication, because in 1939, in a surprising request, Ernest had asked her to comment on what he had written about her mother. Through this request, the daughter entered one of the father's last books.

In her reply written in May 1939, Anya thanked "Daddy" for sending a manuscript copy of his autobiography. She told him that she had made "no major changes," but had "made a few suggestions for toning down places, and I have retyped one page." Then, to soften him, she made a touching and also tactful plea. "You yourself taught me—'Always try to be kind,' and I know you do not wish to hurt someone who was your partner for twenty years and your wife for thirty-nine. You are too big and generous a man for bitterness."[37] So it was that in his autobiography "Miss Grace Gallatin" is described, during the time of Ernest's first meeting her, as "an attractive young woman of aristocratic lineage, a college graduate, and socially well placed." Then come some additional comments about Grace's love of "dress, society, and city life," which Ernest said he did not share, but also admiration of her "as a camper," an area in which "she was a great success, never grumbled at hardship, or scolded anyone. She was a dead shot with a rifle, often far ahead of the guides, and met all kinds of danger with unflinching nerve." The end of the Setons' almost forty-year marriage was handled with the retyped page enclosed in Anya's letter. In *Trail* Ernest used Anya's words to explain that the couple's increasingly "divergent interests" were what "set us ever farther apart." Thus when "our daughter" was "grown-up, married and well taken care of, we decided that we were happier apart."[38] That daughter, Ann, self-made into Anya, in her rewrite of Ernest's words proved herself a dutiful but also skillful handler of his self-promoting saga, in which "Daddy" did decide to "be kind."

Grace Gallatin and Ernest Thompson Seton's writing lives came close to their ends as Anya picked up their trail. *Trail of an Artist-Naturalist* had a printing of only two thousand copies, with World War II hindering sales.[39] Now it can be considered the last important book-length work of ETS's career, but at the time, it did nothing to improve the Chief's diminishing income. In 1939, the year that brought the Houghton Mifflin sales manager to Anya's door, Grace's last book-length work was published. *Poison Arrows: Strange Journey with an Opium Dreamer; Annam, Cambodia, Siam, and the Lotos Isle of Bali, with Photographs by the Author* should be considered the most unusual and entertaining of Grace's seven travel narratives. Although it brought out the best in her, both as an explorer and as a writer, it hardly made a whimper when it appeared first in America and then in England from little-known publishers and with almost no press. What led Grace to pick Indochina for her last venture was her interest in the matriarchal society of the "primitive Moi" tribes of Vietnam. After finishing with its writing by 1932, and for the next twenty years, Grace presided over her own version of a matriarchy at Little Peequo. Meanwhile, without complaining, she surrendered her identity as a popular writer to her daughter.

In 1941, with the hoopla over *My Theodosia* subsiding, Anya thought it was going to be hard to pick up her pen again for another try. After noting Theo's appearance in April, the daughter of writers who between them published more than fifty books complained that "my work doesn't move, partly intellectual slump, partly some loss of confidence because of Theo's slow sale."[40] By the end of the next month, however, an entry noted the important news that she "got an inkling" for a new novel."[41]

A trip with Chan to a camp on the Upper Saranac River in New York State introduced Anya to the Hudson Valley as it had existed in the 1840s and '50s. Lee Barker, as before, was enthusiastic about her idea for a historically based novel, so Anya began her happy pursuit of sources. By October *My Theodosia* had been sold to Grosset and Dunlap for paperback reprinting, another win. Then in December, Lee Barker came out once again to Little Peequo to attend one of the Chases' popular Sunday parties and to check on Anya's progress on her Hudson Valley narrative. The date was December 7, 1941. Lee had gone up to Anya's bedroom to read the first chapters of what they were calling *Dragonwyck* when someone came to the house with the news of the "Japanese aggression" at Pearl Harbor, as Anya called the event in her entry for December 8, 1941. Anya closed her account of the momentous day by looking ahead, with gloom but also determination, as she so often figured out a way to do: "Must get back to my writing," she insisted. "Much encouraged by Lee's enthusiasm, but how can anyone write anything when we are at war, and the future hazed in by black fog."[42]

6 | MONEY MAKER

ONE YEAR INTO THE NEW DECADE America entered what was now a total world war, leaving Anya, who was working on her second novel, to wonder whether it would matter to anyone at all. By the time the war ended, she had published *Dragonwyck* (1944) and was well on her way to completing her third novel, *The Turquoise,* which came out in 1946. The war caused upheavals for the Chases as well as everyone else, yet it didn't adversely affect Anya's new popularity. Doing her financial calculations, on May 4, 1944, she estimated that *Dragonwyck* had thus far earned her close to an astonishing $63,000, although she was quick to add, "But of course I don't net anything like that. Nearly half in taxes."[1]

Anya could begin 1942 with some optimism. The declaration of war brought gasoline rationing, butter shortages, daily accounts of battles won or lost, along with trains, buses, and hotels crowded with soldiers. In May 1943, looking through her journal notes written during the war's first full year, Anya noted how little she had mentioned the huge conflict, musing that it really didn't seem to "touch us" except for "mounting and niggling restrictions."[2] But finally there was joy for her, as for everyone, when at last 1945 brought the celebrations of V-E Day and V-J days. Anya wrote that when the news of Germany's surrender came, while she was working on *The Turquoise* in her New York apartment, the city was filled with the ringing of church bells, and she "saw sky white with floating paper."[3] With son Seton and her maid Adele, she joined others throwing paper from their tall building windows to fill the air.

Anya's presence in her own New York apartment for the V-E celebrations was a result of a decision she and Chan had made in the fall of 1942. With

Pam and Seton safely stowed away at boarding schools (Milton for Pam, Putney for Seton), Anya and Chan began to plan a part-time escape from Little
Peequo and its demands. This decision meant that eight-year-old Zizi would
have to be a weekday boarder at Edgewood School in Greenwich. Drawing
on her own frequent childhood separations from her parents, Anya felt that
for Zizi, weekends with her parents in New York or at Little Peequo would
provide enough family time. Grace was close by too, with the ever-reliable
Hanna to care for her. This left Anya and Chan free to sign a lease on a New
York apartment at a good address, 310 East Forty-Fourth Street, Manhattan.
The apartment was in what was known as the Beaux Arts building, an apartment hotel with a first-floor dining room. It looked to be the perfect refuge.

Moving to her own place in the city, Anya wrote, was going to be "an
answer to a long-delayed prayer." For the first time, she could go out to buy
curtains, china, and pillows, arrange furniture to her liking, and put her things
wherever she wanted. The apartment, she noted, brought her "full circle," since
she had been born, she noted, in "the other" Beaux Arts building, "6th ave
and 40th st." With her usual cautiousness about money, Anya calculated that
her 1942 earnings "from my pen" of $3,500, along with savings in gas and
transportation costs to and from New York, would make the move affordable.[4]

The Chases found that they fit naturally into the city that was both the literary and investment mecca of the country. In many ways, however, the apartment did not fulfill its potential as an urban retreat from the obligations Anya
had resented while living in Greenwich. During the four years that she and
Chan held their own in Beaux Arts, usually from late fall through late spring,
distractions and crises of all dimensions abounded. In November 1942, Grace
suffered heart failure and, according to her doctors, could have died at any
time. Anya was with her for a monthlong recovery, first in rooms downstairs
at Beaux Arts and then at Little Peequo. By Christmas, Anya herself had caught
the mumps, "of all the infuriating, idiotic, meaningless breaks."[5] Although Zizi
never came down with the dreaded illness, a bored little daughter had to be
quarantined at the apartment for the first three weeks of January 1943.

During the Chases' time as residents in New York, all three children came
to stay at Beaux Arts with somewhat frustrating regularity. The apartment
became a new center for ritual holiday and birthday celebrations, which Anya
was never going to abandon. Pam and Zizi were generally enjoyable visitors,
but son Seton caused continual problems. He was kicked out of Putney for

smoking. Returned to Edgewood in Greenwich, he was involved in a much more serious escapade when he attempted to sell some property of the school's science lab. Chan managed to keep criminal charges from being sought and had a long talk with Miss Langley, Edgewood's kindly headmistress. Seton was allowed to return briefly, and although a few years later he was given a high school degree, it was indeed a gift, since he never actually finished his studies there. His parents and stepfather Chan found partial solutions to the troubled son's frequent crises in a tutoring school in New York, then a stint in the merchant marines, and finally brief service in the US Army—all before he turned nineteen. As Anya, Chan, and Hamilton figured out each alternate plan for him, Seton was quite content to haunt the New York apartment.

The war years also brought two handsome younger family relations for extended stays. Chan's younger brother Charles and Anya's cousin Gallatin Powers, her mother's older sister's son, were both serving in the military, Charles as a US Marine Corps fighter pilot captain and Gallatin as a US Navy lieutenant. They joined the Chases frequently when they were on leave or ready to ship out, bringing with them both excitement and some tension, as both enjoyed flirting with Anya and pursuing attractive girls all too glad to be escorted. Given all the distractions of family and wartime visitors, Anya's comment in her May 4, 1944, journal is not surprising. She wrote, "Sometimes I feel cut in little pieces trying to respond to the demands of mother, Chan, and my three children."[6]

In a letter to one of her own numerous male friends, dated September 26, 1944, mother Grace supplied a slightly different version of what her own and her daughter's lives were like as the Chases went back and forth between Manhattan and Greenwich. A September hurricane had caused a need for major repairs at Little Peequo, Grace told friend John Dewicki, so "somebody has to pay for it, and I have a suspicion I know who that person is." She continued to describe financial woes, albeit with good humor. They included the fact that "the grandchildren, bless 'em must have their crust of bread and their movies and their funnies." Anya, as Grace too now called her daughter, was headed back to New York as soon as the children went back to their schools. "She will leave me in a week or so and move her typewriter back to New York (and it's home wherever she hangs that [the typewriter])." The family, she concluded, would sometimes "descend *en masse* for weekends," leaving her the need to "recover from it, something like a gentle air raid, I fancy."[7]

Family, however, was not the only consideration for the Chases as they alternated between city and suburban existence. Even before the move Anya had feared that the frenetic pace and glitz of the city might cause her and Chan to get in "over our heads."[8] From her niche in the Beaux Arts, Anya found it far too easy to cultivate her set with daily cocktail lunches, dinners, and parties, some hosted at Beaux Arts, others attended at the swank dwellings of friends and business contacts. Within their first two months, she and Chan were seeing "lots of glamorous people."[9] By 1945, Anya could hold forth confidently during dinners and cocktail parties with writers Sinclair Lewis, John Dos Passos, Lillian Smith, and Lloyd Douglas. Other Houghton Mifflin authors Esther Forbes, Faith Baldwin, and Ben Ames Williams, all fellow historical novelists, became longtime friends.

In a journal entry for January 18, 1945, Ann listed some of the attendees at a party that she and Chan had hosted in their apartment the night before. Her list demonstrates the Chases' rise to social prominence in New York's frenetic wartime years, for the group mixed valuable literary contacts with "evanescent" celebrities, as Anya would later call this kind of coterie. One guest was revered journalist Dorothy Thompson, who befriended Anya and introduced her to others of her insider set. Another was "pretty" Mary McCarthy, whom Anya liked in a "first impression," but whose "constant smile" she soon found to be "meaningless—grinning, a smile with fangs." Paul Mowrer, a famous war correspondent during World War I, was there, looking "old and tired," along with a "brisk wife," Hadley Richardson, whom Anya did not name but identified only as someone "who used to be married to Ernest Hemingway." The most "conspicuous" guest, to use Anya's term, was African American journalist Roi Ottley, who had recently published a bestselling book about Harlem, *New World A-Coming.* He was gaining acclaim as the first black correspondent to cover World War II for major papers, and he brought the woman whom Anya identified as his white wife with him. Anya noted that the wife "seemed nice," while also commenting on her own guilt for having some "unworthy thoughts" about the mixed marriage.[10]

What the Chases' continual round of star-studded social events meant, as Anya wrote by January 14, 1943, was that she and Chan had "been drinking too much. Everybody does."[11] Frequent fights between the two, again fueled with alcohol, marred their time in the big city. For Anya, stress and drinking contributed to more chronic illnesses. Most debilitating was bladder pain connected to cystitis, a condition that throughout her life was treated unsuccessfully by a series of specialists. There were the other familiar ailments too—vertigo, tooth pain, and ear ringing, all of which, she admitted, were almost certainly symptoms of "neuroses." One consultant told her, "I think you must accept 'it' as part of the creative temperament."[12] Anya did not explain if "it" was her psychosomatic pains or her increasing consumption of alcohol. In her journals of this period, she refused to link her sometimes daylong drinking sprees to any of her closely documented ailments.

Despite the intrusions, medical as well as domestic, Anya had been able "doggedly" to work throughout the fall of 1942 on the novel that she wanted to call *Dark Fountain* but which ultimately kept its working title *Dragonwyck*. In October, shortly before the move to Manhattan, she indicated her pessimism about this second novel. She was "under the writing strain, agonizing over Dragonwyck, which is going to be a disappointment to everyone, especially me. I have a hunch that my third book will be the real success." Her one comfort, she joked, was that even if the family ran out of money, "at least I have a backlog of warm coats and shoes for the lean times ahead."[13] On January 14, 1943, she reported that two days earlier, "at three o'clock I finished 'The Dark Fountain'" and had turned her rough manuscript over to her typist. Looking back at her effort, she recalled that "this book was on the fire for eighteen months as I signed the contract July 1941. And got the idea that May, but during illnesses [I] lost months. I guess the writing took a year though and it doesn't seem possible." She had managed to finish the novel even without the presence of her most important professional supporter, as she also noted. Not long after he had started reading the earliest drafts of *Dragonwyck*, Lee Barker left Houghton Mifflin. It was understandably "a blow to me,"[14] as Anya put it, for Barker more than anyone was the person who had consistently encouraged her and shepherded *My Theodosia* to publication.

Although she wondered how "HM" would respond to her second novel without Lee Barker there as advocate, by March Anya found that she needn't have worried. "Reaction from Boston on *Dragonwyck* was ecstatic wild enthusiasm," she reported. "Magnificently written. . . . Full of the romantic sense of doom which makes the Brontes so wonderful. A natural for sales," they told her.[15] It would be almost a year before *Dragonwyck* was published, in February 1944, but Anya didn't rest on her laurels for long. A "conception of new novel—Santa Fe Cameron," had come to her by the end of June 1943. "Great joy as always. Wrote first pages July 31ˢᵗ," she reported in August, about her idea for a novel whose initial setting would be her father's treasured southwest territory.[16] She and Chan visited Colorado and New Mexico for several weeks in September and October 1943, a time that deepened her love of western land-scapes, before returning to their Manhattan whirlwind, where Anya reported that she was "on fire to get started on Fey," the name she had given to the heroine of her southwestern saga.[17]

The Chases' move to Manhattan in late 1942 would seem to have paid off, at least monetarily. Houghton Mifflin's excitement over both *Dragonwyck* in 1943 and two years later over the "Santa Fe" novel, *The Turquoise*, meant that all the stars seemed aligned, as Anya might have put it. She was, after all, the daughter of successful writers who also believed in destiny, along with some help from sheer determination. Grace and ETS's child had chosen, or had been lucky enough to come upon, the right genre, the right publishers, and the right cultural moment to make her move into the marketplace. As she moved from *Dragonwyck*'s completion to *The Turquoise*'s beginnings, Anya allowed herself to be more optimistic than usual, with a team of enthusiastic editors, money coming in both from stories and her first novel's sales, and admiration from many quarters.

Beginning her career at the end of the 1930s, Anya was able to profit sub-stantially from a new book marketing industry. Advertising agencies, dedicated specifically and exclusively to the science of selling, came into prominence at the start of the twentieth century, and by the 1920s, literary agencies had found a powerful niche as advertisers. When Lee Barker started "handling" Anya's career, one of his first stops with her was to the literary agency of Curtis Brown. The agency had been founded in England in 1914, with an author list that included major figures ranging from D. H. Lawrence to A. A. Milne. By 1926, it had established a profitable New York office. Barker introduced Anya to one of its best agents, Edith Haggard, who became her author representative until Haggard's retirement thirty years later.

Naturally it was Edith's job to get along with her clients, which she did supremely well. She had been hired, and was well paid, to sell Anya to news-papers, magazines, radio shows, film agents, reprint publishers, and others, but she also seemed to have a genuine fondness for her client. Like most literary agents, Haggard handled everything Anya wrote, but as one of the best in the business, she also had a willing and wise ear for this particularly needy client.

She read manuscripts, gave editorial advice, and introduced Anya to a variety of useful luminaries. For *Dragonwyck*, she arranged serial publication in one of the most important 1940s women's magazines, *Ladies' Home Journal*, with an offer of $10,000.[18] With this development, Anya came full circle in another way. *LHJ* had been the premiere woman's magazine as far back as the early 1900s, when it paid Ernest Thompson Seton handsomely for a series of influential articles on the boys' outdoor movement.

Serializing novels was a lucrative step for writers, with the only drawback for a novelist being a delay in publication. For the Chases in early 1943, the extra income was worth the wait, and for their publishers, magazine publication could mean extra sales when the novel did appear. What looked like a winning move for everyone, however, had one calamitous result that almost ended Anya's career. A popular writer whom Anya had used as a source for *Dragonwyck* read her serialized version and threatened her with a charge of plagiarism. Anya had met Carl Carmer in September 1942 at a party given by mutual friends, Maud and Eustace Seligman, a power couple in both the New York and Greenwich social scenes who seemed to know everyone worth knowing. Anya hit it off immediately with Carmer, who was at the time riding high in his own writing career. He was the popular author of *Stars Fell on Alabama* (1934), a personal interpretation, based on travels and interviews, of the diverse people who lived in one of the poorest and most racist states in the country. He had followed up his eloquent envisioning of this place and time with several other similar studies of his home territory, upstate New York. In 1939, he published one of the most popular of his regional works, *The Hudson*, for the prestigious *Rivers of America* series, and at the time Anya met him, he had become the series' editor.

As Anya put it in her journal for September 8, 1942, "*The Hudson* was the springboard for my Dragonwyck," so she was eager to meet its author. She described Carmer as "a nice man in his late forties with a crumpled face and a sense of humor. We talked together for about an hour." However, in a side note penciled next to this description, she wrote, "Had I but known!" along with the date of this later comment, "6/21/45."[19] At issue in the potential scandal was Anya's rendering of the scene of a well-documented Hudson River steamboat race disaster, which she planned to use to bring *Dragonwyck* to its cataclysmic end. On October 3, 1942, still working on her final draft, she had written, "Dragonwyck has got me down. I'm trying to write the climax chapter on steamboat race but am having trouble. Can't get the necessary quiet concentration yet."[20] It was no coincidence that she had met Carl Carmer a few months earlier, nor that she failed to mention him when she described "having trouble."

All seemed well until Carmer read the magazine serial and wrote to Houghton Mifflin, telling them that he was sure her copying him had been simply an "innocent mistake." Still, he threatened exposure unless he received a "quiet" payoff. The alternative, he vowed, was to "sue or take 25% of royalties." Anya was sick with anger at her own carelessness, writing on December 2, 1943, that a phone call from Hardwick Moseley on November 29 had told her of Carmer's threat, which gave her "the worst trouble ever" of her life. She immediately compared her description to his and could see that she had in several places copied him almost word for word. "Incredibly stupid of me," she admitted, "and so easily avoided—damn it." With good reason, she was terrified that "my career is ruined forever."[21]

Immediately, along with her guilt, Anya began to marshal excuses. Before she had turned in her manuscript, she had told Carmer that she used his version of the steamboat disaster, and he said, "I'm flattered." She had given him credit, profusely, in interviews and her author's preface and "thought he gave me sanction" to borrow from him. Still, HM immediately called in lawyers and told Anya to "grovel." She did, however, get up "some fight," and spending two days in the library, discovered that Carmer had taken much of his material "word for word" from newspapers in the public domain.[22] Lee Barker's replacement at the firm, Paul Brooks, showed up to handle the bargaining with Carmer.

In the end, however, it was husband Chan who saved the day. As Anya told the story in one dramatic journal entry, Chan decided to go on his own to see Carmer and "soothed him miraculously. Good will radiating except that the gentleman still demands 2000 secret dollars next summer." Evidently Carmer had some legal troubles himself with *The Hudson*'s publishers, so he was fairly accommodating. "There is nothing in writing," Anya reported in her entry. This was a "gentleman's agreement," and the lawyers felt "C. seems much more interested in the dough than in any of the cardinal virtues." Before Christmas the crisis was over, with Anya describing meeting Carmer soon afterward at a dinner, where "he kissed me" with what she described as "a $2000-dollar kiss." She spent "36 frantic hours re-writing" the steamboat race scene for

Dragonwyck's approaching publication date, happy that Paul Brooks thought it "as good as original version." In her ending to the drama, she remarked, "All quiet again and hope to God this is the end of it."[23] The silver lining involved renewed admiration for Chan, a hero to balance a new villain. It is of some interest that as she worked on *The Turquoise* Anya included, in the character Terry Dillon, a falsely charming, greedy blackmailer.

With Carmer satisfied, Anya could move on with a new novel while waiting to see how *Dragonwyck*, with its rewritten climax, would fare in the marketplace. However, she had already received a financial boon that must have influenced Carl Carmer to seek his reward. Anya was able to cash in on one more development in the bestseller business, the interest of Hollywood in the possibility of turning print bestsellers into film box office hits. Beginning with *My Theodosia*, Anya's publicity directors at Curtis Brown contacted film agents during the prepublication period to see if they were interested in movie rights. *My Theodosia* found no takers, but 20th Century Fox bought *Dragonwyck* for $25,000. Anya's portion was $19,125, which allowed her, she said, to start "paying bills like mad," while also earning back Carmer's $2,000 payoff.[24] Less than three years later, in December 1945, she could report that Warner Bros. had bought the rights to *The Turquoise* for an astounding $125,000. "Here words fail me," was the author's shocked response. Curtis Brown sent flowers to help her celebrate, a gesture that prompted a mixture of pride and cynicism. "'Prize Pampered Pup.' That's Anya, for the moment anyway. Who'd have thought I'd be a money maker!"[25]

The film rights to *The Turquoise* far eclipsed the $50,000 that Margaret Mitchell had been paid for her 1936 novel *Gone with the Wind*. That blockbuster film came out in December 1939. Mitchell's long historical saga of Scarlett and Rhett, Tara and Mammy had become a national obsession that carried over into every aspect of its casting and filming. When the film version of Anya's *Dragonwyck* came out in 1946, its marketers not so subtly promoted it by announcing that its antebellum Hudson River Valley estate was as splendidly re-created "as any southern plantation."[26] Literary and film agents formed strong alliances that produced enormous profits for all concerned, and Anya, her agents, and her publishers were beneficiaries.

One more phenomenon was also to help Anya's star to rise. In the 1920s, the idea of mail order book clubs had been invented. The Book of the Month Club and the Literary Guild, the two most prominent of these, had been started in mid-decade to capitalize on a new population of middle-class readers. By becoming members, or subscribing for a fee, book lovers received by mail a certain number of works at regular intervals. The books themselves were chosen by a selection committee or editorial board that took the guess work out of a hungry reader's process of choosing what to read. Also, for a good price, publishing houses allowed the clubs to print their own company-designed editions and to offer them at the same time as the publishers' assigned publication dates. By the time Anya entered the marketplace in 1940, to have one's book chosen by one of the prominent clubs was a mark of distinction, as well as an additional way to profit monetarily. *The Turquoise* was the first of her novels to earn the distinction, with one of the less esteemed clubs, but other, better offers would come before very long.

Book clubs and film rights gave Anya revenue streams that kept flowing her entire career. Beyond these supports, if she were to succeed in attracting a substantial audience, she also needed to understand and pitch to her reading market. Ernest Thompson Seton had been a master in this department, especially with the collections of animal tales and "boys' exploit" fiction that made his fortune. Other seemingly innate gifts also linked Anya to both parents, particularly her ability to enliven her narratives with meticulous attention to historical detail. Like Ernest and Grace, she gloried in the task of exploring whatever sources might give substance to the universe within her books.

However, despite *My Theodosia*'s effective use of research to build the lives of historical characters, Anya did not repeat that method in her next novel. She was aware that her decision to write a totally fictional plot for *Dragonwyck* might cause her difficulty. Nicholas Van Ryn, she wrote in July 1942, was "a stinking hard character to do, and I'm not getting him. I understood Aaron so well, but then he was ready-made. Here I must spin everyone from my own psyche."[27] *The Turquoise*, too, would be just as different from both of its predecessors in terms of time, place, and conceptions of character. Anya could never be accused of not following spontaneous instincts as she came up with each new narrative line. Still, while she created fictional plots for the four novels that followed *My Theodosia*, all of them relied on extensive exploration of historical and geographical sources. For *The Turquoise*, she even wrangled permission to visit New York's famous nineteenth-century city prison, the Tombs, which had recently been replaced. Research, she always said, was the main joy of her life.

Following her treatment of the expansive geographies involving Aaron Burr and his daughter, Anya did the opposite with *Dragonwyck*, making its setting fittingly claustrophobic. A foreboding, multitowered, walled-in manor is the scene of most action. The great stone pile of the Van Ryn manor house looms high above the Hudson on an estate dominated by a magnetic but also psychotic lead male character. Nicholas, the heir to a Dutch feudal patroon dynasty, holds a reign of terror there over both tenants and family in early nineteenth-century New York. As one reviewer commented, the novel creates its own genre, "Hudson River Gothic."[28]

For *The Turquoise*, Anya followed her father's great passion for the Southwest, re-creating Santa Fe but sending the town back to its early frontier years. Dirt, dust, mountains, and sagebrush replace the formal gardens, dark rooms, and deep forests of the Dragonwyck estate. The first setting of *The Turquoise* reflects Anya's extensive personal experience with the West, both as a girl traveling with her father and later as a married woman visiting ETS and Julia in Santa Fe and Chan's parents in Silverton, Colorado. Anya was glad to capitalize on the parental connection. In one radio interview she joked that "Daddy should like" her newest book, if for no other reason than "at least it has Indians in it."[29] American Indians became a common marker in her novels. Earlier she had rather gratuitously added a Native figure to *My Theodosia*. *Foxfire* (1951), however, made the history of the Plains tribes central to her story, and later in *The Winthrop Woman* (1958) she chose the Native Telaka as an heroic major character when she traced several New England tribes' battles with the colonists.

Another whimsical trademark of Anya's fiction was the inclusion, mostly in bit performances, of American writers who lived in the time her novels were set. For *My Theodosia*, it is a young Washington Irving who flirts with Theo in early scenes set in her father's house, Richmond Hill, in Greenwich Village, New York. Nicholas Van Ryn in *Dragonwyck* feels such an affinity with Edgar Allan Poe that he takes Miranda with him on a visit to the sad home that the poet shares with his young wife, Virginia Clemm, and her mother. However, Nicholas is disgusted to discover that the impoverished and consumptive Poe is not philosophically at all like him. In *The Turquoise*, Fey and Simeon Tower entertain James Fenimore Cooper at a dinner where he is an important guest, invited as part of the Towers' attempt to break into Manhattan society. Later, a carefully researched Geoffrey Chaucer is one of the sustaining characters of *Katherine* (1954), based on the life of his actual sister-in-law, and *The Winthrop*

Woman (1958) features a pantheon of Puritan writers—from John Winthrop and Cotton Mather to Anne Hutchinson.

The one other obvious similarity connecting Anya's first three novels is that each traces the life of a beautiful, sexually inexperienced girl determined to find a great love while also grasping at everything the wide world might offer. All three ambitious ingenue characters are soon forced to learn hard lessons that come only when they accept disillusionment, responsibility, and suffering. As more than a few negative critics liked to point out, her three damsel-in-distress plots followed most of the romance basics of the period. Her detractors, however, missed how Anya embedded her own pointed critique of the romance genre into her treatment of romantic heroines.

When we first meet Miranda in *Dragonwyck*, for example, instead of being inside helping her mother, she is out sitting under a tree, devouring "the fascinating pages of 'The Beautiful Adulteress,'" without having "the vaguest notion" of what kind of "horrifying behavior" would make one an "adulteress."[30] Miranda is enthralled to read just the kind of sentimental melodrama that some of Anya's critics accused her of producing, but *Dragonwyck*'s immature heroine pays dearly for her enchantment, and her book's title foreshadows her own temptations with her married cousin. What put Anya in a different class from the true romance writers and onto the New York bestseller lists were characters who were not simply ingenues, villains, or tall, dark, handsome rescuers. The lives of her characters, both men and women, often take surprising turns, and most of them believably evolve into people who command readers' sympathies. In any case, none of her novels, from the first to the last, has anything like a happily ever after ending.

In *Dragonwyck*, Nicholas Van Ryn invites his young, distant cousin Miranda to his estate to be his daughter's governess. Bored with provincial life on a Greenwich, Connecticut, farm, chafing under the rule of a strict Calvinistic father, Miranda is eager to be off. Blind to many overly obvious warning signs, she quickly becomes her cousin's infatuated handmaiden, overjoyed when he proposes marriage the day after his wife dies. The sad, terrified, corpulent first Mrs. Van Ryn, before her terrible death, grows in the reader's eyes from a gluttonous caricature into a fully realized portrait of the terrors that an abused wife must endure. Dressed and schooled to be her husband's next victim, Miranda, with self-centered naivety, is complicit in bringing her own fantasy world crashing down.

The novel's conclusion features a swift progression from one calamitous event to another. First there is a fight close to the death between Nicholas and Doctor Turner, who has befriended Miranda. Both survive and escape, but Nicholas pursues Miranda, who is fleeing on the Hudson steamboat, the *Mary Clinton*, that her husband owns. He is able to flag down the boat from his dock and, to Miranda's horror, confronts her on the deck. The captain of the *Mary Clinton* is eager to race another steamboat close behind them. With some of his passengers rousing him to dangerous speeds and careless piloting, the captain causes a disaster that kills many of the *Mary Clinton*'s passengers. Nicholas, however, rescues Miranda and tries, in one act of selfless heroism, to save others, but he is lost, and his body never recovered. Dr. Turner subsequently finds Miranda near death from shock and pneumonia. The two find peace, with a transformed Miranda concluding, "The evil in me brought out and abetted the evil in Nicholas."[31] As a few critics noticed, Miranda exhibits a few touches of Charlotte Bronte's Jane Eyre and Daphne Du Maurier's Rebecca. Miranda feels no great joy at having survived the torment she endured with Nicholas, and she recognizes her costly failures of sympathy and judgment.

Writing *The Turquoise*, Anya wanted to make her next heroine, Santa Fe (Fey) Cameron, a character who would be taken more seriously. Still, while having a more colorful start to life, Fey at first seems little more than an exotic, multicultural version of the usual late Victorian Gothic damsel in distress. Her lovely young Spanish mother dies giving her birth, and her grieving father, a transplanted Scots doctor, succumbs to fever soon afterward. Fey, a grey-eyed, dark-haired beauty, barely escapes a plight of eternal drudgery as the ward of a poor Hispanic family. When a handsome drifter, Terry Dillon, comes along, she seizes her chance to flee. Through various shady schemes, the two make their way to glittering New York City during the time of Tammany Hall and the rise of a new metropolitan class of millionaire crooks. Terry and Fey are both intent on making their fortune in a place where integrity has no value. *Dragonwyck*'s plot trick of ominous hints of disaster is replaced in *The Turquoise* by Fey's spiritual gift of second sight, through which she can see into people's past lives and predict their futures. Despite the warnings of a shaman, she nonetheless trades her spiritual faculty for the opportunity to gain control over her circumstances.

It is at this point that Fey grows more complex, in part because Anya gives her a foil, a kindly Quaker doctor who takes her in after she is abandoned, pregnant, by Terry. Dr. Rachel Moreton is the most finely drawn maternal character that Anya had yet produced, an advance on the sympathetic mother Miranda chooses to leave when she follows her romantic desires to Dragonwyck. Rachel begins to make plans for Fey to follow her into a medical career, given Fey's natural abilities as a healer. She also shows Fey how to be a good mother to Lucita, the child born from Fey's supposed marriage to the drifter Terry Dillon. Blind and ambitious as *Dragonwyck*'s Miranda before her, Fey ignores the path to happiness that Rachel opens to her, deciding instead to catch one of the city's most eligible bachelors, Simeon Tower. Again, like Miranda in *Dragonwyck*, she can be chastened only by a tragedy largely of her own making.

Simeon Tower is not the egomaniac that Nicholas was but rather an insecure social climber taking advantage of the corrupt practices around him. He has none of the aristocratic breeding of Theodosia's husband Joseph Alston, but he is as obtuse as Joseph in reading his wife's true feelings. Anya's first three novels are at their best when dramatizing the tensions that grow between mismatched husbands and wives in small, intimate, telling scenes. Fey, like Theodosia, at last begins to find common ground with her husband only when it is too late. In *The Turquoise*, when Terry Dillon returns to the New York scene, Fey falls all too easily under his spell again. The melodramatic, penultimate portion of *The Turquoise*, like that of *Dragonwyck*, demonstrates that when Anya was not depending on history for events, she tended to turn from realistic emotions and motives to sensationalized calamities. Terry sees that Simeon is the perfect target for blackmail, given Fey's murky past. Understandably, Simeon is both infuriated and desperate when he learns that Fey has probably had some part in bringing Dillon to their door threatening complete ruin. In a blind rage, he kills her former lover while his elite dinner guests feast in the next room and then flee the Tower mansion in horror at the scandal.

Simeon's rescue from a guilty verdict at his trial depends on his wife's decision, borne of deep repentance, to confess to adultery. Her action brings public shame and retribution but also redemption. In its last scenes, *The Turquoise* consequently moves rapidly from murder to courtroom drama and finally to domestic and spiritual allegory. Fey has grown from a willful girl looking for excitement and riches, then briefly into a dedicated mother given a chance to be a servant for good. Her abandonment by Terry and need for control turns her instead into a bitter, self-promoting cynic before finally she becomes a fallen, penitential wife approaching the status of a martyr. As she finally faces the destruction she has caused, Fey, like Hester Prynne, becomes a little too much of a saint.

Anya plotted Fey's story as a long progression from innocence into experience and then to redemption in the belief that she could deepen her novel by transforming her ingenue character from stock romance heroine into a woman of moral substance and nobility. Basking in the glow of praise for *Dragonwyck* and flattering attention to her authorial self, she started her third novel with great faith that it was going to be her best. One instance of the kind of head-turning adulation that she received came in a review from the *St. Louis Post Dispatch*, which was supposedly highlighting *Dragonwyck*. The clearly smitten reviewer hardly mentioned the novel except to report erroneously that its movie rights had been sold for a "reported $100,000." Instead, in an almost full-page long essay, the reporter wrote a mini biography of "Miss Seton." Among other tidbits that she had revealed to him was of course the fact that she was the daughter of "Ernest Thompson Seton . . . one of the most prominent authors of his time." Her interviewer pictured Anya's charming childhood in a vignette showing her helping the Chief to perform a "deodorizing" operation on the pet skunks at Wyndygoul. In the account that Anya fed him, she began writing only to make money during the Depression, after brief stints as a model and doctor's assistant. Now, in the article writer's words, she was "content to gather wispy, silken threads that can be woven with her imagination."[32]

The farther away newspapers were from New York, the more likely *Dragonwyck* received positive reviews. At a prepublication party on February 17, Anya said there were "about 70 people all telling me how wonderful and beautiful I was," but as for *Dragonwyck*, there was "no danger of getting a swelled head because the NY reviews were pretty bad. . . . Got lambasted for 'melodrama,' 'Victorian plot,'" and even for "being box office." As Anya reported, Orville Prescott, who would for many years afterward be one of her most negative critics in the *New York Times*, wrote in *Cue Magazine* that she had written a "Preposterous historical novel," a "crude imitation of *Rebecca*."[33] When *Dragonwyck* appeared, neither the bad nor the good particularly bothered Anya, who was already working optimistically on *The Turquoise*. She figured that earnings from "the little golden dragon" came to close to $60,000, so she asked herself, "Who am I to think I should have done better and fuss about three bad reviews even though they WERE important ones. I think what I want most for Fey is good press."[34]

Paul Brooks gave her Houghton Mifflin's best contract for *The Turquoise*, a $5,000 advance and top royalties, so her moneymaking skills were not in question. But more than "another financial jackpot," she wanted *The Turquoise* to be recognized as good literary fiction. *Dragonwyck* had been a struggle from start to finish, but she believed in "Fey," expecting great things for it without her usual pessimism. "How about it Anya? You've always gotten what you willed and wanted. Can we pull this one off? Book of the Month I suppose as a final goal, or is it Lit. Guild, maybe?"[35] By January 1945 Anya was mostly pleased with Paul Brooks, writing that "I like him so much, there is quite a bit of playful sex between us." They remained within bounds during their almost thirty years relationship, but even at this early stage, Anya lodged the one complaint that she would often voice about Paul and other editors: "I don't get any serious critical help on Fey, which is what I want. I need the stimulus."[36]

By June 21, 1945, Anya announced that she had "this minute finished *The Turquoise* revision. . . . A weepy feeling, and a loss," a common emotion after months of hard work. "Some of it's good I know—and I *feel* it," she insisted, certain that it was better than *Dragonwyck*, which she now assessed as having "only synthetic emotion." She was nonetheless realistic enough to add that she would "deliver [*The Turquoise*] finished next week, and then the bitter reality begins while the outer world gets going."[37] When the Literary Guild did not honor *The Turquoise* with a bid, Anya felt it "a bitter blow," but she could be consoled when it was picked up by the Peoples Book Club, which paid $10,000 for the honor. So, she said, "Somebody loves my Fey."[38] As she wrote *The Turquoise*, Anya had very intentionally added an element of what she called "spiritual delving" to give her heroine more seriousness of purpose and destiny. After the Literary Guild turned the novel down, and when bad reviews started coming in after *The Turquoise* was published, Anya continued to insist that Fey had "beauty and dignity and spirituality."[39]

New year 1946 began with more acclaim when Anya was feted at opening night celebrations for 20th Century Fox's production of *Dragonwyck*. "My name came up on screen," she reported on January 26, "and there was a party to end all parties." For the young actor Vincent Price, playing Nicholas Van Ryn in his first starring role, the film provided a lifetime of leading parts as a creepily alluring villain. His costars Jessica Tandy, Walter Houston, and

Gene Tierney rounded out a stellar cast, directed by an up-and-coming young director, Joseph Mankiewicz. For this night, at least, Anya could bask in the limelight, but she was too wary to feel much satisfaction: "it's gratifying but no heady joy about any of this," she wrote.[40] The fate of the movie was not unlike the fate of the novel in most respects. Panned by many critics, it was still a box office success. While *Life* magazine wrote of Vincent Price that he "gives us an excellent performance in an innately ridiculous role," the magazine still made the film its "Movie of the Week," insuring more useful publicity.[41]

On Valentine's Day 1946, there was more good news that Anya should have been able to celebrate, as she reported that "*The Turquoise* had advance sales at 52,000" copies, which was "the biggest advance H.M. has ever had," even more than competing male author Lloyd Douglas had recently earned for his highly praised *The Robe* (1942).[42] Still Anya felt little pleasure. A few months earlier, she had already had the premonition that "the smart little New York boys loathe books so tainted with advance money."[43] She was right. When *The Turquoise* came out, no one loathed the book more than smart Edmund Wilson. He was, at five feet six inches, a little man indeed, except as a literary journalist, where he was generally regarded as the giant in his field. Wilson had become the weekly book reviewer for the *New Yorker* in 1944, just in time to catch *The Turquoise*. He arrived after stints with two other important literary magazines, *Vanity Fair* and the *New Republic*. At a time when New York book reviews possessed tremendous authority for much of the informed reading public, Wilson was able to threaten the future of any book coming out, and *The Turquoise*, as he admitted, was a book he decided to destroy.

Wilson decided that his goal was going to be "Ambushing a Bestseller," as the title of his review announced, by finding one example to show everything that was wrong about popular American taste. He had perused several issues of *Publishers Weekly*, looking to catch a book designed "to sell hundreds of thousands of copies," and there he found advertisements for Anya's third novel, which he assumed "will be widely read." After naming *The Turquoise* as his target, Wilson launched into a long plot summary of the book. Fey with her "picaresque" adventures is a "heroine" straight out of the current craze of "women's magazines." These, Wilson went on, were "so much a standard commodity that it is probably possible for the novelist to pick it up at the corner drug store along with her deodorant and her cold cream."[44] His way with words was inimitable, at once colorful, down to earth, and biting.

Wilson finished up with scathing remarks in the same vein. Written "by a woman for women," novels such as *The Turquoise* laid "a bait for masculine readers, also, by periodically disrobing the heroine." But *The Turquoise* was worse than most of this type because it contained "not even a crude human motivation of either the women or the men" in it. At the end came his recommendation: since "the whole thing is as synthetic, as arbitrary, as basically cold and dead as a scenario for a film," Wilson asked, "Will real men and women, in large numbers, as the publishers obviously hope, read this arid rubbish?"[45] Not a week before Anya read what Wilson meant to be a deathblow to her novel, she was already reeling from other bad reviews, so much so that she wrote, "Maybe I'm not a writer, not dedicated enough—and yet I suppose I can't stop."[46] Literary America's most famous reviewer provided the most serious test that this resolve would ever confront.

7 | HEARTH AND HUSBAND

ANYA'S FIRST REPORT of her response to Wilson's review was, after a "first night of anguish," fairly sanguine. She wrote that with the help of her HM team, "I suddenly developed a shell. He over-reached himself in using so much space and the whole thing is so unfair, vicious, and directed against best-sellers and Houghton Mifflin (he practically admits it) that I thought what the hell."[1] Her journal reflected a soothing letter that she had received from Lovell Thompson, Houghton Mifflin's director. Wilson did not like his publishing company, Thompson said, but more importantly, the *New Yorker*'s intimidating reviewer wanted to go after the "Lion" of bestsellers in order to attack the whole phenomenon, so of course he had "picked you as the biggest lion he could find to shoot at. Congratulations."[2] His "overreaching," Thompson hoped to convince Anya, had nothing to do with the merits of her book but merely reflected Wilson's prejudice against popular novels, which he found to be a symptom of America's hopelessly provincial tastes.

Wilson frequently overreached, as targets as various as Ernest Hemingway, Vladimir Nabokov, and the entire conclave of detective fiction writers could attest. This after all was a critic who in his study of Civil War literature, *Patriotic Gore*, grouped Abraham Lincoln with Lenin and Bismarck as examples of modern dictators. *The Lord of the Rings*, he pronounced, was "balderdash," so Anya could take some comfort in her company. Wilson was one of the first promoters of Joyce and Proust, and a steadfast admirer of one of his close Princeton college friends, F. Scott Fitzgerald.[3] What made him so important for so long was that he spoke with sharp wit and clarity about an astonishing number of subjects. He could certainly be wrong, but he was never dull, stuffy, or hard to understand. In an obituary tribute to Wilson, the *New York Times* explained, "There was, inevitably, some question as to whether he was the most sagacious or the most perceptive but there was no doubt, as the years passed, that he was the most didactic and probably the most influential."[4]

One interesting coincidence is that Wilson was a Princeton man two years ahead of Hamilton Cottier, and Anya later wrote that the two were friends, although she had never met him.[5] Wilson's favorite Princeton professor was Christian Gauss, who chaired the department of romance languages when both Wilson and Hamilton Cottier were students. Cottier later became Gauss's assistant dean of the College of Arts and Sciences, while Wilson was so fond of Gauss he often came back to sit in on some of the professor's famous, informal seminars. He also wrote in a piece after Gauss's death that he had learned his lifelong literary preferences from this mentor.[6] The connection between Wilson and Anya's ex-husband is symptomatic of the way that her life often circled back to old influences.

Whatever Cottier and Wilson's relationship, he and the other critics who lambasted *The Turquoise* left deep scars on their target. In her journal, Anya struggled to move beyond the negative reviews. Asserting that "surely the public is the answer," Anya's final word on the subject was something that she might have learned from Hamilton Cottier. "*The Edinburgh Review* may have killed Keats," she added, "but I hope I'm tougher."[7] By May 1946, she had proved that she could call on that toughness and that it was indeed impossible for her to stop writing. In her journal she recorded, "Have been thinking about the new novel." It was going to be set in the sea town of Marblehead, Massachusetts, and trace the fictional history of several generations of women who managed an inn called the Hearth and Eagle. "Hesper Honeywood," she recorded, was what her new heroine "wants to be called."[8]

Not only did Anya have a new writing project during the summer of 1946, but she also had a new place to write it. She and Chan were tired of the frenetic pace of their lives in Manhattan, and after the attack by Wilson, Anya had said that the city was no longer a good place to do her writing. The reviews had made her ask, "What is happiness, Anya? Certainly not this frantic up and down vulnerability, nor the dining and wining or the feeling of being some sort of a celebrity."[9]

Money from *The Turquoise*'s film rights sale to Warner Bros. might go a long way to buying that happiness. It had enabled the Chases in 1945 to buy a summer house they named "the Inlet," set above a cove overlooking Long Island Sound in Old Greenwich. Anya's June 11, 1946, journal recorded that "at last an entry from a home we own. And it's lovely."[10] Not only had she and Chan bought the Inlet house, which cost thousands to remodel, but Chan had insisted that they also purchase a property in front of it that was directly on the Sound. This property, long called Moon Rocks by the locals, guaranteed the Inlet an unobstructed view of and access to the water. Moon Rocks later would be the place where the Chases built their permanent dream home.

The year 1946 turned out to be as much a roller coaster as 1938 had been for Anya. The great shock of Wilson's review was followed by the joy of beginning a new novel and being able to move to the Inlet for a first summer on the water. Dealing with Grace's unhappiness over the move, which left her alone with Hanna back at Little Peequo, was not pleasant, but as Anya reported, "Mother is mournful but trying to be reasonable." The two had agreed that the Chases would return to Little Peequo in the fall and use the Inlet only as a summer house.[11] By August Anya was "doing some work," she said, finishing most of *Hearth*'s first chapter. She had her usual doubts, feeling that "there isn't the surety of the others." The consolation, she hoped, was that she had become "far more aware of good writing than I was."[12] Edmund Wilson's diatribe had perhaps been of some value. If he demanded characters of more depth, she would create them.

The Inlet, as a summer place, very quickly became too crowded and busy with family and friends to be a useful writing place. Thirty-one people had shown up for a Fourth of July party. While Anya said that "I like it, showing off the place, swimming, sailing, croquet, badminton," she admitted that "it's hard to work"[13] She was "fired over Hearth and Eagle," but a month later worried more about finding the time to write. "This is a play place," she realized. While she felt "triumphant" that she was providing her children with a playground for friends, a place where she could be "extroverted and hospitable," she added, "but I'm not working right."[14]

Shortly after making this comment, Anya received her HM contract for *The Hearth and Eagle*. With a promise of 15 percent royalties and a $5,000 advance, she remembered "smugly" back to when "a $250 advance sounded good." She could also brag that *Dragonwyck* had been sold "to 8 foreign countries" and "*The Turquoise* so far to six," prompting Paul Brooks to congratulate her on being "a World author."[15] Extensive partying at the Inlet continued through

Labor Day, but now, with a contract, she admitted that she would be "glad to crawl into the Little Peequo hole."[16] Pam would soon go back to a new job in New York and Zizi back to Edgewood. Seton, on September 9, was off to Camp Dix, having been sworn into the army at age eighteen. By September 15, calm had been somewhat restored to Anya's life, and she was happily working on *Hearth and Eagle*, remarking that "the purest pleasure in life is intellectual delving—historical delving."[17]

Soon, however, there was another dark cloud. Daddy, in Santa Fe, was very ill. At eighty-six, given a life of constant, extraordinary physical and mental activity, he was finally breaking down. Talking with him by phone in September, Anya reported that he "sounded normal and affectionate" but also "remote."[18] Barely a month later, on October 24, she wrote that he had died the day before. While her shock was great, she began to organize a public memorial service for him at Little Peequo, writing on October 30 that she felt "sadness and love" while picking out songs and reading the many "heartwarming" letters of sympathy. The service took place on November 10, 1946, attended, Anya said, by over one hundred mourners, many of them the old friends from the earliest Woodcraft days. Hearing the songs "Beulahland" and "Home on the Range," Anya broke down but felt "proud and humble."[19] Beyond that, she wrote nothing of her mother's feelings, and her own remained ambivalent. In psychoanalysis, she was to blame him for many of her neuroses while in public pronouncements related to her writing, she continued to spin positively the father-daughter bond.

The year ended with Anya able to report that she was making great progress on *Hearth and Eagle*, and she also found that she had made an income of $94,000 for the year, an "appalling" portion of which would go to the loathsome taxes.[20] On New Year's Eve, she and Chan returned to New York and Beaux Arts, which they had continued to rent but sublet. Almost immediately, two problems that had not afflicted her during the six months they had been away returned—her bladder pain and the excessive drinking that she refused to connect to her health. Alcohol also led inevitably to more friction with Chan. By March she reported that he, at least, was worried enough about his drinking to attend AA meetings, a decision that Anya "loathed" since she refused to see any good in it—for him or for her.[21] The fighting caused Anya to think seriously of a separation, but she countered that "every instinct is against it" because of "all we've had and meant to each other and still do, but at least I'm facing it instead of shutting my mind in fear."[22]

One decision that Anya did count on to improve her life was shutting the door on their Manhattan residence. By May the Chases had given up their lease at the Beaux Arts, where they had spent most of a glamorous but also tumultuous five years. New York City, Anya had decided, was far too hectic, as well as heartless, and Chan was happy enough to go along since he could go there for business whenever necessary. Henceforth, when they both needed to be in the city, they could afford to stay in the best Manhattan hotels. They were relieved to be grounded in Greenwich, especially with an extension to Old Greenwich, where the Inlet made them more popular than ever.

At their summer play place, Anya was still able to complete a very rough first draft of *Hearth and Eagle*. However, as she reported on August 29, 1947, she received word from Paul Brooks that he was "disappointed" with the manuscript. Anya agreed that "the thing sags like a hammock in the middle," and described her solution—ten days in Marblehead alone "doing exactly what and when I wanted." Her return home, after a productive time, made her conclude that "I love my family, but so many worries, so many constant jabs to prevent working."[23] She still struggled, noting by November 1 that "this thing is *much* harder than the others. Keyed lower," and that it was still "evading" her. She was revising more than usual, with her "verve" still intact enough for her to work several hours at a time, usually beginning at six AM.[24]

The command performance of Christmas 1947 as always put a halt to writing. Pamela, who had graduated from Vassar the year before, now had a job and her own little flat in New York City, but she came home to help celebrate. Seton could not attend, and as Anya reported, he "hated the Army," but the fact that he was "being taken care of" mattered most. Zizi, at thirteen, had become an active and attractive teenaged girl, enjoying town friends, dancing lessons, and some increased stability now that her parents were back in Greenwich.[25]

Anya, who still vowed that she loved all the "domestic things," did sound one complaint: "What simple lives women live who aren't also trying to write." The sentiment echoed one that she had expressed two months earlier as she thought about her work. There was, she pointed out, a "cleavage between writing and living."[26] Anya Seton the novelist was becoming increasingly aware of the conflicts between being a woman, with all the expectations associated with her gender, and being a writer, free to give her energies to her craft. She was also much more aware of how gender affected the reception of her work. Edmund Wilson's choice of her as a target for scorn was part of a growing hostility in the field of American literary criticsm that disparaged not just women's writing but their themes and their readers.

If Edmund Wilson's insults had done nothing else, however, they made Anya more determined than ever to write a book that would prove him wrong. No longer wallowing in bitterness as she worked on *Hearth*, she exhibited some of the same pure stubbornness that had always characterized Ernest Thompson Seton whenever he felt unjustly criticized. When John Burroughs and others called him a "Nature Faker," ETS fought back with his four-volume *Lives of Game Animals*, a production so knowledgeable that it won him the John Burroughs Medal. Anya was doing something similar when she began working on her *Hearth*, pointing out in her journal that it was very different from her prior works. It consisted mostly of "some quiet drama," she said, meaning that "nobody could possibly call this melodrama."[27] By March 1948, she was working on a "final revision" of a work that had grown to five hundred pages. Frantic to finish, she was at her desk about seven hours a day, not complaining because, as she said, "the process is always satisfying. Need nothing else." The book's theme as she saw it was "rugged endurance come what may."[28]

A new editor at Houghton Mifflin, Helen Everitt, came out when Anya was completing last revisions and "was so deliriously enthusiastic that it scared me." Despite steeling herself for the expected criticism, Anya began dreaming of the Literary Guild or "serial or movie—all that business again." A movie was not possible, Anya predicted, given that her manuscript came in at some two hundred thousand words. Yet Everitt's praise for Hesper Honeywood— "you've made her continuously more aware"—helped Anya to feel, again, that she was countering Wilson's criticism. "At least Hesper grows and develops," she insisted.[29]

The Hearth and Eagle does break entirely new ground, with a very different kind of female hero and a plot for the most part much less sensational or sentimental than the previous two. The narrative of Hesper Honeywood, from her childhood through the 1850s to her death in 1920, dominates the drama, meaning that she does grow and change over her long life, gaining depth as she goes. Always, Hester develops within the dynamic circumstances facing Marblehead, so that the town and the character are intertwined. Anya creates a multigenerational "family chronicle" in which the characters generally stay in one place, over three generations. Both the town and its old inn, like Hesper, have the force of character that combines the warm stability of "hearth" and the adventure-seeking of the "eagle." The fulcrum for this long narrative span is the Hearth and Eagle Inn, an anchor for a series of strong women figures who keep it going for more than two centuries.

In the first chapter, set in 1846, we meet Susan Honeywood, the innkeeper's wife, as she serves customers on a night when a fierce storm is raging. Three weeks later, young Hesper follows her anxious mother down to the harbor, where they hear the news that several ships had gone down during what history named the Great Gale, a storm in which eleven schooners were actually lost. On one of them, the fictional Honeywoods' two sons served as young crewmen, and disappeared forever with sixty-five others. This opening is the best of the four Anya had produced, combining rich local color, suspense, and the tension between a mother's grief and a little girl's uncomprehending puzzlement.

Anya uses Hesper's grandmother in this chapter to set up a flashback that grounds all the later action, a strategy that, at first, Anya's editors resisted, given that the foreboding energy of the first chapter seems to urge the reader to push ahead. The flashback goes back to the first of Hesper's women ancestors, Phebe Honeywood, as Hesper's grandmother retells her arrival on one of Puritan John Winthrop's ships arriving in Massachusetts Bay in 1630. Like all the future Honeywood women, Phebe has dutifully followed her husband, in her case to New England. While this segment might seem to interrupt the flow of Hesper's forward-moving saga, it contains one of the book's most absorbing history-based dramas, and Anya was not willing to cut it. She relished her research on Marblehead's early history and was able to relate her later women characters' fates to that of this young wife, soon to be widow, determined to build a promising future for her children.

The end of the 1630 flashback sets up Anya's portrayal of the continuous sparring between young Hesper Honeywood's parents, which is at heart a quarrel about the value of the past. Mother Susan Honeywood, a realistic and dynamic character, is usually inflexible, always resilient, and sometimes tender in spite of herself. Her partner as well as opposite, husband Roger Honeywood, is an unassuming scholar whose obsession with Marblehead's history leads him to retreat from the troubles of the present. Susan has no use for the past which has, she believes, turned her husband into a timid weakling. Still, despite her scorn for both Roger's passivity and her daughter's romantic notions, Susan fiercely protects them both. Roger is a new kind of male character in Anya's pantheon. This "college man," with his passion for the Romantic poets and for writing his own epic poem based on the myths of Marblehead, resembles bookish Hamilton Cottier, a retiring scholar who loved Keats and Shelley and spent his later years as a serious book collector.

Hesper is unlike either of her warring parents. In her teen years, she grows into a willful redhead, with "a lot of bosom," whose greatest desire is for love, defined primarily by sexual passion.[30] In this yearning, of course, she sounds not unlike the young Ann Seton. Over the course of her long life, Hesper has three different lovers. Engaged at nineteen to the handsome, virile Johnnie, at this point she is satisfied to be a Marblehead fisherman's wife. When he is killed in the Civil War, Hesper becomes at first inconsolable and then bitterly rebellious against everything Marblehead represents.

An avant-garde bohemian artist is Hesper's second lover. Edward Redlake seduces her with an offer of marriage that will allow her to escape Marblehead. They live in bohemian squalor in New York until the shallow, unstable Redlake abandons Hesper soon after she miscarries their expected but unwanted child. Back in Marblehead, with her marriage annulled, Hesper reluctantly accepts another rescuer, local shoe factory owner Amos Porterman. Marriage to a man she doesn't love is Hesper's way of providing stability for herself and her mother, who still runs the inn. While Hesper learns to care for Amos and has two children with him, her life continues to be torn by various upheavals. The excessive number of the novel's late intrigues include a nymphomaniac mother whose son bears several grudges against the Portermans, a violent attempted murder, and a fire which destroys Porterman's factory and much of the newer sections of Marblehead.

All of these sensational events clash with the quiet drama that Anya first envisioned for the novel, but she manages to save her *Hearth* from *The Turquoise*'s excesses by a stronger grasp on her characters' motivations and responses. One of Hesper's illuminations echoes Anya's perceptions of her own practice of blending past and present: "Why," thinks Hesper, "did the olden times seem so romantic—while the present never did? She had a vague realization that this night's work would also seem romantic someday, but it didn't now. That's because I don't know the ending—she thought. Things you hear of from the past, you know what's happened, you don't have to worry. Yet at the moment, she wasn't worried. She felt contempt, mastery, inner excitement, not worry."[31]

Both Hesper and her creator shared a longing for the stability of the past, a world that could be romantic because one could know the ending. The current world with its uncertainty could be agonizing, but it was also where, if one risked danger and failure, she could feel most alive and masterful. Anya, the chronic worrier, always expected the worst, especially as writer and mother, but like Hesper, she never quit forging ahead. When she sent her last revised draft to her editors in Boston, she agonized over its reception. She was only partially comforted when Dorothy Hillyer, one of her most valued editorial readers at Houghton Mifflin, wrote, "It lived with me overnight and continues to occupy my mind. It is so real and strong a world it is hard to come out of. I think it is a wonderful book, and your best. There is no question of its success." After copying these comments into her journal, Anya added, "I hope she's right."[32]

It was not long before worry was replaced by an exhilarating experience of the "mastery and excitement" Hesper had felt. Anya told the story in her journal entry for May 11, 1948: "Yesterday at the hairdressers Paul called me from Boston. The Literary Guild has taken the Hearth and Eagle for their December selection. Their peak of the year, Christmas book. I can't believe it. Happy, yes, And frightened. This means that I've got everything I ever set out to do in the writing line. Have grabbed all the plums. A real established Best seller. Better press would be nice. I wonder. Today it seems that anything at all is possible."

And for a while, it was. She and Chan were leaving the next day for England, a trip that she had anticipated but also worried over for more than a year. John Beecroft, the powerful head of the Literary Guild, wanted changes in the final chapter, so she was going to have to rewrite Hearth's ending on the ship. Although this was "a nuisance," Anya did not much mind. "Bon Voyage," she told herself, and "Avanti."[33]

The Chases sailed on the America May 12, visiting Paris, then touring England. Chan flew back to the States early, leaving Anya happily on her own in England for the last several weeks. There, she visited Pam, who was taking some summer courses at Oxford, and enjoyed more touring and "extroversion" before she boarded her ship in Southampton. The result of her voyage home by herself was the fulfillment of another desire that had been cautiously expressed in many entries over the last several years, and one that for a brief while gave her great satisfaction. The day after her July 8 return home, she wrote that the trip had been "fun with Chan and fun with Pam and superheated fun alone." All things considered, it was "perhaps the happiest two months of my life. Every damn thing I wanted came true. Beauty and romance. People and experience."[34]

On the "boat," Anya gloated, everyone had thought her ten years younger; she received the "adulation" that she always craved, and then there had been "sex excitement" with an air force colonel named Bob Hare. He fell in love with her at first sight, he told her. Almost immediately too, he wanted to marry her. "I love you terribly, worship, adore," were words that Anya recorded in her journal, adding her own cryptic response, "Ah well." This romantic interlude was inevitable, given Chan's current "remoteness" both physically and emotionally; and always, when on her own, Anya attracted admirers and potential seducers. Colonel Hare arrived on the scene at a particularly propitious moment.[35]

The romance continued after the ship docked in New York but was carried on almost completely by an exchange of letters. Bob had served with the 8th Air Force during World War II and had received injuries that continued to need treatment when he returned to the United States. He left Anya to go to Walter Reed Medical Center in Maryland to receive care for physical problems connected mainly to eyesight and ears, wounds, Anya noted, that he had never explicitly explained. After several weeks there, he returned to his home base at Maxwell Airfield in Montgomery, Alabama. Anya knew little of his private life, only that he had at least one son and that he was deeply embittered by wartime experiences that he also never explained. He insisted that he had money beyond his colonel's pay and could always take care of her and the daughter he thought was her only child. For many reasons, Anya had never told him about her two older children.

In writing of the affair immediately after her return, Anya wrote that she was "thrown off a bit" by it, but also that "I needed this and I've no regrets for once."[36] However, it wasn't long before she felt the inevitable ambivalence. For a short while she was certain that Chan was her only true love, but it wasn't long before she felt "reversion now to deep hostility" towards him and "consequent guilt." She retained feelings for Bob, upset when she didn't receive letters but doubtful when she did. By July 20, she wrote, she had begun to see a therapist, "To try to find out how to conquer my fearful ambivalence towards Chan."[37]

The therapist Anya chose was Dr. Helen Flanders Dunbar, already a renowned psychotherapist, who seemed well-suited to her. The theory behind Dunbar's clinical treatment was her groundbreaking work on the psychosomatic nature of physical illness. She had advanced degrees from both Columbia University and Union Theological Seminary and studied clinical psychiatry at Yale Medical School as well as with experts in Vienna and Zurich. Eventually she attained the title Mother of Holistic Medicine because of her emphasis on the work of integrating body, mind, and soul in order to heal both physical and mental disease. She had also written a study of medieval religious psychology that had some influence on Anya's thinking about psychological motivation when she wrote *Katherine* several years later.[38]

Early in her treatment, Dunbar, according to Anya, noted that her patient's bladder problems were symptomatic of her flawed relationship with Chan. As Anya reported her words, "I think you resent the terrific sex bond with someone who is not on your mental or spiritual plane." In following visits, Dunbar diagnosed "free floating anxiety" and "repressed 'hysterical rage.'" Anya's response was that "I knew that too and would like to get rid of it."[39] Dunbar, per Anya's notes, encouraged her to see Bob Hare to clarify her attraction and advised her not, at this point, to reveal the relationship to Chan. After several inconclusive meetings with her lover, Anya found his presence less and less thrilling. By December she was writing in her journal that "it doesn't seem finished, and where can it lead? I certainly don't want to marry him." Trying to please both husband and lover, "having my cake and eating it too," was not fair to either of them, she admitted, and for her, "both cakes crumble a bit."[40]

By Christmas, Anya wrote that after more than thirty interviews with Dunbar, costing a total of $450, she was ending her visits. The sessions had not resolved her marriage troubles although the physical ailments that so often afflicted her had improved, and she had followed her psychiatrist's advice concerning her affair. Now, she also calculated, she better understood the "neurosis" that had been caused by "my messed-up childhood."[41] In a series of typed "Childhood Memories" preparing for her Dunbar visits she expressed her attraction-repulsion for her father, her frequent experiences of loneliness and rejection, and the "female dominance" issues that resulted from her relations with her mother.[42]

In January 1949, Anya left both husband and lover, traveling cross country by train to California, where she visited friends and promoted *The Hearth and Eagle*, which had been published on October 28, 1948. During her transcontinental travels, she heard frequently from both men. Bob Hare sent telegrams leading to a plan for him to rendezvous with her in Los Angeles. As fate would have it, Chan arrived there a day early, on January 13, the night before Hare's expected appearance. She and Chan "fell into each other's arms, into bed, and it was wonderful," she enthused, writing out the scene a month later. Like something out of a piece of fiction, as Anya described it then, the phone rang shortly after midnight. It was Bob calling, and of course, Chan asked who it was. "So it all came out," Anya wrote, and both men "were swell."[43]

If Chan's mild reaction was surprising, perhaps it was because back in 1943 he had confessed to several one-night stands during stays alone in New York, and while Anya wrote that it was a blow, she had quickly forgiven him.[44] Somehow, at that time evidence of his virility mattered more than his cheating, and now, perhaps he did not mind her doing the same. In any case, during the rest of their time together, the contented couple hardly mentioned Bob, although Anya did somewhat disingenuously let her husband see a letter she received from her lover. They drove east together as far as Arizona, enjoying western scenery as they always did. In Phoenix they met up with Chan's brother Charles and his second wife. Anya had always found Charles to be very attractive. She had enjoyed numerous flirtations with this brother, who was younger, taller, and more athletic than Chan. Now Charles became interesting for a more professional reason—the story of his short-lived first marriage.

Unlike Chan, Charles had followed his father into the mine management business. During his work, he had met a girl named Polly, the daughter of a wealthy mining investor. Like Anya she was a well-bred eastern girl, who quickly fell "under his spell." However, once she was "taken out of her element in the eastern horsey set, she had with [Charles] only a short run in a small copper mining town" near Arizona's southern border with Mexico. Not long after the birth of a daughter, Polly decided "she had enough of CHC's [Charles's] immature behavior," and she left for California with their child and never looked back.[45]

The story contained the kind of romance that would pique Anya's interest, if not as an idea for a novel, at least as something that sounded rather like material for a pulp magazine. After Charles and current wife returned to Colorado, and Chan flew back to New York from Arizona, Anya had time alone to ponder many things. She greatly preferred to travel by train, and on her way back east planned to visit now-married daughter Pam and husband Pete Forcey in Wisconsin, where Pete had a teaching appointment. For several days by herself she enjoyed "a beautiful desert room" outside Phoenix where she could mull over her own marital relationship and take in the powerful influence of place surrounding her. While out hiking a mountain trail, she came to a dramatic decision about her marriage, as she reported: "It's Chan you idiot." In the same journal entry, she also recorded an idea for a fifth novel. "I think I got an idea for a new book. Apache Dart—Lost mine. Mining," she said.[46] The story of handsome Charles and his stormy marriage to Polly would become the core of the plot for *Foxfire*, although the young wife as she was developed was based on Anya's own earlier self, Ann Seton, while Charles was transformed into the part-Apache Dart and also, in personality, into husband Chan.

Now, in the spring of 1949, Anya the writer was headed in a completely opposite direction from the one that led to *The Hearth and Eagle*. That novel's debut had taken place the previous October, so she had been dealing with its editorial completion and debut for the entire period of her romance with Bob. Before publication, *Hearth* had received not only the Literary Guild selection but serialization in *Woman's Home Companion*. Immediately after the publication parties, Anya, true to form, started to worry over whether the book would hit the bestseller lists and how long it would stay there. In this respect, she was to be disappointed.

The Hearth and Eagle was a novel that for many critics did prove Edmund Wilson wrong about Anya Seton's talent. Anya was able to boast that "the press is much the best" she had ever received for any of her novels. However, the book did not sell as well as she or her publishers hoped. The Literary Guild selection, the serialization, and the good reviews could comfort them, and at least Anya was free to move on to a new effort. Out in the Arizona desert by herself, Anya was ready to go again, beginning her tenth year as a writer whose career was a growing success story but whose real life was turning into the ever more vexed melodrama that her next novel would reflect.

8 | WHERE TO GO FROM HERE?

AT THE END OF A JOURNALING BOOK COVERING the years 1942 to 1949, Anya provided a brief summation of the seven years recorded in its pages. There was satisfaction that the three novels published in that period, *Dragonwyck*, *The Turquoise*, and *The Hearth and Eagle*, had made "an incredible amount of money." Beyond that success, she noted somewhat wistfully that her children had "grown up." Her travels, which took her across the Atlantic and across the American continent, gave her great pleasure. The final year, 1948, had been "rich romantically," with "Europe and Bob." Marriage, despite "bad moments" as she assessed it, "still holds." Wrapping up, she claimed somewhat surprisingly, "there has been no great soul-shaking change, except my writing success." Her concluding question was, "Now where [do] we go from here?"[1]

The lives of Anya's children had changed a great deal, "soul-shakingly" or not, in the later years of the 1940s. Pam, on her own 1948 Atlantic crossing to England, had met and developed a close relationship to a Princeton graduate, Charles (called Pete) Forcey, who would soon be a fellow student at a summer program in Oxford. Her mother did not approve of the romance, echoing her own mother's disapproval of first husband Hamilton Cottier. Both Hamilton and now Pete were committed to lifelong academic careers, which Anya seemed to distrust on principle. Like Grace, however, she came around, as her eldest child, very much like her, was determined to become engaged anyway. The marriage took place on June 19, 1949, with a reception at Little Peequo. Anya was proud of how "beautifully" everything had gone, with "150 people, sunshine, champagne (6 cases)," and at the end, "boozy sentiment."[2]

Son Seton had been discharged from the army and had tried halfheartedly throughout 1948 to make some money. Most of the time, however, he was a very restless, unhappy resident of Greenwich with an equally frustrated Anya and Chan, or with father Hamilton. By the fall of 1949, however, he became a twenty-one-year-old freshman at Oberlin College, a good turn of events for all. Zizi too would be off in 1949, starting her first year at Abbot Academy for Girls (later Phillips-Andover). While the children were taking big steps towards their futures, Anya and Chan's relations, after almost twenty years of marriage, were in "a state of flux." Both were in psychotherapy with high-powered New York psychiatrists, Chan with Dr. Henriette Klein and Anya with Dr. Helen Flanders Dunbar, but by July 1949, Anya felt that her own treatments were no longer helpful, and she was always doubtful about Chan's.[3]

As for the glimmer of an idea for a mining novel set in Arizona, Anya had written in March 1949, from Little Peequo, that she was trying "to get into it" but wondered "Is it all silly?"[4] By the next week, she had a title, "Fox-Fire," and had completed a ten-page outline. Still marital difficulties, outlined in the same entry, were getting in the way, as usual. She and Chan talked of divorce not, she indicated, because of the terminated affair with Bob but because, as Chan reportedly pointed out, "there is nothing to hold us together now except mutual desire." Anya, returning from Arizona by herself after the cross-country interlude with Chan, had resolved to try harder for harmony, but soon gave up: "I can love him so much when I'm not with him."[5]

After mentioning an outline for "Fox-Fire" in her entry for March 9, 1949, Anya said nothing more about novel number five, which she abbreviated as "FF," until writing in her new journal in August. Then, with Pam's wedding successfully completed and the usual summer move to the Inlet, she wrote that "I am having trouble with Fox-Fire, won't jell, not enough plot, central drive not under way."[6] She hoped that a planned fall trip to Arizona would help, and it did. For over two months, from October 2 to December 9, 1949, she enjoyed her western haven where the usual "joy of research" was augmented by "friends, side trips, coyotes, Apaches, and mines." Except for twelve days of touring with Chan, she was alone for one whole month, relieved that he had left and being, as she put it, "pure and intellectual" without him.[7]

Anya returned to Little Peequo from her second trip to Arizona with a rich collection of materials but also with the prospect of a "wretched time" with Chan. Their relationship alternated between "battle royales" and "semi-truces."

She looked forward as always to Christmas but also to the chance to "start work on Foxfire," with a big *if*—"if only I can achieve marital calm." As was the case with the two characters whose marriage was shaping the plot of Anya's novel in progress, part of the problem with her and Chan's marriage, she believed, was that "in a way we both care too much."[8] Their mercurial moods, swinging between episodes of seething anger and intense lovemaking, found their translated way into the developing drama of *Foxfire*.

Anya's fifth effort was the only one of her ten adult novels that at least seemed not to be set primarily in the past. She and Chan had married in 1930, during the same early Depression era in which *Foxfire* takes place. The main characters are a newly married couple, Jonathan "Dart" Dartland and Amanda Lawrence, who come from vastly different backgrounds and geographies. Dart is "one quarter Indian," the son of a Harvard-educated scholar and a wife who is half Apache. From a brief backstory, readers learn that Dart's father hailed from a blue-blooded New England family. When poor health led him to Arizona, he met and married a "half-breed" Apache woman, Dart's mother. After his father's death, Dart's mother Saba returns from her husband's home in the East to the reservation to live according to her own father's tribal traditions. She insists that Dart follow the white way, as she and her husband had agreed, by going to college and pursuing a career in his father's more socially acceptable world. Dart graduates from the School of Mines in Tucson. Chan Chase, somewhat similarly, had attended the University of Colorado, but followed a very different academic focus, wanting nothing to do with his father's profession as a mine manager. Dart's choice of a wife, however, is similar to Chan's, since *Foxfire* heroine Amanda Lawrence is a Greenwich girl who, like Anya's daughter Pamela, attended Vassar College.

A more intimate parallel that connects Anya and Chan with Dart and Amanda involves the fact that the fictional characters are drawn to one another by sexual attraction, which remains their strongest bond. Another source connecting Anya's fictional couple with her own family history is the shipboard romance that results in Dart and Amanda's marriage. Anya's parents, Grace and Ernest met, like Amanda and Dart, on a ship making an Atlantic crossing (although in the opposite direction), and they too had been quickly attracted to one another despite their mismatched backgrounds. Anya's own shipboard romance, with Colonel Bob Hare, was undoubtedly lingering in her mind. In *Foxfire*, Amanda's family and friends are horrified by her whirlwind shipboard courtship and subsequent rush into marriage with a stranger of unacceptable parentage.

Foxfire begins as the newlyweds drive their jalopy along dark, mostly dirt roads toward Lodestone, Arizona, where Dart has found a job as foreman of a gold mine in the eastern Pinal mountains. As they make their way, Amanda's memories provide the details of how the two met and the rush of events that led to their marriage. Still completely in love, with no idea of what lies ahead, Amanda now feels a sense of foreboding. Behind her are all the comforts and pleasures of her former life, including the mother who had always been her protector. Amanda's mother is in fact a close facsimile of Grace, with her quiet wisdom, her fatalism, as well as her generous support of her daughter. Grace had done her best to prevent Ann's marriage to Hamilton Cottier, feeling that her daughter, like character Amanda, was far too inexperienced with life or love to take such a precipitous leap with someone she did not really know. *Foxfire*'s fictional mother-daughter pair provided Anya with a way to explore her past, especially through a heroine whose early womanhood experiences echoed her own.

Married life for Amanda and Dart begins in a dingy bungalow in Lodestone, a town full of tough old-timers along with a parvenu class of mine managers. They are suspicious of Dart and scornful of Amanda with her fancy manners. Unable to break the ice with the mine workers or their bosses, Amanda is completely isolated. She and Dart both change, Amanda becoming a clinging outcast and Dart an uncompromising he-man absorbed in his job and impatient with his wife's unhappiness. Lovemaking is all that holds the two together, with arguments a daily fare. Dart becomes so insensitive that it is hard to understand what he had ever seen in Amanda, while she responds increasingly as a victim with little will of her own.

In a fairly early 1950 draft that she sent to Houghton Mifflin, Anya made Dart so heartless that Paul Brooks "wanted him softened."[9] The final version of Dart does exhibit a more benign side, particularly when he thinks of his lost relationships with his stoic mother and fierce grandfather, Tanosoy. At least physically, Dart is his creator's ideal man, very different from husband Chan as he looked to his critical wife after close to twenty years of marriage. Tall, lean, athletic, and darkly handsome, Dart has the bearing of certain men for whom Anya often voiced admiration in her journals. In his meanest moments, however, Dart might very well have been serving as a stand-in for Chan in his 1950 personality. Both the fictional and the real husband, as Anya described them, exhibit moody preoccupation and uncompromising stubbornness, often responding to their wives only with blunt criticism or surly silence.

Amanda, without husband Dart's sympathy, begins to look for any kind of company and finds it only with two characters whose isolation is as complete as hers. Calise Cunningham is the self-imprisoned widow of the mine's first owner. A well-educated beauty who married beneath her, she has hidden herself away in her thirty-room house in order to pay for a terrible sin. As a bored young wife, Calise had taken a lover, inviting him to her bedroom, where they were discovered by her husband. Enraged, the husband kills the lover and soon dies of a stroke, leaving Calise to mourn in a crumbling gothic mansion. Amanda also sometimes seeks out Hugh Slater, Lodestone's irascible, hard-drinking physician, who introduces himself as "a goddam combine of midwife, bonesetter, and veterinarian."[10] He too is in exile because of past tragedies and crimes. Calise and Hugh are colorful but flat characters trapped in overdrawn memories that impede rather than advance a coherent plot.

Anya spends a good deal of time psychoanalyzing the unlikable Amanda, her Greenwich-born ingenue character. Looking back to her girlhood, Anya seems, with Amanda, to be satirizing herself as young and foolish Ann Seton. On June 30, 1950, the anniversary date of Ann's marriage to Hamilton Cottier in 1923, Anya commented about herself as that bride, "I was a vegetable."[11] Like Ann back in 1923, Foxfire's Amanda knows all about popular psychology, including Freud's theories on the dominant sex urge. Sheltered and secure, she is easily hurt when others do not immediately like her. Like young Ann, she also tends to draw on her store of worn quotations from romantic poetry. If accused of naivety, she admits simply that she is incurably romantic. Through Amanda, Anya dissects some of her own girlhood self-absorption, but does so to the point that her character's late transformation into a courageous and resourceful helpmeet for Dart is hardly plausible.

Writing Foxfire gave Anya almost nothing but trouble. By February 1950, moving toward the climax, she described what she had produced as a "vast inchoate mess." Still to be accomplished was the task of writing out most of a plot that she had only outlined: "the arrival of Amanda's family and Tim, Saba's death, Dart's disaster in the mine, search for the Pueblo Encantado all ahead."[12] As she "sweated" her way toward a conclusion, close to two months later, Anya figured out a way for Hugh and Amanda finally to lure Dart into a quixotic search for treasure supposedly hidden in sacred Native American territory.[13] At this point, the narrative takes many improbable turns. The motivation for the doomed quest involves dark intrigue when Dart, fired from his job and accused of sabotage, quickly turns not only against the mine. He also, for no credible reason, denies his spiritual inheritance from his shaman grandfather. Only violence and Amanda's newfound empathy give him renewed inner strength. Finally, every conflict is resolved in an all-too-happy last chapter. Anya recognized some of these problems, writing to herself that "I don't know if it stinks. Too much emotionalism."[14]

Foxfire's simplistic finale might have been due to Anya's other preoccupations at the time, especially the turmoil engulfing her marriage. She was impatient to move on, at least with the novel, and rushing to finish a final draft, she began to refer to her work as "Fox-Flop." Her staff at Houghton Mifflin, she noted when she created this nickname, were asking for almost no changes as she turned in her work, but she did not trust them. "They're always kind. Too kind?" she feared.[15] She dreaded Paul Brooks's critique, but when he gave her "only a few minor points" of criticism, she was shocked. Brooks revealed HM's general mindset when he responded to her surprise by saying, as she quoted, "Apparently you're disappointed because I don't tell you to write it all over again, but you've *done* what you set out to do." Either he did not understand, or he discounted, the fact that Anya was not satisfied with what was faint praise instead of insightful critique. In her journal entry's response to Brooks, she crafted a mock *Time* magazine review: "Miss Seton's mystical mush of mining and melodrama, all the stale ingredients right from the store, etc.," adding "at least I've said it first." She added that she was "not proud" of *Foxfire*.[16]

Anya's distress over her current effort was not a new reaction. Even before the critical failure of *The Turquoise*, she had wished for more time and more constructive editorial advice. Her publishers, unfortunately, were in their own rush simply to get out another Seton book. They rather cynically knew, by this time, that *Foxfire* would sell even if it did not meet high literary standards. While Anya had dreaded the publication of "Fox-Flop," she had to be pleased when it was accepted for the Sears Readers Club and for serialization with *Woman* magazine. The book came out on January 2, 1951, and the overall response "was not Foxflop at all," she marveled. Her book sold better than expected, hitting both the *New York Times* and the *New York Herald Tribune* bestseller lists within ten days. With many good reviews, Anya could laugh when the *New Yorker* commented simply that she was "incessant."[17]

Foxfire made it to number six on the *New York Herald Tribune* list almost immediately after its debut, the highest she had ever reached on any list, as she reported. Still, she commented, "the big line critics will have none of me." Given that her editors did not seem to care, she wished, "if only some good critic would help me!" One of her most negative reviewers was a "good" one, she thought, who ideally might have given her the kind of help she wanted to get for herself *before* a book came out. The critic she had in mind was Catherine Meredith Brown of the *Saturday Review of Literature*. Brown had given *The Hearth and Eagle* perceptive praise in 1949, which had especially pleased Anya. In *Foxfire*, however, Brown saw only "under pressure writing—hurried, repetitious, pedestrian," as Anya quoted the review. She was hurt not only because she admired Brown, but also because she saw some justice in the critique. Writing about Brown's comments, she said that "I have to accept them," vowing with determination, "I must study more."[18]

Another of Anya's disappointments about *Foxfire* had nothing to do with the lambasting that it received from some critics or the failure of her editors to help her improve. At an early stage of writing *Foxfire*, she had asked Chan to provide her with some information about the technicalities of mining operations. She was hoping not just for advice but also, she admitted, for "a word of praise. . . . I got neither," she added, even though "he grew up in mines, worked with them." A deeper motive for her questioning him, as well as for picking the western mining culture and plot for *Foxfire* in the first place, came to the surface when she added, "I chose this theme partly and unconsciously so that we might share a little, in something." As she saw it, Chan was not interested in having a part in her writing life. He was only "resentful."[19]

Whatever anyone thought, *Foxfire* sold better than any of Anya's previous books. "I want to write better," she said as the novel made it to "Number 4 on Trib list," but, "if I did would anyone recognize it?" She was admittedly in "a writing depression," feeling that she would "always be second rate of course."[20] As would almost always be the case, the depression that Anya felt over her writing would lift as soon as she began to see the light of a new project, and after "Foxlight," as she also liked to call it, the wait was not long. It would also have been hard for her not to be consoled when *Foxfire* provided an extra bonus for her and her handlers, the sale of film rights to Universal Pictures.

Her agents had worked to sell the novel to Hollywood since she had finished her first draft in 1950, and they were finally successful in 1953. "Universal bought for $8,750," she wrote, which was "peanuts," she added, compared to the incredible amount she received for *The Turquoise*. Still "all movie stuff is ga-ga," she acknowledged.[21]

In 1955, Universal presented an almost unrecognizable redo of the novel. Young Amanda, whose shining gold hair was part of Anya's symbolism for *Foxfire*, ended up being played by much older, dark brunette Jane Russell after June Allyson, who had first been hired for the role, dropped out. Jeff Chandler, playing Dart, also coproduced the film, perhaps interested because he had done well in a starring role at the warrior Cochise in the 1950 film *Broken Arrow*. Chandler even wrote a song for *Foxfire*, which he sang during the film, something Anya's Dart would never have done. Much of the movie was filmed in California, and in its Hollywood version, Dart is a raging, jealous husband while Amanda is the always plucky, as well as very sexy, heroine. Anya, like most audiences, thought the movie to be the real flop. When the *Andrea Doria* ocean liner sank on July 25, 1956, its passengers were watching *Foxfire*, which Anya said was "spooky. . . . It could only have made the victims' ordeal worse," she thought.[22]

Despite the low regard in which *Foxfire* was held by its author and most later readers, it has some distinctions that have never received adequate recognition. In the typescript of an article she wrote after *The Turquoise* was published, Anya explained that her inspiration for starting a novel was always "a sense of place," even before a "vivid interest" in history or "a particular character."[23] One passion that Ernest and Grace shared was their love of the outdoors. Grace made herself very much at home out in the wilds of many countries, as all her books demonstrated. Ernest not only introduced Anya to places of great natural beauty, but he also gave her a vocabulary of appreciation with which to describe them. When Anya first met Chan, one of his attractions was that he loved his western roots and had none of the eastern stuffiness or reserve that constrained so many of her Greenwich acquaintances. The two were always happiest together on their many western trips. Sense of place was Anya's springboard for *Foxfire*.

During their marriage, Anya wrote glowingly of her western journeys with Chan, which usually included visits to her father in Santa Fe as well as to the Chase family in Silverton. After she had conceived the preliminaries of

Foxfire on her first stay in Arizona, she returned to the historic mining town of Globe the next year to fill in the gaps. This locale, she said then, made her "intensely happy." Her agenda was to leave her room in the Dominion Hotel and drive a rented "little Plymouth" eastward while taking in all that she saw and heard. Her route took her through the Sonoran desert and then higher, toward the Mogollon Rim where *Foxfire*'s most exciting scenes were to take place. Always she was drawn to the startling contrasts between "mesquite-studded desert and stark rock-walled mountains," moved by "the spiritual beauty of sunsets and rises."[24]

From the opening paragraph of *Foxfire* to the closing sequence, the fictional viewpoint on these landscapes is self-admitted tenderfoot Amanda. On the evening of her first drive with Dart towards Lodestone, she sees the high Pinal range ahead as a "somber enigma." She voices her uneasiness to Dart, telling him that for her, "the country's overpowering." She lists its "spooky" features: "Canyons, cactus, empty, vast, lonely."[25] In the novel's last section, when Amanda with Hugh and Dart find the Anasazi cliff dwellings, her response, as Anya crafted it, is self-consciously lyrical. "Across the little canyon on the eastern wall," Amanda sees the "yawning" cavern "opening like a mouth on a little city of stone," where the buildings "floated in a mist of enchantment infinitely still and awesome."[26] She and Dart very quickly become hesitant to disturb the cliff dwellings' mystical aura.

Anya's ability to make the territory of her novel both tangible and poetic was closely connected to the way she combined the past and present worlds of the Apache. The first edition book jacket for *Foxfire*, which she either wrote herself or authorized, emphasized how she came to her knowledge. As she had often done before, she provided her attractive myth about the name Anya and its supposed adaptation from Anutika, the address bestowed on her as a little girl by a visiting Indian chief. The book jacket also reports that "during her childhood," Miss Seton "spent much time in the Southwest, on a ranch which was owned by her father, Ernest Thompson Seton." The ranch of her early years was of course the Connecticut woodlands of Wyndygoul, with Seton's New Mexico Castle, also never a ranch, not yet even on ETS's mental drawing board.[27]

More factual are the credentials the book jacket provides concerning Anya's personal knowledge of the geography that was such a force in *Foxfire*. To prepare, her readers were told, she had gone "over the whole of Gila County," south and west of Globe, Arizona, even "staying on the Apache reservation" located not far from there.[28] With this information, the book jacket functioned much as Anya's usual author's prefaces do to establish her source material. Yet nowhere did she provide details of her most significant sources. These were the experiences that she absorbed during her life with her father before her marriage, a time during which he brought many Native peoples, from dozens of tribes, to his various Woodcraft campgrounds in Greenwich. Then too, she clearly applied knowledge supplemented by what Ernest wrote in extensive coverage of American Indian life over his more than four decades of witness.

Even during her teenaged years with her father at DeWinton and Little Peequo, Ann Seton participated as Black Wolf held his audiences spellbound with stories of American Indian beliefs and exploits. Before her marriage, Ann Seton had met one of Ernest's closest, lifelong friends, a Dakota Sioux also of French and English descent, who greatly influenced Black Wolf's thinking. Dr. Charles Eastman, whose Native name was Ohiyesa, often visited the Setons during the DeWinton years, enjoying canoe rides on Peequo Lake.[29] In the 1930s, Eastman and Seton worked tirelessly together to change federal policies toward Native Americans. Both *Foxfire* and later *The Winthrop Woman* would incorporate Ernest's tireless activism into vivid Native American women characters.

Grace made a Plains Indian maiden outfit that Anya sometimes wore, as a teenager, at Council Ring ceremonies at DeWinton and Little Peequo. The dress closely fits the description of one that appears in *Foxfire*. In the scene on Dart's family's reservation, a teenaged girl proudly shows her ceremonial dress to Amanda. At the memorial service for her father that Anya organized at Little Peequo in November of 1946, daughter Zizi wore the dress once worn by her mother, so it was fresh in Anya's memory when she created the scene for *Foxfire*.[30] Promoting and celebrating Native American ways was a family affair for Ernest, Grace, and Ann, likely contributing to their most animated and cooperative times together. *Foxfire*'s evocation of those ways represents a kind of elegy through which Anya paid her respects to a rich inheritance.

Foxfire's delineation of the historical past as well as the present of the Arizona Apache comes most substantially through Dart's reminiscences of his revered grandfather, warrior and shaman Tanosay. A kind of composite Apache chief, "related to the Great Cochise," Tanosay tells his grandson of his participation, as a young man, in one of the tribe's last raids against the invading white settlers, admitting that he killed everyone traveling in one lone covered wagon, except for the family's young daughter, Nellie. Years later, after this girl has grown up and assimilated within his tribe, Tanosay and Nellie marry and have a daughter, Saba. Saba is sent to the San Carlos reservation agency school and soon marries the white Dr. Dartland, with whom she has one son, "Ishkinazi," or "Dart." Like his mother, Dart is sometimes pejoratively known as a "half-breed."[31]

Dart consequently inherits two opposed racial worldviews and tries to craft an individuality beyond belonging to any race.[32] The novel, however, comes down on the side that Anya's father "Black Wolf" promoted when he wrote, "The culture and civilization of the White man are essentially material; his measure of success is, 'How much property have I acquired for myself?' The culture of the Red man is fundamentally spiritual; his measure of success is, 'How much service have I rendered to my people?'"[33] Anya imbues the *Foxfire* chapters set on the reservation with the same tone of ardent distaste for land as property and reverence for its spirituality. The sentiment expressed there, which Dart embraced through his grandfather and mother, makes it hard to believe his abrupt, albeit temporary, decision late in the novel to desecrate his tribe's sacred ancient burial grounds. Finally chastened after his challenge at the place his people held as inviolable, he returns with Amanda to Lodestone restored to dignity and wholeness and to his birthright belief in the gospel that Ernest preached.

Using her store of experiences and Ernest's writings as primary sources, Anya carefully acknowledged some of both the past and present worlds of the Arizona Apache in her novel. When *Foxfire* is viewed as her only work not set in the past, what is missed is the witness that Amanda becomes when she visits the reservation with Dart, who has been summoned to his dying mother's bedside. Amanda is at first horrified by the "filthy," primitive conditions she sees but learns a new perspective when she helps the women grind corn while left on her own. As one of them tells her, "It's good for women to work together." With these words of initiation, as Amanda toils alongside tribeswomen, she discovers a previously unimaginable "freemasonry of women" that she is generously invited to join.[34]

The Apache women tell her that they "like to live pretty much in the old way, keeping the customs," because "it made one happier. . . . For the good of the tribe," they have their own "expeditions" that take them out to the plateaus or the plains "to gather acorns, yucca, cactus fruit, and mesquite pods."[35] They have carved for themselves a fulfilling labor independent from but neither better nor worse than their men folks'. Amanda is observing something similar to what Grace had found among the matriarchal Moi tribe of Vietnam. Grace had written that in the Moi, or Mnong tribe she visited, women existed within a clan culture that was "strictly egalitarian." "Here," she added, "is a division of labor and both sexes are interdependent."[36] As Anya describes the Apache women, in a paragraph that is much more anthropological than novelistic in its tone, her interpretation of their labor is strikingly similar to her mother's. "The women," Anya's readers are schooled, "were on equal footing with their men, they held positions of dignity, their work was of equal importance in the structure of the clan," a description that is not filtered through Amanda's eyes.[37]

The impressions that Amanda gains on her day of belonging to a free-masonry of women "faded very soon into a dream."[38] *Foxfire* has many chapters to go, containing increasingly heavy-handed drama that allows no return to the way of life among the women "who work together." In the novel's conclusion, Anya chooses briefly to focus instead on a modern model of companionate marriage, in which supposedly Dart and Amanda will be respectful equals. Was Anya thinking of her own marriage? Whatever the inspiration, she was not able to stick to the ideal of an egalitarian marriage for the Dartlands. When they return from their ordeal, everyone in Lodestone notices a happy change in the once miserable couple. Almost immediately, however, as they are asked to tell their story, Dart tells his wife to "Hush," which Amanda meekly does.[39] For a finale, Amanda in turn tells her husband that she will be happy anywhere he is, especially now that she is going to have a real bathroom in a much better house in Lodestone. Her deference and shallowness have inexplicably returned.

The ending of *Foxfire* dispels the brief glimpse that Anya provided of a creative, woman-centered, but also primitive societal organization. Yet in her next two novels, set in societies and centuries far apart, she recovered some of *Foxfire*'s uneven depiction of a fulfilling kind of mastery that women might achieve. Her heroines in *Katherine* (1954) and *The Winthrop Woman* (1958) are based not on a feminist or even on a matriarchal idea of power, but on one that might best be called maternal. The real-life Katherine Swynford was mistress and finally wife of the powerful fourteenth-century Duke of Lancaster, John of Gaunt. With fierce love and determination, she was able to be much more than his lover, as she became the director of her estates and a shaper of her children's destinies. In the history that Anya drew on for a novel set three centuries later, Elizabeth (Bess) Winthrop was one of the first women in America to purchase and to hold, in her own name, a significant amount of real property in what was called the New World. That property was Greenwich Point, Connecticut, also called Elizabeth's Neck, one of the places in Old Greenwich that Anya loved best.

Anya noted in her journal that once she finished *Foxfire* she was going to write another biographical novel, as *My Theodosia* had been ten years earlier. The difficult fictional plot of her Arizona novel had been a constant and unsatisfying struggle. In her next two adult novels, she re-created the experiences of two courageous women from history who achieved unusual social power while still being strictly defined as wives and mothers. Between them, Anya wrote a young adult novel that also fit that pattern. These novels, completed in the 1950s, became the vehicle through which Anya imagined the possibility of women's lives reaching well beyond traditional roles. Struggling with many inner demons, Anya did not have much success in ordering up the personal life she wanted for herself as Anya Seton Chase. But as she sat at her desk in her study in 1952, tracing and then designing her interpretation of a fourteenth-century woman's heroic maternal destiny, she became very much in charge.

9 | MIDWAY

BY THE SUMMER OF 1950, Anya had finished most of the work of *Fox-fire*, although the novel would not come out until the following January. She already had another of her "glimmers" of an idea for a very different kind of novel. "Next time," she vowed, she was going to do "a biographical novel again I think. Some theme and characters so big they'll carry themselves."[1] Trying to plot an imaginary story for Dart and Amanda had showed an old weakness that had been part of the problem for *The Turquoise*. Still, Anya had achieved an enviable stature by mid-century, with the five novels written in ten years, each more successful, at least commercially, than the last. Now halfway through her career, at age forty-six, she could hope to do even better. Her next group of adult novels, the five published between 1954 and 1973, would take twice as long to produce but would also exceed previous records for both commercial and critical success. Soon there would be changes not just in her status as a writer, but also in all her other roles, especially those involving family—daughter, mother, and wife. Some of these changes were inevitable, a few for the better, but more, as time went on, a consequence of increasingly self-destructive choices.

By 1950, Pam had married and moved to Madison, Wisconsin, where husband Pete was beginning doctoral studies in American history at the University of Wisconsin. By August, Seton was at Oberlin, and Zizi was starting her last year at Abbot Academy near Boston. The Inlet, basically a summer cottage, was sold in October, so Anya and Chan began to plan a permanent residence on their adjacent Moon Rocks property. By deciding on the move to Old Greenwich, Anya was severing ties with the home, Little Peequo, that had been her refuge since she had graduated from Spence School, except for her years with Hamilton in Oxford and the first two years of her marriage to Chan. She was leaving her mother and Hanna behind too, the maternal figures who had been her rocks at every stage of her life. During the 1950s, Grace would become increasingly dependent on her daughter in an inevitable role reversal that was hard for both, especially given that they had for so long shared not only a home, but a vocation and mutual feeling that father/husband had abandoned them.

The inevitable transition connected to her children's distancing was also a difficult change. While raising them had often taken her away from her writing life, she enjoyed the dominating role of motherhood. The elaborate ceremonies that she scripted for birthdays and holidays provide one example. They were dramas not to be altered. Christmas rituals took place over three days, with a creche presentation and placement, traditional songs and meals, personal note reading, wassail, and a prescribed order for gift giving. For Thanksgiving, there were gratitude lists. For New Year's, there was a public reading of resolutions, which might be critiqued. In one of her childhood memories Anya had written that her parents had been "good at festival feelings," and her festivals might have been a way to recapture or revise some childhood occasions.[2] They were also, however, a means of asserting control over her family

Approaching fifty, Anya was still an attractive woman. She made friends easily and craved positive attention, which kept her worrying about her looks, especially her weight. From the 1930s on, her journals kept a close watch over pounds lost and gained. Nearing mid-life, sometimes she approached 160 pounds, to her horror, but through dieting, even foregoing some of her highballs, she could usually get closer to her ideal of 130. The passes that so many men had routinely made in her earlier years were not as regular, but she didn't want or expect them as she once had. Once established in Old Greenwich, one of the East Coast's most socially elevated towns, she and Chan fit easily into a new, more powerful social set, despite the odd architectural design they chose for Sea Rune. Here, Little Peequo's secluded environment was replaced by a close-knit Old Greenwich neighborhood. All kinds of company were within walking distance, and the Chases' glass house, perched so close to the water, became a magnet. When hurricanes were forecast, all the neighbors arrived at Sea Rune to catch the best view of whatever the storms brought in. Particularly interesting were the unmoored boats that often washed up on the

Chases' private sandbar. Anya had loved cooking and entertainment back at Little Peequo, but now her culinary skills and welcoming personality kept her regularly in the hostess limelight.

Chan, too, liked the new social status and Sea Rune's location. He loved sailboats, and soon owned two that he could take out from their sheltered cove into the open water of Long Island Sound. There was a new group to enjoy swimming and water sports with the Chases, one no longer dominated by the teenagers who had swamped the Inlet. Although Sea Rune was not meant to be a party house, it was seldom without guests, both neighbors and friends from near and far, especially on weekends and holidays. This hospitality meant, more than any other enticement, the pleasure of liquor. By this time, Anya's regular, "medicinal" four evening highballs were heavily supplemented whenever guests appeared. Chan, who had been going on and off the wagon since the mid-1940s, continued that pendulum swing. The result was predictable. The two Rs—Rage and Remoteness—that had already often marred the Chases' marriage, became almost daily occurrences.

The journals that Anya kept beginning in 1951, through almost the last one that ended in 1972, contained page after page documenting a marriage that was to remain dangerously off course for the next seventeen years. Anya's journaling was becoming more and more dedicated, she said, to offering "catharsis and release" from Chan's insults and her own guilt.[3] It was a means of self-analysis and perhaps, like her drinking, self-medication. With these functions, the entries began to linger on every scuffle, or reconciliation, or major tempest with Chan. Anya was also still much involved with her children, nearby or not, as well as mother and friends, to say nothing of writing, so it is unlikely that her marital woes took up as much time as she gave them in her chronicles. Yet the opportunity for a blow-up was always there, as was the fuel that liquor added.

The cycles of drinking and fighting created another menace: Anya's health problems. While she was almost always willing to admit that her physical ailments were mostly psychosomatic, she took each pain seriously, as did the doctors who prescribed a variety of pharmaceuticals to treat them. The journals throughout the 1950s and beyond listed almost endless maladies, including vertigo, blocked ears, no menstrual bleeding or too much, stomach pains, and stiff joints, to name the prominent ones. The blood pressure readings that she recorded were increasingly high, but she never quit smoking. As with her fights with Chan, it is doubtful that her infirmities took up as much of her focus or time as her journals implied. In her notes she continued to cover conversations with editors, public appearances, funny comments to and from friends, Binney Lane gossip, and happenings out in the world. These illustrate that Anya somehow continued to be a lively, popular, hardworking woman who was living, as she said soon after moving to Sea Rune, a "bifurcated, trifurcated life."[4]

The month of November 1950 illustrates how Anya's vistas as writer and woman seemed to be changing. *Foxfire* was finished although not yet published, so she was between books, which usually meant an "extroverted" time. Sea Rune was in the design stage. On November 7, with Seton and Zizi settled at their schools, Anya could boast of the "glitter-glamour life" she and Chan had been leading. After mentioning that the Korean War was going on with the "Chinese Reds," she launched into a description of a two and a half week stay with Chan at the Berkshire Hotel in New York. They dined at Sardi's and the plush Versailles, paying an exorbitant "$105 for dinner without dessert!!!" They gave and went to cocktail parties with the HM team, also with agent Edith Haggard, Chan's financial partners, and old friends such as wealthy civic leader Eustace Seligman and wife Maud, Lee and Adelaide Barker, and "the Isabel Lords." Anya particularly admired two new literary acquaintances, writer Elizabeth Bowen, "a woman to admire," and Harrison Smith, influential editorial writer of the *Saturday Review of Literature*—"a bit opinionated but I like him."[5]

Back at Little Peequo, waiting on the new construction to begin out at Moon Rocks, Anya reported that she and Chan "continue to meet VIPS." At the top of the list were Gloria Vanderbilt and her husband, conductor Leopold Stokowski, famous for directing the Philadelphia Orchestra, the NBC Symphonic Orchestra, the Hollywood Bowl, and the New York Philharmonic. Gloria and "Stoky," as Anya called him, were married in 1945, and when the Chases became their friends in Greenwich; the couple, he at sixty-eight and she at twenty-six, had recently become parents of their first child, son Stan, born in August 1950. At their first meeting, Anya wrote that she and Gloria talked "childbirth and mysticism," becoming fast friends, even though Stoky was somewhat a "cold fish." Anya and Chan were pleased when these new friends invited them to dinner, although Anya wondered if they were becoming "snobs, both dazzled in a way by success with VIPs."[6] Anya remained close to

Gloria, sharing her joy in a second pregnancy and "the funny bond we have," noting two years later, as Gloria's marriage to Leopold became strained, that she was having many affairs, and "who could blame her.[7]

Anya did not completely neglect her writing during the "extroversion" she enjoyed in the fall of 1950. While still working on *Foxfire* the previous spring, she had also been reading a newly published book about Geoffrey Chaucer and noted on June 30, 1950, that she was "delving into Chaucer's time. Would love to write it, maybe." In her long journal entry for November 7 of that year, describing all the parties with celebrities, Anya also noted something that would end up being much more significant. Because she was so taken with a book called *Geoffrey Chaucer of England*, which had come out in 1946, she took the time during her New York visit to write a "fan letter, cold," to its author, Marchette Chute. "Miss Chute" immediately invited Anya to tea, where they bonded over "blissful 14th Century talk." A long friendship began that day, with Anya describing, in her first impression, that Marchette, as she would soon call her, was "a fine thoroughly channeled woman, with delightful humor," and perhaps more pointedly, a supporter who was "Most Helpful." Before leaving New York, and energized by Chute's encouragement, Anya bought "one hundred dollars' worth of source books" to add to her collection. Anya greatly depended on Chute's work, glad that Marchette, unlike Carl Carmer the *Dragonwyck* nemesis, seemed genuinely pleased to see her new friend rely on her own impressive research.[8]

Back at Little Peequo with her stacks of books and maps, Anya recorded, still on the same date, "I don't know what I'm doing yet, but I'm fiercely interested. Excited. Will little Blanche Swynford be the heroine?" Then all the distractions returned. She and Chan were frequently meeting with Stamford architect Tony Sherwood, who was drawing up plans for the new home. Thanksgiving and even Christmas were already on Anya's radar, so that she agreed with what her therapist told her earlier, that "I DO have a complicated life."[9] However, only four days after this entry, the curtain came down on both researching and partying. News came from Abbot Academy's physician that Zizi had experienced several fainting spells and seizures which he thought might indicate epilepsy. "This blow, this blackness nearly the worst, not THE worst thank God, and I must have faith," Anya noted on November 26, 1950. The episodes had begun on November 11 and continued for two more weeks, while Zizi underwent every kind of medical test. None provided any answers or protocols, leaving Anya and Chan to feel "mutual guilt, fear, hostility—how could we have done such a bad job where we both felt steady love and maturity."[10]

The numerous specialists called in could see only some kind of what they called "conversion hysteria" as the cause of Zizi's "attacks," but what that diagnosis meant was unclear to all. Zizi remained at the school infirmary, even attending some classes, but by December 12, she was home for the long Christmas break. Her parents had no guarantees about her future, only the threat that another attack would mean she could not return to Abbot. Anya continued to see this crisis, as she had said when she first confronted her daughter's illness, as "the most shattering real trouble I've ever faced."[11] Christmas passed with all the children there but without any of the customary record of celebrations. Zizi remained at home for the long holiday and was with her mother in New York when *Foxfire* made its debut on January 2, 1951. In her entry for that day, Anya wrote that "#6," the barely started Chaucer novel "is far away. To hell with my psyche—it's a bore. Pray for strength for the coming brick bats. I'm not in the mood."[12]

Life for the Chases during the spring 1951 months did settle down enough to improve Anya's mood. *Foxfire* surprised everyone with its success, and Zizi returned to Abbot for her last semester. She graduated cum laude in June, even after having skipped a year and "despite the month's strange illness last fall," as Anya pointed out.[13] With *Foxfire* listed as number four on the *New York Tribune* bestseller list by March 2, Anya could confidently get back to her writing. Still, at this time she felt that she was second rate, a typical self-deprecation when reviews were appearing. She did partly blame her own priorities, asking "How can any woman of my type do better. Chan and family first and demands—mother—social—and my own sexiness and extraversion [sic]." These were always going to interfere. Comparing herself to the women whom she considered "A-1"—Willa Cather, Ellen Glasgow, and Esther Forbes, all of whom had won the Pulitzer Prize for literature—she rationalized that they were "semi-hermits and husbandless, childless." This sense that women with traditional domestic and social lives could not do it all became a more frequent refrain in the coming years, while Anya's output would prove that she could, when deadlines loomed, become something of a semi-hermit herself. At this point she consoled herself with the resolve, "Anya you CAN'T have everything, accept, and work harder."[14]

With this intention, on April 27, 1951, Anya wrote, "Don't feel I'll ever write again, but I will." That resolve would be tested throughout the summer, during which "wallops from Reality," as she called them, came roaring back.[15] There was increased acrimony with Chan, who had gone off the wagon in March. By August, according to Anya, he was "depressed, irritable, unreasonable," sometimes taking the car and driving off into the night, as he had years before when he was drinking. This time, both realized that "Liquor" must be "cut out," which meant Anya foregoing her regular four highballs before dinner. As was to be sadly the case so often, a doctor, in this case her longtime personal physician Gray Carter, told her, that she "needed some before dinner to relieve tension" and suggested, "Why don't you sneak a couple" (at least according to her own account of the conversation).[16] Anya's experiment with abstinence lasted two weeks.

The most serious problem of the summer, however, was not Chan but almost eighty-year-old mother Grace. On July 22 she broke her hip, an injury so severe that it was questionable whether she would ever walk again. She was in the hospital for nine weeks after multiple surgeries to implant a plate in the hip and an agonizing time in traction. Even with this setback, the Chases carried on with their home-building project. They were approaching the last stages of Sea Rune's construction, which inevitably triggered hassles with their architect, rising costs, and frustrating delays. Anya resented Chan's indecisions, in these scenarios wanting a more assertive, take-charge man. "I want to be cherished and protected and feel I have a strong arm to lean on in all these worries, mother, house, financial, and my God, how can I WORK in this mess."[17]

The big day of moving into Sea Rune finally arrived on September 14, 1951, with much celebration and many details still to manage. A housewarming party that took place on October 14 brought in many gifts, with Anya listing the best ones. She naturally included Gloria Vanderbilt's "iron candelabrum and Stueben glass." Ten days later, on October 24, 1951, she announced in her journal that she had gotten back to work again on "Kath." Her report of that day's activities marks the opening notation of what was to become her most complete record of daily progress in writing any of her novels. First, she "thanked God" that she was back to her "Kathy" research, continuing,

The yearly chronology. Tracing Jog [her abbreviation for John of Gaunt]. More grasp. Frustrated because maps—English—somehow lost in move. WHY do I so love maps and dates and actual history? Fitting my story to what did happen and what might have happened. A bastard form, I'm afraid, like the little Beauforts, but they DID get legitimated in the end. Great thrill Sunday. Final discovery of logical convent Kath. could have been at, a Benedictine priory on Isle of Sheppey. Fits all the requirements including nearby Ed. III and Jog castle of Queensborough. A tiny advance like that makes me happy—good pure unambivalent pleasure.[18]

From this time on, John of Gaunt went by his nickname while Katherine DeRoet Swynford, his mistress and later the third Duchess of Lancaster, was Kath or Kathy. A new Chevy purchased for Zizi as she started her college years at Wellesley was named "Jog." In her journals, her almost familial connection with the novel's characters indicates how deeply she was immersed in this project. She began giving much more than her typical accounting of how far she was getting and what she was thinking about both her method and her story.

There were interruptions, some of them professional. On October 23, 1951, she gave one of her canned talks for the Darien Book Club. She entitled these, privately, "How can I do it too?" but still cared about her housewife would-be writers' opinions. For the occasion, she wore "a red beret, gold jewelry, an orchid they pinned on me, minks—whipped together at home." She assessed her performance by comparing herself to Daddy, remarking that like Ernest, "I know I can turn it on when I want to," and she was pleased that "at least I made them laugh several times." Then on November 8 there was a "tougher" performance, when she joined a panel on "Pitfalls of Writing" for what she called a "jury of her peers test" because it also featured friend Marchette Chute and hostile critic Cleveland Amory, a *Saturday Review of Literature* writer who was soon to become commentator for the NBC *Today* program. Anya felt she held her own, even though there was a "ghastly idiotic moderator."[19]

Anya's prestige was growing, which added to the pressure, for as she said, "So many things keep me from work, Or I think they do. But I AM working some." The note that she WAS working launched two years of journal entries that trace the broad sweep of her production of *Katherine*, "Number Six." On November 16, 1951, she wrote, "The blessed mornings—Chaucer, Froissart and a few yellow pages covered of the 1st chapter. Katherine and her journey, but thin as yet, no texture, and so much so terribly much to know."[20] By

Thanksgiving, while jotting down her traditional gratitude list, she included, "Thankful that I'm working, that Kathy becomes a trifle realer, and thankful for old Dan Chaucer whose Ballade of Bon Conseil I've 'translated' this morning to read in the ceremonies," by which she meant the family's traditional inspirational Thanksgiving readings. Thinking of spiritual messages for the day, she also drew on a saying by Julian of Norwich, soon to be developed as a central character in *Katherine*: "It is only because of our self-willing that we do not hear and see God."[21] At many points in her life, Anya read religious books and attended several churches without joining them. It was not surprising that while she was absorbing the religious focus and practices that dominated the fourteenth century, she gave more attention to her own seeking.

By the new year, Anya had negotiated her HM contract and advance for "Kathy," after a conference with Paul Brooks during which "he was charming—bucked me up so." With that boost, she went on to write "a complete outline, rewrote 1st pages—5000 words in a day or so."[22] She also began to plan a trip to England, an essential research quest. February 1952 was both productive and frustrating. Anya read Chaucer's *Troilus and Cressida*, both in modern and middle English, proud of her growing proficiency in that language. *Troilus and Cressida* was important to Anya's conception of her characters because she believed that Chaucer's 1380s epic poem, dealing with the tragic love affair between the Greek hero Troilus and the Trojan maiden Cresyde, might have been prompted in part by the illicit love affair of his sister-in-law Katherine and Chaucer's patron, John of Gaunt.[23] A few days after the enjoyable reading of Chaucer's implicit take on Katherine's love affairs, Anya was back to complaining that her work was stalled. "Katherine goes so badly," she brooded. "I haven't got into it. I can't get at them. Pale flabby tripe comes out. I've been putting words down but there's no sweep. No elan."[24]

On February 6, the same day as this complaint, Anya wrote out a two-page summary of what a "fairly typical working day" looked like at this time. Her sketch demonstrated why concentration was difficult.

> Awoke and got up at 6, eight hours of sleep are enough for anyone.
> Made Chan's breakfast and mine
> Then sat here by the window in sunlight and read Troilus and Cressida,
> both translation and original, looking for phrases, endearments,
> speeches, an angle.

Got writing by nine, can't get Jog in the round or anyone, derivative tripe.

Interrupted by Mildred (maid)—kitchen door won't shut. Jasper came and fixed.

Thanked Paul for $5000 advance.

Back to work except for watching oxtail stew.

Ate big lunch at one and read Barnes's "Passionate Drood?" Richard I. Not so good but she has detail that's escaping me.

Then nap for 20 minutes.

Phone call from Zizi—wanted to come home with roommate Janet. New Chevy, ecstatic.

No more nap. Went for walk, talked with neighbors.

Blanche first appearance in her solar. Kath a static goon/ gave up at 6 cooked noodles etc. for dinner/ got drink and I'm back to the old 4 a night before dinner. Jigger and soda each

Did double crostic in Sat. Review had bath, read Walpole.

Bed, Seton phoned not coming, sick.

Another comment for this day was, "Oh for an office life. Icebox, humidifier on blink, furnace, electric blanket ng [no go]." Her wish for a place to write away from her home was never resolved into the creation of an office life, but Anya did keep close to this work schedule, which fit her other ideal of being a proper 1950s housewife.[25] From this time on, weekday mornings—after fixing Chan's breakfast—were her most productive time. Bedtime, except for parties, was early, and the early evening drinks were essential to allow her to relax while cooking dinner.

During the next two months, before Anya was able to get away to England, she concentrated on the research that she could do to use her trip productively. On February 20, there was "So much to know. God. Took two days off to copy pertinent bits in the Register and read more. And am struggling with the tournament. Froissart and Ivanhoe to guide, but it's all so thin."[26] A month later, there were questions: "Trying for first time to sweat out story in resume form, not outline, more detailed, but sketch just the same to see what I need. So much keeps appearing. Was the wedding night with Hugh in Walton? Where the hell WAS the great North Rd. and Ermine Street in 1366," she asked, followed by the frustrated curse, "Damn being a woman."[27]

Ten days later, she was on her way to find answers, as well as some freedom from being just a woman, as she boarded a flight for London.

Anya, who was terrified of flying, took this flight by herself on March 30, 1952, which was, she noted, Zizi's eighteenth birthday. She did not record the details of her trip in her journal until two days after her June 10 return. Her excursion had started badly. As she noted, "Was sick on flight, continued even in England to suffer for two weeks with teeth first one side then the other, sinus. . . . Relief finally came" when she "at last found divine dentist and doctor." For the first part of her travels, she was accompanied by one of her oldest friends, Isabel Garland Lord. The two had known one another well growing up and had recently become friends again when Isabel moved to New York after her divorce from her second husband. She often stayed with Anya at Sea Rune when Chan was out of town, which was a mixed blessing since Anya reported that "Isabel drinks too much," without adding whether she did as well.[28]

Isabel was the daughter of one of Ernest Thompson Seton's closest friends, writer Hamlin Garland. As children only a year apart in age, she and Anya were often together, sharing similar experiences of living in the shadow of famous, overbearing fathers. Isabel, like Anya, was a writer, although not a very successful one. In the 1960s she wrote a memoir about life with her domineering patriarch father, entitled *A Summer to Be*. It was not published until 2010, many years after Isabel's death. Her niece Victoria Doyle-Jones, who wrote the foreword, described Hamlin Garland as a "high-achieving narcissistic alpha male of his era," which would fit Ernest Thompson Seton as well.[29] *A Summer to Be* provides a glimpse of the kind of book that Anya might have written about her father, a project that evidently she never contemplated.

By 1952, Isabel had experienced even more chaos in her life than Anya. She had made it through two marriages, the second one to Mindret Lord, a writer who started out, like Anya, by writing pulp fiction. Mindret became increasingly involved in film writing after their 1937 marriage, which made Isabel very unhappy. She was invested in their dual writing career, which involved cowriting short stories under the name "Garland Lord." Anya and Chan had visited the Lords in California during their happier years, and Isabel came back into Anya's life after her rocky marriage to Mindret failed in 1947. The two friends became frequent travel partners. Isabel never remarried and was shattered by Mindret's suicide in 1955.

On their first journey together in the spring of 1952, the two friends had some "rocky moments," as Anya reported, "but we got through them," enjoying many good times. They had gone separate ways for some of the time, with Anya recording "10 necessary days alone" during which she lived in libraries and church archives. As always, the country of her father's birth enchanted her, evoking such rhapsodic descriptions as "England and the golden dream—in Kent the mists, the golden light, the mossy walls and wallflowers I petted, the new born lambs, the first cuckoo, I heard on the Wye—with my hand on a bank of violets and primroses. . . . the river and swans."[30] The sense of place that was a hallmark of *Katherine* reflected Anya's lifelong love of the English countryside, which she had first described in the journal that she kept during her first residence in 1923, as a nineteen-year-old bride living in Oxford with Hamilton.

In 1952, it was second husband Chan who appeared to join his wife in England in early May. They traveled to Holland, following John of Gaunt's trail as the duke, with his older brother, the "Black Prince," led several inconclusive skirmishes with the French during the Hundred Year's War. Anya and Chan spent most of their time fighting as well but reconciled before he flew home ahead of her. Anya had another brief time alone in the country she adored and chose the ship *Queen Mary* for her return, this time avoiding any shipboard romances. A few weeks after her return, she and Chan put in the required presence at Seton's wedding to Oberlin classmate Susanne Hunt on June 22, 1952, spoiling the festivities at least for themselves by constant squabbling.

By August Anya was back hard at work, both on her "sick marriage" and "Kathy." The novel in progress evidently was the easier task, as she wrote, "I must protect myself from further turmoil or I can't work, and I have been, hard, spurred a little by Pam's return today to type Chapters." Here she also put down a foundational statement of what she saw as the vision for her brand of historical fiction:

> Kath is fearfully slow. There is so much to be told, to bring out. I can't seem to skip things—just finished Bolingbroke episode and tackling birth of Blanche. The story hasn't started and I'm on p. 182. Also I know I lack tension—conflict, no matter I must plod on as it comes—and then tighten, but at this rate when can I finish. February looks absolutely impossible. I'm writing at least plausible history, I

couldn't blithely say as so many of the Hist. novelists do, 'I've taken some liberties etc. The white tower wasn't actually built in 1070 but it suited my purpose to put it in.' If it wasn't built and you're telling the lives of real people—you can't use it.[31]

Katherine and the novel that followed, *The Winthrop Woman*, adhere to this principle with a force that distinguishes them from most other historical novels. Some readers have criticized the history in these works as too heavy, but for most, Anya's great respect for what might be called the knowability of the worlds she was bringing to light is their greatest asset.

On August 29, Anya recorded a visit to Isabel Lord in her new penthouse in New York and to Chan's office at Scudder, but told herself, "Go to work Anya, you're stalling." That directive allowed her to finish part one of the novel and to "tackle 1369," but there were still intrusions that made her add, "Hell and Blast."[32] One important distraction involved trying to find a buyer for ten acres of Little Peequo so that Grace could afford to stay there, even though her home of over thirty years was showing signs of "cruel attrition." Comments about Chan in the same journal entry continued to show only resentment. He made "continual jabs" at her work, she said, for instance telling friends during one dinner party that "Anya is dumb about anything but the 14th century."[33] "He spits out his venom and leaves me with it," she added on September 15, an entry in which she also voiced her concern about their joint finances, worried that "Katherine may not sell at all."[34]

Since the early Depression years when she and Chan were first married, Anya had worried about money. The Inlet and Moon Rocks were expensive real estate ventures that, Anya bemoaned, although not honestly, Chan wanted more than she. From his earnings, Chan gave her "800 a month for expenses," presumably the household ones. But it was her "bonanza," the huge Hollywood payment for *The Turquoise*, even though never filmed, that paid the big expenses. She listed among these, stressing that they came out of her pocket, the monthly mortgage on Sea Rune, as well as provision for all Zizi's expenses, including her tuition at Wellesley, her clothes, allowance, and the car payments on her beloved Chevy.[35]

Chan was a capable financial advisor who presumably understood the family's monetary situation well enough, but Anya characteristically did not completely trust him. The Chases always managed to meet their financial obligations and had never been in debt once Anya started earning money through her writing. Still she was in many respects an inveterate penny-pincher. Her miserliness might have reflected her father's worries during the early 1920s, when he was not bringing in his usual income and begrudged all of Grace's extravagant travels, or the Setons' and Chases' struggles during the Depression years. Anya often would not buy new clothes, angering Chan by wearing older, frumpy dresses because she hoped to lose weight before spending money on anything new. Still, like Grace, Anya never considered doing without a full-time maid and a gardener and, after 1948, always booked her stays at the best Manhattan hotels.

Anya's fretting over expenditures never lessened, no matter what shape her finances were in. Her income taxes always infuriated her. For 1952 she calculated that she and Chan had been making a "vast sum" in income, "averaging $45,000 a year between us," but the taxes and expenses meant that they still had "so little to live on.[36] No matter what her monetary worries, Anya kept close to "Kathy," in part because she hoped that the novel's success would solve money problems. She reported on September 17, 1952, that Paul Brooks "called from Boston—wants to see whatever I HAVE done—First eight chapters. He'll pick MS up in NY. I'm pleased after first panic—and fortunately new typing lady [Marian McClelland] seems good albeit no historical knowledge or much humor. Spent day going over those 70,000 words of part one and readying."[37] Finishing was financially important not only to her but to Houghton Mifflin, so they hurried her along. Anya was moved to tears when Paul and Dorothy responded to her part one draft with unqualified praise, especially for her use of historical sources, allowing the "reconstruction of the period (alive, colorful, wonderful)." Prophetically Paul wrote that "this is your big book. Don't be scared of it."[38]

By the time Anya received Paul's encouragement, she had moved ahead, able to tell herself that "I do think the Plague chapter 10 is pretty good." Her depiction of the tragic death of Duchess Blanche, John of Gaunt's wife, she also said, was "Not too bad."[39] The month of October demonstrated how she could work feverishly when she gave herself the time, and especially when Chan stayed out of the picture. As she wrote on October 2, 1952, "Feverish hit or miss scurries back and forth in source books, piece here, piece there, forced into looking up each reference in the Registers—and in consequence my Latin is improving too."[40] Her source books were extensive, complex, and even contradictory, leaving her sometimes no recourse but to guess or to invent.

The two fourteenth-century contemporary sources essential to Anya's reconstruction were John of Gaunt's *Registers* and Jean Froissart's *Chronicles*. The *Chronicles* were the French writer's minutely detailed history of the chivalric worlds of France and England during the Hundred Years' War. Thus he had much to say about Edward III and his sons, and what he wrote of John of Gaunt, the Duke of Lancaster, was particularly positive. Froissart also covered the Peasant's Revolt and many of the royal scandals of the period. Even more important for Anya were the many volumes of John of Gaunt's *Registers*, available to her in the editions published by Armitage Smith beginning in 1911. These provided an immense record of most of the duke's fourteenth-century life, documenting all his expenses, including payment to his retinue, gifts made to courtiers and family, costs of building and renovating his many castles, and much more.

The *Registers'* minutely detailed records were one of Anya's most important guides for the chronology of her characters, providing an especially clear way to trace the duke's relationship to Katherine through his many gifts to her. They revealed his appointments of her and her children to his service as well as all the financial arrangements related to both her children by Hugh Swynford and the four that were the offspring of her consorting with the duke. The *Registers'* wealth of information is what made Anya write in her own record, "Constantly slowed by slavish adherence to facts. This thing so SLOW. Only one half page yesterday. This thing as I've always said Just a little bit too hard for me. And too damn much source material."[41]

For much of October 1952 Chan was in Colorado, trying to help his father, Charles Chase, who had to deal with the closing of the Silverton mine that he had skillfully managed for over thirty years. At Sea Rune, Anya noted Chan's absence on October 11, 1952, by writing, "so heavenly without the tension," as she struggled with the powerful first sexual scene between John and young Katherine. The two had been brought together in their grief for his lost wife, Duchess Blanche, during the great plague. In Anya's scene, they move slowly toward the inexorable fulfillment of their long suppressed passion, to use Anya's language. She herself said that she was "floundering through love scene at Savoy, saddened at so much written and so much left to do. And is it dull?"[42] Generations of future readers would answer that this love scene was anything but dull.

LEFT: Anya Seton's mother, Grace Gallatin Thompson Seton, in 1921. Note indicates the photo was signed to Hanna Engstrom, her longtime personal maid. RIGHT: Anya Seton's father, Ernest Thompson Seton, around 1920.

Wyndygoul, estate house built by Ernest Thompson Seton, largely completed around 1904 in Cos Cob, CT. It was the first of three Seton homes he designed and built in Greenwich Township.

ABOVE LEFT: Ann Seton and Grace
Thompson Seton sitting in a window at
Wyndygoul, around 1908–1909.
ABOVE RIGHT: Ann Seton outdoors
with Ernest Thompson Seton at
Wyndygoul around 1911.
LEFT: Ann Seton in "Indian dress"
dancing at Woodcraft League
Ceremony, around 1918.

ABOVE: Ann Seton, portraits signed for fiancé Ham Cottier, 1922. RIGHT: Ann Seton and husband Hamilton Cottier at their wedding reception, held at Seton home DeWinton, in Greenwich, CT, 1923.

Hamilton Mercer (Chan)
Chase, second husband of
Anya Seton, around 1960.
*Courtesy of Clemency Chase
Coggins*

Anya Seton's children Pamela
Seton Forcey, Seton Cottier,
and Clemency (Zizi) Chase
Coggins, around 1937.

Ernest Thompson Seton and second wife
Julia Moss Buttree Seton, 1945–46.
Julie Seton

Anya Seton and Grace Gallatin Thompson Seton, around 1955, while vacationing
in Florida.

Pen and ink sketch of Sea Rune, showing the home after renovations were completed around 1957. *Courtesy of Forcey-Toussaint Private Collection*

Anya Seton and Hamilton Chase, with Grace Gallatin Seton, children, and grandchildren in their living room at a Thanksgiving gathering, 1958.

Wednesday. October 24ᵗʰ 1951.   Sea - Rune.

#6.   Suddenly on Friday started to work again
           thank god. Research - the yearly chronology -
many   tracing Sog - more grasp. Frustrated because
things lost maps - English - somehow lost in move. Why do
& later found. I so love maps and dates and actual history?
shoes,   Fitting my story to what did happen and what
Can. licence, might have happened, a bastard form I'm afraid
These maps like the little Beauforts, but they did get legit-
but many   imated in the end! - Great thrill Sunday -
still lost final discovery of logical convent Kath. could
sort of an have been at, a Benedictine priory on Isle of
epidemic   Sheppey - fits all my requirements, including
of losses. nearby Ed. III - Sog Castle of Queenborough. A tiny
           advance like that makes me happy - good pure
           unambivalent pleasure. There is no g.p.u. pleasure
           like intellectual interest, except perhaps appreciation
           of nature - scenery? or making things - the golden
           bath. - But I must get to England
           which frightens me. Isabel wants me to go
           with her in April, ditto Chan. Some of me would
           like to be alone, and a big part of me wants
           to take Zizi - and in any case I don't know
           exactly what we use for money.
Chan.   He continues to be fine I think constantly
           rejoicing and fondling Sea - Rune, and I continue
           to be remote, miles away and critical. In this
           bed where we thought we'd be "close" why
           aren't we? What is the cold sort of impersonal

colder - quieter in all ways than L. P. - my I feel here & didn't barrier? Baffles and discourages me, there were about 36 hours last week when it was better, stimulants of course affect but not really deeply. I feel no impulse to go back to Tiebout - I maybe so blind but it seems to me all my neurosis - is this and only this and always has been, and I don't see that he helped it much. And that too - weekly trek now, would play hell with the quiet rhythm I must have to work. Bad enough trekking over to see mother - poor lamb.

Froth -
Yesterday I did one of those ladies gatherings - ego pamperers - Darien Community House - Book Club lecture - except they let me sit down - about 75 females in a semi-circle gazing at me waiting to be amused, curious, waiting to be told the "secret" - how can I do it too, and to this I'm sympathetic. I chattered and answered questions on my 5 novels for 1½ hours and remember none of it. I'm spontaneous, jolley, ingratiating, and quite honestly minimize - they say such nice things, queer to hear a Mrs. Hopkins reading excerpts from Toni - fire in a hushed voice. My characters so real - all had re-read my books - each had favorite "Heagle" - "Turquoise". Mrs. geiswer the chairman "My Theodosia" - "Foxy Too" and I came "Dragonwyck" but not so many for which I was grateful. Anya in red beret, gold jewelry, orchid they pinned on me, minks, - plush horse - whipped together in 20 minutes at home

Anya Seton's October 24, 1951, journal entry, continued.

By the end of the month Anya had placed Katherine on a ship bound for Bordeaux, where she had been called to nurse ailing husband Sir Hugh Swynford. A knight attached to the duke's service, Hugh had been wounded in one of his lordship's battles across the channel in France. "Can't imagine what happens next, and don't feel like finding out," Anya recorded on Halloween. Still she forged ahead, reporting by November 17 that "somehow I've murdered Hugh—and the 6 chapters they haven't read go to Boston today for discussion next weekend."[43] In having Katherine's husband murdered by the duke's body servant, Anya was taking some liberties, although there were no recorded facts in any of the contemporary histories to explain exactly how Hugh died. Whatever actually happened, now would come "the bedding (at last)," of "Kath and Jog," which Anya confessed she was "way off mood" for writing.[44] Perhaps her mood had something to do with Chan, who was home from Colorado, preoccupied and uncommunicative, although neither of them were drinking at this moment. By Thanksgiving Anya had a comforting visit with her editors in Boston, on a "heavenly day" when she received "such PRAISE for Katherine," but had only one wish: "All I want is to WORK in Peace."[45]

In January of the new year 1953, Anya was in the mood to work, but without much peace, at least with Chan. She had completed her narrative of Katherine and her duke's long bedded interlude in peaceful Aquitaine, while his army waited for him to return to his war. By January 15, she managed to get her heroine away from the duke and home to her children at Kettlethorpe Hall, which, as Sir Hugh Swynford's widow, she now owned. Anya made this progress even while contributing to "neurotic shenanigans" with Chan, in part caused, she admitted, by "my own aggrievement, disappointment, self-pity, and irrational hostility."[46] At least some of her hostility was understandable. She was under great pressure, completely engrossed in the most demanding project she had ever undertaken. But as she had written back on January 7, 1953, she would "work if Chan will let me."[47] The "if" and the "letting" were key words. At least in her mind, Chan made demands on her time because he was jealous of her passion for her work. She was certainly not the young, sexy girl he had married, whose passion, in the early years, was always sexually driven, and all for him.

February brought no relief in the conflict between the writer and her husband. "Work Work Work," she wrote, desperate for a schedule that would be "uninterrupted by Chan or any emotions." What she needed most was "my own routine—work rhythm," as she wrote on February 13. The ideal day that she described in this entry would be to start around 6:30 AM with source reading, then going "to typewriter about nine, depending on how much household matters first," and writing nonstop if possible until "about one." After lunch and napping, she was "back to work 3:30 and recently good productive afternoon time to about 6:30." After this came the stop "for three drinks while fixing dinner." With Chan home, they would "dine at eight," and she would head for bed "about 9:30 after last cigarette" and be asleep "by 10:15." Although she was usually a friendly and relaxed neighbor, now Anya even took to "chasing trespassing kids" off her property, because they "disturb my work."[48]

Approaching the crisis-filled years of John and Katherine's lives in the 1370s and 1380s, Anya had plenty of documentation for the period's political upheavals but complete gaps in terms of her characters' motivations and emotions. These years constituted the most tumultuous period of the great Duke of Lancaster's life, a time when he became the most powerful but also most hated man in his kingdom. For him, Katherine was often an afterthought during this time, even though she had borne her lord two children. When he finally returned to England after no conclusive victories over the French, John brought back a new wife, Catherine of Castile, whom he married only in hopes of someday becoming the king of Spain. Katherine knew that this marriage was inevitable, and Anya is at her best in dramatizing the hidden mistress's bitterness and fatalism. Katherine belongs to the duke, who is now the declared, although not acknowledged, king of Castile. The desires of a mistress carried no weight. John himself is returning to his country with the stigma of military failure. Now he must try to protect his failing father, King Edward III, who is threatened by a rising tide of rebellion because of his many excesses. John's loyalty to the throne only makes him even more disliked than his unpopular marriage and disastrous wars, especially when he dismisses "the Good Parliament" that had demanded reforms.

In *Katherine*, Anya sought to deepen the psychological motivation for John's unusually cruel and politically unwise vengeance against the reformers. The rationale she came up with had no supporting documentation, but she was determined to add what she saw as a plausible Freudian twist. Anya relates John of Gaunt's cruelty to a rumor surfacing, during the time of the reform, that this great duke, Edward III's third son, was his mother Queen Phillipa's bastard. The falsehood, in Anya's version, was something John had heard before but always repressed. Now the tale sends him into a black fury. Katherine, in Anya's fictional casting of this episode, is asked by John's sister-in-law to try to lead him back from his breakdown. Katherine gently draws out his fear and shame, managing to banish his despair more through therapy than love. In her journal, Anya explained, "Finishing analysis of Jog at Kensington. Will it wash? Doesn't come off? I don't know. Pretty psychiatric but I had to do it.[49] Some of *Katherine*'s critics have questioned her twentieth-century psychoanalysis of a fourteenth-century prince's imagined psychosis. Here, however, as with Katherine's pilgrimage to Julian of Norwich later, Anya felt free to go where intuition led, when interpretation could be sanctioned by missing evidence.

What lay ahead for Anya's narrative were monumental challenges. "STILL all the Revolt and Pilgrimage ahead. God," she cried, as she considered that the most violent and emotionally draining episodes were still to be written.[50] By now she had changed her mind several times about the title as well. The novel would not be called "The Enchantress," her early choice, but instead "Goddess of Fame," the name of yet another Chaucer poem. This title, she thought, was appropriately both "elegant" and "cynical," perhaps "pretty grandiose but more dignity than Enchantress."[51] Throughout April and May she kept on "sweating," listing each milestone as she moved "doggedly" along. By May 5, 1953, she had done the Peasant Revolt in two chapters, afraid it wasn't "any good" because "my brain's a mush." The killing of Wat Tyler, the peasants' leader in their catastrophic pillaging of London, was accomplished by May 11.[52] Yet at this point, Anya's editors weighed in, treating her in ways that were both irritating and disheartening.

On May 11, 1953, Anya complained that Paul Brooks was not reading carefully enough and that Dorothy Hillyer thought there was "too much history" in the recently completed chapters. Before Anya could act on her disappointment, however, her editors provided a solution that would be a blessing to their jittery author for the rest of her career. As Anya reported on May 20, they came up with a huge boon in the person of "Mrs. Anne Barrett," a recent editorial assistant hire, to help Anya complete the rest of her manuscript. After meeting with "Mrs. Barrett" for lunch, Anya described her as "6 ft" tall and "around 60ish" in age, "with nervous mannerisms but I like her and thankfully left ms for her fresh intelligent reading. Can work with her and she'll come down June 4."[53] Anne Barrett was often going to be HM's ace in the hole, not only for Anya Seton but for other writers to come, including J. R. R. Tolkien and Pat Conroy.

With the aid of Barrett's masterful skills, Anya was able to keep "struggling on and on," and by June 19 she was "frantically trying to create these last hard chapters (I'm almost through Lady Julian. God, mawkish perhaps, so damnably hard, flabby)."[54] Anya was hardly mawkish in this instance, and in fact was at her best in handling the circumstances that led Katherine to the anchorite Julian of Norwich, well-known historically in the fourteenth century for the eloquent writings she produced about the spiritual vision she received during a critical illness.

On July 10, Anya wrote the last entry in her 1951–1953 journal book, recording that "Kath is on the penultimate chapter." Still, she had promised a finished manuscript by August 15. On Tuesday, July 28, 1953, the day after the Korean truce was signed, Anya was able to say that she had beat her deadline. To mark the occasion, she provided one of her usual, self-critical assessments of what she thought right then of her accomplishment. There were three weeks left for her to try to improve her "yellow sheet draft" of *Katherine*'s last three chapters, but, as she declared, "the skeleton is complete."

> One year of actual writing and three months in England. Three years research and chasing and Notes. Since June 30th entry 1950 at Inlet *"No. 6? Delving into Chaucer's time. Would love to write it, maybe."* I've written something about Chaucer's time all right and I wonder if anyone will want to read it. I think at the moment it's disappointing, thin and undramatic. I've stuck to historical fact at every point which means I had to pull punches. And the damn writing is undistinguished. If I could take another year to polish, I wonder if I could improve it much. There's no suspense, how can there be when the genealogical table shows Katherine gets her duke in the end. I should love to have it received as an honest not over-romanticized new view of an important bit of English history plus the helpful spiritual lessons of Lady Julian. They cannot honestly say it's lewd, cheap, or bosom-y. But they aren't honest.[55]

Of course, there was much more to come—cutting and more cutting, a serial offer that contradicted her doubts, publication to great fanfare, and the reviews, some not only honest but admiring, and some not. "Enchantress," "Fair Katherine," "Goddess of Fame," and finally *Katherine*, midway in her career this sixth novel gave Anya Seton her permanent place in the pantheon of American literature. In July 1953, she nonetheless was not satisfied, nor would she ever be.

10 | HERSTORIES

THE NOVEL THAT ANYA wanted to call "The Enchantress" or "Goddess of Fame," but never *Katherine*, proved her wrong in almost all her predictions. First, on October 9, 1953, came the call from *Ladies' Home Journal* "begging" to serialize the book. For Anya, this meant "agony of mind in decision, and bleak astonishment, shared by everyone." Learning the news, she listed every reason why she had assumed that the book could not ever receive such an invitation: "14th Century, too long, Catholic, foreign background, unwed mother having bastards, everything against it." *LHJ*'s offer meant that publication of the novel as book would have to be postponed, but Anya, always anxious about money, "couldn't turn down $27,000 sure and to top it all Woman's Journal in England wants it too, 1000 guineas." The "saddened" folks at HM "gave in," she said, "even though I've already got galleys, and was happily correcting."[1]

As it happened, everyone connected with *Katherine*'s future could afford to be patient. Anya's November 5 entry noted that the Literary Guild had asked to have *Katherine* for their 1954 list. John Beecroft, the guild's blunt editor in chief, told Anya, as she noted, "You've really done it this time. I never thought you could. I hate medieval England, all that jousting and stuff, but you've done it awfully well." Soon came news that 20th Century Fox would buy the novel's film rights for $100,000 dollars. Like *The Turquoise*, *Katherine* was never made into a film, but the price tag just for rights, Anya figured, were going to give her $25,000 a year for ten years.[2] A year ahead of publication, Anya wrote of her Kathy, "She has everything that can happen to a book."[3] With these assurances, HM had almost a year to build up her hopes as well as their own for good sales a year down the line.

With so much good news, and her family relatively settled, Anya made a "Wild Plan" to take off on an almost six months' trip to Europe. She was particularly glad to leave behind her "empty feeling" about having no new "urge" for another big book.[4] She had written on September 14, 1953, that one of her main rivals in the historical novel genre, "Tom" Costain, had exclaimed when he heard Katherine was finished, "Do you mean that you haven't a dozen projects calling you?" Anya responded, to herself, that "four years with no other work pursuit but 14th century England" entitled her brain to a rest.[5] She departed by ship on December 10 and did not return until June 7, 1954. For some of the winter abroad, Anya had Zizi with her in Italy, since her youngest was able to take a break from a year's stay in Paris with a Wellesley study abroad program. Isabel Lord also accompanied her for a time, and Chan came over in May for tours of Ireland and Scotland.

Three days after her return home on June 7, Anya was already fretting about how Katherine would be received on its publication date in October. "How to protect myself against injustice in Katherine reception?" she asked. Based on the serial version, Hedda Hopper, the flamboyant Hollywood gossip columnist, had reported that Anya's heroine was a "temptress redhead," and the book "pure romance adventure." Her comments, to Anya, devalued the book as serious literature, and she fumed, "Just not true. If people will READ Katherine, impartially forgetting the extraordinary price tag around her poor neck, willing if possible to admit that a book of popular appeal may also have merit even though written by a woman."[6]

As so often before, Anya felt that critics responded unfairly to her work because of her gender, but this time, she was also incensed that they seemed to see Katherine only as a "lurid, sexy book. . . . My own HM, to my fury," she wrote, had "posted a notice in Publishers Weekly" that the novel was "gaudy, uninhibited," and all about "cruel times, magnificent love story between King and Commoner."[7] On July 8, 1954, Anya reported that she had protested personally, on a trip to Boston where she made her feelings known concerning HM publicists' "incredible, cheap and lurid" plan for advertising Katherine. She must have blown in like a hurricane, since she was able to conclude, "Think I squashed all this crap and directed Kath's presentation towards more dignity."[8]

Anya spent the rest of her summer "chasing my tail," as she put it.[9] Grace, completely incapacitated, needed almost daily nursing visits, even though she had other full-time help. Then in early September, the Chases weathered two actual hurricanes, Edna and Carol, which also brought the inundation of friends who showed up to see the storm shows. Finally, on September 27, 1954, Anya began preparing in earnest for the four-day New York extravaganza that would celebrate "Kathy's" coming out. A new concern, one she had never voiced before in her journals, involved how to handle her drinking. She wrote down her choices. "Either I drink and smoke too much without worrying about it and pay the penalty or—." The alternative would be to "ration" the cigarettes, but she doubted that "I can hold liquor to less than three" before the big evening parties. "I can try for greater moderation," she admitted, "but have scant hope of caring."[10] Increasingly, Anya was becoming more fatalistic about her liquor consumption. Her old faith in her willpower changed into an insistence on her need to drink to "get through" a day, an evening, or any anxiety-causing event.

By October 3, Anya could report making it through all ordeals, one way or another. On September 28, 1954, at the Houghton Mifflin dinner at "21," she enjoyed "perhaps the most terrific night of my life." The list of the attendees was a roll call of the people who had been her most important supporters, many who had been with her for her entire career. At her side to celebrate her achievement were Paul Brooks, Lovell Thompson, Hardwick Moseley, Karl Anderson, Thomas Costain, John Beecroft, Louis Auchincloss, Edith Haggard, Helen Everitt, Hal Smith, and Esther Forbes, among others. There were "liquor, orchids, Cornish rock hen, and adulation," and no descriptions of hangovers or other "penalties."[11]

As for the long-dreaded reviews, most were admiring or even "wildly enthusiastic," but Anya of course "chewed over" the negative ones. The *New York Times* review, always one of the earliest to appear, lived down to Anya's expectations when it appeared on October 1, 1954. This time, however, she was particularly insulted by the *Times'* choice of a reviewer. It was written by "a Nardi Campion, of whom *no one* has ever heard," she underlined. This "unknown young lady," Anya wrote, had clearly "pre-judged" the novel, only "skimmed it here and there," in order to come up with "grossly unfair nonsense. . . . None of this would matter," she finished, "if it weren't 'The Times' and the rank injustice of some little pipsqueak being given so much power."[12]

The pipsqueak turned out to be the wife of Thomas Baird Campion, who had become the director of operations of the *Times* in 1948, and that connection probably explained her power. Although she was not well-known at the time, her status would change very shortly. Her first book came out a year after *Katherine*. Titled *Bringing Up the Brass*, it was coauthored with her brother and told a lively story of their growing up as army brats. It soon reappeared in the form of a hit movie, *The Long Gray Line*, directed by John Ford and starring Tyrone Power and Maureen O'Hara. Nardi Campion went on to write eight other bestselling books and was a nationally syndicated columnist up until her death, at age ninety, in 2007. One of her own later reviewers was her close friend and fellow Wellesley alumna, Hillary Clinton.

The early example of her reviewing skills in her critique of *Katherine* does display a degree of harshness not shared by other reviews of the book, even negative ones. As Anya summarized, Campion "puts 'historical' in quotes, she says 'no characterization,' 'nothing but sex.'" This "nobody" even attacked John of Gaunt as a "caricature."[13] Because of Campion's take, Anya expected more bad press from the *New Yorker*. It too was "mostly nasty, of course," she reported on October 24, but could be dismissed as only "silly." The claim that *Katherine* "did not deal with human beings" was, Anya commented, "for the birds."[14]

These two brickbats by the New York literati were more than balanced by praise. There was "divine" notice from the usually derogatory *Saturday Review*, and even *Time* magazine "wasn't bad," Anya reported on October 3. To more than make up for the *Times*, there appeared on the same day as Campion's review a front page spread in its rival, the *New York Tribune*, which also provided a "dream review." The next day, October 2, the *Tribune* even published a second notice, "to offset the ridiculous Times," Anya thought. This one, she quoted: "The gifted Miss Seton," it read, provided "a pageant remarkably combining splendor, honesty, enjoyment, and learning." The only "slap" in the commentary was the humorous one that the author had too often employed the expression "God's nails."[15] This point, she admitted, was deserved.

All in all, Anya had successfully come through the book launching storm, and she did have something new to do. A year earlier, on September 23, 1953, she had received a letter from Alice Pigeon, a Doubleday editor and colleague of Lee Barker. Anya announced that "she asks me to do a 'young adult' historical novel about Eleanor of Aquitaine for their new series."[16] The series was

Cavalcade, which Doubleday had recently designed to offer young readers educational but also entertaining fiction about historical heroes and events. It proved to be a very successful series but was as yet an untested one. Anya did not want to write about Eleanor in any case. She had been thinking of writing a biography, especially if she could choose a personage who would allow her to use the fourteenth-century research she had accumulated. When Alice Pigeon came to visit her a week later, however, Anya found that "suddenly while talking to her," she had an idea involving a much earlier period in Britain's history.[17]

The hero Anya picked was Boadicea, the Celtic warrior queen who around 60 AD rallied a powerful coalition of Celtic tribes to drive out the Roman legions that had acted as brutal conquerors for the past two decades. Anya's research on Chaucer had led her to one of Chaucer's sources, the Roman historian Tacitus, who wrote of the famous queen in a work that became available in France and England around 1360. If Chaucer read Tacitus, then Anya felt she had to read some Tacitus too, whether or not his writings would become a useful source for her. With her Cavalcade project, he now brought her another woman's history, from a fascinating, mythical time about which little was known. Houghton Mifflin reluctantly loaned her to their rival firm, and Anya looked forward to the treat of working with old friend Lee Barker. Writing a book of only sixty thousand words, with a guaranteed payment of $6,000, would mean, she calculated, that she would make ten cents a word, easy money with no worries about reviews or sales. "I want to do it," she said.[18]

She did not want to do it right away, however. Anya left the Cavalcade project behind along with other obligations during her six-month escape to Europe, although she did look up some Celtic history while in England. Not until the summer of 1954 did she begin to make a tentative start on her book, now called *The Mistletoe and Sword*. She loved this beginning stage, "the peculiar process of writing a first draft which is almost as new and startling as *reading* a new book."[19] As soon as the public fanfare over *Katherine* ended, she went back to her work to introduce a historically based woman who was the opposite of the dutiful third Duchess of Lancaster.

Not long before Anya picked "the Warrior Queen" of early Britain for Cavalcade and very shortly after she finished her final draft of *Katherine*, Anya made one of her most revelatory statements about her personal relation to her creative work. "I suppose I write myself over and over again in the heroines" of her books, she mused.[20] She was bound to have had Katherine in mind, but she seemed also to be looking backward to her earlier novels and might have been looking ahead as well. The myself that she was considering in her comment appears in the two heroines whose lives she would soon be shaping, Boadicea and Bess of *The Winthrop Woman*. Between 1950 and 1955, when she was struggling with more tensions as both woman and writer, Anya created three women living in distinctly different circumstances and cultures. Yet their stories were all her stories through what she called her "empathy and elan" with them.[21] As she had written some years earlier, "The details of living change fast, but people change slowly and emotions not at all. It seems to me that a story set in any period may have validity and meaning for the present."[22]

In writing herself, first came Katherine's story, a long saga of the passionate, steadfast, often tormented mistress and finally wife of John of Gaunt, one of England's most powerful leaders.[23] Katherine transgresses against one of her society's most rigid, but also most often broken, social and religious taboos when she yields to her passion for John of Gaunt. In her other private relations, however, she epitomizes the ideal of the good mother to six children and the dutiful helpmeet of her dominating lord and lover. Her pride, as Anya shows, is never completely sacrificed during the years of their adulterous affair, when she becomes increasingly dependent upon the duke's largesse because of the children they have together. At one point, "Katrine," as the duke calls her, "looked at him in gratitude, yet lifting her chin proudly, for she would not be a dog fawning after a bone for all the watching meinie to see."[24]

Katherine is also capable of unshakable determination and great courage, becoming as she matures a wise steward of her properties, a tenacious advocate for her children, and a shrewd bargainer with the men who underestimate her. Running her own manor alone, she takes on the cathedral prelates and the local businessmen to keep her assets secure. She begins to free her serfs, convincing her son Thomas Swynford that they now work "more efficiently" than they had under "the old servile system." As she turns down a marriage request from the richest landowner in Lincoln, she explains, in words echoing Anya's belief that she could not forget the past, "For me, it's not the past—it's still the present."[25] In the years after the duke's supposed public repudiation, she grows into a stoic but also resolute woman of great religious faith as well as sturdy self-reliance, epitomizing the character that Anya often longed, but could not manage, to be.

How else might Anya have written herself into Katherine? She too was an adulteress. Like Katherine, as a young wife stuck in a bad first marriage, she had at first resigned herself to motherhood and acceptance of a man who fulfilled none of her desires. Even during the increasingly hard times with second husband Chan, she often in her journals, although seldom in behavior, expressed guilt for her hostility toward him. In most ways, she tried to arrange her life to meet the housewifely expectations of her husband and her class. The love affair of Katherine and her duke is also reflected in Anya's issues with male dominance. Both Hamilton and Chan disappointed her in that department, perhaps because she inevitably compared their masculinity to that of her overbearing, manful father. Chan resembled Ernest only in his black rages, she came to feel, especially as he aged.

In some respects John of Gaunt is a physical copy of Ernest Thompson Seton in his role as the Chief, the imposing, attractive leader of intrepid bearing and supreme self-confidence. However, for Anya, the duke is mostly an ideal that neither her father nor her husbands adequately modeled. Katherine's lord and master, for all his faults, is the tall, handsome, powerful, decisive protector who remains emotionally committed to the woman he adores. He embodied an ideal that women readers of Anya's own time found enticing. *Katherine* could not have been more different in almost every respect from Ayn Rand's blockbuster, the pro-capitalistic propaganda novel *Atlas Shrugged*, published three years later in 1957. Yet John of Gaunt could appeal to women readers of the fifties in the same manner that Rand's tall, rugged, imperious heroes did. The duke's vulnerability and moments of great tenderness with Katherine ultimately make him a very different masculine model, over the years a much more admirable character for female audiences.

Katherine as mother seems much closer to Anya's heart than Katherine as mistress or wife. This can be seen especially in the attention Anya gave to her heroine's despair over losing her beloved daughter, Blanchette. Zizi's mysterious illness brought Anya constant anxiety during the time she was working on this novel. The Katherine with whom she perhaps most identified was the one who is transformed after the shock and despair she experiences when Wat Tyler's mob attacks the duke's great Savoy Castle. Blanchette runs away during this scene, maddened after hearing John of Gaunt's pious confessor, just before his death, name her mother as a responsible party in Hugh Swynford's death. Grieving the loss of her daughter and overwhelmed with a guilt that now involves not only adultery but murder, Katherine responds by making a sacrificial pilgrimage of repentance and petition to the cathedral of Walsingham.

Anya fully captures the depths of Katherine's wretched disappointment when her petitions fail at Walsingham. As she dramatized Katherine's illuminating encounter with Lady Julian at Norwich, Anya feared that her depiction would be viewed as maudlin or emotional. Still, the sequence was too important in its relation to her own search for peace to be restrained. As she wrote, "I'm writing of God. Katherine to find something I haven't got myself. The great higher LOVE."[26] Whenever Anya felt called upon to defend *Katherine*, she highlighted the spiritual dimension of her heroine's interactions with Lady Julian. She had overused the notion of second sight in earlier novels, notably *The Turquoise*, and had learned from reviewers that such seers were reasonably viewed as awkward foreshadowing gimmicks. Fourteenth-century European Catholicism provided rituals, mystical visions, sanctions, and convictions that Anya built into the religious belief system of her characters. From the nuns who take her to London from their shabby convent to the friar who takes her to the anchoress Julian, Katherine's journeys are propelled by the theological determinants of her faith, and she accepts these precepts, even if she cannot follow them.

All her life Anya sought the comfort of spiritual faith, toying with everything from varieties of mysticism to Christian Science. She intermittently attended different churches, usually Episcopal or Anglican, and when she was in Manhattan, often went into St. Patrick's Cathedral to light a candle. Every year she marked the beginning of Lent by receiving ashes and noting what she was going to give up for the season. How she developed her idiosyncratic brand of Christian practice is hard to trace. Her parents had no interest in churchgoing although they allowed Ann to follow any doctrine she pleased. Ernest had reacted to his father's uncompromising Presbyterian creed by disowning him and designing his individualized "Gospel of the Red Man." Grace closely studied the Eastern religious systems prevailing in the countries she traveled and later became a dedicated disciple of Yogananda, one of the first Indian gurus to bring the practices of Yoga meditation to the United States.

Throughout her life, Anya enjoyed some of her mother's spiritual habits, which included seances and numerological calculations. In her last novel, *Green Darkness* (1972), she presented a sympathetic picture of her mother's spiritualism at a time when her own life was taking its bleakest turn. Her own seeking is reflected in the fact that almost every year, in her journals, she noted the coming of the season of Lent as a time that she turned to meditation. A journal entry written not long after she was so devastated by *The Turquoise*'s rejection provides a look at what her frequent turn to prayer, religious writings, and churchgoing meant. "Part of my fear and depression," she wrote, "is because there's always been the feeling—'well if things get too bad I can always pull myself out with the spiritual.' Now I have turned to the spiritual and I get scanty answer." The only answer she found at the time kept her seeking; "perhaps I didn't try right or enough," she concluded.[27]

Particularly when Anya faced conflict, disappointment, or crisis, she turned for inspiration and comfort to readings that were based on some form of spirit-mind-body connection. In 1957, as she described her library to Frank Taylor, who was writing a profile of her, she highlighted "the mystical shelves, from Vedanta to William James, to Zen and Evelyn Underhill, and C. S. Lewis." She added, "This is a strong interest for me and certainly comes through in my books."[28] It was during the 1950s that her own quests became more intense as inner peace became more elusive. During the post-*Katherine* period her professional success should have given her more confidence, but instead she kept falling back into old fears, accompanied by all the debilitating physical symptoms. As she said, however, for her "the antidote is always work,"[29] and the great Celtic rebellion against the Romans was there for her to pick up as *Katherine* made it to number two on the New York bestseller lists and then declined.

For *The Mistletoe and Sword*, Anya provided none of the introspective journal entries that accompanied her progress with *Katherine*. Tacitus's history gave her few details to factor into a full portrait of the warrior queen, and while she credited some subsequent authors who speculated on the facts, she also noted that "I have used my own interpretation."[30] Her focus was not primarily the queen, although she provided sufficiently startling descriptions of her. "Queen Boadicea was a majestic, full-bosomed woman, over forty but her hair, which cascaded down to her knees, was still the color of ripe wheat. Her face was broad, with high cheekbones; above them her eyes glinted a proud ice-blue." When the "puffy" Roman procurator has her mercilessly whipped, she remains "stone quiet, her face gray as ashes, her eyes sunken and terrible as those of a corpse."[31]

The novel's subsequent action is more concerned with the young Roman standard bearer Quintus, who falls in love with Boadicea's adopted daughter.

He is on his own mission but bears witness to the Romans' misdeeds and the destruction wrought by the revengeful Celts. Still, the fierce, brooding, enraged female leader of the Celtic forces appears often enough to be a haunting presence as she carries out her vow to slaughter every Roman in Britain. Boadicea is driven by the motive of just revenge, as the honorable Roman generals who must track her down admit. She became almost a mythical goddess to later Britons, including Prince Albert, who in 1856 commissioned a bronze statue of her that was installed near Big Ben in 1902. His intent might well have been to suggest an identification between the ancient warrior queen and his own Victoria.

Boadicea's story, for Anya, can also be seen as an identification, an instance, even though a minor one, of how she could write herself in one of her heroines. In this respect, as would soon occur in *The Winthrop Woman*, Anya embedded in them her growing frustrations with her life as a professional woman writer struggling in what she saw as a man's domain. The Romans who were trying to subdue the British tribes discount Boadicea primarily because of her gender. "We'll spank all the little dears and send them home to their pots and pans," one of Quintus's friends boasts.[32] In January 1951, Anya recorded some words on this matter spoken during a CBS radio interview following the publication of *Foxfire*: "You know, the business of being an author is much different for a woman than for a man. [A man] can just close the door and go to work, knowing the household will be taken care of. The woman has no one to protect her from interruption."[33]

On July 1, 1954, while Anya was working hard to finish *Mistletoe*, she again expressed in journal format her frustration with being unable to give all her energy to her work. "Why," she questioned, "is it so hard to keep a steady quiet work tempo for me? Things keep happening that must be done. Wouldn't if I were a man. People would insulate me. Well, I'm not. Is this penis envy?"[34] Boadicea, as Anya concluded her history, felt no need to envy the manhood of "insulated" Roman generals and died a hero's death on her own terms, on her chosen battlefield. One of the wise Roman generals refuses to allow her body to be desecrated, lest she become a martyr, a status that she still achieved in her country's history.

On September 20, 1954, a few days before *Katherine*'s successful debut, Anya wrote that she had "ploughed through to the last chapter" of *The Mistletoe and Sword*. Writing it had taken her only three and a half months, and the revisions, she predicted, would be "Duck Soup."[35] She followed the book's fortunes while watching *Katherine*'s place on the bestseller list and could happily report on January 9, 1955, that Doubleday editor Lee Barker's reaction to *Mistletoe* was "startled praise" that included a decision to "send it to England for serialization." The easy young adult book had turned into a profitable adventure for her writing career in more ways than just its commercial success. Anya was able to envision in Boadicea a heroine whose indomitable will could be further explored, even though Anya had "no creative urge" as she finished this book.[36]

On January 9, 1955, with a new year ahead, Anya wondered "when I'll get a new idea and if I can DO a straight biography."[37] What might have motivated her to try a straight, factual narrative of some historical figure? It is possible that after her foray into history with Boadicea as well as after the huge amount of research she had been able to gather for *Katherine*, she decided to try staying closer to a re-creation of history without adding the creative interpretation that seemed less appreciated. Only nine days later, she was ready to move on to another full-scale book project without deciding between biography and fiction for its genre. She wrote on January 18, 1955, rather unenthusiastically, that she was "delving a little without spark in the US Colonial period." By March 2, she followed up by acquiring "30 odd sourcebooks," including five volumes of the "Winthrop papers" at a cost of twenty dollars that were "on special." With "all the Winthropia" in her library, she could announce that "something stirs."[38]

The stirring came in the form of Elizabeth, born Elizabeth Fones, the daughter-in-law as well as niece of John Winthrop, who led his Puritan flock from England to New England on the ship *Arabella* in 1630. Whether or not Anya was going to tell the story as biographer or novelist, she could at least say, by March 2, 1955, that "yes I'm afraid I DO want Elizabeth." Two days later, she added Elizabeth's married name, Elizabeth Feake, to her journal, explaining, "I 'bought her' yesterday by written agreement with Lydia Holland. I paid $500 down and promised to pay another $500 if and when I used Lydia's research in published book—much too generous, as Lydia said."[39] This time, Anya was taking no chances that a historian, in this case her Greenwich friend Lydia Holland, could object, as Carl Carmer had back in the *Dragonwyck* days, to any facts that she might use in her own work. The exorbitant price was her insurance.

For a few more months, Anya kept toying with the idea to write biographically about the woman she began to call Bessie. On March 10, she seemed to be wavering. "Am I prepared for small sales and a quiet flop, and scant money the way I'm used to? I'm going to start out biography," she still asserted.[40] The question as well as the determination remained on April 1, when she queried once again, "Can I POSSIBLY do her as a biography? I want to." However, without explaining her last decision, by July 17, 1955, she had made her choice. On that date, she announced that she had begun her project with a fictionally rendered scene. It was set in John Winthrop's Groton manor, in Suffolk, England, where young Bess lives as her uncle's ward. The scene depicts the brutal whipping that Bess receives from her uncle as punishment for her incorrigible willfulness. The whipping scene, Anya said, "came to me in the strange way those things come, and oh the joy—straight unambivalent joy, of this stage and the startled feel, 'I'm doing it.'"[41] Straight biography could not provide the kind of joyful energy that Anya derived from crafting a full, dynamic picture of history as she was seeing it, with a fiction writer's mind.

Anya had done a bit of Biblical research, in the King James Version, to prepare her for the painful scene of Bess's public punishment. In her July 17, 1955, entry, she described how she found the harsh command of Ecclesiastes 30:1 and gave it the usual colloquial translation as "Spare the rod, spoil the child." That injunction, she inferred, "must be what influenced my puritans and helps with that first chapter I've just so pleasurably outlined."[42] She might also have been turning back to another book for inspiration, a scene in the novel she had recently published. Bess's whipping has a close parallel in *The Mistletoe and Sword*, when Boadicea receives her terrible flogging from the Roman conqueror.

Boadicea and Bess are publicly punished in order to assert the superiority of men who see themselves as the containers and administrators of all law. In *The Mistletoe and Sword*, these men are the primary villains, as Anya promotes the practices of the ancient Druids as morally superior to those of the corrupt Romans. She would soon do the same with the Sinoway and Pequot tribes when she moved on to colonial New England in *The Winthrop Woman*. In both novels her sympathy is all for those who struggle against an oppressive, materialistic "advanced," conquering culture. It was patriarchal proscriptions, she felt, that also limited her ability to work, and to have her work fairly recognized, in the 1950s.

Anya produced in Boadicea and in Bess Winthrop two women characters who experienced the dismissive, demeaning attitudes of male governors. Katherine had been much more fatalistic about her circumstances, as a wife and mistress living in a world overseen by Catholicism and the divine right of kings. At least, through Anya's telling, Katherine's heroic steadfastness results in her becoming the foremother of one of Europe's greatest ruling dynasties. In the conclusion to *The Mistletoe and Sword*, Anya looks far ahead to a new kind of civilization that would, through the marriage of Roman Quintus and Druid Regan, allow the daughter's more matriarchally ordered society to mediate the supposed advancements offered by the Romans. "From such as you," the Arch Druid foretells, "will come the new race in Britain."[43]

Like Ernest Thompson Seton, daughter Anya questioned whether her own culture was an improvement on more primitive ones. She does not completely provide an answer in *Mistletoe*. She was, after all, writing to educate young adults, whose parents would expect the glories of Roman civilization unequivocally to win the day. Anya did, however, insist on at least a mitigation of the "Civilizers'" influence when she ended the novel with the unrealistically harmonious meeting and mutual admiration of Arch Druid Con Lear and the chastened Roman general Petillius.

Anya's questioning became more ardent in *The Winthrop Woman*. Boadicea is replaced in the next novel by a Sinoway chief's proud daughter, Telaka. Telaka receives a similarly brutal torturing, but as a central character in *The Winthrop Woman* she engineers a much happier fate than the Druid queen. Branded as a witch, Telaka bears what she must but never capitulates, and she actually gets the last word in the novel. She is only one of those whom John Winthrop singles out for attack, and one of the few who overcomes her suffering. Winthrop's inflexible wielding of what he interprets as his biblically ordained authority victimizes not only other sects and the "savages" of the New World but also the women of his own faith and family. His kinswoman Bess Winthrop finds herself terrorized and abused by the strict devotion to Puritan ideals demanded by its ministers. Anya included in her narrative the crusade and tragedy of Bess's friend Anne Hutchinson to stress the fate that the Puritan lawgivers inflicted on women who dared to challenge their authority in a supposedly new world.

On a bright spring day in 1952, when she was immersed in her research on *Katherine*, Anya had interrupted her train of thought to burst out, "Damn being a woman." The last sentence of this entry indicates that she was not really thinking of her novel. The sentence is a command to herself, "But get to work—make bed, dishes,—Kathy."[44] The novels that Anya published in 1954, 1955, and 1958 proved that she could get back to her writing work, and get beyond cursing her gender, to imagine women taking on some of the most difficult battles she faced, not only with others but with herself.

11 | DICHOTOMIES

ANYA BEGAN WORKING on *The Winthrop Woman* in the spring of 1955 and finished it in the summer of 1957. To sustain her confidence during this time, she could point to the great success of *Katherine*, which rose to second on both of the New York papers' bestseller lists and stayed there for seven months. On August 26, 1954, with *Katherine* finished but not yet reviewed, and *The Winthrop Woman* not yet imagined, she had written, while thinking of her writing process, "I don't want to sound smug—or tempt fate—even to me—but perhaps there IS a secret—for popular success—or even masterpieces. The fertile fancy, imagination, empathy, elan, dramatic timing rush vs. the meticulous (yes) proofreading, detailed, plodding, carefulness side. The pendulum swings from one mechanism—dichotomy (fond of that word!)."[1] Her fondness for this idea of paired opposites, of a pendulum swinging her energies and focus between disparate poles, was understandable. She had for years defined her world as divided between a writing life and a real life involved in a continual tug of war. Turning fifty-one on January 23, 1955, Anya could see other dichotomies approaching, many involving stark changes connected to the real life that so often challenged her writing time.

In the months before she took up Bess Winthrop's story, Anya as usual took more time for her extroversions, as she called her social activities, but also for more reading, of both novels and books on philosophy, religion, and psychology. She used the latter to seek answers for both her physical malaise, as she now called it, and to bolster the spiritual and mental conditions that she always tied to her various ailments. In August 1954, finished with both

Katherine and *Mistletoe*, she became particularly interested in the writings of Alan Watts, who in 1938 had moved from England to America in order to study Zen. Not long after his arrival, he took the path of being ordained as an Episcopal priest and began a prolific writing career. Anya admired Watts for the strain in his studies that echoed her other favorites—Rollo May, William James, C. S. Lewis, and her own first psychotherapist, Helen Flanders Dunbar. Like them, Watts was focused on what he called "bridging" the oppositions between mind, body, and spirit. During the months between publishing *Katherine* and starting on *The Winthrop Woman*, Anya closely studied Watts's *Myth and Ritual in Christianity*, which he published in 1953. She started a correspondence with him and later met with him, finding the real man less inspiring than his theories.

One of Watts's pronouncements in *Myth and Ritual* particularly caught Anya's attention because it spoke directly to how she understood her personal relation to her fiction. "The Past is the creation, the empty echo of the Now," were the words that she quoted and underlined in her journal.[2] Although the past was hardly "empty" for her, it was she who filled it through her self-directed research, and she was becoming more conscious than ever of the confluence between her lived experience and the worlds of her created characters. As she said later, "Factual as I've been the interpretations are me."[3] Elizabeth Winthrop became a kind of composite of other Seton heroines but also an expression of Anya's ideal sense of herself. Her two previous biographical heroines, Theodosia and Katherine, were, like Bess Winthrop, forced into unhappy marriages that served as a prelude to romantic fulfillment with other men. Yet in *The Winthrop Woman*, Anya intricately combined struggles against patriarchal domination with Bess's more successful efforts to find worthy love and autonomy. As Anya began to study Bess's rebellious life in Puritan New England, the Winthrop woman in several respects echoed the never quite realized "Now" that her creator desired.

Elizabeth Fones Winthrop Feake Hallett's three husbands gave Anya several streams through which she could examine her marital relationships. Bess's first two marriages incorporated past experiences that Anya was being reminded of more directly at this time. In the summer of 1955, she brought from Little Peequo her diaries from the 1920s, and in her current journal she began perusing them, examining in particular the first months of her relationship with Chan. Remembering those passionate times, she noted the tension between now and then, which measured "the usual tragedy of aging—so much of me is still that girl, still unchanged."[4] When Bess makes her rash decision to marry her cousin Henry Winthrop, she is a naive girl looking for escape and completely absorbed in the sexual ecstasy her new lover and future husband affords.

After Henry's death on the Puritan fleet's journey from England to New England, Bess loses any chance to choose a compatible mate for herself. John Winthrop doesn't take long to get his embarrassing daughter-in-law and niece, and now widow, married off again. So Bess is given in marriage to the gentle, effeminate Robert Feake, who is at least kind and represents security within the confines of Puritan judgment. Bess becomes patient and compassionate but also resigned and frustrated as she tries against her own instincts to please a husband terribly conflicted about the marital act. Her thoughts are similar to those of Mrs. Ann Cottier, living as a faculty wife and mother in Princeton, who sighed as she wrote in her journal that she supposed she and Ham were as happy as most married couples she knew.

Anya knew all too well the clash between romantic expectation and sexual disappointment and dramatized the oppositions in her biographical characters when she felt free to embellish the traits of their husbands and lovers. Both Bess and Katherine, as well as Anya's first biographical heroine, Theodosia, are forced into marriages that allow them to develop only in the traditional role of mothers, caring maternally not only for their children but also their unsatisfying husbands. Ann Cottier's husband and husband-to-be were as different, especially in terms of sexual intimacy, as Joseph Alston and Meriwether Lewis, Hugh Swynford and John of Gaunt, or Robert Feake and Will Hallett.

In Anya's new novel, Bess becomes the woman character who breaks free in ways that neither Theodosia nor Katherine could have contemplated, given the restrictions of their times, places, and stations. Bess finds her courage out of necessity when husband Robert Feake is incapacitated by his mental breakdown. Still she has few qualms when faced with the decision to leave Massachusetts, both to secure her family's future as well as to give herself a new start. Additionally, there are new spaces to head toward in the seemingly vast frontiers of America. Settled in the Greenwich area of Connecticut, as the first woman to hold property in the British colonies, Bess Winthrop Feake can find in Will Hallett the equal partner she desires and deserves. Although they will not be able to marry for many years, she discovers in him a man with whom she is willing to brave scandal and persecution.

In the first months of tentatively sketching out her Winthrop woman's biography, Anya was focused mostly on a situation that also gave her some similarities to Bess—her penchant for homebuilding. The tidy fortune that *Katherine* had brought in the previous year allowed a second project to start almost simultaneously with the research stage of Anya's new writing project. On April 1, 1955, she recorded, down to the penny, the "appalling amounts" of money that she and Chan had made during the previous year, a total of $107, 677.74. Of that amount, $35,261.55, "all income," came from "my writing," she stated pointedly. Her ability to earn such a substantial sum on her own might have influenced a resolution that she made in June 1955: "stop clinging to Chan."[5]

While the Chases couldn't understand "where it all went," they launched that spring an ambitious expansion of Sea Rune. In barely four years, they had outgrown their custom designed home. Anya's April 1, 1955, entry recorded that "outside our bedroom door" there was a four-foot drop, an excavation begun with a bulldozer now sitting in the yard. The new wing would provide a master bedroom suite called the Snail because its windows curved to provide the best view of the sound.[6] More important for Anya, there was going to be a large study, big enough for her father's huge desk, which she had brought out from Little Peequo, and for a whole wall of bookshelves. About her father's desk, she recorded that "he wrote many of his books at it," and she celebrated that "now it's here, and mine, and I love it. A root to settle me here."[7]

The Chases had hardly been at Sea Rune a year when they realized that their new home, so long anticipated, would not fit either their family and social life or Anya's professional work. Between 1951 and 1955 there was a steady stream of overnight guests—many friends and, later, the two older children, Pam and Seton, with their spouses. Zizi came home frequently from Wellesley, bringing school friends for weekends and holidays. Isabel Garland Lord often stayed, especially when Chan was out of town. Chan's brother Charles, who had moved east with his second wife and three boys, often appeared. The appeal of a house with a small private beach, two or three boats to sail, and lawn space for croquet and badminton, made the house on the Moon Rocks a magnet, even for close neighbors, most of whom didn't have the view or the beach that Sea Rune afforded.

Their home's popularity increasingly became a source for arguments between its owners. Chan wanted parties there on evenings and weekends, even when Anya was hard at work, and they often disliked each other's invitees. The new wing was designed to solve many problems, and even frugal Anya had no qualms about spending money on it. On April 1, she noted "with what joy I've been working and buying books at Barnes and Noble like a mad thing." She would be able to call up her advance for "Bess" from Houghton Mifflin whenever she liked. "It's fun to get up in the morning again [to] twin excitements of wing-building and WORK," she wrote.[8] At that moment, the two activities were not in opposition, but if one had to be put on the back burner, it was going to be the book.

As summer began, the new study was not close to being ready for all the source books Anya had bought. When her internist, Dr. Carter, told her to "Get to your work" to cure her ongoing "megrims" and vertigo, she wrote, "But I can't, when the house needs so much and we are living from suitcases, plumbers, painters, carpenters, delay, and everything is pro tem."[9] Even with a new wing under construction, she and Chan were hosting a "summer country club life" for too many people. Anya found guests in her shower, "using my comb," and grumbled that "they might say 'May I.'" Her complaint list was extensive: "They drink our liquor, smoke my cigarettes, float on and ruin our life-cushions," leaving her feeling "a bit exploited. Nobody seems appreciative."[10] With the weather somewhat cooler, and in spite of intrusive guests, Anya turned a little of her attention towards Bess by August 15 when she wrote that "I have been getting deeper in, and more grasp." Her British publisher Ralph Hodder-Williams disappointed her by being "non-committal" about a Winthrop novel, but she vowed to persist, replying, "Well, maybe Bess a flop but I love doing her."[11] Part of her enthusiasm might have been related to what she was able to fill in about her young colonist, who became her strongest woman character. The "interpretations," as she said, "are me."[12]

During the summer, the extroverted Anya often left Bess to go to New York for plays or to socialize with an increasingly exclusive set of Greenwich friends. She was happiest when attending gatherings hosted by old friends such as the Seligmans, who had been close since the Chases' early married years at Little Peequo. After one of their always elegant affairs, she wrote with contentment, "They always make me feel a little larger than life, but apparently I DID look prettier than usual," she gloated on July 31, 1955. A descriptive self-portrait followed: "Hair very curly brought forward over the ears (!), fluffy bangs, old peacock cotton print, blue Chinese ear-rings, that momentary hush of approval from men, appraisal from women when I entered." Chan reported that one of the men at the party remarked, "Your wife is a very beautiful woman." In Anya's telling, he relayed the compliment "only grudgingly." He was "not proud of 'his property,'" she surmised, "not sure of it and afraid I might get conceited i.e. less submissive."[13] Her deep need to be admired for physical attractiveness and her distrust of her husband's attitudes were not getting better with age. Resentment that her spouse could think of her as his property was something Bess might have felt as well.

The arrival of autumn meant a partial dispersal of the summer crowds and the completion of the spacious Sea Rune additions. Still Anya had little urge to go to work, reporting on September 2, 1955, "Bess is not very close, the house is lovely, but I am operating creakingly—something holds back." Family could always be counted on to distract. Loyal Hanna, now approaching seventy, had broken her hip the winter before. Both she and Grace were severely incapacitated, and it was finally time for Hanna to have a different living arrangement. Anya looked sadly on the "long bondage broken" between Grace and the woman who had come to Wyndygoul as an eighteen-year-old girl to look after little Ann.[14] That the very loyal Hanna had never left, for marriage or a less dependent situation, meant that she was as much a Seton as any member of the family.

When Ann had begun boarding at Spence School around age ten, her "second mother" took on a new and long career as Grace's shadow, her cook, her servant, and her fellow traveler, though never called companion. Anya found Hanna a subsidized New York apartment and arranged for payment of a monthly pension as well as nursing assistance when needed, but these boons did not placate the family's dependent, who was very resentful. As Anya wrote, Hanna had "no affection left for Mama and vice versa," a dismal end to a more than forty-year relationship.[15] Much happier was the announcement of the engagement of Zizi and Cecil Coggins, who, in another one of those uncanny coincidences, used the nickname Pete, as did Pam's husband, Pete Forcey, whose name was Charles. Names were an endless source of upset in Anya's family. Pete Coggins was finishing his studies at Harvard Medical School and would soon start his residency. Anya also took some time, as summer waned, to do some shopping. Her purchases included a mink stole, priced at $1,100. The mink, she felt, was "the badge of success." More than that, she added, "I earned it myself though felt guilty."[16] Back and forth her moods went, from self-assertion to fear of judgment.

When Chan took a business trip to Europe, Anya went to Boston for three weeks, planning to do research on the city's early Puritan roots and to spend time with Zizi. There were a few grand days but also periods of "anxiety and guilt—panic," and struggles with vertigo that were relieved only by doses of Seconal. It was Anya's barbiturate sedative of choice now, always accompanied by a swig of vodka, which she began keeping in her purse in an aspirin bottle. Zizi was distant, trying, it seemed, to keep her mother away from her fiancé, which left Anya to write that "it seems to me I have no one in the world to lean on."[17] She had a terrific attack of vertigo in Boston, so bad that she had to ask a stranger for help finding her way back to her hotel. Her response was, at last, to go into psychotherapy in Greenwich, and again with Harry Tiebout, whose patient she had been briefly in the late 1940s.

"I don't know what else to do," she said, on October 25, 1955, when she made her appointment with Tiebout.[18] It was a date that began a dependence on doctors and drugs that lasted the rest of her life. Harry Tiebout had long been connected with Blythewood Sanitarium, where Ann Chase had worked briefly in the early 1930s. He had retired from Blythewood in 1950, mainly to concentrate on his professional interest in treating alcoholism through some of the Alcoholics Anonymous principles that he had embraced through his association with Bill Wilson and his AA "Bible." Tiebout was particularly interested in the prospect of helping alcoholics to heal through complete repudiation (which he called surrender) of their dependence on a narcissistic craving to return to a tyrannical infantile state. Tiebout did not press Anya about her drinking, but he began working on what he said bluntly was her "immature control of her emotions."[19] He also started her on Thorazine, very new to the drug market and now considered the first antipsychotic medicine. It was geared primarily toward the treatment of severe mental illnesses such as schizophrenia, but was also thought, even without clinical trials, to help with acute anxiety, long a discernible trigger for Anya's incapacitating vertigo.

On the same day, November 4, 1955, that Anya mentioned her new drug, she wrote that a few days earlier, on Halloween, she "somehow reeling and staggering, started the creative draft" of what she called "W.W."[20] During the next months, she saw Tiebout at least once a week. She was taking "50 grams a day" of Thorazine by November 14, along with one Seconal in the morning and afternoon, "and then liquor." This was a combination "which helps," she thought.[21] Moving toward the hectic Christmas season, she was able to get

Grace and a new assistant off to Palm Beach. December 12 brought only a quick description of her work, as she complained, "I'm just not 'in' to it at all, three quarters of first chapter and dull work. Hope to God after Christmas."[22] What bothered her most was that she had gained eight pounds in two months, something that could very well have been caused by the Thorazine. Her own explanation was that liquor was "doing worst of it," the one drawback of her favorite medication.[23]

New year 1956 did promise a chance to work on "WW," but only after Anya dealt with "a house to be tidied and tax mess to be gone over."[24] Over the next months, with "many interruptions," she made "very slow" progress. The sessions with Tiebout continued with some success to treat her vertigo, and there were fewer rows with Chan although he was often depressed, telling her at one point, "I hate my life." By February 23 she could report, "Finished yellow draft of 2nd chapter *hier* [French for "yesterday"], it's thoroughly 'Seton,' my style bores me, but I can't help it. Work is joy anyhow."[25] By April she had completed chapter three and still found that "the creative moments are blessed," but she was taking three Miltown sedatives a day, and asked herself, "If a simple chemical can cut all that syndrome, and let me feel normal, what IS psychoanalysis all about?"[26] Being able to write productively while continuing both the therapy and the chemicals seemed to work. Soon, however, events from the real world curtailed the work and increased the drug dependence. On May 11, Grace had a "cerebral spasm" while Anya and Chan were vacationing at a resort called the Chattahoochee Ranch in the North Carolina mountains. Anya rushed home from Asheville to tend to her mother, worried not only about how to care for Grace but also about her Miltowns. She was "afraid of dependence," she wrote, as she was "taking 3 or 4 a day."[27]

Summer brought Zizi's June 23, 1956, wedding, which Anya reported two days later as an extravagant affair. "And so our beloved Zizi is married. St. Paul's 4 pm. Reception at Riverside Yacht Club. 250 people." She had to include, for herself, that "I looked 'beautiful,' everyone said so. Our own baby has a good husband. . . . WW," she added, "feels a million miles away."[28] Summers had seldom been a good time for Anya to write, and this year the season was just as difficult. By July Anya was vowing, "MUST get to work again, it's nearly 3 months. The wedding is OVER."[29] Unfortunately, other problems loomed. Her internist, Gray Carter, became worried that the Miltowns could cause damage, so told her to cut back. Chan was going through his own agonies, saying one night, after drinks, that "it can't go on like this," by which he seemed to mean his business worries but a comment that could also refer to their marriage, which had now been going up and down for more than eight years.[30]

Late July brought an international drama that played out close to home. Like millions of others on both sides of the Atlantic, Anya and Chan were transfixed by the sinking of the celebrated Italian ocean liner, the SS *Andrea Doria*, on July 25, 1956. Its collision with a Swedish passenger liner, the *Stockholm*, three hundred miles east of New York City, resulted in over fifty deaths and a monumental rescue effort to save close to a thousand other passengers and crew. The dramatic news, enhanced by the availability of television, brought some odd publicity for Anya, who learned through the extensive coverage that many of the *Andrea Doria* passengers had been watching the film version of her novel, *Foxfire*, when the disaster occurred. It was not the kind of publicity she wanted.

Just before the *Andrea Doria* captured the public's mesmerized attention, Anya and Chan began to see hints of a disaster much closer to home, again coming from their younger daughter. Less than a month earlier she had been a happy bride. Making her new home in a small apartment in Boston, with husband Pete often away for days at a time as a resident at Chelsea Naval Hospital, Zizi was now "overwrought and depressed,"[31] Anya reported. Within a few weeks she was much worse, and Chan went to Boston to check on her.

Alone at Sea Rune, Anya described August 2, 1956, a day spent in anticipation of news about Zizi's condition. She "awoke after miltown and nembutal night," the latter a drug added because worry over Zizi made getting to sleep harder than usual. She made calls to daughter Pam, to Grace at Little Peequo, and to her editor Anne Barrett in Boston, talking with all of them about ways to help Zizi. Then she went into Greenwich to get her hair done and do her marketing, rather amazingly with "no trouble driving, but still sedated." Back home, she read some of a novel written by her friend Nora Lofts, ate lunch, napped, and then scanned the afternoon mail, which included a "disappointing" letter from Alan Watts.[32]

By 3:30 PM, Anya continued in her saga, she was able to do some writing. "I pulled myself together," she wrote, "and tackled hard part of 4th Chapter, WW, showing Mass. Bay Co. men in action, preliminary to migration. This meant much consultation with source books." "Hard work" continued until 6:15 PM, the time that she almost always began drinking her ritual highballs.

When Chan arrived home, they both continued drinking, consuming "five highballs in two and a half hours." At bedtime she again took "one miltown and three-quarters of a nembutol, though the latter is rare." So a day that began with sedation that she had needed to get through the previous night ended the same way. It was also a day in which Anya swung back and forth between worrying, handling several chores, reading source books, writing, and drinking.[33] It was not an atypical day for this woman of great stamina, determination, and neediness.

Throughout the fall, Anya's days were dominated by Zizi's illness, which had progressed to a hospital stay, but she was also able to work intermittently on "WW." Although a longed-for trip to England seemed impossible in August, Zizi stabilized enough for Anya and Chan to fly to London on September 6. Only six days later, however, the news came that their daughter was in a coma in a Boston hospital, being tube fed. Anya did not report this news until October 25, 1956, since she and Chan had rushed back home immediately and stayed in Boston to help Pete Coggins tend to Zizi for the next five weeks. None of the specialists provided an adequate diagnosis. This was at a time when medical treatment of such severely damaging physiological symptoms, inexplicable through the kinds of tests available, was clearly inadequate.

When Zizi was able to return to the Coggins's Boston apartment, with nursing care for a while at home, Anya returned to her novel. On November 7, 1956, she vowed, "I *can and shall work* on Bessie, have done one half of fifth chapter." Watching her mother's self-pitying decline, in part due to hip surgeries that left her badly crippled, Anya had another reason to try to busy herself with work, now itself a distraction from worry. "I don't want to be like that," she wrote of Grace's situation, "and God forbid I should ever be dependent on my children." It was a plea that carried the weight of a dreaded inevitability.

The world beyond Greenwich echoed the chaos in the family. Anya noted that with the Suez Canal crisis and Hungary being overrun by the Soviet Union, "the world looks a mess, but I don't think there'll be War."[34] Dependable Eisenhower had been reelected, with the help of Anya's vote, while at home circumstances slowly improved.

By Christmas all children were present for the familiar rituals, with Zizi almost back to her good-natured, energetic self. On New Year's Eve 1956, Anya concluded that "W.W." had been "in the long fallow period" that usually stalled her novels during the holidays.[35] A month into the new year, she found herself "groping, can't understand the inconsistent Puritans," but she was "sweating hard," complaining as she had with *Katherine* that "it's so damn long."[36] Her three children and their spouses arrived at Sea Rune to celebrate the Chase parents' twenty-seventh wedding anniversary on February 25, 1957, a gathering during which Anya could be "proud of my six handsome children." Still, all the shifts in family dynamics caused her to feel that "nothing stays put," and the partying also made it "so hard to work but will try."[37] By March the big news was Zizi's pregnancy, not entirely happy news, since her parents wondered whether she had recovered enough from her traumatic illness. The news was also hard for Pam and her Pete to hear, since Pam had not been able to conceive and had recently undergone two operations for fibroid tumors, a problem that Anya had also had to treat through surgery years earlier.

Anya stayed close to her study and her work through the spring, and by June reported that "I'm pressing so, write, write, write," and that she had the "awful feel of being nowhere near end." Yet she had gotten Bess, her husband, her children, and her "Indian servant" Telaka as far as Greenwich, where they could live without the harassment of the authorities in Boston. In the territory that would become Greenwich, Telaka returns to her tribe, the Sinoway, who are willing to sell land to the Feakes. Soon Anya reported that she had "killed off" one of the Feakes' co-settlers, the family's great friend and protector Daniel Patrick, who had been banished from the Massachusetts colony before they fled.[38] He had also been Bess's cosigner for land purchased from the Sinoway, although she was sole owner of "the Neck."

By this time, even though there was still a great deal of history to pour into her novel, Anya was far enough along to receive an offer from the *Ladies' Home Journal* to serialize a novel they had not seen. It was an offer she refused, wanting to "Try it without for once."[39] This was an unusually stubborn stance, but as she reasoned, she and Chan did not need the money, and too much of it would simply go to taxes. Anya worked steadily through the summer of 1957, a season when, between the heat and the summer socializing, she usually gave up trying to get much done. This summer, she was "too driven by my work" to "care about anything" else, even her "*entreintes*" with Chan, which were few and far between. Everything was "far away" except "this book," an "unwieldy mess" as she called it, "sometimes good, sometimes lousy."[40]

That summer Anya witnessed the "general patterns" of her family life irrevocably changing. Most disruptive was the planned sale of Little Peequo, the home of Anya's girlhood and also that of her own growing family over a period of thirty years. She had "no notion" of what housing or nursing-companion assistance to provide for Grace, whose permanent address had been Little Peequo from the time Ernest left in 1927. Grace's health continued to deteriorate, while Anya pushed on with "W.W," despairing of her August 1 deadline. The summer routines "go on and on," she reported, "too much liquor weekends, and always W.W. push, and my defensive (?), proud, grim obsession about including, recreating, interpreting the damn *facts*."[41]

In the same July 4 entry in which she bemoaned her obsession with facts, she wrote an answer for herself and also for Paul Brooks, who she said had asked her, "Who cares?" "But I care. I'm not a grade A creative writer. I'm a Grade A imaginative interpreter of fact. A funny bastard talent but mine own. Last night did Robert [Feake's] final departure for England, not very well. Had to figure from the evidence just how 'distracted in his wits' he was. Well, Avanti."

Anya was approaching the last two hectic years of Bess's life and knew this period had many improbable aspects, but as she said, "like Mt. Everest I have to do it because 'it's there.'" Anne Barrett came out to reassure her that the book was "marvelous," but Anya as usual discounted the praise.[42]

On this Fourth of July, Anya also recorded the opening salvo of a drama that would consume her professionally for two months, while she also tried to deal with getting Little Peequo sold and her mother's living situation clarified. It all began with a call from good friend John Marquand, whose wife Adelaide had been her friend since their teenaged years. Marquand had won the Pulitzer Prize in 1938 for his novel *The Late George Apley* and had others made into popular films. Now he happened to be one of the five judges who picked new novels that would have the distinction of being chosen for the Book of the Month Club. He wanted to have the first look at *The Winthrop Woman* as soon as Anya could get it to him. At Houghton Mifflin, Paul Brooks did not approve, since John Beecroft, the director of the Literary Guild, who was the sole decision maker for that club, had already called for the book. It would have been the third of her novels to be so honored, following *Katherine* and *The Hearth and Eagle*. Brooks was afraid to antagonize Beecroft, but Anya had always believed that B.O.M. Club's approval would give her the one thing she had so far lacked, the validation of her talent by prestigious fellow writers.

Anya had never experienced anything like the competition for an unfinished novel that *The Winthrop Woman* was receiving. The *Ladies' Home Journal* actually threatened her about serializing the novel, hinting that she might not get offers in the future if she didn't accept this one. She refused to back down, and her reasoning was sound. She did not want to delay publication, but more important, she quite shrewdly calculated that "this book's strength is its documentation, all of which would be cut, L.H.J. hurts book sales, and any dough would go to the U.S." With her traditional prepublication pessimism, she also speculated that while the demand was "flattering . . . probably nobody will want it when they've read it, except, and here I know I'm lucky, my two publishers" (Houghton Mifflin and in England, Hodder and Stoughton). For her, at least for the moment, "That's enough."[43]

Luckily, or perhaps tellingly, Anya's vertigo bothered her very little as she concentrated intensely on finishing her book. From July 6 to July 17, she "hid away" in a little motel called Stonehenge, near Norwalk, Connecticut, because "I cannot get sustained concentration for last chapters here [at Sea Rune], when too much going on. Phones, Mama, Terrace being reset, Driveway just 'gray topped,' Garage roof repaired, people, people." At Stonehenge, Anya reported working seven hours a day, spending four hours eating and drinking alone, and sleeping peacefully nine hours a night. "I simply loved it," she said.[44] Her hermit existence was an indication of what she might have accomplished if she had been able to go into hiding more often for the sake of her work.

Back home in her study at Sea Rune, Anya moved Bess and Will Hallett to New London, but as she charted their historical course, she had to ask, "Will I *ever* creditably finish this book!!!" Two weeks later, she had "only one and a half chapters to go." She was pleased that "I have just got Bess and Will married at last in New Amsterdam as I'm quite sure they were." There was still the wind up to handle, and her plan for the finale included "the spiritual I want to get in somehow without going mawkish."[45] On August 16, 1957, she wrote that two days earlier she had "creditably" finished this "long damn" book, at "the stroke of noon on Daddy's birthday." There was the usual "strange shivering exultant lost empty relief" and the immediate pessimistic predictions of Bess's reception. "I don't suppose that anyone will give the thing credit for what it is—a tour de force—VIVID (?) tightly plotted novel somehow evolved from a slavish meticulous following of fact."[46]

As she almost always felt compelled to do with a newly finished work, Anya assessed what she thought she had accomplished with "Winthrop Woman." Her critique was not unlike earlier ones she had penned when she had reached a novel's finish line:

> Only twenty people will care about all this. I suppose the reason I care so much to have the *research* recognized is that I have no illusions about my writing. It is swift, competent, pictorial, emotional, and I'm a storyteller. I'm not very original and have no subtleties of style. And like my parents before me I'm in danger of "sentimentality."

The mind trick behind her self-deprecation was, of course, a cushion. If she sold herself short, she might keep at bay the critics who would otherwise, she suspected, take on that task themselves.[47]

On August 15, Anya had received a phone call that momentarily gave her some uncharacteristic optimism. She reported all the details in her long August 16, 1957, entry, so it served as a kind of uplift from her self-critique. The call was from Clifton Fadiman, a popular radio and television commentator who had been chief editor for Simon and Schuster and editor of the *New Yorker* book review section. Most important, at this moment, he was another of the judges of the Book of the Month Club selection committee. Like John Marquand, he wanted a sneak peek at the book. Because there were five judges who would not make their decision until September, Anya was sure that John Beecroft would be able to "snatch it up" with HM's approval. But Fadiman told her "to let him read it as a friend, over weekend." She disingenuously "finally agreed, feeling naughty and sub-rosa, and decided not to bother Paul with this since he's terrified of Beecroft's resentment." Her rationalization was that Fadiman would "probably hate the thing," the "word" would get out, and she would be "in the soup." But the risk was worth it because, as she said, "I WANT B.M.C. this time, always have, naturally."[48] A week later, Paul Brooks too agreed to send a "photostated" copy to the judges. They would have to hope for the best.

Anya wrote, too, on August 16 of her dismay in hearing that Edmund Wilson had chosen his "Ambushing a Bestseller" diatribe on *The Turquoise* to include in his recently published Doubleday Anchor collection, *Eight Essays*. The Book of the Month Club judges' interest gave her a way to recover from this unexpected, returning blow, for as she said, "if my writing is really so awful, why should men like Fadiman, Marquand, Gilbert Highet, John Mason Brown, Basil Davenport, even CONSIDER me?"[49]

The final roller coaster ride, with all the agonizing critical dichotomies in play, now began in earnest. Clifton Fadiman provided heady praise, sending word that it was "a fine book. Subtle, strong characters, wonderful feel of period, English part a 'stroke of genius,' homosexual element beautifully handled, good *muscular!* [Anya's italics] style. The men all excellent."[50] By September 5, however, the news was bad. Paul had a "most unsatisfactory conversation" with one of the judges. The tally now was "two judges are for, 2 against and one on the fence."[51] The judges would meet to decide on Friday, September 13, not a good omen, and Anya prepared for the worst. She agonized over who might be the naysayers and fretted especially because she herself did not like the book's ending.

Telling herself "to face unpleasant facts," Anya predicted catastrophe. "I KNEW there was too much pre-build up. WW won't make money, CAN it be a total flop? No sales and the cruel critical reception too?" After tormenting herself through the last week, she received some slim hope, which she recorded on September 9. "All is not quite lost," she explained, because she had "a most helpful talk with Marquand who said WW was 'extraordinary reconstruction, perfectly marvelous job.' Would vote for it Friday the 13th at meeting and so would Gilbert Highet. John Mason Brown on fence." The fifth judge, Basil Davenport, evidently hated it, leaving the big question, "how would Fadiman vote?"[52] Anya took the risky step of calling him, and he was very brusque, so down she went again.

At last, on Saturday, September 14, Anya wrote that she had been "in a pretty continuous state of prayer" until finally, "Paul called at 6 pm" on the "bad luck" Friday evening. He simply said, rather cryptically, "Everything's dandy," then explained, "They took it. Feb. or March selections." For Anya, the floodgates opened. "I could not believe it," she wrote. "In a way the shock of joy was as upsetting as disappointment. My strongest reaction was a trembling. Tears of gratitude and thanksgiving. Humility and Awe." She permitted herself to gloat, and even to look a little higher. "Top for my profession (except maybe Pulitzer)! Never dared look higher but now picked by a jury of my peers and superiors; the sure money pleasant but the achievement is all I care for." Up she went, contemplating the next rung on the ladder, the Pulitzer. Then she stepped down, commenting, "With my usual dichotomy half of me sneers at childish superstitions."[53]

Now all Anya had left to do were the revisions, particularly to work on the ending that she had never thought was quite right. By September 23, 1957, she said she had "revised last 4 chapters last week. I know I improved them, and rewrote pages which in detachment embarrassed me by their amateurishness. Can't imagine how BMC *took* the thing, *nor* why nobody's apparently been revolted by the mystical outburst at the end."[54] She retained some of that mystical "oneness." It was inherent in the novel's last word, which she retained in her revision. "Monakewaygo" expressed a spiritual merging with the great universal Whole, a concept that Telaka had shared with Bess. When Anya wrote of finishing the first draft of her ending, back on August 16, she was feeling that exultant faith.

> Monakewago—I know mysticism is. I increasingly know the moments of joy, heightened perception—beauty that seems to come from nature mostly for me. I spent 2 delightful hours on "Elizabeth's Neck" last week, and I "heard" the haunting chant I've dared put in W.W. Mo-na-ke-way-y-y- go." And it goes on from the farewell of Hiawatha, I guess. "I am going—going—on a journey."

On her visit to the Neck, Anya had found the site of the pool, and the actual deeply overgrown site of what she felt sure was the Sinoway fishing camp. She had asked herself, "It was so lovely in the woods—and *did* Bess feel it?" Then the historian had weighed in. "Actually our only real lead," she pointed out, were the words in the old Greenwich records of "her particular purchase." Only one question remained on August 16, before the hullabaloo of the book club wars began. "Ah well, where do I go from here?" Anya asked that day. "What do I do next?"[55]

There were a variety of answers to that question. "I suppose I'll go into an extraverted swing now," Anya prophesied about a month later. "Look like hell, and must do *something* about it," was another challenge.[56] There was also another coming event to anticipate. "Zizi baby due," she wrote, on September 23, and then, "My study—I love it. I'm happiest in it though the big news [about the B.O.M.C. honor] came in the living room. Not all of life's surprises are unpleasant."[57] The triumphs of *The Winthrop Woman*'s reception would arrive before long, but first came the momentous occasion of the October 29 birth of Chase Frederick Coggins, who would turn Anya into the doting grandmother of "the most beautiful baby in the world."[58]

Just before her fifty-fourth birthday in January 1958, Anya went to Boston for that other birth, reporting, "I first saw my book, and the jacket is lovely." She had the signal honor on this occasion of being treated to a grand lunch by all of Houghton Mifflin's directors, "me and sixteen men," at the Union Club.[59] For a while, she could dispense with the usual dichotomy and bask in her good fortune, before her world became divided again.

12 | THE GLASS CRUTCH

WHEN ANYA FINISHED THE JOURNAL BOOK containing her entries from 1955 to 1958, she wrote on the last page, "These years, three and a half in this journal, have been toughest, most agitated of all. Dare I hope that the next journal will be more serene?" The second half of the 1950s had indeed been an emotional seesaw, even though financially the years provided a windfall from *Katherine* and *The Winthrop Woman*, Anya's two bestselling novels to date. The worst for both Anya and Chan had been Zizi's puzzling 1956 illness, necessitating prolonged hospital and home care. Her crisis point had brought them hurrying back from England after only six days into their planned excursion. The best for Anya was the news that came on Friday 13, 1957, when the Book of the Month Club judges decided to take *The Winthrop Woman*. Anya wrote as she summed up 1958 that their vote had been "the happiest event of my life, perhaps."[1] Right after hearing the news, she had been moved to vow, with all her superstitions intact, that "A very good girl I will try to be. Modesty, awe, and gentleness."[2]

A week later, however, Anya admitted to being "critical and unloving" to Chan, continuing the more frequent occurrence of rows that had much to do with making the years 1955 to 1958 tougher than any before.[3] Chan was staying on the wagon with some slips through these years, while Anya, especially at the parties that were now such a staple of their lives, drank more than ever, often mixing her drinks with various barbiturates. On December 6, 1957, she recorded going to a party at the home of new acquaintances on Binney Lane, Allan F. Kitchel Jr., and his locally known actress-socialite wife Hylah. Allan

Kitchel, always known as Tim, was the grandson of Edwin A. Binney, the man for whom Binney Lane was named when he built his beautiful mansion there in the 1890s. Usually Anya enjoyed these neighborhood gatherings with Old Greenwich's wealthiest residents, but this time she complained, "I felt neglected, unloved, heavy. Conscious of age."[4] The comment was an eerie foreshadowing of events that would reach a traumatic climax for both the Chases and the Kitchels ten years later.

Almost certainly Anya drank too much on the night of the Kitchel party. On January 27, 1958, after another evening of excess, she had written, "Vodka too much I guess. Alcoholism would certainly be horrid. In fact everything seems horrid today."[5] By the end of 1958, she was writing, "Cut out daytime vodka except two emergencies, *no* drink at Sunday lunch cocktails. The usual four whiskey drinks at night. I allow five hundred calories for the liquor as Gray [her longtime primary doctor] said."[6] In May 1959, she was still trapped in the "Modus vivendi I deplore," calling her dependence on her "vodka routine" a "Glass Crutch [which] has been going on at intervals a long time."[7] By the time this year was drawing to a close, Anya reported a consultation with another of her longtime physicians, Dr. Johnny Bolton. She shared with him "my shame at the quick ones" that she would swig sometimes before breakfast and always, now, "the daily lunch ones." His response, which she put in quotation marks to emphasize exactly what she heard, "Pooh. No alcoholic ever talks the way you do. I've never met one that would reveal his fears or his pattern, or admit he was in any danger or that he <u>might</u> lose control. And don't be afraid of seconal addiction either." Thus the destructive pattern was again validated, the glass crutch remaining the "only help," Bolton reportedly said, "for these 'psycho-motor storms.'"[8]

Professionally, Anya seemed to be at the top of her game as the 1950s moved toward their end. *The Winthrop Woman* debuted in early 1958 to many excellent reviews, but of course Anya fussed over each negative one, especially a "savage attack" in *Time* magazine's notice on February 15, 1958. Among other defects, the reviewer objected to all the "prithees and forsooths," which made Anya go back and count them. This "false" criticism was balanced when she made "the Cover Girl" for the influential weekly literary magazine *Saturday Review* the same weekend. *SR*, as it was known, also honored her with a "lovely review" by the esteemed scholar, editor, and literary critic Edmund Fuller. In Boston there were "interviews, radio broadcasts, Colonial Society party with all the Winthrop descendants," all the "adulation," as Anya liked to call it, that a major writer could ask for. Summing up the attention that bringing out a new book always involved, Anya concluded, "All this glitter and crashing and froth, what does it really matter. Withdraw to the calm center."[9] But family matters and alcohol were going to provide major obstacles to any withdrawal or calm.

The final separation from Little Peequo brought the new year's first upheaval, with the closing on January 2. Hanna had been moved to what to her was an unsatisfactory residential hotel in New York a few months earlier. Since the first of December, Grace had been safely stowed away at her winter retreat in Palm Beach, Florida. After months of struggles, Anya had finished getting the old house emptied of its treasures and junk. Grace, of course, had wanted to keep everything, and her help, the loyal maid and chauffeur "Bee and Bryan," who had lived on the property for over two decades, also had to be dealt with. The house was bought by Stewart Brown, a New York advertising agency executive, and his wife, Betty, for $370,500. Anya recorded that she "took Betty for a drink at the Pickwick Arms" after all the papers were signed and then went home to Sea Rune to cry.[10] Betty and Stewart raised their children at Little Peequo, and Betty continues to live there in 2019.

"A great many patterns have shifted," as Anya noted on her 1955 to 1958 journal book's final page. Closing up Little Peequo, she thought sadly about what the house had come to mean, personally and professionally, over the forty years of associations there. She had lived at "LP" as a teenager looking for a beau, often with Grace far away and her father busy with his writing and his secretary. Her two children with Hamilton Cottier had grown up there, as had Zizi, her child with Chan who had been conceived there, she noted. "My first words of *Theodosia*, my first book, were written there," she also recalled.[11] Now Anya had only four months to construct a cottage for Grace that when completed would become known as Lotilot, built on land that the Chases owned next to Sea Rune. Grace had insisted that her grandchildren call her Loti, loathing the idea of being old enough to be a grandmother. She also insisted that the new home named for her be built right next to Sea Rune, since she was being "forced" to abandon Little Peequo by her daughter, to say nothing of her health. As Anya was being feted and "pampered" through the month of February for her achievement with *The Winthrop Woman*, she was also dealing with the construction of Grace's cottage, which needed to be ready for her ailing mother by April.

Having Grace live a few steps away, even with full time help—as soon as that help could be found—was not a happy prospect. A much more pleasant task at Sea Rune was caring for first grandchild, Chase Coggins, "the Coglet," whenever Zizi would let her. She and Chan got along as grandparents much better than they did as husband and wife. Anya also had another writing commitment to replace "Bess," since in October 1957 she agreed to write a biography of Washington Irving. It was to be another Houghton Mifflin book, one of a group edited by Sterling North for the firm's North Star series, which was conceived to bring out biographies of American heroes for younger audiences. Anya did not start writing her biography for several months, but Irving, an early American literary luminary, was no stranger to her. She had researched his life in order to create his cameo appearance as Theodosia Burr's first suitor and later her sympathetic supporter in *My Theodosia*. Circling back to him almost twenty years later was an easy task.

By May 1, 1958, Grace was back from Palm Springs, but Lotilot was not yet prepared, so she and her new assistant Lily Dickmeyer were ensconced in the guest room at Sea Rune. Anya could hear them singing "Holy Holy Holy" while she tried to work on Washington Irving, so she gave up and joined in. The Cogginses were often there as well, so the house was also filling up with baby things, with Chase providing "a love that loosens the heart," Anya said.[12] Once moved to Lotilot, Grace complained and demanded changes, but for Anya, the unhappiness of her new tenant could be countered with the ego-boosting fate of *The Winthrop Woman*, which stayed number two on the *New York Times* bestseller list for several weeks. She also finally had reliable service from another "Polish pearl" named Janina, who would end up staying with her beyond the next ten years of almost continual crisis.[13] Anya also shared a second helper, Beth Raymond, with her mother, who when not tending to Grace provided Anya with chauffeuring and help with other tasks, including babysitting. Anya still drove herself to do her errands in town, never without taking a seconal with a swig of alcohol, the only combination, she felt, that somehow "steadied" her behind the wheel.

Anya now employed a housemaid, a gardener, and an assistant and could easily afford them. Calculating her finances on June 19, 1958, she wrote that "WW has made about $10,000 to date. Kath's $25,000 still running." To her it seemed all "fairy gold," and besides, as she sang in her usual refrain, "the US grabs all." She had by this date "batted out an outline" of her Irving biography to send to editor Sterling North while she continued to read *Winthrop Woman* reviews now coming from England. They, too, were mostly positive, but "I totally discount the 90% pleasant reviews," she admitted, fuming especially at one that said Bess Winthrop was a "Jayne [*sic*] Mansfield" heroine. The criticism affected her ability to get on with a new project. As she put it, "I wonder if other successful writers are as emotionally family involved as I. For sure my creative side is abeyant, and it is as hard as ever to have confidence in the face of contempt, injustice" of negative reviews. She took these very personally. There was something about her, she decided, that "infuriated" her antagonistic critics, "because I'm too successful partly I suppose, and these are always MEN."[14] There was some solace in this resolution, whether completely true or not.

In addition to her Irving biography, Anya was now thinking about genealogy, especially her father's unshakable belief that the Setons had descended from a legitimate peerage, the earls of Derwentwater, the first of whom was Sir Francis Radcliffe. The Radcliffes were ardent Catholics who found themselves on the wrong side of history when they supported the deposed Stuart king, James II. This James lived in exile in France with his son, who became known as James III or James the Pretender after protestant William of Orange was granted the British crown. With many others in the far north region of Northumberland county, the Radcliffes became Jacobites, who engaged in a long and fruitless quest to restore the Stuart line through James III. With no new novel idea perking, Anya decided on a trip to Northumberland, where the earls of Winton had lived at their manor, Dilston Hall. It was going to be, she said, a journey "to clear up Seton mystery once and for all."[15]

Ernest Thompson Seton had been born in the Northumberland village of South Shields, and an aunt who had remained there after his family immigrated to Canada urged him to reclaim the family's lost inheritance. The theory was that the Thompsons, including Ernest's father, were the legitimate descendants of the illustrious Radcliffes. In particular their line could be traced back to the second earl of Winton's two Jacobite sons, James and Charles Radcliffe, who had come into tragic conflict with the British royals during the first and second Jacobite rebellions, dated 1715 and 1745. Ernest's branch of the family had supposedly decided to avoid the sad fate of the Radcliffe brothers, both of whom were beheaded, by moving to London and hiding themselves, assuming the name Thompson. Thus the peerage was lost to them, an injustice that Ernest had always wanted to correct.

In late summer 1958, Anya's plan to trace the story back to its roots was threatened "by marines landing in Lebanon, war with Iraq," as she reported. At Sea Rune, she waited undeterred, writing "Northumbria calls me. I've spent the last days in it reading avidly, taking notes. Short of WAR, I'm determined to go. I must go, I yearn for it."[16] By the first week of September, her determination won out, and she was able to spend ten weeks abroad, some of it with Chan but some of it happily engaged on a solo genealogical mission in her "beloved England."

Back from her trip by November 1, 1958, she summarized what she had found. There was no evidence that the Setons were connected to any peerage, but that hardly mattered. While hunting ancestors, she had begun to think that something more creative was stirring "among the moors" of England's most isolated, rugged county. The idea had to be put away, since back at Sea Rune there was the inevitable "stress of homecoming."[17] Two crises had progressed to a critical stage during her absence. "Mother feebler," she reported, and also, "Pam, my darling child, worst of all, she and Pete breaking up." Still for a few days, Anya tried to delve into the possible next book during the few times she could be alone in the "serene quiet" of her "green study. . . . All I've got," she wrote, were the names "Northumberland, Derwentwater, and Virginia," and the date "1714." However, at least "something's fomenting somewhere." There was, she added, "my commitment" to Washington Irving to consider. "I think I can do him, but he's cold as a mackerel right now."[18]

No matter what was happening around her, Anya could in any case celebrate that "my own long slow rhythms are back thank God, no wish for lunch drink, happy with my books."[19] The heady feeling that a writing opportunity always engendered could keep her afloat as it always had. She also could look forward to a night of "Triumph" coming up on November 12, 1958. It was a banquet in her honor, where she was to receive the Society of Colonial Wars' top annual award, a bronze medal, for *The Winthrop Woman*'s "contributions to Colonial history." While she sat on the dais with "some twenty-five men," she noted that Chan was "at a table below," and that although he seemed very pleased, he exploded following a slow burn when they got back to Sea Rune. They had both been drinking at the banquet, and now he told her that he was "sick and tired of my problems," that she had "no consideration for him, only for others, no appreciation of how busy he is." Drinking, she saw, "seems to be a large part of the problems. His, of course, and partly by projection, mine."[20] As Anya saw it, any drinking was disastrous for Chan, while for her, drinking remained necessary medicine. While Anya continued to try to see herself honestly in the journals of this period, the dependence on her glass crutch, coupled with the consumption of each new drug her various doctors tried out, made her far less capable of clarity concerning her health and her medicating habits.

As Anya closed out the year, she turned more to her journal as her sole therapy, trying to "write out the anxieties" that were flooding her. Grace needed to be readied for her annual migration to Palm Beach, at a time when her health was especially precarious. She would be attended by loyal Lily and Beth, her steadfast companions following Hanna, with a four- or five-month stay planned. Their departure from Lotilot was going to provide Anya some relief from her mother's "Pity Me" lists, for as she said, "I [am] inwardly resentful" of those complaints, "thinking, I suppose, 'Pity ME.'" Watching her mother's deterioration, she became more anxious about her own condition. "There *is* more to withstand, there is increasing health worries. There is less careless courage to meet threats of insecurity, there seems to be more fear. Does there HAVE to be? Every brave and hopeful reaction helps as much as the frightened ones pull [me] down."[21] Anya's alternation between brave determination and fearful insecurity was becoming the defining struggle of her life. By November 26, 1958, saying good-bye to her mother, she was able to say that Grace was still trying to be "her best self" and "very brave," bolstered partly by a positive "message from 'on High,'" meaning words arriving from her current guru, who went by the exotic name Mustapha.[22]

With Lotilot empty, Anya was able to work, thrilled that she had sold a story, "The Lady and the Miner," to *American Weekly*, a Sunday supplement of the Hearst newspaper chain, for $1,000. Now she could turn to the idea that had stirred on the moors, starting the project of "reading Northumberland Table Books" while she also got back to Washington Irving, "on which I've done two and a half chapters."[23] "Good-Bye 1958," she wrote in a rare optimistic mood. "You have been a good year for us."[24]

The following year did not continue the trend. Chan, preoccupied with work, completely forgot the rituals always connected to her January 23 birthday, which was supposed to begin with kisses and a "spanking," along with a card and gifts. He had been "too busy," he fumed, leaving her to lash out in the way she always regretted. "You treat me like garbage," she told him.[25] At age fifty-five, with her blood pressure often as high as 190 over 100, she was now taking more pills than ever, swigging from the glass crutch more often, but also able to vow, "I must get to WORK. It is my salvation and I'm letting myself spread too thin."[26]

Three months into the new year, on March 11, Anya surprised herself as she recorded that Washington Irving "seems to be finished." Weighing in at nine chapters, Anya assessed it as "a workmanlike, pretty static job," saying that "most of it bores me." On second thought, she gave herself more credit. "I *have* given his whole life, quoted a lot from him direct, mentioned all his books in the proper places and yet kept to the word limit." She had, moreover, "developed fondness for the man, and startled discovery that he was never dull." Houghton Mifflin's editors for the North Star series were more effusive, accepting the book immediately, so now the familiar end-of-project tremors arrived. This time, her way of putting the question was shortly to prove tragically ironic. "Where do we go from here? I wish I knew," she queried. "No person has appeared, no theme. All I have is the usual pull to place. Northumbria? Virginia? And an idiotic veering between 1715 etc. and 1815 etc. Shall Read and Read now as usual. Hopping around until something hits."[27] A week later something did hit, one of worst traumas of her life, for on March 19, 1959, Grace Gallatin Seton died, peacefully but suddenly, in Palm Beach.

The death of eighty-seven-year-old Grace was not a surprise. In February, Anya had been called to Florida by the news that her mother had a blood clot and needed surgery. It turned out to be "a false alarm," so Anya could go back to Greenwich and complete the Irving biography.[28] Her trip turned out to have been a blessing, since a massive coronary occurred exactly a month later, and Grace was gone. By her hospital bedside on February 16, Anya had prayed, "Quick, soon and easy, dear Lord," and so it turned out to be. "No fears. No pain. No awareness," and thus no suffering, Anya and Pam found out when they flew down the night of March 19 to Palm Beach. The indomitable big game hunter and celebrity suffragette, the proud wife never overmatched in will or vision by her formidable husband, looked, when Anya saw her that night, "20 years younger," with her "secret little smile."[29]

Writing out of her grief on March 25,1959, she affirmed, "Now I know death and it's not the way you think. There is even something funny about all this. Pam said she looked in control as she would have loved it, but I think it was more 'mastery.'" So much of what Anya been able to learn about mastery, of both self and circumstances, had come from Grace. She continued,

> I know she's near me. Oh mama—what is that secret you know now. Can it be that all the things we thought and tried to believe in are *true?* "Yes, but not quite the way you think." Mama, I asked you long ago if you got there first to keep an eye on Zizi. I know you will. I don't know why you had so much fear and pain at times all your life. But whatever it was you've worked through it now. You must still help me to conquer the fear thoughts.[30]

Grace was taken back to Greenwich and buried next to her mother, Clemenzie Rhodes Gallatin Duffy, on a hill in historic Putnam Cemetery. A large marble cross was erected by August, bearing an engraved lotus flower, Grace's special symbol.

Grace's death provided Anya some peace of mind, only because she no longer needed to worry that her mother would face long years of increasing incapacitation. What Anya had not foreseen was the devastating emotional impact that losing her mother was going to have, which took a while to manifest itself. Grace had been the one human being whom she could count on from the time that Ernest had left them in the late twenties. Fiercely independent for the next twenty years, Grace had ruled the roost at crowded Little Peequo, but in some ways, her presence was what allowed Anya the freedom to begin her own writing career. Along with Hanna and her other servants, Grace provided care and attention for three grandchildren, and she covered many necessary expenses. Even when they were fighting, usually over some of those expenses, Grace never turned away when her daughter sought sympathy or counsel. When the Chases moved to Sea Rune, Anya saw or spoke by phone with Grace nearly every day. Neither involved themselves in the other's writing careers—probably a good thing. If there was any professional jealousy between them, Anya did not document it. Their letters to one another throughout the years were full of gossip, inside jokes, and affection. Without Grace, Anya was without her most trusted sounding board and closest confidante, and no one would ever replace her.

Two months after Grace's death, Anya could barely start thinking about her new project. On May 16 she wrote, "I'm still too scattered. I think about #8 of the big books. Wash. Irv[ing] is in Boston, finished and praised," but "I'm bored with it." More clearly and pleasantly in mind was the book beginning with the letter "D." Like Grace, she liked to play with mystical patterns in names and numbers, and now she had "Devil's Water," "Derwentwater," and "Dilston. . . . What is this person I'm pursuing. Is it really Charles Radcliffe's bastard?" she asked. The aftermath of her mother's death meant that "I can't get at it, yet! People, people, letters, bills, estate problems. No time."[31] Yet she moved ahead, "collabing" with various history buffs and "cerebrating," delving, in other words, which was "a Salvation."[32]

In late April, Anya and Chan had received announcement of another loss soon to come. Zizi, husband Pete, and little grandson Chase, Anya's most effective mood booster, were moving to Cyprus in August for a prolonged stay while Pete completed his navy medical service. Some consolation was coming too and arrived in the form of a second grandchild, Busey Seton, born to Seton and Susanne Cottier. This welcomed baby wasn't quite the same for Anya, in part because her son and his wife were often much more remote, geographically and emotionally.[33]

Nonetheless, when the Coggins trio did leave for Cyprus, Anya was able to admit that while part of her wanted them "to stay," there would be "relief when they go." Sounding a little like the confident writer she had sometimes been in earlier years, she celebrated that "I am my own woman and free to work."[34] For the next six months, she did just that.

Chapter one of novel number eight was begun by August 19, 1959, with its title decided. It would be called *Devil Water*, a local variation on the name of the ancient stream that flowed through the Radcliffe manor lands surrounding Dilston in Northumbria. By the end of the month, Anya could say, "I'm stuck on the beginning of 2nd chapter. Have to read, read, read, straighten out the multitudinous characters, at Beaufort, in London, but that work I love. 6-7-8 hours a day."[35] On September 10, she hit a snag. "The work is a mess," she fretted, "writing against grain. No elan. No plot. And I'm afraid I've bitten off more than I can chew." She had to have a heroine, she felt, but the one she had in mind could not enter the scene until a great deal of earlier history had been planted. As she said, "structurally it's a mess with baby still unborn."[36] The baby was going to be Jane or Jenny Snowden, the daughter of Charles Radcliffe, whose existence had been hinted at but never substantively verified in public or private records.

When Anya chose the two Derwentwater brothers, James and Charles Radcliffe, and the Jacobite rebellions for number eight, she didn't seem to realize at first how much she was going against the grain of all her standard storylines. "DW" would be the first of her novels to have no female character to grace the scene from the start. As she said in her long summary of problems on September 10, 1959, "Can't seem to get out of Chas's [Charles Radcliffe's] mind, unfree." She had consulted British historian, Ralph Arnold, who had written a book on Charles's brother, James Derwentwater. He "upset me in a slightly waspish letter," she wrote, because he was "demanding proof of Meg and Jennie Snowdon." Meg Snowden was Charles Radcliffe's mysterious lowborn wife, according to a few suggestive historical notes, and Jennie, sometimes spelled "Jenny" by Anya, was his daughter by Meg. "I had already told him no proof, just hunches and tiny corroborations," she groused. Then, in her journal, came a turn from what she usually demanded of herself as a historical novelist. "But supposing the whole sub-plot is imaginary which I don't think, as I am also presenting *all* the *human* facts of the Radcliffe lives. Isn't this permissible? Of course, but it's got to be a good story too, and I can't get *at* it." The most telling comment was the question, "Can I write it when I can't feel it?"[37] Jennie had virtually none of the historical documentation that filled in Anya's imaginative connections with Theodosia, Katherine, and Bess Winthrop. She was going to have to invent a good story, and was at a loss.

By November, Anya had given in to the fact that "I must be honest and admit her [Jennie's] insubstantiality." That shouldn't "really matter," she reasoned, except that it "weakens my inspiration." Putting it bluntly, and truthfully, Anya wrote, "It doesn't come naturally."[38] New Year's Day 1960 brought more doubts from another source. At a party that day, she met up with one of her most irritating literary reviewers, Orville Prescott of the *New York Times*. Sometimes he had praised her work as a historical researcher but more often, as in his review of *The Winthrop Woman*, he consigned her to a lower rank as a novel writer. Approaching him, what she had in mind was to "Placate placate the hostile male who looks like an elegant white wasp," but when he asked her what she was doing now, "I told him both Jacobite rebellions and he said it was a tall order, should be two books."[39] His comment haunted Anya throughout her writing of the novel.

In saying that she had too much history for one novel, Prescott did not know that she had bitten off even more. There was the first Jacobite rebellion, during which Charles's beloved older brother, James Radcliffe, was captured at the Battle of Preston and beheaded for supporting James III's attempt to claim the British crown. There would also be the second one, during which Charles met the same fate as his brother some twenty years later for attempting to join Bonnie Prince Charlie at Culloden. Between these two, Anya was going somehow to tell the story of Charles's daughter, Jenny Snowden. This third strain would include getting her off to colonial Virginia in the company of none other than William Byrd II. The historical records showed that the patrician Virginia colonist had spent much time in England, looking for a wife among the noblewomen of Queen Anne's court at a time when Jenny could have been there as a friend of his daughter Evelyn. Anya's idea was for Jenny to go back with the Byrds to William's Westover plantation on the James River.

Prescott's words and Anya's dilemma were bluntly expressed when Anya wrote on January 15, 1960, that while she had written Jenny's birth, "I can't get into a woman where I belong until Jenny grows up. And I'm haunted by that damn Prescott saying what I fear myself. Too much."[40] "Where I belong," she felt by instinct and experience, was inside the head of a young woman whose individual life could be interwoven into a personally meaningful historical context. The one dimension that Anya did powerfully develop with Jenny was not her romance with Rob Wilson, which never caught fire, but her relationship with her father, Charles. Creating the close bond of a father and daughter was something she knew how to do, and in this pair, Anya had the complex historical figure of Charles to work with. Partly she had this filial plot line down because she had done it before, with Aaron Burr and Theodosia. She also had the deeply felt experience of her own relationship with Ernest, another mercurial figure driven most by his desires and his causes. Like Charles Radcliffe and Aaron Burr, ETS could show great affection to his daughter, but she believed that his expectations of her were based mostly on what he needed for himself.

With Aaron Burr and Charles Radcliffe, the physically expressed love for their daughters is often too close for comfort, which was never something that Anya indicated about her relationship with Ernest. Her fictional fathers' link to Anya and father Ernest involved abandonment and self-promotion more than incestuous innuendos. Charles comes and goes in Jenny's life, always putting himself first, swearing his love but leaving her to fend for herself when other opportunities call him. When Anya was searching for the good story to tell with Jenny, she found it in this father-daughter plot, where the attachments, loyalty, desire, and betrayal come through most strongly.

Anya had done most of her work with Charles's and Jenny's time together before January 1961. Her overall discomfort with where she had to go next—getting Jenny and future husband Rob to Virginia—made it easy for her to leave the novel-in-progress behind for almost four months. She had a good excuse, since she needed to be able to attend the coming births of two new grandchildren on different sides of the Atlantic. Zizi and Pete Coggins's second son and Anya's third grandson, Daniel Coggins, was born in Cyprus on March 22, 1960, with Anya and Chan present for support. One month to the day later, Anya's Pan Am flight landed in New York "at 1 p.m.," where she found that her first granddaughter had arrived several hours earlier. Blythe Forcey, Pam and Pete's long wished-for baby, "was easily born at 3:54 am," Anya recorded, adding, amazed, "What a day."[41] For the Forceys, baby Blythe was a special miracle. They had tried for a pregnancy for ten years and not two years earlier had been separated for several months.

Anya's own timing had been perfect. An enthusiastic grandmother, she willed herself to be with both daughters when their big events occurred. "All the prophecies happened," she crowed, in a tribute to Grace's faith in her gurus' fortune-telling gifts.[42] Anya's record of Daniel's and Blythe's births was written a year and a month after the March 25, 1959, announcement that Grace had died in Florida. As she planned her trip to Cyprus and back, Anya had asked Grace's guru, Mustapha, to predict her daughters' and their infants' fates. He soothed her with assurances that she would be where she was needed and that the babies would come with health and bring happiness.

What a difference a year made, at least in some ways. As Anya finished her double grandchild birth narrative, she reflected on the completed two months' journey to Europe and back. "Two grandchildren and 16,000 miles and at least six flights later!" she was back on the ground at home. The months had seemed "a year in emotion and variety," she thought, so much so that the future might look like a new page. Yet she also had to add, "with the help of liquor and barbiturates I managed all those flights."[43] The adage that she so often liked to quote, "The more things change, the more they stay the same," was true once more.

By June 1960 Anya was back at work on *Devil Water*, finishing one of the narrative's most dramatic scenes by "polishing off poor James's decapitation."[44] The summer contained interruptions, especially those involving caring for the two stateside grandchildren, Busey Seton and Blythe Forcey. By August Anya still had not figured out a way to get Jenny and Rob, her heroine's chosen lover although only a lowborn native of Northumberland, into a romance that would take them eventually into married life in Virginia. There was to be one more major Seton family drama to survive before *Devil Water* could be finished, and this one, uncannily, involved Anya and her father. In August, Anya and son Seton went out to Santa Fe for ceremonies that Julia Buttree had organized as a final memorial for Ernest on the one hundredth anniversary of his birth in 1860. Although Anya wrote that the trip went well, she also recorded that "many folk in Santa Fe told me . . . 'nobody accepts her [Julia] but the toadies.'" Julia, she went on, "will have none of me. I was a horrid threat to her."[45]

Anya was galled that she had to beg her stepmother to give one of Ernest's paintings to his namesake grandson. Seton did get a central role in the memorial, as he, with Ernest and Julia's adopted daughter, Beulah, now in her twenties, went up in the airplane to scatter the Chief's ashes over his last domain. Seton saved a pocketful of ashes for Anya to carry back to Greenwich, where they were later buried in a little box in front of Grace's cross in Putnam Cemetery.[46] "Daddy's wind-up," the more proper one for Anya, took place on October 3, 1960, when the ETS Boy Scout Reservation was dedicated just beyond Greenwich on Riverside Road. The "emotional binge," wrote Anya, "is over."[47]

Now, Anya had nothing to do but to get back to work. The question before her was, "When do Rob and Jennie marry, and *can* I get her back to Charles in one final chapter?"[48] The answer to the second question was no. The rest of 1960 was spent dealing with more real life problems that always allowed evasion. She and Chan, with their children all too far away or too involved with newborns, spent Christmas alone, but at least it was in Williamsburg where holiday spirits ran high. Anya abandoned her home rituals with surprising ease, under the lights of the hospitality and admiration of the other guests at their cozy inn. She hardly mentioned *Devil Water* again until the next February (1961), when she wrote that Paul Brooks was putting pressure on her to finish soon or "we lose next January publication." A week later, on Washington's birthday, she finally got back to "that most difficult wedding scene, Rob and Jenny," and realized that this novel was "thinner—smaller scale—less dramatic than Kath. and W.W., Not as good."[49] She was right, but nonetheless she was going to complete what she had started, no matter what the result would be.

"Devil Water is virtually finished, the creative part," Anya wrote on March 19, 1961.[50] She didn't note that this date was exactly two years to the day since Grace's death. Paul Brooks sent queries regarding this draft, the most incisive having to do with one of the incidents that Anya had to invent. Near the novel's end, Jenny Snowden (Radcliffe) Wilson is happily married to Rob and living with him on their snug farm in the Shenandoah Valley region of Virginia. Word reaches her that her father was captured as he tried to join Bonnie Prince Charlie at the start of the short-lived 1745 Rebellion. Now Charles asks for Jenny to come to him in London, where he awaits trial in the tower. Rob is enraged that Jenny would let the proud, aristocratic father Radcliffe try to lure his wife away. When Jenny insists on going, Rob beats and rapes her, with hardly any provocation. In the final chapter a penitent Rob shows up in London just as Charles is executed, in time to catch Jenny as she collapses while watching her father go gallantly to his beheading.

Paul Brooks believed correctly that when Rob savagely hits Jenny, "we lose all sympathy with him, write him off, so to speak, and then at the very end we are asked to accept him again."[51] Anya agreed immediately to "warm up" Rob a bit, in a letter sent back to him that still argued, "Some females don't mind Rob's behavior in clouting Jenny."[52] Overall, Houghton Mifflin was pleased. Anya wrote that Anne Barrett "wept at [the] finale. Paul has sent me two wonderful letters," saying "best yet." Now Anya could look again at the future, having finished off her retelling of a past replete with historical figures that her father claimed as kinsmen. "How desolate I shall be without DW to interest me," she wrote, wondering as she always did at the end of a project, "what to do next creatively, I haven't a clue."[53]

Back in October 1960, with most Americans, Anya had participated in the making of American history as she watched Richard Nixon and John F. Kennedy in the first ever televised presidential debates. "I am fascinated," she said.[54] The sixties were going to be a turbulent time, she felt, but as Anya began a new journal book on March 12, 1961, her own future looked better than it had for some time. She and Chan were for the time being "on the same wave length," affectionate and "cooperative," and Anya recorded that on that day in March 1961, they played one of their favorite songs together, he on the organ and she on the piano. The song was "Smoke Gets in Your Eyes." The lyrics, "when a lovely flame dies, smoke gets in your eyes," had never quite gotten through to Anya before, she said, and now she saw their application to many past times. Without her suspecting it, those lyrics were also foretelling a story of her future that the rest of the decade would confirm.[55]

13 | THERE IS NO AVALON

ON MAY 9, 1961, Anya wrote that she had nearly finished the revisions to *Devil Water*, so the novel could soon move on to marketing. For her, however, the next months were a complete blur, beginning almost immediately with one of her undiagnosable illnesses. On May 15, she started her journal entry with that one word, "Bed: the real wallop on the day I last wrote [May 9]. At 3 p.m. so dizzy could hardly walk. Undressed and went to bed and have been there more or less ever since. 6 days." She had held herself together, after Grace's death, in order to write, to be present for the births of two grandchildren, to see *Devil Water* to completion, and now, it seemed, she could let go. She saw nothing ahead but trouble, with Hanna complaining and Chan worried about his job. As her vertigo began kicking in, Anya dreamed of her mother and woke to remember one of Grace's many sayings, "Satan has his fingers crossed."[1]

Chan was anything but supportive, for as she noted on May 15, "I still don't know what Chan means by separation. Where would he go—what do with boat. What tell people? Does he mean it or is it just a threat to hurt me, as has happened often enough. There is too much strain between us, always has been."[2] For close to a year, Chan had pleaded "impotence" to explain his total lack of sex interest, which could be one factor in their troubles, since their sex life, Anya had often said, was the one thing that kept them together. Two weeks after she wrote of the double wallop she had received, she was finally, although unsteadily, on her feet. "The 16th day and I have at last put on slip, girdle and stockings. I still wobble and sway, but can walk alone. And better than last week. . . . am certainly getting a pint a day of hard liquor—mostly vodka—through the day."[3] The die was cast this time, for there would be no permanent recovery for her physical ailments, her drinking, or her marriage. All dragged on for years, sometimes better and more often worse.

One indication that Anya's state of mind was fragile was her willingness to accept a message brought to her by her mother's longtime guru, Mustapha, whom she continued to consult through the coming years. Meeting with her on May 16, he told her that the power behind her illness was Julia Buttree. She quoted him as saying, "The woman in Santa Fe, with your father's ashes, she is making this trouble." Anya thought that this was "true in part. 'Black magic' not exactly—partly unconscious perhaps, but I've given her power by hating her and shall stop." Whether his pronouncement was valid or not, Anya took "all the spiteful Julie publicity and her photos etc. and I burned them up in my little fire. Not in revenge. Simply with a desire to let it purify in the living flame."[4] Anya's perception of the power, through her own hate, that Julia Buttree held could have been extended to include the power that Ernest Thompson Seton also held. With her father, however, her feelings were always going to be too complex and ambivalent to exorcise.

By June 8, Anya had a brief relapse, despite her effort at a mystical cure. This time, she made a different diagnosis, writing, "I need a new project, I know that. No Direction."[5] Unfortunately, this best of medicines did not arrive for well over a year. For a while she thought about writing a biography of Edgar Allan Poe, a sympathetic character as far back as *Dragonwyck*, but he eluded her. Chan, meanwhile, ignored his wife's "summer blues" and bought a bigger sailboat, *Dauphine*, without telling her. Anya's fear of boating was one cause of Chan's frequent disgust, so this time, she made the attempt to go out in it. On June 13, she went aboard *Dauphine*, "and we were sailing. My first sail in 10+ years. I like it too. And I was impressed by Chan's skippering." As bad luck would have it, however, she fell and gashed her leg during the ride, starting an infection that left her with a wound that required stitches and left a permanent "hole in my shin."[6] While the leg was still swollen, she had made it to Boston to do some final copy work with *Devil Water*. All her editors, she reported, "really seem to think it my best," although "I don't," she responded bluntly. Especially pleasant to her was praise from Paul Hodder-Williams, the editor in chief of her British publishing company. *Devil Water* "reads as of English origin," she quoted him as saying. "She really seems to have gone home to write it. . . . Ah yes—I did," she replied in her journal. "Don't know what'll come of it in the outside world but at least so far everything lovely."[7]

What she was facing when she returned to Greenwich from Boston was far from lovely. Chan informed her that he had borrowed $13,000 from their account to "put into the business" and that he had invested in some land in Massachusetts as well as in "an airplane 707," which would later prove a bust.[8] Increasingly he was going his own way.

In August the Coggins family finally returned from Cyprus and moved to Palo Alto, California, for another navy posting. Before their move, all the children and grandchildren came for a reunion at Sea Rune that, as Anya said, "Can hardly soon occur again." There were ten visitors in all, "somehow housed and fed," counting Anya's three children, their three spouses, and four grandchildren, with "two little highchairs" taking over the kitchen.[9] Anya loved these gatherings, welcoming the visits from her children, who now provided some appreciation in the face of Chan's persistent criticisms. Settled in California, Zizi and Pete brought another granddaughter, Christa Coggins, into Anya's world a year later.

A few days after the 1961 family invasion, Anya got the news that the Book of the Month Club would not take *Devil Water*. It was not surprising to her, and at least she had the Reader's Digest Book Club already in hand, which would pay $80,000, half of which would be hers.[10] Later the Literary Guild made an offer, but since it would mean a delay in the novel's publication, both Anya and Houghton Mifflin went ahead with the Reader's Digest Book Club, pleasing Anya especially because they would not "cut a word."[11] The fall proceeded without dramatic upheavals, although the Chases took separate vacations, he to France and she to Vermont, Quebec, and Boston. Anya stayed with friends, including her Houghton Mifflin editor and always supportive friend, Anne Barrett, and her son Seton's family along her way. In November she noted that "I have done no writing for six months," a long dry spell.[12] By December 14, she was autographing prepublication copies of *Devil Water*, and in the new year, the novel about the earls of Winton who were not, after all, related to her Setons finally had its debut.

While other novelists made their mark as 1962 BOMC and Literary Guild selections, Anya this time was on the sideline, with her usual "miserable, jealous watching of the competition." She steadied herself for the coming reviews, writing, "What goes way up always recedes, but there's life in this old girl yet."[13]

Another source of comfort to Anya as she waited for the critics to weigh in was Virginia Woolf's diary. It was "a help," she wrote, especially as Anya read "how she suffered from every adverse review—and there were plenty. Nobody remembers that now." To this favored writer she spoke, "Ah yes, Virginia, I know. Praise and blame."[14]

Yet Anya also cried out, "Won't anyone take the book seriously? Won't anyone realize the plus value in my undoubted story-telling skill?"[15] Many reviewers, did, but like Virginia Woolf, Anya was always less likely to enjoy the praise than she was to suffer from adverse notices. In addition to reviews, she also had to assess the kind of books that were being awarded top honors. This month, the Book of the Month club's choice made her compare her work to her friend Barbara Tuchman's *Guns of August*, the Pulitzer Prize–winning study of the prelude to World War I. Anya's relationship to Barbara was close in part because the historian had lived at Wyndygoul after her parents, the Maurice Wertheims, bought it from Ernest in 1912, the year Barbara was born. The "fiction competition," Anya believed, was also "heavier this time than I've ever had it," with the added problem that "my style is out of style. Except [for] 'Agony and Ecstasy' [there is] nothing like me on the list."[16] Irving Stone's novel about Michelangelo, within her own domain, was a very big competitor.

Anya respected other authors' success but seldom gave any grace to negative critics. The worst sting this time, as usual, came from the *New York Times*. "They gave it to some English instructor, University of Virginia," to review, she seethed on February 22, 1962. In her journal she recorded the crux of this upstart's remarks. According to her version, he wrote that "I have no sense of drama, indulge in mumbo jumbo psychic stuff, scolds me for not putting hell-fire sequence on stage, then shows off as to how he'd do it. Finally scolds me for not being Walter Scott. A dull humorless stupid review," she decided. "Dear Robert Scholes, whoever he is,"[17] turned out to be a young English professor who would begin to make his mark four years later with an influential book (coauthored with Robert Kellogg) called *The Nature of Narrative* (1966). In later years he became a noted literary theorist, author of many books on semiotics, structuralism, and teaching literature. He made significant points about *Devil Water* that echo some of the problems Anya articulated in her journal as she was writing the novel.

Scholes did praise Sir Walter Scott in what was not exactly a fair comparison, saying that "Miss Seton goes so far as to invade Scott's own territory and his favorite period" and praising Scott because he "was truly steeped in the history of this time and place." By contrast, Scholes wrote, "*Devil Water* too often seems a tepid and precarious union of fact and fiction, each at odds with the other." He did add some faint praise when comparing this novel to her earlier fiction, naming *The Turquoise* in particular. "Like Anya Seton's earlier novels, *Devil Water* is a blend of fiction and history," he notes, adding that because in this novel, "the blend emphasizes history, it is one of her better performances."[18] As a rising scholar, Scholes was happy to show off his knowledge of Scott's famous *Rob Roy*, and like most of her other academic critics, to turn up his nose at Anya's brand of historical romance. Yet she too had admitted that there were many troubling gaps created by her insistence on the almost completely fictional character of Jenny, which had to be "pieced," as Scholes put it, into the historical drama of the Radcliffe brothers. As Anya said, Jenny's "insubstantiality," while it "shouldn't matter," did "weaken my inspiration." With Katherine and Bess Winthrop, she had not faced this challenge, and as she said, the story of Jenny "doesn't come naturally."[19]

One of the best sections of *Devil Water* occurs when James Radcliffe agonizes over conflicting loyalties after he is called upon by brother Charles and other Jacobite leaders to join the campaign of James the Pretender in 1715. While his heart is with those eager for "the Rising," he knows that the cause will fail. He stops by the Devil Water stream on his way home to Dilston Hall one night, where he prays for strength but nonetheless senses a grim message from the water as he tosses a red leaf into the rippling current. "He knew then," Anya writes, "what the Devil Water had come to mean to him, why it referred not to this beautiful burn but to the black waves which had been swamping him. The devil's water was uncertainty. No the devil's water was fear."[20]

By contrast, one of the most troubling moments in the novel, and least credible, is the much later one that Anya felt called to include—the scene depicting Jenny's desire to return to her father. Rob's response, beating and raping his until-then beloved wife, is both a horrifying and puzzling response, as Paul Brooks had pointed out to Anya after reading her first draft. Anya left it in, writing back to Paul only that she had "softened" Rob in some ways.[21] So many of Anya's novels contained rape, including several by infuriated husbands. The prevailing values of the 1950s did not generally find such scenes objectionable. The attitude represents a commentary on the passive roles that women were expected to play in the face of male prerogatives, which allowed men wide latitude in how far they would go to assert dominance. Then too, the "titillating" reputation that was often applied to historical romance novels, a category that critically often included Anya's works, made the threat or the actuality of forced sex an expectation.

In creating both James Radcliffe's moment of awareness and Rob's violent attack on Jenny, Anya was bringing her own sensibilities to bear. One of the differences in the psychology of the scenes is that the earlier was rooted in a historical context and the latter entirely made up. James Radcliffe's sad epiphany by the stream echoes Anya's frequent uncertainty and fears at this time—her fear of aging and being abandoned—especially after she lost her mother, the mainstay of her life. Accompanying these fears was her growing dependence on her "devil water," the vodka and highballs that got her through the day. Her experience of fear and dread matches James's as he stares into the stream that spells out his suppressed feelings. Jenny's rape scene, especially as it is the consequence of her husband's fury, accessed some of Anya's resentment of Chan and what she saw as his verbally violent abuse. Robbie openly acts on his "black rage," the expression that Anya often used for both Ernest's and Chan's anger. She, on the other hand, could seldom be openly angry, at least as she described her responses in her journals. She buried her resentment by writing those descriptions, or by breaking into tears, or by stalking out of the room. This was what she would have been expected to do by her class and culture.

Ironically, while she was beginning to worry most about her drinking and Chan's snarling comments, the couple joined the Riverside Yacht Club on January 30, 1962. Chan was on the wagon now, but liquor was the most popular staple at the high-class club, and Anya was never going to be able to turn down an evening's innumerable rounds of cocktails. After one party that the Chases hosted at RYC, where Anya admitted being "naughty," there was a typical "Row" during which Chan showed "Fury," as Anya capitalized it, when she asked him to put down his paper and "talk to me a while." Her description of his lashing out included his accusations that "I was rotten spoiled and conceited with all my publicity and speeches," that their relationship was "no good," and again, that he didn't like living with her.[22] A week later, calm seems to have somehow been restored, since the Chases bought tickets on March 26, 1962, for another European trip during which they planned to be together for at least several weeks.

As Anya had once remarked, with Chan "it goes on and on, so puzzling up and down."[23] By this time, however, at age fifty-eight, Anya was much more insecure about herself than she had been in earlier years, when she often, in her journals and in remarks to Chan, called critical attention to some of his defects, including physical ones. Now she often felt herself to be unattractive and thus had much more to fear from her husband's lack of physically expressed affection. Her weight, now at 150 "ugly" pounds, and the inevitable signs of aging that were, she felt, making her less desirable to any man, resulted in self-hatred and more neediness. So many of her reactions to men were founded on her craving for attention, and up until this period she had counted on her sexiness to bring admirers, if nothing else did. When Marilyn Monroe committed suicide on August 4, 1962, Anya's comment was, "Dismal moral in that." She did not go further with the thought, but went on to record her weight and comment, "I'm a mess around the middle."[24] She identified with Monroe's depression, especially as it might relate to her own insecurity.

In April 1962, Anya could at least relax about her current professional work, since *Devil Water* reached number five on both New York bestseller lists and was the number-one seller in England. She had also started on another book for Sterling North's North Star series, this time a biography of one of the early British explorers of Virginia, John Smith. She admitted that she was "driven to it to keep sanity."[25] But by mid-April she gave up this assignment after hearing from her editors that her first chapter draft was "too condescending and tentative." Their view upset her, but she had at the same time been complaining that she could not get into this biography, so pulling out was easy. As she explained, "I can't write as though I knew what happened, semi-fictional. And I'm losing interest."[26]

Necessity, however, became the mother of invention. Something more interesting began to "quiver" primarily because of the coming trip with Chan to Switzerland and, of course, to England. Beginning with *Katherine*, Anya had always used travel to her "beloved country" as a means to do research for a novel, and she didn't want to "waste the trip" this time.[27] As she was making a last-ditch effort to settle on some historical theme for "Number Nine," on May 17, she wrote, "Have bought many Anglo-Saxon books. Think I'm in 10th century. But I'm scattered. Blind staggers and no plot or people clear. Just Holy Grail and Wessex. And baptism at a Holy Well. And King Edward's murder."[28] A week later, on the day before she was leaving to join Chan in

Geneva, she enthusiastically reported more solid inspiration. "Farewell for a while. Off tomorrow for 10 a.m. flight TWA to Geneva. Glad to go. Glad to meet Chan. . . . #9 gave me a pleasant shock *hier* when I found that Alfred's granddaughter had married King Louis of Provence. The first link. So much to learn. The hero is their son, I think. Romien. The girl *n'existe pas* yet. But the villainess [is] Alfrida."[29] Thus *Avalon*, number nine, was born after an almost three-year creative stall.

The Chases' time abroad was not satisfying when they were together, often quarreling, but Anya's weeks alone in England, she wrote after her return, were, as always, a joy. "My England," she sighed, "the long southern tour alone. It was heaven. I never in my life had a better time."[30] The rugged, almost completely sea-surrounded county of Cornwall, located in the southwest corner of England, was an entrancing location for her to explore. Its coast would provide the opening setting of the new novel. Anya had already schooled herself well through books and old maps that illuminated the complicated history of Anglo-Saxon England, with its internal fighting over land boundaries and its battles against the invading Vikings. She also, with "Romien," again had a male, historically verifiable hero in mind but did not know who the absolutely necessary "girl" would be. This time she did create an immediate role for the novel's leading female character before starting chapter 1, so that the first person we meet is Merewyn, a young Cornish girl who believes she is descended from King Arthur. In this belief, she is terribly wrong, for her father was killed during one of the terrible Viking raids on Cornwall, and she is the product of her mother's rape by the band's leader, Ketil. The lie about her ancestry will haunt Merewyn's life.

The story of Merewyn's early years in Cornwall is almost immediately submerged under the story of young "Romien," soon to be called Rumon, who finds her while he is wandering lost on the coast of Cornwall after being shipwrecked. In the tenth century, Cornwall was an isolated region of what was loosely known as England and had its own difficult Cornish dialect. The very civilized Rumon considers Cornwall's distinctive culture, within which the Roman Catholic faith had the barest of footholds, appallingly primitive. His assessment includes Merewyn. This Frankish prince, as Anya develops his character, has left Provence on a quest to reach the seat of English power. A vision at his home in France has directed him to travel to the Wessex center of England called "Mercia," which combined the cities of London and Oxford.

This was the land where Rumon's grandmother had been born. Rumon, who dislikes his native country because of its own distasteful wars, is enchanted by the legend of a place of peace and joy called Avalon. The shipwreck that has landed him in Cornwall is an irritating impediment, but when Merewyn's mother dies while Rumon is recovering in her manor, he must unhappily deal with another. He is entrusted, as a chivalrous prince, with the unwelcome task of taking Merewyn to her aunt, a nun residing in a convent in Romsey, not on his planned route.

For much of the rest of the novel, Rumon and Merewyn's adventures overlap and alternate on the novel's stage, which becomes a launching point for an intercontinental travelogue replete with missed connections on both sides of the Atlantic between these star-crossed lovers. They move from Cornwall to Glastonbury where they meet the great Catholic archbishop Dunstan before being presented to the royal family of King Edgar. Here Rumon falls into besotted love with the wicked English queen Alfrida, who has married King Edgar after both of their spouses have been set aside. Not until after Edgar has died, and his son Edward murdered by the boy's evil stepmother's servants, does Rumon realize his folly and also, too late, his love for Merewyn.

The much-enhanced object of Rumon's newfound affection, meanwhile, has returned through a myriad of events to Cornwall, where she becomes the victim of a Viking raid and is almost raped by her own Viking father, Ketil. He discovers in the nick of time that this now beautiful young woman is his daughter, the child born of his brutal rape of her mother Breaca. At this point the settings move across the Atlantic, to Iceland (Merewyn) and to the narrow coastline of what will eventually become New Hampshire (Rumon). Ketil takes Merewyn back to his Icelandic post, where eventually she marries a suitable, lordly warrior named Sigurd and lives a hard but contented life, bearing two children in this pagan marriage. Rumon too crosses the Atlantic on his search for her, yet when he finally finds her in Greenland, he is spurned by the woman whom he once had spurned. Separated again, they both eventually get back once more to England, where their mismatched attraction began.

Rumon, chastened by his fruitless journey, once back in Catholic England, embraces his true vocation and becomes a saintly monk. Merewyn, following the death of her husband and the failure of the Viking outpost in Greenland, also returns to England, where she searches for Rumon. When he refuses her request to see him, she marries the wealthy thane Wulfric and does not meet Rumon again until he is dying.

The dizzy geographical and emotional crisscrossing of place and emotions turns *Avalon* into a kind of mythic saga, certainly something different from a historically based double quest. Too many threads are picked up and dropped, often with flimsy explanations, for the actions to be credible. It would have taken much more intense concentration for Anya to complete a coherent narrative, something that she only dimly suspected as she trudged ahead.

Anya began writing novel number nine on August 1, 1962. "Avalon?" she questioned, thinking of a title. "I wonder. I'm happy when I'm working on it. It is my escape, my anodyne. But I've no idea how to handle the thing. Mysticism. Merewin (?) Rumon. Alfrida. What are they? The Holy Grail. The Quest." Old friend and advisor Lee Barker "thinks Avalon a good title," she wrote. "It came as I sat with happy highball on the back porch, four days ago."[31] And so the project began, for the next three years alternating between her highballs and her green study. All the while there were other both personal and national blows to slow her work down to what she called, several times, "a trickle."

Chan's volatile changes of attitude were a constant. After one crisis, Anya wrote, "Work is the answer, but Avalon is still churning. Can't get the story line or direction quite. Reading and research—the clarity in the morning, but I fill my afternoons with Bridge, etc. or that food glut jumps on me."[32] Increasingly, playing bridge with her coterie of friends became more of an anodyne than writing, taking up most of her afternoons. She was also receiving little guidance from her Houghton Mifflin team. Hardwick Moseley, out at Sea Rune for an "alcoholic and boring" weekend, told her that "it would be tough to do, so far back and everything." Her response was, "Thud, as usual."[33]

World affairs also became a way to procrastinate. Anya did not like John Kennedy, whom she called "that sleazy-eyed, devious young man."[34] His turbulent presidency provided easy distractions, all captured on television. In late October 1962, it was the Cuban missile crisis. Anya was "glued to TV" for the high drama. As for "Avalon," she mentioned, "I bat out a few lines, but the world crisis is too much."[35] A year later, of course, it was Kennedy's assassination that paralyzed the entire country. On November 25, 1963, Anya described where she was when the news exploded. "Friday at one p.m. I was sitting at lunch with my guests," she wrote, when someone called to say, "The President and the Governor of Texas have been shot. . . . Like everyone," she went on, "my reaction was 'you're kidding.' We turned on the radio. In 10 min. 'The President is dead.'" Then there was the funeral, and the killing of Lee Harvey Oswald. "My God, what a weekend," Anya said, speaking perhaps for most Americans. All animosities about this too flashy young president were forgotten, for as Anya put it, "Shame everyone feels—at this ghastly, senseless violence."[36] "Avalon" was put aside. "I simply can't work," Anya said on November 30.[37]

In the agonizing year between these two "strenuous" historical events, as Anya once called them, there were many family events that made work on Anya's new novel difficult, if not impossible. She recorded an all-too-typical occurrence on December 8, 1962, describing a recent night on the town with Chan that went very badly. After being bawled out for ruining the evening with her unbecoming behavior, she lashed out at Chan for his own prim regimen: "no cigarettes, no liquor, and now no sex." His response was his own brand of "Fury," as he shouted that "I was too fat, I was drunk. He hated my wig." The fight's end was also typical, with the threat that now always hung between them. "If you value this marriage—shut up!" he screamed, and "I did," she conceded.[38] Anya admitted to much more worry during these times about her drinking, weight gain, smoking, and abnormally high blood pressure, none of which she was able to control. "Are there any happy people?" she asked.[39]

Family incidents that took place in these years were personally distressing for Anya. Pam, pregnant a second time, was dealing with two-year-old Blythe, financial worries, and Pete Forcey's increasingly undependable behavior. Seton was exhibiting the first signs of unmistakable mental instability. Neither situation was going to improve, although the appearance on April 21, 1962, of a fifth and last grandchild, Pam and Pete's little boy Peter, was cause for celebration and a temporary truce between his parents. Yet the following autumn, there were new explosions in both the Forcey and Seton Cottier families. On November 12, Anya wrote that her daughter-in-law Susanne had called to tell her that Seton had a full-blown "psychotic episode" in New York, requiring psychiatric care. On November 22, three hours before Kennedy was shot, Pam met with Anya to tell her that she and Pete were divorcing. Even though Blythe was only three and "Peterkin" only six months old, this time no reconciliation was to be considered. The worlds around and within Anya were collapsing. Perhaps there was little wonder that she was working on a novel about a man's search for the idyllic Avalon.

The trajectory of Anya's progress on *Avalon* during the same one-year period did, however, show some success. Anya had been happy to have heard from Paul Brooks, who "has now sent contract and nice letter praising my project which I am not doing on account of social and Xmas."[40] The new year also brought some promising signs. Anya reported on January 5 that she was "back with it [*Avalon*] a bit. Must find a Viking." On January 11, 1963, her news was that she had spent a few happy hours with Merewyn, her fictional heroine, and with Eric the Red. She was glad to have found this particular Viking, a historical figure to develop, because "I need a Dane to give the thing unity. And data on those Vikings so hard to sieve out."[41] On January 29, optimism continued, her plot was "coming clearer," because, she said, "I have much more of the pleasant fact-correlating to do."[42] In these entries, Anya was writing out the problem that Robert Scholes had identified in his *New York Times* review of *Devil Water* a year earlier. He had written that "the embarrassing moments in the narrative come from her [Anya's] piecing out of the gaps inconveniently left by history."[43] When she was working within a historical framework that she could correlate and with historical characters, whose lives provided knowable data, she was much more certain of her skills. With such characters, she found it easier to create underlying motivations and emotions anchored in some history-based plausibility.

Anya's optimism did not hold. From March to July of 1963, her characters, set into motion on in their various journeys, moved hardly at all; in fact they and she were "stuck," as she put it on March 19. Settings from the faraway times and places also remained frozen, despite the fact that Anya and Chan made a two-week exploration of Iceland in May. The summer that followed, like most earlier ones, was a hard time to write. Anya always hated the heat and now had fights with Chan even about how low she could turn the air-conditioning. Her writing work was hardly mentioned again until September 16, 1963, when she noted that "Avalon is a mess" and that she needed "insight from somewhere." Three days later she did see what one of her problems was, although not an answer. "Worried about uncharacteristic lack of scene in Avalon," she wrote. "I can't seem to visualize clearly their surroundings."[44] In part, the inability to visualize her characters' environs was related to Scholes's comment about gaps, since the settings she had chosen, like the characters, did not provide her usual imaginative connections with place or history, except for the enchanting Cornwall. She was blocked both by the lack of familiarity with such ancient settings and "data on those Vikings," as she put it.

It was not only Kennedy's assassination, Pam's looming divorce, or Seton's psychoses that caused Avalon to move so slowly in the last weeks of 1963, but other blocks of longer duration. She felt little of her usual relish as she worked on her book during 1964. Most of her comments recorded, "Avalon slow" (March 12), Avalon slow "but trickles" (March 20), and all sorts of problems "play hell [with] Avalon" (May 1). By midsummer she was doing some "painful creeping on to Merrimac,"[45] as she tried to construct a chapter during which Rumon was to find himself in future American, actually New Hampshire, territory. Anya also frequently admitted that she was drinking heavily at this time, often twenty ounces of vodka a day, and escaping regularly to afternoon bridge parties.

One professionally useful interlude broke up the unproductive routines. In 1964 Anya joined the faculty of the well-regarded annual summer Indiana University Writers Conference (IUWC), which had been holding its week-long workshops for both beginning and working writers since 1940. Over the years such luminaries as Tennessee Williams, Robert Penn Warren, and P. G. Wodehouse had been in residence. Anya was terrified of the faculty, of how she would do with her workshop students, and whether she would find enough liquor on the campus. She need not have worried. Most of her students, she found, appreciated and enjoyed her, especially her "100 word" exercise, which she didn't go on to describe. In the evenings, there were not only readings by faculty and students but "cocktails everywhere."[46] Anya was proud that she had not missed one of her classes and that she had attracted some never unseemly flattery from male students. The nicest of her fellow faculty, she wrote without elaboration, was Kurt Vonnegut.

Back from the writers' conference by July 13, after a week that she had enjoyed more than she expected, Anya had to deal with Chan's new and even bigger sailboat, named *Gudrun*, and the social activities it involved. In August there was a "long marathon" babysitting session with Zizi's Christa and Pam's Blythe and Peter, who descended upon Sea Rune (along with several babysitters) without their parents for several days. After their departure, she commented, "I am very tired." While Anya did drink during the children's time with her, their parents seemed to find her care, with assistants, to be adequate. As Pete Coggins told her by phone, when she was caring for two of the children who had stomach bugs, "You're a good coper."[47] Whenever the grandchildren visited, which was often, Anya seems to have gladly put everything else on hold, especially her writing, without complaint.

By December 1964, Anya was moving toward the final section of *Avalon*, with Anne Barrett coming out on the fifteenth of that month to see what she had accomplished. She wished she had "more to show," while she was "stuck in Greenland with Merewyn," but her next comment indicated at least partly why she was managing only a "trickle." She had developed a "new habit," now needing to drink her liquor in order to write, another sign of growing dependence. "It comes out better after vodka," she disclosed, with swigs beginning in the morning and "stretched throughout the day, more than a pint but not much." Sometimes, "of course I show it," she admitted, but the swigs gave her "exhilaration, ease, not depression."[48] The end of December 1964 saw the first of another new trend, a stay in Greenwich Hospital. This was a stay of short duration, ordered by her doctors in order to do "every test [they] could think of" related to fatigue, high blood pressure, and intermittent severe stomach upsets. All tests were "negative," leaving Anya with a continuing array of physical "woes" and no acceptable answers, including "no directives even on the drinking."[49]

A first draft of *Avalon* was somehow brought to completion through dogged persistence. Anya worked as hard as she was able between January 15, 1965, when she pushed her narrative to the year 1000, and April 26, when she wrote that "Avalon finished and is now in both countries" (with publishers Houghton Mifflin in Boston and Hodder and Stoughton in London). Now she could await their verdict before starting revisions. Her own judgment was, "I think it's a fairly good job. 500 pp including afterword."[50] Paul Brooks, who had not seen even the early chapters of her draft until the beginning of April, had written in a letter dated April 12, 1965, that he was "enormously impressed." He had particularly liked "the character of Dunstan, his conflict with Alfhere, and the handling of the rivalry between the Church and the temporal lords."[51] In other words, he thought that her best work was with the historically documented drama of Anglo-Saxon England.

Paul was unusually delicate when he questioned Anya's development of the character of Rumon, who seemed inconsistent to him, especially in her handling of his "sex drives." He asked, tactfully, if Rumon might not be "more convincing and more interesting if he were a normally-sexed young man from the start," and wondered perhaps if "the reader would take to Rumon more quickly if one sensed a strong character whose 'religious drives' (for lack of a better word), whose yearning for the ideal, are in conflict with the earthier facts of life." In this very gentle tone, he finished by telling her not to worry about revising "right now," but to go ahead and get the narrative to its end. Perhaps most significantly, he had crossed out the word "Yours" as he signed his name, and wrote instead the word "love."[52] Anne Barrett, who had been with Anya most often in recent months, might very well have urged him to provide this extra warmth.

In any case, by May 7, 1965, Anne Barrett, Anya's most stalwart defender, had given the green light to improvements in Rumon's character. With her HM editors' blessings, Anya sent her British publishers a revision, telling them to throw out the old first chapter. "Anne Barrett," she informed them, had said, "joyously, from Boston, 'The changes you have made in Chapter One make all the difference. This is beautiful craftsmanship, and a joy to watch happen.'"[53] Throughout Anya's work on number nine, Anne Barrett became an essential emotional replacement for Grace Seton. In the early going of the novel's construction, Graham Wilson, one of Anya's Curtis Brown editors in their London office, objected to the way the plots of Rumon and Merewyn had been "split apart." Disagreeing, Anya replied that "as Anne Barrett said, it [*Avalon*] is a book about BOTH of them."[54] When the final draft came in, Anne had written a memo to Paul, copied to Anya, summarizing the major accomplishment of the book. It was, Anne wrote, "a most impressive blending of scholarship and imagination," through which "the historical characters come alive in a way that is unforgettable."[55]

Unfortunately, Anne could not cure what was most seriously wrong with one of Houghton Mifflin's biggest stars, and the one whom she had taken under her wing most carefully. When Anya sent off her *Avalon* draft, she asked in her journal, "And now what to do."[56] The answer, unrelated to any writing work, was not long in coming. By May 19, 1965, she was experiencing a failure of muscle reflexes and was "very frank about vodka problem" with "all doctors" when she was examined. They now agreed with her that alcohol was "the central problem." Chan's diagnosis was most blunt: "If you won't go on the wagon, I'm leaving. . . . You're deteriorating."[57] By May 22,1965, Anya was booked into Greenwich Hospital for twelve days. This turn of events was a replica of the collapse that had occurred when she finished *Devil Water*. Again, it was as though she had held herself together to see *Avalon* through to the completion of the first draft and then let herself quit, physically and psychologically.

Anya returned home on June 3, 1965, from another inconclusive time in the hospital, which had at least been "an Asylum" from Chan's continual barrages. She had been "sedated a lot," more than her doctors and "darling" nurses knew, since she confessed only to her journal, "I had swigs 'smuggled in' by faithful housekeeper Janina." Once she was back home, Chan was not coddling but demanding, even though Anya had agreed to see a new psychiatrist, David Morley, whose specialty was helping patients addicted to alcohol. Chan told her, "'If you don't go away, I won't stay.' What I think he meant," Anya added, "was that 'if you don't go to Silver Hill and get on the wagon, I'm leaving.'"[58] Silver Hill was a fashionable nearby drying out facility, to which Anya attached the stigma of shame. Dr. Morley tried out hypnosis, soon coming to her house for lunch, she wrote, and then putting her into "light trances" while she lay on her bed. The treatment helped her depression but was not enough to take away her craving for alcohol, however, so back to Greenwich Hospital she went, where, unlike a stay at Silver Hill, supposedly no one would have to know she was drying out.

Anya reported in her journal that she was in the hospital for "22 extraordinary days," August 21 to September 12. "And after the first week in which I must have been sort of balmy, my memories are of TLC, kindness, lots of attention, small amusements like my painting, the divine bed-bath and back-rubs."[59] At last, she had a refuge, people who seemed to really care and who mothered her in a way she had not known since Grace's stronger times. For Anya, "the hospital was a good period. Sheltered and I had so many compliments. From patients, nurses, and doctors." Here she was called "Beautiful, sparkling, courageous." Here she even managed to correct the British galleys of *Avalon*, although "not very well," she worried. Once home, she was faced again with Chan, who had no interest in nursing her ego. Ending her long description of the "good period" in the hospital, she vowed, in her entry for September 15, 1965, to stay sober and "live one day at a time."[60]

In the final scene of *Avalon*, the monk Rumon, who filled his last years with good works, summons Merewyn to his bedside to hear his dying plea. He wants her to confess, to her rich husband Wulfric and the English court where she is a welcome guest, that she is not the daughter of the great King Arthur, but the bastard child of a hated Viking. Merewyn agrees to carry out his wish, expecting banishment or worse, but she is met, astonishingly and unrealistically, with acceptance, at least by the sympathetic Queen Emma and by Wulfric. As she leaves the court in the novel's last scene, Merewyn thinks of Rumon and "felt his words like a benediction." Responding to this intuition, she whispers, "My dear, dear love."[61]

On September 19, 1963, at an early stage of writing *Avalon*, Anya had written that she had been thinking of Chan one evening when he was not coming home, and she had been spurred with "wonder & puzzlement" to say out loud, "my dear, dear Love."[62] Two years later, trying to finish the novel, those words came back to her, but not with any certainty that Chan could be, unambivalently, the one who should receive them. During their last interview, Merewyn says sadly to Rumon, "You were always questing, searching for a blessed place called Avalon. I see that you have not found it." He replies, "Unless it's here. In this little garden, or anywhere that one can find peace."[63] It is a stoic, resigned answer for this couple who could never reach a happy ending together.

Anya found peace, after finishing *Avalon*, only in Greenwich Hospital, and only by becoming an invalid. After she was discharged, she stayed on the wagon, more or less, for two months, buying new clothes and enjoying compliments. She looked "fifteen years younger," friends told her. *Avalon*, when it came out in October, was "far more successful than I expected," she reported, even getting a good review from the *New York Times* and another run in Readers Digest Book Club.[64] Her meticulous research, as usual, was praiseworthy, especially given that she was reconstructing "an era so far removed from us," as she put it in her afterword to the novel.

Her afterword also summarized some of the events that followed the tenth-century period she had chronicled, and as usual she listed the people who had been particularly helpful "personally," including British Arthurian scholar Geoffrey Ashe. In addition to sharing his groundbreaking knowledge about geographies connected to King Arthur, Ashe was probably the one who introduced her to the intriguing story of a sixteenth century "walled-up girl" whose remains had been discovered in castle ruins in Kent. Anya would hardly have been able to resist the idea of expanding on this mystery in a book, which eventually did become novel number ten. She later sponsored an American lecture tour for Ashe, proud of her association with a popular writer and speaker. In her afterword, she also thanked Charles Michael Boland, an American amateur historian whose well-regarded book *They All Discovered America* (1961) argued for the Vikings' presence in the territory of New Hampshire. He too would have a place in her life later.[65]

With Avalon published in November 1965, Anya faced the Christmas holiday season. For so many years a season that she filled with celebration, this year it was marked only by her descent, once again, into "compulsive drinking." She and Chan joined the Coggins family for festivities in their new home in Cambridge, Massachusetts, where there was little joy. She was back in Greenwich Hospital on December 26, acknowledging that this was her fourth stay in 1965. As with her two previous rounds of treatment, she insured that Janina's smuggled flasks would counteract cold sobriety. Return to Sea Rune with a nurse came after two weeks of "asylum," on January 8, 1966, but Chan met her there with the news that he had sublet a flat in midtown Manhattan. The handwriting in her journal for the previous three months had been, for the first time, terribly irregular, and her writing life now disappeared from sight.

14 | INTO GREEN DARKNESS

WHEN ANYA REPORTED THE DEBUT OF *AVALON*, number nine of her "big" historical novels, she had been upbeat. The November 11, 1965, occasion brought the usual fanfare or, as Anya called it, "razzledazzle. Flowers, liquor, adulation. My beautiful party at Carleton House and later the best dessert of my life—Grand Marnier soufflé." It was a sadly telling detail—a dessert with a strong liqueur. Anya "drank some through all this and WNYE [Radio] broadcast" which took place "in City Hall where Chan and I were married. He was sort of quiet through all this."[1]

The silence should have been deafening. It took two more years for the worst blow to fall, but the signs had long been everywhere. "The blackest day of my life," as Anya described it on November 22, 1967, had occurred on November 20. Chan told her that he was "in love with someone else" and wanted a divorce.[2] The woman he wanted to marry, as Anya already suspected, was Hylah Kitchel, one of her frequent bridge partners who lived up the street with husband Tim. Chan had talked more than once about his attraction to her, and Anya had seen Hylah's pictures in his briefcase.

For the two years after *Avalon*'s publication, before Chan's divorce announcement, Anya fought a losing battle against drinking and was treated with drugs such as Ritalin, Valium, and Librium. After a vacation in Martinique, she haltingly started a new novel about Josephine, the wife of Napoleon, concentrating on the empress's earlier life there. But after Chan broke his news, her efforts at regaining her health or moving ahead with a novel project came to a bleak halt. As another now dreaded Christmastime approached, she expressed overwhelming grief and brutal honesty about what she now faced.

> It's the loneliness. The having no support [or] assurance of help from a husband in sickness and trouble. It's the feeling of being a pariah, "the formerly married." It's the destruction of a whole pattern, a diminution, and it's the love loss. Pride terribly hurt, but love too. His clothes, his interests elsewhere. No more "withness" with people, no more morning papers, or joint letters, or telephone [calls]. It's the horrified pity of my friends and family too. Everything said, everything in this home reminds me of him who wants to pull out—for another woman.[3]

Binney Lane, or Sinney Lane as their street was often called, had seen this story before, and would again, but Anya's shame was compounded by her heavy reliance on her seductive appeal to men as one of her chief assets. To be publicly cast aside by her husband of almost thirty-eight years, for an attractive younger woman who was also a supposed friend and a neighbor, completely destroyed her already fragile ego.

Four years earlier, thirty-eight-year-old Pam had come to Anya on November 22, 1963, the day of John Kennedy's assassination, to tell her of her own coming divorce from Pete Forcey. In 1967, soon after Chan's blow, Anya compared herself in her journal to both daughter Pam and mother Grace. "Divorce—I could take it at 40," she wrote, but "Not now. Mother's age," she wrote on November 22, referring to the fact that Grace's divorce from Ernest occurred when she was almost sixty-four, the same age as Anya was soon to be.[4] Grace's mother, Clemenzie Gallatin, was also a divorcee, which meant that Anya was now part of a four-generation pattern. She and Grace, who paid such close attention to numerology, were both divorced by their husbands after close to forty years of marriage, another sad coincidence.

Hylah Kitchel was almost fifteen years younger than Anya, a pretty and confident part-time actress who in marrying Tim Kitchel had joined the Binney clan, a founding family of Old Greenwich. According to Anya, neighbors had taken note of Hylah's predatory interest in Chan and considered her to be the villain in the Chases' breakup, which was little comfort to Anya.[5] She never speculated on Hylah's motives for leaving Tim but did note that Tim sympathized greatly with her own situation, telling her that "nothing would induce him to take [Hylah] back, even if Chan changes his mind." Anya recorded Tim's sympathy on her birthday in January 1968, also indicating that she was departing that day, with newly hired companion Muriel Hynes, for a long trip that would "leave a clear field to Hylah." She did not know "what I really want, except not to suffer."[6] She headed for California by train and stayed in several resorts there, also visiting with her lifelong friend Isabel Lord.

Anya did not return to Greenwich until March 15 and somehow lived through "D-Day," as she called April 18, 1968, the date when her marriage to Chan was dissolved through legal decree in Juarez, Mexico. Although she wrote in her journal entry on the occasion, "I'm the plaintiff o.c. [of course]. Incompatibility," this turned out not be the case.[7] In her next entry, April 25, with surprising complacency, she wrote that a mistake had been made, whereby Chan charged "cruelty" and "me incompatibility." It was simply "Dopey," she added, without suspecting any malice on Chan's part.[8] On her return home she had discovered that Chan and Hylah insisted on continuing to live in Greenwich, in a home Hylah owned, making Anya's encounters with her husband's lover around town inevitable. Hylah and Chan were married on April 27, 1968. "I hope they suffer," Anya remarked as she thought of their coming nuptials. "I've endured too much."[9]

As her journals showed her, when she went back through them during this agonizing time, Chan's and her long marriage had given them both much to endure. The first serious rows and threats had begun in 1936, only two years after Zizi's birth. Neither had much interest in the other's professional life, with common interests largely confined to children, finances, and mutual friends. Their closest bond was sex, with affection not often enough expanded into compromises made for the partner's sake. Anya did attend readily to her obligations as housewife, social director, and nurse. A 1962 article appearing in the *New York Herald Tribune* as *Devil Water* was about to appear bore the headline SUCCESSFUL NOVELIST WAS HOMEMAKER FIRST. It ended with the reporter saying, "The children are grown up now and Miss Seton says her husband is 'sympathetic' about her work and the inevitable clutter it brings to the house. 'But,' she says, 'dinner is still on the table at 7:30, or else.'"[10]

Anya might have meant the implied threat to be a joke, but it contained a revelatory subtext. Chan could be intolerant and verbally abusive over small as well as big things. He brooked no criticism of his purchases or his behavior and was easily hurt by pressure from his bosses at Scudder or derogatory comments from social acquaintances. Also difficult were his relations with his stepchildren's families. When Pam or Seton arrived with spouses and children, he argued with Seton or Pete Forcey, or he simply disappeared.

One area where he and Anya generally, but not always, got along was their finances. Despite the fact that she often second-guessed him, Chan invested her funds as well as his own, continuing to handle her investments after the divorce. Anya had willingly used her income to pay the mortgage on Sea Rune and Zizi's education expenses. Her general penny-pinching was a lifelong habit that Chan seems not to have encouraged, while she resented his spending on luxuries. Both spent a good deal of money on treatment with psychoanalysts over the years, something she minded much more than he did.

As she often admitted, Anya could be hypercritical, especially when drinking, and her not very subtle jabs led to Chan's anger and recriminations, most often when he too was under the influence. In the last years of their marriage, he had been able to stop completely, leading him to more active attempts to "police" Anya, as she saw it. She bitterly resented his oversight, which only helped to drive him away. Both wanted their own work to come first and their tastes to be indulged. For almost four decades, they put up with each other through wave after wave of tension. They stayed together because even without sex in the last years, neither wanted to give up their home, their relationships with family, or their social standing. Neither wanted to face being alone, but Chan found in Hylah his way to solving that problem. "So this is how the story ends," Anya wrote on the day of the divorce. "The long stormy marriage. 38 years lived in a dream."[11]

Immediately after the April divorce, Anya wrote that she felt little except "dreadful waves of hurt and yearning. . . . Numbness was setting in" too, she said, as she prepared to depart on yet another trip with Muriel Hynes, this one a voyage abroad on the ship *The France*.[12] All she could see ahead was a future devoid of joy. But a very different outcome awaited.

Anya designed her trip to provide a "safe escape" from the wreckage of her marriage that lay behind in Greenwich. Her European wanderings, which encompassed time in Ireland, France, and England, lasted four months. On her return, Anya began a journal entry recounting her experiences with one word, "Incredible." Traveling in "beloved England," she had engaged in two torrid affairs, according to her retelling. The attentions of two engaging, admiring men, Anya wrote, "saved my sanity, though I still don't see how I could alternate as I did." Her long, explicit journal entry for August 24 reviewed some of the "magical midsummer madness" with them and concluded with the assessment that "few people have lived so much so fast in 8 months."[13]

The phrase, "too much too fast," became a chorus lyric for many of the entries of the following years. It was her explanation for the collapse that had landed her back in Greenwich Hospital two days after her return from England on August 9, 1968. During her travels, she had never been "a day without sickness," she wrote, the one exception being her times with the two men "who loved me in their fashion," as she put it.[14] Greenwich Hospital kept her for nine days before she returned to Sea Rune frail but sober and, again, temporarily with no desire to drink. Taking trips that ended with hospital treatment had become and would continue to be a routine that Anya subconsciously willed. When she was away from home, alcohol was the anodyne that she relied upon. Her doctors were not within easy reach, parties were the order of the day, and no one with her could stop her. In her journal, she had even started calling alcohol by its scientific chemical name, whose elements were symbolized by the letters "RoH," a useless ploy to stress its function for her as medicine.[15]

The doctor that Anya most counted on to treat her in Greenwich was her psychiatrist, David Morley. As early as October 1966, she asked herself a rhetorical question: "I have everything to make a woman of my age happy. A good husband except sex. A lover-doctor except total sex. Good children, especially Zizi. What then is eating you?"[16] When Anya used the word "lover" for Morley, she was in no explicit way indicating a sexual relationship. In the context of the question she wrote to herself, she was pointing out the contrast between a husband who no longer felt any sexual attraction to her and a physician who was giving her sympathetic attention that may very well have included praise, even flattery, translated by her as "love." She never indicated that he crossed any ethical doctor-patient boundaries. Dr. Morley had come into Anya's life in 1965 specifically to help her achieve sobriety. However, for her he became the man she "most loved" for at least the next decade, according to her journals and some typed "reports" that she wrote but possibly never gave to him. After a time she seemed to feel completely dependent on his treatments. These included his prescribing medications as well as giving her "verbal" signs of her attractiveness, at least as she recorded their interactions in her journals. The degree to which she was exaggerating his behavior cannot be confirmed. The years of their doctor-patient relationship were the time when her ego was at its most fragile, and her blurring of reality and wish fulfillment most acute.

Describing the start of his work with her, Anya wrote that Morley set up weekly hypnosis sessions with his patient. As Anya described them, they took place in her bedroom, with him seated by her on the bed, holding her hand. "Do you suppose David makes love—verbally—with other attractive females?" she asked in her October 27, 1966, journal. Her answer was that "he says not. But he is not consistent. I'm sure he has his own problems. He did say in excuse that sleeping with me would be a regression for him."[17] For her, their sessions came close, but never actually arrived, at "spontaneous combustion," as she later called it.[18]

DLM, as Anya often called Morley in her journals, was a necessary fixture in her life. When he wasn't affectionate or available enough, she felt abandoned. Kind words or help with her own or other family members' health crises were effective in pulling her out of depression. She wrote in journal entries that she shared with him all her conquests of other men, but he seems to have been neither judgmental nor encouraging about her sex life. Her reported conversations with him had several dimensions other than sex, for he often spoke to her of her need to rely on a higher power and to call on her spiritual resources. She reported that on occasion he gave her small gifts which sometimes she found too impersonal.

After her divorce, Anya began several sexually based relationships that she documented at length in her journals, and evidently to Morley. These were, she felt, the only way she could find life bearable, a sentiment she had voiced far earlier, when she found no sexual pleasure in her marriage to Hamilton Cottier. Her always vulnerable ego and the fear of being thought undesirable had also been heightened during the many years of strained or denied sexual activity with Chan. Now she had "freedom" to accept physical signs of affection, something she noted in her entry for April 25, 1968, a week after the divorce was finalized. She was able somewhat to counter her misery then with the realization that "I'm Free. And there are so many men—if I want them."[19] The men whom she chose to want might have been taking some advantage of her, but their company was stimulating, comforting, and simply fun. As she wrote in October 1968, "I want almost any man's loving arms. And to be held."[20] With a male friend staying the night, she did not have to endure the loneliness of an empty house. Often, she could call on her love interests to escort her to the parties and events she enjoyed. In her circles, a lone woman created social awkwardness, fairly or not, as she well knew.

Anya began to describe several intimate relationships that she developed in Greenwich around the time she admitted her need to be held. Her compatible overnight visitors joined her in a rearranged bedroom, with its new queen-size bed. There were two particularly close companions, Stefan Salter and Charles Boland. Charlie had turned up in April 1968, just before she left on her trip to Europe. He had been one of the consultants she thanked in her *Avalon* afterword. Anya had enlisted him to help her tour Viking ruins on the coast of New Hampshire while she was working on *Avalon*. In April 1968, newly divorced himself, Charlie showed up "out of the blue" to visit.[21] By October 1968, they were intimately involved. Charlie knew almost as much history as she did, and he could be wonderful company, though per Anya's records over the next several years, his increasing health problems hurt their romantic relationship, although they remained friends.[22]

Anya began an affair with Stefan Salter around the same time. He was a German-born, highly respected book cover designer who now, in his early sixties, was legally blind from diabetes. Physically he was a big "bear" of a man whom Anya did not find physically attractive. She "found comfort in his arms," however, also delighting in his "good mind" and endless supply of entertaining stories.[23] The men whom Anya chose for her longer-term relationships all possessed the qualities that Chan most lacked. They had lively intellectual interests that paralleled hers, and they enthusiastically gave her all the attention she could desire.

While Anya was exploring newfound sexual freedom, she was also seriously attempting to get on with a project that she was calling "The Marsdon Chronicles." When she had made her post-divorce 1968 trip to England, she built in the possibility of research on the legend of the "walled-up girl" supposedly discovered during renovations at the historical Igtham (pronounced *Item*) Mote, located in County Kent. Just before that trip began, she wrote the name "Celia" in her journal, along with the name "Igtham Mote."[24] "Help me find my Book," she prayed as she left.[25]

During her "incredible" visit to England in 1968, Anya had "squandered" her research time with her romances, she wrote later.[26] It was six months afterward, in Greenwich, that she returned to the story of "Celia" and Igtham Mote. Now she was bolstered in her research by a creative "first glimpse" of the "Cordrays," an ancient England family who had settled in Berkshire County. This, she determined, would work as the childhood home of her possible heroine, now named Celia de Bohun.[27] Between trips and trysts with her admiring male friends, she worked "a little" to shape "Celia,"[28] then groaned that "it's slow" as she tried to "re-do the first chapter."[29] By the spring of 1969 she was exultant about a rare period of health and attractiveness. "I am *Free*," she said again, "to give and take beauty." That freedom did not carry over into her hopes for writing number ten. The "whole concept" was "still unclear," and Anya "doubted that I can pull it off."[30]

A year later, in April 1970, Anya was still fumbling with possibilities a bit, trying to straighten out her story line. She recorded that "I delve and delve," while realizing that "I've done so little in a year. Doubt if [even] a third. *Pressure*."[31] Now there was the additional pressure of having a signed contract, which spurred her to write sometimes for as many as eight hours a session. At these times she was so "happy working" that she could even say "men recede."[32] She was on her game again, seeming in most ways to be as sharp as ever, at least in her writing life. August brought inspiration for a different title. "That's *It*," she said of the words she chose, "Green Darkness."[33]

Anya delighted in finding a literary source that for her perfectly expressed her novel's theme. She had wanted to use a quotation of Poe, "Dark Fountain," for *Dragonwyck*, and one taken from Chaucer, "Goddess of Fame," for *Katherine*. This time she turned to words from a poem by Stephen Phillips, a little-known British poet popular in the 1890s. He was the author of an almost completely unknown poem called *Marpessa*, a very long blank verse narrative that contained the image of "green darkness."[34] Anya quoted the relevant section in her journal, and in her novel's final chapter, she has Lily Taylor, the mother of the modern-day Celia, quote the lines from memory. They somewhat illogically come to Lily as she thinks about all her daughter has been through, as Celia Marsdon of the sixteenth century.

All these complicated time frames were the results of Anya's decision to use reincarnation as a device to precede and close the story of the doomed Celia de Bohun of 1540. It is during the novel's time-leaping last chapter, when Celia

Marsdon has come back almost literally from the dead, that modern mother Lily turns to the lyrics written by a poet she calls "Somebody Phillips," whose lines she had "learned" in school:

> T'was the moment deep
> When we are conscious of the secret dawn
> Amid the darkness that we feel is green . . .
> Thy face remembered is from other worlds,
> It has been died for, though I know not when,
> It has been sung of, though I know not where. . . .

Lily goes on to say to her companion, "Awfully romantic . . . but then I was romantic at fourteen, and I felt—felt—well, that there is something *true* about it."[35] Anya might have called up the poem from memories of one of her literature classes at Spence, or she might have read some of Phillips's work with Hamilton Cottier, who specialized in the study of late nineteenth-century British poets. It is doubtful that Anya had ever made her way through the whole thing, a feat which only a very dedicated scholar would take on.

Anya now, in 1970, had an inspiring new title, and she was committed to starting her novel not with the sixteenth century but with 1968, the year of both her devastating divorce and her discovery of freedom. For this first section, set in the near-present, she created a decidedly odd cast of modern characters who would be matched, through reincarnation, with earlier selves. Part one of the narrative opens with a gathering of misfits at a house party hosted by the recently married Celia and Sir Richard Marsdon. As Richard says, "Nobody would fit this extraordinary house party."[36] The weekend inevitably proves to be a disaster, setting into motion Celia's total collapse and Richard's madness, with other houseguests scurrying away while an ambulance takes Celia to the hospital. By August 1970, Anya was able to settle her modern crew and tentatively move back to the sixteenth-century section of Celia's narrative. "Some of it," she judged with faint praise, was "not so bad."[37]

Off and on the work went forward, so that by the new year 1971 she was able to say that "Celia" is "my real job."[38] She had a new advisor from British publishers Hodder and Stoughton, editor Robin Denniston, to whom she was able to give the first nine chapters on January 23, 1971, her birthday. Anya's life was "very full," she said on March 21, but she forged ahead, even though the following months saw the serious illness of her son Seton.[39] That spring, after many tests, he was diagnosed with pancreatitis, and he stayed with her for tests and the first of many surgeries. Still, she did enough on "GD" to be able to report, on August 4, 1971, that Anne Barrett and Houghton's new editor in chief, Richard "Dick" McAdoo, were pleased with what she was able to show them. She had brought the material through chapter 13 to Boston, where she was staying near Seton and Susanne during his second operation at Massachusetts General Hospital.

As Anya's journal entries noted her progress, it was clear that she had found the kind of energy for writing that had eluded her for almost five years. Consistent work carried her through to the following year. By January 22, 1972, she had returned to her present-day characters and was "struggling with the denouement, how to kill Emma/Edna." This was the evil, demented villainess who as sixteenth-century Lady Emma Allen was responsible for the horrible fate that Anya envisioned for Celia de Bohun. Returned to the present as Edna, Celia's nemesis is a hostile houseguest tormented in reincarnation by what she had done at Ightham Mote long ago.[40] Not quite a month later, *Green Darkness*'s first draft was finished. "Some of it is good," Anya surmised, asserting rather strangely and with no further explanation that it was a "highly moral" book. Illicit love spurred on by witchcraft, a tragic suicide, a king and queen given to slaughtering thousands for their religious beliefs, would not seem to contain helpful moral lessons.[41] But for the modern characters, there is forgiveness and reconciliation.

Anya had been able to write for "five hours a day," some "700 manuscript pages," during the "final sprint." While she knew there would be revisions, the moment, she said, called for "Trumpets." As she looked back, she saw that the novel had taken four years, beginning with "mention of the 'walled-up girl'" in 1968. It had progressed slowly through "two not entirely successful research trips to England—lovers—so many—ill health—collapses."[42] Anya's sporadic creative effort during these stormy years resulted in a novel that was indeed full of tumult, some of it horrifically related to dim history and some of it a kind of parable of the inner darkness in which Anya had so often felt trapped.

The twists and turns of *Green Darkness* involved not only time travel but also the dizzying religious reversals that sixteenth-century subjects of the royal families of England suffered during the reigns of King Edward VI and Queen Mary. Edward VI was the Protestant heir of Henry the VIII, followed after his death at age fifteen by his half-sister, the Catholic Mary Queen of Scots. With characteristic diligence, Anya weaves her characters' fates into the historical events that upended so many of England's families during what became known as the Reformation, a time when many destinies were determined and destroyed according to which faith they were thought to profess. Anya Seton was at her best in re-creating such dramas.

Celia de Bohun, the mostly fictional center of the historical drama of *Green Darkness*, has been raised a Catholic. That upbringing doesn't prevent her from dangerous infatuation with her tutor Brother Stephen, an intensely devout Benedictine monk who wants nothing to do with her attentions. When they meet, she is a beautiful fourteen-year-old, a poor relation living with her aunt, Lady Ursula, at the Cordray manor of Sir Anthony Browne. Sir Anthony, a staunch Catholic, is at the novel's opening in 1552 trying to impress young Protestant King Edward. He has come to Cordray for the barely disguised purpose of checking out Sir Anthony's loyalty to the Crown. Celia takes in all the pomp and circumstance but is already interested only in how her beloved Stephen must be hidden away during the royal visit.

It will be seven years later, after near-rapes and marriage to a kind but impotent older man, that Celia manages to fulfill her obsessive aim of firing Stephen's lust. Over the same period, persecuted Catholics such as Sir Anthony become powerful English counselors after young Edward's death and then see themselves plunged again into fear and uncertainty after Catholic Queen Mary dies with no heir. The stage is set for the rise of Henry VIII's other daughter, young Protestant Elizabeth, who is allowed only a brief appearance in Anya's narrative. The politics of English royal history move forward as tortuously in *Green Darkness* as they had in *Katherine*. In the 1954 novel, however, almost all the characters had been garnered from historical records. In *Green Darkness*, while Anya found some of her characters documented through her source work, she had to match up the main actors from the sixteenth century with fictional, reincarnated descendants. Reincarnation provided a fascinating new method for attaching the past to the present, but it also required tangled plot threads and shaky constructions of cause and effect. Finishing up, Anya knew she might be in for some negative reactions in her own near future.

When Anya sent her completed draft off to Houghton Mifflin, she addressed a note to Paul Brooks, who had been her editor for decades, and Anne Barrett, who had joined her editorial team back when she was working on *Katherine*. "Here it is," Anya announced with her manuscript, going on to list all the portions that were "historically accurate," including "of course all the royal doings." She proclaimed, too, that "all of the places are as I have portrayed them," with the exception of Medfield Place, her composition of Sir Richard Marsdon's manor in 1968, which was "of necessity fictional." She stressed that "all the characters in 1968" were also "fictional." Anya argued strenuously for "the theme of reincarnation" in her novel, saying that "those who are limp on this central theme (which I imbibed with my mother's milk)," should take it as a perfectly acceptable "time gimmick." After all, she reasoned, the popular "Maurier," referring to competitor Daphne, had used time travel in a recent novel. Anya thought that her own "gimmick" had more "pith" than DuMaurier's.[43]

In spite of Anya's insistence, not everyone agreed that the reincarnation theme was going to work. Anya's note to her editors was dated February 15, 1972. A week later, in an internal memo, Anne Barrett wrote a lengthy critique to Paul Brooks. Anya's most stalwart fan within Houghton Mifflin, Anne was uncharacteristically negative in her reaction to *Green Darkness*. She began by noting that Anya's best novels were biographical, but that this one is "a romantic gothic novel," therefore not what her readers would expect. Anne had "tried to persuade" her author to "compress the 20th century part into a prologue and epilogue," but Anya "would have none of that; it had to be now, for reasons that I think were personal to her."[44]

Anne Barrett perhaps understood very well the most personal motive making Anya adamant about using reincarnation. When Anya stated that she had imbibed reincarnation "with my mother's milk," she was, for herself if no one else, invoking Grace Gallatin Seton's presence. In the novel, Grace is recast almost perfectly as the novel's past and present mother figures, reincarnated in Lily Taylor of 1968 and, from the sixteenth century, in Lady Ursula, Celia de Bohun's motherly aunt. Anya also worked into the novel the mysticism that had been Grace's abiding preoccupation since her hands-on explorations of world religions in the 1920s and '30s. Grace died in 1959, but for the rest of her life, Anya dreamed of her, prayed to her, and in *Green Darkness* reincarnated her.

Lily Taylor arrives in chapter 1 to visit her recently married daughter, now Lady Celia Marsden, at the Marsden manor of Medfield Place. Lily has brought with her "one of those exotic characters she was always finding." If there were no other clues, Lily's appearance with an exotic Hindu would be the tipoff that her character was based on Grace Seton. Grace had brought many such figures to Little Peequo, often for long stays. In the novel's reworking of this strain, modern Celia remembers that she had not liked many of her mother's "collection of swamis, numerologists, astrologers, and mediums," but tolerated her mother's "sudden enthusiasms" and "naivete" with good-humored "indulgence."[45] Physically too, Lily as described in the novel also resembles Grace in her later years. Lily is "past fifty and did not look it," slender, with "expert tinting" that "kept her hair blond."[46] In all her appearances in the novel, Lily also has Grace's air and personality. Lily too is always well-dressed and well-mannered, a capable manager of events and a gentle stoic.

Lily Taylor's fictional companion at Medfield Place, luckily for its modern owners, is "a Hindu" named Dr. Akananda who "practiced yoga," Celia notes, but was also "a doctor of medicine." Making him even more socially respectable, he had "studied at Oxford" and wore "well-tailored" English clothes.[47] Grace Seton had a long association with one of the most famous of Hindu gurus, Paramahansa Yogananda (his spiritual name), who brought his yoga practices to the United States in 1920. Grace visited him at his California Centers for Self-Realization in Los Angeles and Encinitas, and from the 1930s through the mid-1940s, she assisted him in the work that brought his practice a large, eager following. Grace was especially helpful in editing many of the center's newsletters.

Yogananda was not a medical doctor, but he was handsome, youthful, dark haired and dark-skinned, an athletic man with kindly eyes, just like Anya's Dr. Akananda. Yogananda died in 1952, at the age of fifty-nine, of heart failure. Anya transferred these details too, into her Dr. Akananda, who is "about 60," the novel tells us, and who realizes at the close of Green Darkness that his heart is failing, primarily due to his exertions on behalf of the Marsdens. By channeling the sixteenth-century Italian medical doctor and astrologer Julian Ridolfi, Akananda in Anya's plot is able to save Richard and Celia from death and madness by experiencing, with them, their lives as Celia de Bohun and Brother Stephen Marsdon. At the end, it is suggested that this effort might cost him his own present life.

Anya indicated in the preface to Green Darkness that Celia de Bohun and Brother Stephen were "harder to document" than the other historically-based sixteenth-century characters, but "they existed," as did Dr. Ridolfi.[48] Celia de Bohun, whose spellbinding beauty captivates virtually every man who sees her, bears some similarities to the self-centered, naive heroines of Anya's earlier novels, especially Miranda from *Dragonwyck* and Santa Fe Cameron from *The Turquoise*. This Celia differs, however, in that her passion for Stephen is her sole motivation throughout *Green Darkness*. With so little depth of character, she remains one-dimensional. Brother Stephen is capable of only two emotions, intense devotion to his religious vocation and equally intense guilt for his inability to withstand Celia's seduction. Anya throws in some flimsy dark magic to explain Stephen's helplessness when he succumbs to Celia, inventing a water witch whom Celia consults supposedly to help her husband John Hutchinson's impotence. The device partially excuses Stephen, but makes Celia even less a sympathetic character.

When Celia seeks out the strange water witch, the grotesquely deformed woman also gives Celia some "hemp" to chew. Anya might have been having some private fun with this, while also courting a younger generation of readers, when she describes the effect of this stimulus. Celia finds herself feeling that everything around her "glowed and pulsated" beautifully, while she smelled "a sweet, musky smell, sweeter than any rose."[49] Anya too sometimes enjoyed pot, as she called it, mostly indulging with younger friends. Slyly, she concludes the water witch scene by stating that Celia, briefly soothed by the hemp, did not use the "love potion" for its intended purpose with her husband. Thus it is easy to foresee that the powder is going to be saved for Brother Stephen. She receives no more hemp to enjoy.

During the entire time that Anya was working on this last adult novel, she wrote obsessively in her journal about the sexual tension she felt as she was treated by David Morley. The fantasy of illicit love in *Green Darkness* becomes a tragedy ending in shame, punishment, and death for its doomed lovers. Anya did not approach illicit love with Morley, who she knew opposed it. Still, she did draw clinically on their frequent hypnosis sessions as she created the scenes in which Dr. Akananda hypnotizes Celia Marsdon to help her go back to her earlier identity and later to return redeemed. Anya would find her own experience of both hypnosis and temptation useful again when she developed the problematic relationship between a high school student and her teacher in her last published work, the 1975 young adult novel, *Smouldering Fires*. In the preface to *Green Darkness*, Anya acknowledged "several kindly physicians" who helped her with the novel's "medical aspects," adding that "to one physician in particular I owe very special gratitude."[50] It perturbed her when Morley admitted that he did not read the novel in which she made this anonymous allusion.

The usually savvy Anne Barrett did not think that *Green Darkness* would attract a new kind of audience. She believed that Anya's readers traditionally "did not include members of the counter-culture," nor would this work bring them in. "Yoga and mysticism in general are fashionable now," she acknowledged, but Anya's readers, as well as reviewers, would be "looking for another *Katherine*" and were going to be "turned off by the opening chapter." Anya was "so good in describing the mores of another age," she argued, "but out of tune with those of today." Anne also revealed in her memo that she had preferred the title "The Marsdon Chronicle" to "Green Darkness," but that she "couldn't budge" Anya on that matter either. She wondered "how much revision" they would be able to get from Anya, reasoning that "if we ask too much, we will only succeed in upsetting" her. She was also irritated that the British publishers, "notoriously uninterested in revisions," wanted to move quickly ahead.[51] Anya did work hard on revisions for the next three months, but what she fought to include stayed in, which had not always been the case in her frays with her publishers.

By 1972 Paul Brooks, still helping out with Anya, was no longer editor in chief of Houghton Mifflin, a post he had held for twenty-five years. He had resigned his editorial position in 1969 but was available to assist with some of his best clients. His growing passion was his own environmental writings, influenced by his close work at Houghton Mifflin with Rachel Carson. His help with her on *Silent Spring* (1962) was one of the reasons that he received the John Burroughs Medal in 1967, as ETS had some forty years before. Anne Barrett's memo shows that Brooks was still involved with Anya, but it seems clear that Robin Denniston, from Hodder and Stoughton in London, had some increased influence. Anne mentions him, but not with pleasure, in her memo when she tells Paul, "I am happy to see that [Anya] has not followed Robin Dennison's [*sic*] admonition to sex up the scene where Celia seduces Stephen."[52]

In spite of the many reviewers who agreed with Anne Barrett, *Green Darkness* eventually hit number three on the bestseller lists and stayed there "for weeks," as Anya said, clearly attracting new readers who sent "lovely fan mail."[53] Although her audience might not be countercultural, *Green Darkness*'s sales records indicated that her readers did not disapprove of reincarnation or other unearthly dimensions, and they might have recognized nonchalantly the effects of "hemp." The two books that *Green Darkness* could not budge from their higher slots on the charts also indicate why Anne Barrett was wrong about what people wanted to read in the 1970s.

Number one was Richard Bach's *Jonathan Livingston Seagull*, an allegorical fable about a bird who wants to do more than just fly around mundanely searching out his next meal. Number two was a novel that could not have been more different from Bach's or Anya Seton's, *The Odessa File* by Frederick Forsyth. A spy thriller set in World War II, it was full of violence, moving ahead from the horrific realities of the Holocaust into a narrative of revenge and international intrigue. It was dosed up, according to a *New York Times* reviewer, with "quick thrills" and "flimsy melodrama."[54] A new generation of readers at this time had been through a decade of enormous political and social changes, a president's assassination, the church-bombing murders of little girls in Birmingham, and the carnage of the Vietnam War. An over-the-top, made-for-a movie-script spy thriller or an avian fantasy could both be welcome distractions. Whether critics liked the top three on the 1973 bestseller lists or not, readers were happy to pay for a transcendental seagull, a thriller with flimsy melodrama, and Anya Seton's idea of a cosmos within which the justice or injustices of one's present life could be explained by reincarnation.

Anya's happiness over the fate of *Green Darkness* was a feeling that she had not been able to indulge for many years. "Whatever happens at least I've *done* it," she exclaimed. New editor Robin Denniston "sent the most beautiful jacket [wrapped] for G. D.," she gloated. The good results called for some alcoholic toasts. "Am drinking vermouth now. I am thankful," she admitted.[55] By April she had vacationed in Bermuda, which as usual brought her back to Greenwich for another hospital stay. On the mend once more, she reported on April 17, 1972, that she received a "jubilant cable" from her British publishers Hodder and Stoughton and a "lovely letter from Dick McAdoo." They were celebrating that *Green Darkness* had won another turn from the Literary Guild and an offer from *Reader's Digest* to serialize. English publication would now take place in October 1973. "You've done it again in spades," Dick McAdoo told her, and she responded in her journal, "I hardly know how."[56] Anne Barrett, back in cheerleading mode, acquiesced with congratulations. "But you've written a good book, Baby," she replied when Anya attributed all the "plums" to "luck."[57]

On June 29, 1972, Anya announced that *Green Darkness* was going to earn her even more "dough" through paperback rights secured from Fawcett Publishers.[58] Now there was little for her to do but wait for galleys to come in for correcting. Much of her time was filled with concern for Seton, still danger-ously ill. In July he was having shock treatments to treat the deep depression and heavy drinking that contributed to worsening pancreatitis and diabetes. Chan joined her at Greenwich Hospital to visit Seton, and she wrote that four years after their divorce, "the long rapport of that marriage [was not] gone."[59] Chan continued to handle Anya's investments although he sometimes tried to lower the amount he had to pay her in alimony. Generally, they were able to remain cordial.

There was still the "Do" for *Green Darkness*'s American debut ahead, scheduled for December 11 and 12, and Anya managed to survive only "with great strain and too much booze."[60] Most of the reviews that began coming in were predictably "horrid," she reported. The assessment in *Saturday Review*, written by Joseph Karon, "couples me contemptuously," she reported, "with DuMaurier," whose novel *Rule Britannia* had come out about the same time: "we both stink."[61] *Green Darkness*'s official opening sales day, celebrated on January 23, 1973, provided gratifying fanfare and "quite a birthday for the book and me," Anya noted as she reached the age of sixty-nine.[62] The novel had already brought in $78,000 in prepublication sales, still "Fools Gold" to Anya.[63]

The joy that Anya felt over the success of *Green Darkness* was not sustained for long. As so often had been the case, these signs of her stature as a writer failed to save her from herself. The three journals covering her life from 1965 to 1973 became an increasingly sad, cyclic melodrama. Close to the end of the ninth journal, in her entry for June 2, 1973, she wrote that her drinking and illnesses constituted "a long dreary pattern," and that "I'm in a deadlock where I don't want to do *anything*." On the last page of this journal book, she wrote, "Last entry in this book, not yet the last of my life, but one sure prays for a speedy demise."[64] She was not optimistic about what there might be left for her to do as a writer or to experience as a free woman who had enough time and money to craft more good years. While one more successful novel was in her future, there also loomed what she most feared, a slow descent into the darkness of declining health. Journal ten might very well have told some of this story, but that volume disappeared some time before her death.

15 | THE SOURCE AND SHE WERE ONE

ON THE FIRST PAGE of what turned out to be the last of Anya's available journals, she wrote that she began the day in a "sun-rise glow of well-being." This was the ninth of the leather-bound books which, all counted, as she said, "cover nearly 40 years," and she felt "without morbidity that this may well be the last." She was writing early in the morning, as was customary, "in my green study," eating a breakfast that included "coffee, Triscuits with poppy and sesame seeds, broiled grapefruit and honey" while she read excerpts on writing by "Maupassant, Tolstoy, and Flaubert—springboard stuff," she explained. Housekeeper Janina, "God bless her," had just arrived, and Anya described a new tenant who had just moved into Grace's cottage, a "cultured English lady in her late 50s" named Wynne Enderby, whom Anya envied because she had all her "real teeth." On this peaceful morning almost a full year after her divorce, Anya rejoiced that "God opened unexpected doors as one great portal clanged shut."[1]

Four years later, on her journal's last page, one of the last sentences read, "America is in the throes of Watergate." The contents of the book covered April 28, 1969, to June 8, 1973, with the final blank page reserved, as it had always been, for a summing up of the important events of the years recorded. Watergate was the only political story that Anya listed here. For most of her life she had been a good Republican, but she had also always been a pacifist, like her father, so she abhorred President Richard Nixon's escalation of the Vietnam War. Not many of her entries for this period detailed "world and national events," she noted, "because I now view them all with cynicism. They are so phony and change so fast."

She used the book's last page to record personal triumphs and defeats. The best news was the publication of her tenth major book, *Green Darkness*, which had become the most financially successfully of them all. She also named the men who had entered her life, bemoaned her high tax bracket, and mentioned the dire possibility of gas rationing. She did not philosophize about how she had remade her life, moving from scorned wife to pursued and liberated woman, but she did mention a new health problem, diabetes, and one of the best birthday gifts she had ever received, a "darling" cat named Cherie, the first house pet she had owned since her children had enjoyed them at Little Peequo.

Like many people her age, Anya had also lost many people she cared about to death or life events during the last few years. Janina, the most faithful of housekeepers, had moved to Florida, as had Beth Raymond, who had augmented her service staff, as well as Grace's, for almost twenty years. Hanna Engstrom, Anya's lifelong second mother, had died in February 1968. Anya was traveling at the time, but she arranged for Hanna's ashes to be buried within the Seton plot at Putnam Cemetery, Greenwich, where those of Grace and Clemenzie Gallatin Duffy had been placed. Another death was that of handsome naval officer Gallatin Powers, the cousin who had come so often to the Chases' Manhattan apartment during his World War II shore leaves. He had died in California, where he had owned a famous restaurant that bore the Gallatin name, but there was solace for Anya in the current presence of Gallatin's daughter, Sandra Powers, who had moved to New York to pursue an acting career.

The most tragic death of this period had been that of Tim Kitchel, the other spouse left behind with Chan and Hylah's affair and departure. His kindness had greatly comforted Anya in the aftermath of that trauma; they often went to dinner and even to church together. Tim was remarried by 1970, and his second wife, Tish, also became a friend. Anya wrote on December 21, 1972, however, that all the Old Greenwich community was "rocked" on November 30, 1972, when Tim died very suddenly. The cause of death was not made public, but it was a terrible shock to all, "so painful," Anya concluded, that she could write nothing else about it.[2] Her most sympathetic doctor, Gray Carter, had also died, replaced by several other medical consultants, most importantly David Morley.

Closest to home, Seton remained in precarious health and was treated by many of Anya's own doctors while staying at Sea Rune. One of them told her,

"Anya, he has some emotional problems, but he has enormous physical ones," which proved to be only too true.[3] The rest of Anya's family were healthy and close by. Six grandchildren between the ages of ten and fifteen came and went, providing her with glimpses of a startlingly new world.

Also important to Anya were younger adult friends who loved to hang out with the open-minded, funny, and welcoming hostess at Sea Rune. Among these were cousin Sandra Powers, Gallatin's daughter, and her husband, Gabe Grayson, who came out from New York frequently. For a while the couple rented Lotilot, as did a series of younger men who often paid part of their rent by escorting Anya to events, chauffeuring, or doing house repairs. Anya's nephew, Phil Chase, the son of Chan's brother Charles, became with his wife, Gail, perhaps her closest new friends. Phil was completing his MD at Harvard, where he was close enough to visit Anya frequently. He and Gail were the pair who, for a birthday present in 1971, brought Anya her cherished cat, Cherie. Anya worried over Cherie's health and moods as much as she did her own, adoring her extravagantly for many years.

Anya's professional associations were inevitably changing. Paul Brooks and Lovell Thompson, two major Houghton Mifflin champions of her career, retired by 1973. On July 3, 1973, Lee Barker, her first editor at Houghton Mifflin, died suddenly of a heart attack, just a few weeks after Anya wrote her last dated entry for journal number nine. He, like Anya, was born in January 1904, and he had remained in her corner since the time in 1938 when he came out to Little Peequo to talk about Theodosia Burr.

In 1986, Paul Brooks published a memoir about his years at Houghton Mifflin, entitled *Two Park Street: A Publishing Memoir*. It was a humorous and anecdotal account of his many years at Houghton Mifflin, from his start there in 1931 through his resignation as editor in chief in 1969. His memoir saves most of its space for the company's most prestigious authors during his tenure, including Winston Churchill, J. R. R. Tolkien, and the two environmental writers who gave Brooks special pride. One was Tory Peterson, whose Peterson Field Guide Series provided readers with extensive, accessible scientific information, primarily on the international range of different kinds of birds. Peterson was a devoted admirer of Ernest Thompson Seton, whom he named as the one who inspired him to create the popular nature handbooks that became enormously popular. Rachel Carson's *Silent Spring* also merited its own chapter in *Two Park Street*. Brooks noted that his retirement from

Houghton Mifflin in 1969, five years before it would have been mandatory, was due primarily to a request from Carson's literary executor, after her death, asking Brooks to write her biography.

Among the writers who received more than just name-dropping in Brooks's memoir is Anya Seton, something of an honor, given "the scores of novelists" he could choose to include.[4] Brooks noted in his three paragraphs about her that Anya had "certain qualities of the prima donna, fortunately tempered by a warm personality and a sense of humor." He regretted that her "early romantic novels" ended up in her being "typed by some reviewers as a popular writer not to be taken seriously." *Katherine* and *The Winthrop Woman*, he argued, deserved to be considered major historical fiction. He admired the way that "before putting pen to paper," Anya always "plumbed the archives and quite literally covered the ground where the action takes place."[5] He considered his own contributions to her success minor, consisting mainly of "lending an appreciative, if sometimes critical, ear."[6] Brooks didn't say, although he was bound to have known, that Anya thought of him as an essential, valuable friend as well as mentor. She often called him "Boss" in her letters, while in her journals, she wished that he would be more critical than he was.

Paul Brooks was out of Anya's editorial picture by the time *Green Darkness* was ready for its very successful publication in 1972, but Anne Barrett remained to try to keep one of her most profitable HM authors, as well as her good friend, going. As early as September 1972, she suggested a new project for Anya to consider, hoping to help her to stave off the depression that usually attacked after Anya finished a big project. Anne's suggestion was "an Acadian theme," Anya wrote, and it gave her "a flicker, but no green light."[7] Once all the publicity and spectacular sales news for *Green Darkness* began to subside early the next year, Anya agreed by February 2, 1973, that she needed a new project and asked herself if it could be "the Acadians?" Two weeks later, she was reporting, "I'm agonizing over *some* new idea—Evangeline."[8] A week after that she began to make a plan. The "Acadian book, very feeble," had "quivered" more strongly, so she purchased train tickets to leave with companion Muriel Hynes for New Orleans on March 28.[9]

The pair traveled on the southbound Royal New Orleans as far as Lafayette, Louisiana, stopping there for an "impossible effort" to find "Evangeline's grave." Then they flew on to New Orleans, where the visit, like so many others earlier and later, turned into "a Debacle" involving what Anya called three

"V's," Vodka, Vermouth, and a Virus." She and Muriel were back home by April 1, and Anya was in the hospital by 3:30 PM that day. All she had to say about the brief trip was that it was "blotto."[10] In a letter to her brother and sister, dated July 16, 1973, Pam shared her conversations with Anya's family physician, Jim Wood, which indicates Anya's worrisome condition at the time. She was again in Greenwich Hospital, where he was trying to cut back on the number of drugs, including valium, that she was taking and "to put Mother on antabuse, thus preventing her from turning to alcohol when she feels the need of something." This meant that she would have to be told that "she does have a real alcohol problem."[11] There are no journal entries to indicate if or when she was given this self-evident diagnosis, but Anya did write several lengthy typed notes, of which she saved copies, to several physicians after this time that indicate she had continued using her glass crutch of liquor as well as various pills.

On the last dated page of journal nine, Anya again mentioned the flicker she still felt concerning the Acadian project. Summarizing her state of mind on June 8, 1973, she wrote, "I get through quite a lot social, and agonize over a new subject. Longfellow reading right now. But I'm blocked."[12] Those were the final extant words that she recorded for journal purposes concerning what two years later became her last published book, the young adult novel entitled *Smouldering Fires*. It was published not by Houghton Mifflin but by Doubleday and thus appeared not as a major novel but as young adult fiction. This category was more a specialization of Doubleday than Houghton Mifflin, and it was Doubleday who had published *The Mistletoe and Sword* in 1955. In her discussions with her editor during late summer of 1973, Anya sounded clearheaded as well as enthusiastic about her project's possibilities.

Anya sent plans for her Acadia book to Janet Chenery, the children's book editor for Doubleday, in a letter dated August 1, 1973. Chenery was also a writer of many popular books for younger children, so she knew the business well and seems to have been already acquainted with Anya. At least Anya's outline hints that there had been some previous correspondence concerning the Acadian-themed book. It is possible that Anne Barrett had facilitated the switch to Doubleday, believing that what Anya had in mind would be better suited for the young adult market. For this effort, Anya wanted to use time travel again, as she had in *Green Darkness*, and she had settled on a present-day girl of high school age to be her protagonist. In the plan presented to

Janet, she started by saying that "I don't want to use reincarnation again per se, and at present I feel the best gimmick would be hypnotism and dreams."[13] She ended up using all three devices.

As she pitched her plot, Anya said, "Suppose we open in the Greenwich (or imaginary) high school," adding that she had checked "innumerable facts there" as to "when and how they teach American Literature now." The plot that she went on to describe contained much of what the book eventually covered, with a few essential modifications:

> My heroine is 15, chunky, be-spectacled, not very attractive. Her name is actually Ange-Marie Delatour, but known as Amy—her mother's contraction of the "Canuck" name given by grand-pere. Amy is lonely, has no boy-friends, but a tremendous I.Q. Her teacher is a young man of 25, Martin, who has scarcely noticed Amy in class, until she hands in an extraordinary paper on Longfellow and his works. It's so good that Martin calls her into his office after school and asks, "How come?" She says simply, "I love Longfellow."[14]

Continuing her first thoughts of a plot line, Anya says that Amy will proceed to tell Martin every relevant detail of Longfellow's life.

Smouldering Fires developed from this beginning. As the finished novel shows, Amy has sources of information about Evangeline beyond Longfellow's because she has learned the history of the period of the Acadian removal from Nova Scotia through her French-Canadian grandfather. After the Grand Dérangement began in 1755, when the British drove the Acadians away from Nova Scotia, Grandpere's (or Pierre's) branch of the Delatour family were sent, like so many Acadians, to Louisiana. His family had returned to a French haven in western Quebec before he was born. Pierre and his son Louis, skilled cabinet-makers, immigrated from Quebec to Greenwich, where coincidentally, some of the earlier Acadians had been "delivered" by the British in the late 1750s.

Anya's early outline clearly sets up Amy's present-day situation in modern Greenwich. Louis Delatour, Grandpere's son, marries a "Yankee girl" named Sarah Mead. Offstage, father Louis dies in an automobile accident when daughter Amy is eight years old. At the novel's beginning, Amy, with "glum and dour" mother Sarah and elderly Grandpere Pierre, lives in a squalid apartment, where her only joy at home is listening to Grandpere's memories. He kindles her imagination most with his impassioned history of the old days in French-settled Canada.[15]

Anya did not go further than this rough beginning in her 1973 letter to Janet Chenery. Undecided about what to do next, Anya did tell Chenery that she might decide just to write a straight biography of Longfellow. Eventually, as had happened before, she found that her gifts would work best if she used fictional Amy as her vehicle into history. In this mode, Anya went on in her work between 1973 and 1975 to develop the relationship between Amy and Martin based on the potentially healing power of hypnosis, which Dr. Akananda had employed with Celia in *Green Darkness*. Anya's outline showed that she assumed there could conceivably be a romance between the high school student and her teacher, forbidden love perhaps similar to that between Celia and Brother Stephen. As she told Chenery in her outline, she saw a "burgeoning love between Martin and Amy."[16] This scandalous complication was later jettisoned from the narrative. At some point, Anya added a love interest for Martin in the form of a former Louisiana girlfriend, and a boyfriend for once "dumpy" Amy in the form of a popular fellow high school student named Mac Wilton.

Anya's pitch to Janet Chenery ended with her insistence that she was "particularly interested in the French minority ethnic group, in America and Canada." For Anya, this was a significant political point since it provided "another instance of individuality fighting submersion in the all too constrictive melting pot."[17] Here Anya, on a moral crusade, sounded very much like Ernest Thompson Seton, who fought throughout the 1930s for Native Americans' right to preserve their languages, customs, and ways of life in a "constrictive melting pot." She had championed that cause in *Foxfire*, but in *Smouldering Fires* she followed through only sketchily with this mission.

Anya's penultimate assessment of how she came to write *Smouldering Fires* appears in the novel's preface, where she only indirectly mentions the modern Cajun cause, saying that she hoped her readers would become interested in "a largely overlooked minority group. . . . But above all," she added, she wanted to present "a convincing, entertaining story."[18] In a typescript draft of this preface, Anya added a paragraph in her own hand. Here she argued that *Smouldering Fires* "is a book on 2 levels, the present and the past, linked not necessarily by reincarnation as it was in G.D. One may instead think of 'genetic memory.'"[19] In *Smouldering Fires*, Amy's return to the earlier, fictional Ange-Marie is connected to Grandpere's direct ancestor, one of many Acadians over the generations named Delatour. Genetic memory provided a slightly different concept from *Green Darkness* for her character's re-experience of a past life. This time, the time transfer takes place through its linkage to "blood" ancestry.

In *Smouldering Fires*, eighteenth-century Ange-Marie, like Longfellow's Evangeline, is separated from her fiancé as the Acadians are loaded onto ships bound for different locations in the American colonies. Paul Delatour, her husband-to-be, is sent to Louisiana while Ange-Marie is bound over to Greenwich and indentured as a servant to the Mead-Bush family. This prominent family happens to live in a house constructed in 1730, in a section of colonial Greenwich known as Cos Cob. By Anya's present time, also Amy's, the Mead-Bush homestead was a house museum. In *Smouldering Fires*, when visiting the house for her own research, Amy feels the presence of Ange-Marie and the black slaves also quartered there in the old time. It turns out that Ange-Marie was a servant at the Bush home, and her fiancé Paul Delatour was able to find her there. The two marry and begin a good life in Greenwich. With her inclusion of what became Greenwich's house museum, Anya could draw on her familiarity with the old inn that her father had frequented with Cos Cob artist friends, also the place where she still served on the board of directors.

For her young adult novel, Anya wanted touches of Gothic horror that would excite modern teenaged readers for whom Longfellow's *Evangeline* would be very dull stuff. Thus Ange-Marie's fate is as chilling as Celia de Bohun's in *Green Darkness*. A few years after their marriage in Greenwich, Paul decides to go back to Louisiana with their young son to prepare a place where the family can "live free." Before he is able to call for Ange-Marie to join him, she is murdered by marauding Tories known historically as Cowboys in the Greenwich area during America's Revolutionary War. Amy, hypnotized by Martin, recites how she, as Ange-Marie, had been tied up by the marauders and burned to death in the small cabin Paul built for her. Amy's terrible phobia about fire and the blisters that sometimes mysteriously appeared on her hands and face reflect what she endured in her earlier life.

Beyond the 1973 letter to Janet Chenery, the comments of Anya's preface to *Smouldering Fires*, and the handwritten note written sometime after the book's publication, only one other available record exists to reveal how the process of writing *Smouldering Fires* played out. This was Chenery's response, dated November 21, 1974, to a complete draft that Anya had recently turned in.[20]

Chenery's comments provide an instructive demonstration of how editors dealt, at least in her era, with matters such as "current usage." Janet objected to the word "jock," which had too "derogatory a connotation," and thought "big man on campus" somewhat "stiff," but it was the expression Anya nevertheless chose to replace "jock." Chenery also pointed out that some of Anya's discussions of sex in the novel, especially scenes between Amy and her boyfriend, would not go over well. Chenery acknowledged that "even most nine-year-olds" of the 1970s knew a great deal about such things as "sex, the pill, and pre- or extra-marital sexual activities" but that the adults who "purchase books for children still find such realism unacceptable."[21] Certain obscene words that Anya included in her teenagers' vocabulary, Chenery added, would also be objectionable. Those words disappeared, replaced in the novel by such cringe-worthy expletives as "Gosh" and "Jeepers."

After listing Doubleday's "suggestions," Chenery assured Anya that they "are only that." Anya was free to accept them or not. "It is *your* book (and a marvelous one!)," Chenery enthusiastically told her, "and we want you to be entirely happy with it." Doubleday would be able to get the book out "on schedule," she concluded, and so it was, in 1975.[22] There is no way to know whether Anya censored herself or followed someone else's protest when she decided that Martin's interest in Amy would be motivated only by professional curiosity and a "crusading" concern for a very bright but deeply troubled girl. Most important, she builds in his necessary interest both in "para-psychology" and the possibilities of using hypnosis to cure emotional or mental problems. In Anya's switch from her early idea of a romance between teacher and student, she throws in for Martin a former Louisiana girlfriend named Claire who just happens to have a PhD in psychology and is teaching troubled youth nearby in New York City. Clunky coincidences that younger readers would not mind save the day for Anya's plot.

Martin and Claire begin untangling Amy's deeply disturbed psyche and with amazing speed lead her to the discovery that she has been reincarnated from the young Acadian Ange-Marie. Under hypnosis, Amy reincarnates the tragic Ange-Marie, relives her awful death, and is almost immediately cured of her nightmares, fire phobia, hallucinations, and blisters. Through Martin and Claire's ministrations, Amy's "chunky" unattractiveness also starts to be transformed, even before she re-experiences her earlier identity. Her relation-ship with romantic love interest Mac Wilton proceeds to the point that when they are alone in his house, Mac "tore open" her dress—not, it should be noted, a bodice. Amy admits to Claire in a tear-filled confession that she "wanted more."[23] However, she is also filled with shame, especially when Mac ignores her at school the next day.

When Martin hears the news of Amy's bad date night from Claire, he says automatically that "it seems that Amy asked for it," a comment that Claire does not correct. She is only relieved that he will at least ask Mac what happened. Martin's brusque judgment might have been jarring to readers of the 1970s, but the whole affair takes Anya only a few paragraphs to resolve. Whatever Anya's intentions in Smouldering Fires, rapes or near rapes take place in all of her works, a carryover from the historical romance category that she often said she disdained.

The antidote to the tragedy of eighteenth-century Paul Delatour and his Ange-Marie is handled in a maudlin, happily-ever-after Cinderella ending that includes a wedding between Martin and Claire. The setting that Anya provides is full of stereotypical plantation trappings such as hanging moss and the remains of old slave quarters. This is the ancestral Louisiana home Bellerive, still owned by Martin's mother, who holds forth as a belle dame of the Old South sort. Amy and her grandfather have been invited along for the Christmas nuptials so that Amy can be Claire's bridesmaid. In her spare time there, Amy manages to find Grandpere's and her own long lost Delatour relatives. During his joyful reunion with them, Grandpere dies happily and is buried on Christmas Eve among "his people." The wedding takes place as scheduled, supervised by Martin's widowed mother, Azile, a Creole grande dame dismissive of her "nigra" help and lower class Cajuns but otherwise a delightful lady with a heart of gold. In addition to new maturity which she will take back to Greenwich, Amy gains "a dimpled smile that transfigures her." "Jeepers" is all that Martin can say.[24]

In her last journal book, which was never found after her death, Anya might very well have expressed her thoughts about the novel as she was writing it. Some of its shortcomings were perhaps due to her publishers' general disinterest in making improvements. Then too, at age seventy-one and after many health crises, Anya was understandably losing energy as well as acumen. She too wanted some of the fairy tale resolutions that young adult readers enjoyed. Smouldering Fires' original book jacket announced Anya as "author of Green Darkness and The Winthrop Woman." Doubleday naturally counted on Green Darkness's popularity to attract an audience for their light version, and Anya delivered all that was expected. In the handwritten note that she appended to the typescript draft of her preface, she included the sales triumph of the novel. *Smouldering Fires*, she wrote, "has succeeded in selling far more than Doubleday expected (or I did)."[25] That was fairy tale enough for the time being.

Anya's completion of two popular novels by 1975 temporarily gave her the healing anodyne that her writing life always provided. Her life was also enriched by her grandchildren, who found Sea Rune a place to enjoy, just as her own children had loved the Inlet, their summer vacation home of the late 1940s. By the mid-1970s Anya's daughters, Pam Forcey and Zizi Coggins, had become successful career women, not quite as unusual as it had been in the time when Anya presumably could have achieved happiness as a Greenwich housewife and mother. The decade ended, however, with two tragedies that stunned all the Seton family.

Chase Frederick Coggins, Anya and Chan's cherished first grandchild, often mentioned so glowingly as "Chederick" and "the Coglet," was an especially promising twenty-year-old student at Yale University by 1978. He was spending a weekend at his parents' home in Newton, Massachusetts, when a tragic accident ended his life. On February 13, 1978, he had been cross-country skiing on isolated train tracks after a snowstorm near the family's home. He was struck and killed instantly by a passenger train at a time when it was thought that no trains would be running. His death of course left his family shattered.

In the next year came a second terrible blow for the Setons. Anya's son Seton Cottier died on July 1, 1979, never having recovered from the debilitating physical and emotional problems that had tormented him for many years. The cause of his death was never clearly determined. For some years he had been a very successful IBM employee, and he was also a fine artist. He left behind wife Susanne and son Busey in addition to his mother and sisters. Anya's frustrations with him as boy and young man had greatly changed during the years of his illnesses, when she could offer the kind of nursing motherliness that came more naturally to her. Hamilton Cottier died in September 1979, only two months after Seton, but Anya had felt that Ham was too ill to be informed of his son's death. Through the years Anya had retained her affection for her first husband, never speaking critically of him in her journals. In 1979, she was bound to be reeling from the combined blows.

As for writing, Anya continued, after *Smouldering Fires*, to follow up on a few "quivers," including drafts of a novel that was to take place in the city of Castine, Maine, during its turbulent history as both a French and English harbor in the seventeenth century. Yet no steady green light kept her going. She dated, played bridge obsessively, attended or hosted meetings of the Mystery Club, and wrote a series of eight humorous articles, entitled "Greenwich: A Personal Memoir," for the *Village Gazette* of Old Greenwich. They generally concerned her growing up years in three Greenwich houses that were still standing in 1980. About Little Peequo she revealed that, as Ernest was building the house during the Prohibition Era, he included a secret room in the basement that was "loaded with grenadine and a few bottles of gin."[26]

Throughout the 1970s, Anya often carried on her role as prima donna of the board in charge of historic Bush-Holley House, the setting that she re-envisioned through Amy's eyes in *Smouldering Fires*. The home had been built as a private residence for the colonial Bush family, which much later included two United States presidents. Anya became most active at Bush-Holley when she aided in its 1957 purchase and restoration by the Historical Society of the Town of Greenwich (later renamed the Greenwich Historical Society). A life-long board member of the society, she often entertained friends there and was hinted to have presided no matter who else was in charge. She also gave tours of Tod's Point, later called Greenwich Point, a nature preserve on a peninsula that stretched out into Long Island Sound at the east end of Old Greenwich. Part of the area encompassed ruins of an estate built there by railroad magnate John Kennedy Tod in the 1880s, but for Anya it was always Elizabeth's Neck, the cherished spot where Bess, her Winthrop Woman, with one impulsive purchase became the founding mother of Greenwich.

On January 3, 1980, Austin Olney, a friend and by this time the executive editor at Houghton Mifflin, sent Anya a royalty check for $25,000 along with a cordial note. In it he said, "The '70s haven't been the greatest decade, have they? But the '80s have to be an improvement." A last line encouraged her to keep writing, as he expressed the hope "that your health is holding up and that Baron Castine is in your thoughts."[27]

On February 7, 1981, however, the event that Anya had most feared for so long occurred when she suffered a massive stroke. For almost ten more years, she was homebound, needing a wheelchair and the assistance of skilled nurses, her housekeeper Nancy Perry, and a secretary, Audrey Kahout, who had joined her staff in 1973. Friends still came for bridge and grandchildren for visits. Granddaughter Blythe Forcey stayed with her for a week in 1989 while writing a dissertation on Harriet Beecher Stowe that she was completing for a doctorate in American literature at the University of Colorado. Her grandmother, Blythe later commented, was enthusiastic and helpful as they talked about the dissertation, still able to share her own love of "delving."[28]

Anya died at Sea Rune on November 8, 1990, three and a half years after Hamilton "Chan" Chase's death on May 20, 1987. A celebration of her life was held at Bush-Holley House on December 8, 1990, at which several close friends reminisced or read poems in her honor. On December 11, 1990, a traditional memorial service took place at Saint Saviour Episcopal Church in Greenwich, the church she most often attended. Her ashes were interred in 1992 in the family plot in Putnam Cemetery. Pam and Zizi chose a dark pink marble granite Celtic cross monument for her, which faces her mother's cross, of lighter granite but, importantly, the same height. Near them are plaques or stones, flush with the ground, marking the burial places of ashes of Anya's grandmother and Grace's mother, Clemenzie Gallatin Rhodes (with first name misspelled Clemenza), Anya's son Seton, and Hanna (Johanna) Engstrom.

One of the best documented events of Anya's last active decade had taken place on December 18, 1975, when she spoke to an audience of about one hundred at the Greenwich library. A photograph accompanying a news article that appeared in the *Greenwich Time* on December 22, 1975, featured an attractive Anya seated at a table loaded with copies of *Smouldering Fires*, surrounded by a group of admiring fans. Anya's research for the story of Greenwich high schooler Amy was included in the long piece, along with the news that the book was already in its third printing. Anya announced too that an option on the book had been purchased by ABC television. They were proposing a screenplay treatment that was now, she said, somehow stalled. With a "twinkle" in her eye she quizzed her audience on their knowledge of "my town" and waded with good humor into a controversy over what the city was going to do with the old Greenwich High School campus. She tactfully gave the library a plug by saying that although she had "amassed 2,000 research books" still kept in her study, if she couldn't find what she needed in them, "I go to the Greenwich Library."[29] Back in 1941, she had told interviewers that she found her inspiration for *My Theodosia* in that library.

"Sit in the Student Center at Greenwich High School for three or four days," Anya said mysteriously, "and you see things." She claimed that "writing Amy" had not been difficult, since the girl "simply took over." Crossing the generational divide, "at my advanced stage," Anya boasted, was no problem, because "I can well remember my 16-year-old troubles, worries, and miseries."[30] Anya had in fact been imaginatively creating teenaged girls since she produced Theodosia for that first novel. In 1975, with her last novel, this celebratory gathering brought her full circle.

The article noting her thirty-five years of achievement began with a quoted declaration. "The only joy in life for me is writing," Anya said.[31] While this could have served as an epitaph, her daughters chose a different one. Engraved on the Celtic cross of "Anya Seton, Author and Historian" are words from the ending of The Winthrop Woman, "And the Source and She Were One."

AFTERWORD
OTHER ANYAS

FAR TOO MANY YEARS AGO, I gave a talk to celebrate the centennial of Anya Seton's birth, January 23, 1904, at the Greenwich Historical Society. I had not yet fully committed myself to the idea of doing a biography of the writer whose works I had loved reading since I was a teenager. Still, by 2004 I had met Anya's family, had looked at the papers they had donated to the GHS, and had published an article about her for the society's magazine. The archivists were wonderfully knowledgeable and helpful. A large and enthusiastic audience came to my centennial talk, and there to support me, as well as to reunite with many Greenwich friends, were Anya's two daughters, Pamela Cottier Forcey and Zizi Chase Coggins. One of their friends, also a writer, nodded in sympathy when I said how I wished I could have met Anya. In a later email, sent to Zizi but also shared with me, the friend mentioned my wish and then provided her wise perceptions of the woman who was always simply "Zizi's mom to me."

"I think your mom was a very strong person," she wrote to Zizi, "someone who grew a lot herself after shedding a lot of childhood influence. I always admired her focus, her determined way of working at writing." This friend "distinctly" remembered Anya "pounding away at work in Pam's room with the morning sun coming in the window." As others have also said, she thought that Anya "was a very warm person. Empathy. She seemed to understand a lot which she conveyed without words, focusing totally on the person, listening and smiling." As others also attested, this friend loved Anya's "dramatic appearance which sometimes belied her warmth. And I loved the dramatic expression of her sincere feelings." The friend's conclusion: "She knew other people's feelings, probably enabling her to bring her literary characters to life, which she did so well."

At the time Zizi's friend and I met, I had not yet read any of Anya's nine bound journals, which came a good while later. I was even thinking naively that I might do a combined biography of Anya and Grace Gallatin Seton. Ernest Thompson Seton didn't need more attention, but the mother and daughter in this prolific family of writers both deserved their very considerable due. Eventually I realized that Anya was the one I wanted to know, and it was her story that I needed to tell. Once the journals in their entirety were made available to me, they became my way of meeting her, the window through which I could see her and get to know her, exclusively as she expressed herself, largely *for* herself. In the hundreds of pages of her journals, she does reveal herself, as Zizi's friend said, to be a warm, dramatic, empathetic, determined, and sincere woman. The "dramatic" and "determined" side, among other tendencies, could also make her, especially within the privacy her family, a very difficult person, to put it mildly.

Anya, "Mama" to her daughters, was "neither saint nor devil," as Pamela Forcey has written, but "as a mother," she had "a very mixed record." In this other Anya, empathy was blunted by her own constant need for praise and appreciation. All three of her children, as Pam wrote, "ended up with violently ambivalent feelings about her." Her journals demonstrate that this would have to be the case. Anya often gave her children extravagantly affectionate attention, especially during their younger years, but she often, in addition, conveyed constant anxiety as she hovered and tried to micromanage their affairs. She also imparted harsh, insensitive criticism when their behavior did not meet her expectations. She continued those tendencies into her children's adult years when it must have been hard to know which Anya was going to meet them at the door. At least if it was Grandmother Anya, the reception seems always to have been an enthusiastic one.

Especially in later years, as the alcoholism she would never name took over so much of her life, she frustrated and exhausted those closest to her. That time of turmoil is a significant and terribly sad part of her story that must be acknowledged. That she was able to keep researching and completing novels, given the alcohol and pill consumption that she documented, is a testament to the presence of a strong interior force. While she called alcohol "medicinal," she turned, for as long as she could make herself, to the much more powerful, healing anodyne, her writing work.

For me, the abiding question has been how best to get across the legacy of her full life, in all its diverse dimensions. This focus has informed my choice to present her narrative by attending to the voices and viewpoints that come through most vividly—in her journals, in letters written to and from her, and in the conversations and descriptions of those who saw her through a variety of useful lenses.

Late in life, Anya told her public audience that "My only joy is writing." Pamela Forcey has also written that she and Zizi "agreed that she was really happy only when researching and writing her books." I would amend that judgment to say that she was consistently happy only in that creative zone. Still, her journals supply many small, colorful vignettes of other Anyas besides the one pounding away at her typewriter, and some of these could be joyful, grateful, deeply touched by others' interest in her, and glad to help others. Her unique, wide-ranging life was one lived daily, as all lives are, through small habits, fleeting emotions, exasperating chores, reactions to news good or bad, and seemingly mundane decisions that might have big or no consequences. Her journal is a record of that dailiness too.

She had many women friends, with whom she loved to gossip and laugh. Friends often came to her with problems, and she was distressed by their troubles. She was a gourmet chef, for whom food was very important. She loved organ meat and for lunch would fix herself such delicacies as ox-tail soup or kidney pie. She also could guiltily binge on chocolates. Drama was essential to her recipes and her dinner parties, as well as her self-presentations. At Sea Rune she would go out into the water on a float, donning large sunglasses, dressed in shorts and a lowcut blouse, and paddle about while reading a book. She knew that neighbors thought her "balmy" and that to many of the staff at Houghton Mifflin, she was the "prized pampered pup." To fit the part, she would "sweep" into the Boston office like the "prima donna" that Paul Brooks recalled, but in a sense, she was quite simply mocking herself. She could also be embarrassingly frank, intentionally or not, and she appreciated good jokes as well as quick-witted people who would spar with her.

Anya became by the late 1930s a hypochondriac, perhaps as a way to get more attention, and she scrutinized every scratch or pain, projecting dire diagnoses. She also diagnosed her family's ailments, often with more clinical detachment, but prided herself on nursing them back to health. Never was she detached about any perceived illness of her beloved cat, Cherie. She enjoyed her work as an aide at New York and Greenwich hospitals, and later, when she sometimes spent weeks as a hospital patient, she learned her nurses' names and knew their stories. She loved gardening, changing her plantings with the seasons, hated hot weather, and was exultant one October when it snowed.

Anya's daughters laughed and shuddered about her penchant for applying gilt or glossy paint to everything from tables to lamps and antique chests, even telephones. People who dropped by Sea Rune found themselves recruited for impromptu croquet competitions, dinner guests were swept into fierce word and trivia board games, and loyal friends wheedled into joining serious consultations with her Ouija board. In the years following her stroke, those friends still came to play bridge on afternoons when her wheelchair would be pulled up to the card table and her cards propped on a homemade stand that she could reach with her one usable hand. Anya became an eccentric fairly early in both her social and professional life, adopting a persona that allowed her to flaunt her assets and to hide her shyness at the same time. These are all glimpses of Anya Seton, not really another Anya but one who constructed diverse images and costumes for herself, as she did for characters whom she dressed in garb always appropriate to their epochs and situations.

The last other Anya whom I have come so gratefully to know has been granted to me by the two daughters and granddaughters whose lives also filled her journals. I met Anya first as a passionate reader of her books, trading her novels around with my mother and sister in the early 1960s. Then in the early 1990s I met Blythe Forcey (Toussaint), who became a colleague in the English department of North Carolina State University. We were already friends by the time she told me, diffidently, that she would like to write a historical novel. It was an aim, she added, that was connected to her grandmother, whom I "might have heard of." Blythe is successfully pursuing her writing goal while she continues, as a teacher, to be a powerful role model for a new generation of high school students. She gave me my current goal too, but not until I tried to convince her to take on the task of writing the biography of Anya Seton that her legions of readers should have.

I lost the argument to convince Blythe to take on her grandmother's life but won a gift that more than compensated when Blythe introduced me to her mother, Pamela Forcey. Pam had tried but also firmly decided against writing about her mother. Soon I also met Blythe's aunt Zizi and Zizi's daughter, Christa. Christa at the time was living with her husband and two children at Sea Rune, but they were packing up to move to Santa Fe, where they could follow their careers and also build a beautiful home not far from Seton Village. I was very lucky in the timing of my trip to Sea Rune, in 1998, because it allowed me to see Anya's very unusual home before new owners demolished and replaced it with a house much more typical of Binney Lane, one that covers every inch of ground on its plot.

Through Anya I now have the gift of knowing two daughters, two grand-daughters, all highly accomplished in their professions, all researchers and articulate advocates for fields from teaching, writing, and editing to archaeology, art history, and community philanthropy. They are all, most significantly, supportive and loving companions to one another. They continue to constitute, for me, a generous, encouraging, accepting company of women without whom I would never have attempted to start delving into Anya Seton's world. To Anya, again, I give the last words, spoken by a young Native American woman in *Foxfire*, "It is good for women to work together."

ACKNOWLEDGMENTS

MY FIRST AND GREATEST THANKS for their invaluable role in presenting this story of Anya Seton's writing life go to her daughters, Pamela Cottier Forcey and Clemency Chase Coggins. I am so grateful to them for their generosity, insights, and encouragement. To Pam, I owe more than I could ever repay to her indefatigable work as a reader and an editor. Until her death last April, she had read every draft of every chapter, providing information that only she could add and catching errors that only she could correct. To my other invaluable readers, I can say now that only friends as constant as you could have seen this project through. First, to Pam Forcey's daughter and Anya's granddaughter, Blythe Forcey Toussaint, now a friend for decades, I give thanks for the early conversation that opened the door to the lifework of your grandmother, whose novels have brought so much enjoyment to so many. To Deborah Hooker, like Blythe a colleague in the North Carolina State University Department of English, I can say that your editorial skills, your patience as a formatter and interpreter of style codes far beyond my understanding, and your wise perceptions as a reader are the reason I have made it this far.

Many years ago, on my first trip to Greenwich, I was given the gift of Susan Richardson, librarian at that time of the Historical Society of the Town of Greenwich. I will never forget our drive up to Wyndygoul, which had not yet been torn down but was in a terrible state of decay. She shared my passion for historical preservation, showing me all the places where the Seton presence still abides in Greenwich Township. I am just as grateful now to the dedicated staff currently in charge of an even more exciting Greenwich Historical Society, still on the same site at the Bush-Holley House but beautifully renovated and expanded. The new archives and library are a researcher's dream come true, managed with skill and wide knowledge by curator Christopher Shields. Dr. Debra Mecky, executive director and CEO of GHS, and Anna Marie Greco, director of education, have welcomed me often and made wonderful arrangements for my two lecture series there. Thanks to others I met in Greenwich who have helped so much: writer and researcher Divya Summers, who shared interviews she collected from Anya's friends; also Julie Lee, Sandra Powers, and Jo Hubert Williamson, girlhood friend of Clemency, who all provided wonderful impressions of the Anya they knew; and Betty Brown, the current owner of Little Peequo, who opened her home to me and Anya's family, always with gracious hospitality.

In Santa Fe I was so fortunate to get to know Dee Seton Barber—Ernest Thompson and Julia Seton's adopted daughter—who welcomed me several times to Seton Castle before it tragically burned; also David Witt, now curator of the Seton Legacy Project at the Academy for the Love of Learning, who promotes ETS's legacy in a beautifully designed, innovative, and empowering educational facility on the grounds of Seton Village; and Julie Seton, ETS and Julia Seton's granddaughter, who also works tirelessly to keep the Seton vision alive and relevant through the Ernest Thompson Seton Institute. To Christa Coggins, Anya's granddaughter, and her family, I am so grateful to you for hosting my stay at Sea Rune shortly before it was torn down by its new owners, and then for welcoming me to your home in Santa Fe.

I have been blessed with several wonderful editors. These include Lisa Reardon, who was the first to see the promise of this project, and Yuval Taylor, who took all my early drafts and helped to make them coherent and readable. At Chicago Review Press, I have had the privilege of working with editors Devon Freeny and Michelle Williams, and to have the able assistance of editorial associate Alex Granato as well as the press's design and marketing teams.

Last but of course not least, there is my family to recognize. Before his recent death, husband John happily accompanied me on what we called our "Seton treks" to Ottawa, Santa Fe, and Greenwich. He was so delightfully curious about all these places and always my mainstay. Our children, Alex MacKethan with wife Beth, and daughter Karen St. Clair, for so many years have foresworn the temptation to ask me how much longer this project was going to take. Instead they have kept telling me that I could do it and that they would always be there for me, which they are.

NOTES

Author's Note

1. Seton, foreword to *My Theodosia*, v.
2. Anya Seton Bound Journals. November 24, 1956.
3. Anya Seton to Frank Taylor, October 2, 1957, ASP, series 3.2 (General Correspondence), box 19, folder 103.
4. Seton, foreword to *My Theodosia*, v.
5. Ann Seton Diary, September 5, 1921.
6. Anya Seton Bound Journals, February 26, 1946.
7. J. Seton, *By a Thousand Fires*, 87.
8. Seton, 87–88.
9. Anya Seton Bound Journals, August 21, 1953.

Preface: I Was Born

1. Anya Seton to Frank Taylor, October 2, 1957, ASP, series 3.2 (General Correspondence), box 19, folder 103.

1. The Starving Artist, the Heiress, and the Princess

1. E. Seton, *Artist-Naturalist*, 304.
2. Seton, 304.
3. Seton, 343.
4. There are three full-length biographies of Ernest Thompson Seton: Betty Keller's *Black Wolf: The Biography of Ernest Thompson Seton*, H. Allen Anderson's *The Chief: Ernest Thompson Seton and the Changing West*, and David Witt's *Ernest Thompson Seton: The Life and Legacy of an Artist and Conservationist*. Keller, a Canadian, is frequently critical of Seton; Anderson, on the other hand, makes Seton much more of a heroic figure. Witt's work is certainly the most up to date and objective and contains many photographs as well as stunning illustrations of Seton's drawings and paintings, many of

them on display at the Academy for the Love of Learning in Santa Fe. The academy is on the site of Seton's last home, where Witt serves as curator of the Seton Legacy Project.

5. Witt, *Ernest Thompson Seton*, 61.
6. Finz, "Governor's Mansion Empty in Sacramento," https://www.sfgate.com /homeandgarden/article/Governor-s-mansion-empty-in-Sacramento-3248686.php.
7. E. Seton, *Trail of an Artist-Naturalist*, 343.
8. Whitelock, "Ernest Seton-Thompson at Home."
9. Clemenzie Craig Duffy to Grace Thompson Seton, January 21, 1900, ASP, series 2 (Family Papers), box 11, folder 50.
10. Forcey, "Grace Gallatin Seton," 1–2.
11. E. Seton, *Wild Animals*, 9.
12. Garland, *Companions*, 99.
13. Steffens, *Autobiography*, 436–37.
14. Ernest Thompson Seton, "The Story of Wyndygoul," *Country Life in America*, August 1909, 400, ASP, series 2 (Family Papers), box 10, file 41.
15. Roberts, "Home of a Naturalist," 155.
16. *Baby's Record*, 1904, ASP, series 1 (Biographical and Personal Material), box 1.
17. Quoted in Pamela Forcey, draft chapter 1, "Born into a Different World," 11, FTPC.
18. *World Magazine* (*New York World*), February 7, 1904, clipping, ASP, series 1 (Biographical and Personal Material), box 1, folder 7.
19. Of the many accounts of Seton's Woodcraft Indians, the most up to date is "History of the Woodcraft Movement," Ernest Thompson Seton Institute, accessed February 13, 2020, http://etsetoninstitute.org/history-of-the-woodcraft-movement/.
20. Witt, *Ernest Thompson Seton*, 103.
21. "Seton Baby Christened," *New York Times*, July 24, 1904, clipping, ASP, series 1 (Biographical and Personal Material), box 1, folder 7.
22. "Naturalist Seton's Daughter Will Be an Outdoor Child," *New York World*, February 7, 1904, clipping, ASP, series 1 (Biographical and Personal Material), box 1, folder 7.
23. Unidentified Rochester, NY, newspaper clipping, ASP, series 1 (Biographical and Personal Material), box 1, folder 7.
24. Unidentified newspaper clipping, ASP, series 1 (Biographical and Personal Material), box 1, folder 3.
25. Anya Seton, "Childhood: Endeavor to Uncover Possible Experience to Explain Neurosis," July 10, 1938, 3, typewritten notes, ASP, series 1 (Biographical and Personal Material), box 1, folder 3.
26. John Burroughs, quoted in Atta, "Ernest Thompson Seton and the Woodcraft Indians," 9.

27. Bolt, "Seton's Indians," 45.

28. Quoted in Forcey, "Grace Gallatin Seton," 2.

29. G. Seton, *Woman Tenderfoot*, 32, 24.

30. There is no full-length book covering Grace Gallatin Seton's life or work. For an extensive biographical article, see MacKethan, "Profile of Grace Gallatin Seton."

31. G. Seton, *Nimrod's Wife*, 3.

32. Seton, "Childhood," 6.

33. Anya Seton, unpublished obituary for Johanna Engstrom, October 4, 1969. FTPC.

34. Ann Seton Diary, July 2, 1921.

35. Seton, "Childhood," 6.

36. Anya Seton, "Childhood Memories," 1948, ASP, series 1 (Biographical and Personal Material), box 1, folder 3.

37. Mary Holland Kinkaid, "Feminine Charms of the Woman Militant," *Good Housekeeping*, February 12, 1912, 146, ASP, series 2 (Family Papers), box 11, folder 49.

38. Kinkaid, "Feminine Charms," 153.

39. The clearest account of the Camp Fire Girls movement, also the one that most emphasizes Ernest's and Grace's contributions, is in H. Allen Anderson's biography of Seton, *The Chief*, 166–69.

40. For the story of ETS's involvement with the Boy Scouts of America, see David C. Scott and Brendan Murphy, *The Scouting Party* (Brooklyn: Red Honor Press, 2010).

41. Stanton et al., *History of Women's Suffrage* includes Grace Thompson Seton's role in volume 5, 73.

42. "Wyndygoul, a Woodland Estate," *New York Times*, November 17, 1912, clipping, ASP, series 2 (Family Papers), box 10, folder 43.

43. Isabel Proctor Lord to Grace Thompson Seton, November 14, 1912, ASP, series 2 (Family Papers), box 11, folder 52.

44. Clara Spence to Grace Thompson Seton, October 12, 1912, ASP, series 2 (Family Papers), box 11, folder 52.

45. A full portrait of Clara Spence and her school can be found at Elizabeth Titus, "Clara B. Spence: Ahead of Her Time," *Ms.*, March 6, 2015, http://msmagazine.com/blog/2015/03/06/clara-b-spence-ahead-of-her-time/.

46. Clara Spence, quoted in Brizendine, "Words Shared at the 2016 Alumnae Luncheon," https://www.spenceschool.org/2017---bodies-vantage-points-news-detail?pk=849666.

2. Houses Divided

1. Anya Seton, unpublished typescript of biographical sketch, 1965, FTPC.

2. Hamlin Garland, quoted in Anderson, *The Chief*, 71.

3. E. Seton, *Trail of an Artist-Naturalist*, 349.

4. Ann Seton Diary, August 31, 1921.

5. Ann Seton Diary, June 30, 1921.

6. Ann Seton Diary, early June 1921.

7. Ann Seton Diary, September 5, 1921.

8. Anya Seton, "The Treasure Hunt of Research," *Writer* (April 1962), clipping, ASP, series 1 (Biographical and Personal Material), box 1, folder 9.

9. Ann Seton Diary, September 5, 1921.

10. Ann Seton Diary, September 5, 1921.

11. Ann Seton Diary, September 5, 1921.

12. Anne Seton Diary, August 21, 1921.

13. Ann Seton Diary, September 5, 1921.

14. Ann Seton Diary, September 5, 1921.

15. Ann Seton Diary, October 22, 1921.

16. Ann Seton to Hamilton Cottier, April 11, 1922, ASP, series 3.1 (Family Correspondence), box 15, folder 68.

17. Ann Seton to Hamilton Cottier, January 13, 1922, ASP, series 3.1 (Family Correspondence), box 15, folder 67.

18. Ann Seton to Hamilton Cottier, March 27, 1922, ASP, series 3.1 (Family Correspondence), box 15, folder 68.

19. Seton to Cottier, April 11, 1922.

20. Anya's copy of *A Woman Tenderfoot in Egypt*, with Anya's note about not being included, is in the Forcey-Toussaint Private Collection.

21. Forcey, "Grace Gallatin Seton," 3.

22. Grace Thompson Seton, "What the Author Says to the Reader," foreword to *Woman Tenderfoot*, n.p.

23. Anya Seton, "Childhood Memories," 1966, ASP, series 1 (Biographical and Personal Material), box 1, folder 3.

24. J. Seton, *By a Thousand Fires*, ix.

25. Ann Seton to Hamilton Cottier, April 10, 1922, ASP, series 3.1 (Family Correspondence), box 15, folder 68.

26. Keller, *Black Wolf*, 195.

27. Julia Seton, quoted in Therese La Farge, "The Indefatigable, Indestructible Julia Seton," *Santa Fe News*, October 9, 1969, clipping, FTPC.

28. Grace Thompson Seton to Ernest Thompson Seton, January 24, 1923, ASP, series 2 (Family Papers), box 11, folder 52.

29. Ernest Thomson Seton to Grace Thompson Seton, May 24, 1924, ASP, series 2 (Family Papers), box 10, folder 42.

30. Ann Seton to Hamilton Cottier, October 2, 1922, ASP, series 3.1 (Family Correspondence), box 15, folder 68.

31. Seton to Cottier, April 11, 1922.

32. Seton to Cottier, April 11, 1922.

33. Ann Seton to Hamilton Cottier, October 5–12, 1922, ASP, series 3.1 (Family Correspondence), box 15, folder 68.

34. Ann Seton to Hamilton Cottier, October 6, 1922, ASP, series 3.1 (Family Correspondence), box 15, folder 68.

35. Grace Thompson Seton to Ernest Thompson Seton, December 8, 1922, ASP, series 2 (Family Papers), box 11, folder 51.

36. Grace Thompson Seton to Ernest Thompson Seton, October 19, 1922, ASP, series 2 (Family Papers), box 11, folder 51.

37. Ernest Thompson Seton to Grace Thompson Seton, March 14, 1923, ASP, series 2 (Family Papers), box 10, folder 42.

38. *Spur*, July 7, 1923, clipping, ASP, series 1 (Biographical and Personal Material), box 1, folder 6.

39. Grace Gallatin Seton, quoted in *San Francisco Examiner*, n.d., clipping, ASP, series 2 (Family Papers), box 11, folder 49.

40. Ernest Thompson Seton, Journal entry for June 30, 1923, quoted in Anderson, *The Chief*, 205.

3. Dearest Ambitions

1. Ernest Thompson Seton to Ann Seton Cottier, December 21, 1923, ASP, series 3.1 (Family Correspondence), box 16, folder 81.

2. Ann Cottier Diary, June 21, 1924.

3. Ann Cottier Diary, June 21, 1924.

4. Ann Cottier Diary. June 23, 1924.

5. Ernest Thompson Seton to Ann Seton Cottier. July 29, 1924, ASP, series 3.1 (Family Correspondence), box 16, folder 81.

6. Ann Cottier Diary, July 7, 1924.

7. "Alonzo E. Cottier Gets Divorce," *Newark (OH) Daily Advocate*, https://newspaperarchive .com/newark-daily-advocate-feb-22-1896-p-1/.

8. Ann Cottier Diary, May 27, 1927.

9. G. Seton, *Poison Arrows*, 301.

10. Ann Cottier Diary, July 27, 1928.

11. Ann Cottier Diary, January 1, 1929.

12. Ann Cottier Diary, July 27, 1928.

13. Pamela Forcey to H. Allen Anderson, n.d., FTPC.

14. Ann Cottier Diary, September 8, 1928.
15. Ann Cottier Diary, January 1, 1929.
16. Ann Cottier Diary, February 12, 1929.
17. Ann Cottier Diary, March 4, 1929.
18. Ann Cottier Diary, March 16, 1929.
19. Ann Cottier Diary, March 16, 1929.
20. Ann Cottier Diary, April 8, 1929.
21. Alonzo Cottier to Hamilton Cottier, September 4, 1929, FTPC.
22. Alonzo Cottier to Hamilton Cottier, September 4, 1929.
23. Ann Cottier Diary, November 19, 1929.
24. "No. 1 Too Highbrow, She'll Try Lawyer as Husband No. 2," clipping, ASP, series 1 (Biographical and Personal Material), box 1, folder 7.
25. J. Seton, *By a Thousand Fires*, 253.
26. Anya Seton Bound Journals, November 15, 1932.
27. Anya Seton Bound Journals, November 15, 1932.
28. Anya Seton Bound Journals, March 7, 1933.
29. Anya Seton Bound Journals, April 29, 1933.
30. "Mrs. Seton Adds to Books; Husband Rests on Ranch. Greenwich Woman of Amazing Energy Plans Another Volume While One Is Being Printed. Wife of Mr. Seton? She Disavows Reflected Glory," *Bridgeport (CT) Post*, December 5, 1932, clipping, ASP, series 2 (Family Papers) box 11, folder 49.
31. Anya Seton Bound Journals, January 24, 1935.
32. Forcey, "Grace Gallatin Seton," 5.
33. Anya Seton Bound Journals, November 15, 1932.
34. Alma Archer to Mrs. Hamilton Chase, March 6, 1932, ASP, series 3.2 (General Corresspondence), box 18, folder 91.
35. Anya Seton Bound Journals, August 8, 1935.
36. Anya Seton Bound Journals, January 5 and February 4, 1936.
37. Anya Seton Bound Journals, January 5, 1936.
38. Anya Seton Bound Journals, February 4, 1936.
39. Anya Seton Bound Journals, November 12, 1936.

4. From Ann to Anya

1. Anya Seton Bound Journals, January 25, 1935.
2. Anya Seton Bound Journals, January 30 and February 20, 1935.
3. Anya Seton Bound Journals, September 6, 1935.
4. Anya Seton Bound Journals, August 5, 1936.
5. Anya Seton Bound Journals, October 5, 1936.

6. Anya Seton Bound Journals, October 5, 1936.
7. Anya Seton Bound Journals, November 12, 1936, and January 23, 1937.
8. Anya Seton to Nelson Antrim Crawford, September 25, 1937, ASP, series 3.2 (General Correspondence), box 18, folder 92.
9. Anya Seton Bound Journals, June 13, 1937.
10. Uzzell, *Narrative Technique, passim.*
11. Anya Seton Bound Journals, June 22, 1937
12. Anya Seton Bound Journals, September 13, 1937.
13. Anya Seton Bound Journals, October 12, 1937.
14. Thomas H. Uzzell to Hamilton Chase, January 11, 1938, ASP, series 3.3 (Fan Mail and "Interesting Letters"), box 23, folder 131.
15. Uzzell to Chase, January 11, 1938.
16. Anya Seton Bound Journals, February 5, 1938.
17. Thomas H. Uzzell to Mrs. Anya Seton Chase, December 18, 1942, ASP, series 3.3 (Fan Mail and "Interesting Letters"), box 23, folder 132.
18. Anya Seton Bound Journals, July 1, 1938.
19. Anya Seton Bound Journals, July 28, 1938.
20. Anya Seton Bound Journals, July 1 and August 24, 1938.
21. Anya Seton Bound Journals, August 5, 1938.
22. Anya Seton Bound Journals, August 24, 1938.
23. Anya Seton Bound Journals, September 13, 1937.
24. Anya Seton Bound Journals, August 24, 1938.
25. Anya Seton Bound Journals, September 28 and November 21, 1938.
26. Anya Seton Bound Journals, October 25, 1938.
27. Ueland. *If You Want to Write.*
28. Anya Seton Bound Journals, October 25, 1938.
29. Anya Seton Bound Journals, November 21, 1938
30. *New York World Telegram*, November 19, 1938, clipping, ASP, series 2 (Family Papers), box 10, folder 44.
31. Anya Seton Bound Journals, April 10, 1939.
32. Anya Seton Bound Journals, June 6, 1939.
33. Anya Seton Bound Journals, August 28, 1939.
34. Anya Seton Bound Journals, September 4, 1939.
35. Anya Seton Bound Journals, September 1, 1939.
36. Anya Seton Bound Journals, October 14, 1939.

5. Passionate Daughter

1. Anya Seton to Frank Taylor, October 2, 1957, ASP, series 3.2 (General Correspondence), box 19, folder 103.
2. Anya Seton Bound Journals, October 14, 1939.
3. Brooks. *Two Park Street*, 127.
4. Anya Seton Bound Journals, November 1, 1939.
5. Anya Seton Bound Journals, November 18 1939.
6. Anya Seton Bound Journals, December 19, 1939.
7. Anya Seton Bound Journals, December 27, 1939.
8. Arthur Hailey, quoted in "Lee Barker Dead, Doubleday Aide," *New York Times,* July 3, 1973.
9. Brooks, *Two Park Street*, ix.
10. Anya Seton Bound Journals, January 1, 1940.
11. Anya Seton Bound Journals, January 1, 1940.
12. Anya Seton Bound Journals, February 8, 1940.
13. Rowena Wilson Tobias, "Writing a Biography of Theodosia Burr," *Charleston S.C. News and Courier,* n.d., clipping, ASP, series 5.2 (*My Theodosia*), box 26, folder 158.
14. Anya Seton Bound Journals, February 8, 1940.
15. Anya Seton Bound Journals, March 22, 1940.
16. Anya Seton Bound Journals, April 10, 1940.
17. Anya Seton Bound Journals, April 10, 1940.
18. Anya Seton Bound Journals, March 22 and April 10, 1940.
19. Anya Seton Bound Journals, April 10, 1940.
20. Anya Seton Bound Journals, May 23, 1940.
21. Anya Seton Bound Journals, April 10, 1940.
22. Anya Seton Bound Journals, August 5, 1940.
23. Anya Seton Bound Journals, June 27, 1940.
24. Anya Seton Bound Journals, August 5, 1940.
25. Anya Seton Bound Journals, October 17, 1940.
26. Anya Seton Bound Journals, November 6, 1940.
27. Anya Seton Bound Journals, November 6, 1940
28. Anya Seton Bound Journals, November 26, 1940.
29. Anya Seton Bound Journals, December 31, 1940.
30. Anya Seton Bound Journals, April 4, 1941.
31. Anya Seton Bound Journals, May 26, 1941.
32. Marion Leland, "Anya Seton's Ambition Was to Be Doctor, Not to Write, *Greenwich Press*, March 6, 1941, and Rose Feld, "Burr, Mountaineer," *New York Herald Tribune*, March 23, 1941, clippings, ASP, series 5.2 (*My Theodosia*), box 26, folder 158.

33. Jacob H. Lowry, "New Author Contributes Nothing but Splash of Mud to The-
    odosai [sic] Legend," *State* (Columbia, SC), n.d., clipping, ASP, series 5.2 (*My
    Theodosia*), box 26, folder 148. Much more recently, Richard Côté, in a full-length
    biography of Theodosia, still charges that Seton, with *My Theodosia*, shows that
    she "loathed and despised every aspect of the South, its history, and its culture."
    Thus her novel is "a distortion of factual information readily available to any
    researcher of her time" as well as "racist and venomously anti-southern." Côté,
    Theodosia Burr Alston, 298.
34. Biographical notes, back jacket flap, Seton, *My Theodosia* (Boston: Houghton Mif-
    flin, 1941).
35. Quoted in front matter, Seton, *My Theodosia*.
36. Anya Seton Bound Journals, November 26, 1940.
37. Anya Seton letter and enclosure to Ernest Thompson Seton, May 23, 1939, ASP,
    series 3.1 (Family Correspondence), box 16, folder 82.
38. E. Seton, *Trail of an Artist-Naturalist*, 343–44, 349.
39. Keller. *Black Wolf*, 213.
40. Anya Seton Bound Journals, April 4, 1941.
41. Anya Seton Bound Journals, May 26, 1941.
42. Anya Seton Bound Journals, December 8, 1941.

6. Money Maker

1. Anya Seton Bound Journals, May 4, 1944.
2. Anya Seton Bound Journals, May 20, 1943.
3. Anya Seton Bound Journals, May 7, 1945.
4. Anya Seton Bound Journals, October 3, 1942.
5. Anya Seton Bound Journals, December 27, 1942.
6. Anya Seton Bound Journals, May 4, 1944.
7. Grace Gallatin Seton to John Dewicki, September 26, 1944, RIHU.
8. Anya Seton Bound Journals, October 3, 1942.
9. Anya Seton Bound Journals, December 12, 1942.
10. Anya Seton Bound Journals, January 18, 1945.
11. Anya Seton Bound Journals, January 14, 1943.
12. Anya Seton Bound Journals, November 16, 1943.
13. Anya Seton Bound Journals, October 3, 1942.
14. Anya Seton Bound Journals, January 14, 1943.
15. Anya Seton Bound Journals, March 1,1943.
16. Anya Seton Bound Journals, August 23, 1943.
17. Anya Seton Bound Journals, October 19, 1943.

18. Anya Seton Bound Journals, March 1, 1943.
19. Anya Seton Bound Journals. September 8, 1942.
20. Anya Seton Bound Journals, October 3, 1942.
21. Anya Seton Bound Journals, December 2, 1943.
22. Anya Seton Bound Journals, December 2, 1943.
23. Anya Seton Bound Journals, December 16, 1943.
24. Anya Seton Bound Journals, December 16, 1943.
25. Anya Seton Bound Journals, December 17, 1945.
26. Newspaper ad for *Dragonwyck*, the film, *New York Herald Tribune*, March 19, 1946, FTPC.
27. Anya Seton Bound Journals, July 19, 1942.
28. Harriet Colby, review of *Dragonwyck*, *New York Herald Tribune*. n.d., clipping, ASP, series 5.3 (*Dragonwyck*), box 27, folder 171.
29. Radio interview with "Miss Craven" (typescript), 1944, clipping, ASP, series 5.4 (*The Turquoise*), box 27, folder 170.
30. Seton, *Dragonwyck*, 2.
31. Seton, 333.
32. Alvin H. Goldstein, "She Wanted to Be a Doctor. But Peacocks, Skunks, and Grandma Conspired to Turn Anya Seton into Successful Novelist," *St. Louis Post Dispatch*, February 26, 1944, clipping, ASP, series 5.3 (*Dragonwyck*), box 27, folder 169.
33. Anya Seton Bound Journals, March 7, 1944.
34. Anya Seton Bound Journals, May 4, 1944.
35. Anya Seton Bound Journals, May 4, 1944.
36. Anya Seton Bound Journals, January 18, 1945.
37. Anya Seton Bound Journals, June 21, 1945.
38. Anya Seton Bound Journals, November 8 & 20, 1945.
39. Anya Seton Bound Journals, March 13, 1946.
40. Anya Seton Bound Journals, January 26, 1946.
41. "Movie of the Week: *Dragonwyck*," *Life*, March 18, 1946, clipping, FTPC.
42. Anya Seton Bound Journals, February 14, 1946.
43. Anya Seton Bound Journals, December 17, 1945.
44. Wilson, "Ambushing a Best Seller," , 311, 314.
45. Wilson, "Ambushing a Best Seller," 317.
46. Anya Seton Bound Journals, February 14, 1946.

7. Hearth and Husband

1. Anya Seton Bound Journals, February 26, 1946.
2. Lovell Thompson to Anya Seton, February 15, 1946, HMP.

3. An astute assessment of Wilson is Louis Menand's "Missionary: Edmund Wilson and American Culture," *New Yorker*, August 8, 2005.
4. "Edmund Wilson Dies," *New York Times*, June 13, 1972.
5. Anya Seton Bound Journals, August 18, 1957.
6. Wilson, "Portrait: Christian Gauss," 345–355.
7. Anya Seton Bound Journals, February 14 & 26, 1946.
8. Anya Seton Bound Journals, May 19, 1946.
9. Anya Seton Bound Journals, February 14, 1946.
10. Anya Seton Bound Journals, June 11, 1946.
11. Anya Seton Bound Journals, June 11, 1946.
12. Anya Seton Bound Journals, August 15, 1946.
13. Anya Seton Bound Journals, July 16, 1946.
14. Anya Seton Bound Journals, August 6, 1946.
15. Anya Seton Bound Journals, August 15, 1946
16. Anya Seton Bound Journals, September 3, 1946.
17. Anya Seton Bound Journals, September 14, 1946.
18. Anya Seton Bound Journals, September 26, 1946.
19. Anya Seton Bound Journals, October 24 & 31 and November 12, 1946.
20. Anya Seton Bound Journals, December 16, 1946, and January 8, 1947.
21. Anya Seton Bound Journals, March 27, 1947.
22. Anya Seton Bound Journals, August 15, 1947.
23. Anya Seton Bound Journals, August 29, 1946.
24. Anya Seton Bound Journals, November 1, 1947.
25. Anya Seton Bound Journals, December 28, 1947.
26. Anya Seton Bound Journals, November 1, 1946, and December 28, 1947.
27. Anya Seton Bound Journals, July 19, 1947.
28. Anya Seton Bound Journals, March 28, 1948.
29. Anya Seton Bound Journals, April 14, 1948.
30. Seton, *Hearth and Eagle*, 78.
31. Seton, 117.
32. Anya Seton Bound Journals, April 30, 1948.
33. Anya Seton Bound Journals, May 11, 1948.
34. Anya Seton Bound Journals, July 9, 1948.
35. Anya Seton Bound Journals, July 9 & 20, 1948.
36. Anya Seton Bound Journals, July 9, 1948.
37. Anya Seton Bound Journals, July 20, 1948.
38. Dunbar's work is the subject of an extensive analysis at "Profile: Helen Flanders Dunbar," Psychology's Feminist Voices, accessed February 11, 2020, http://www .feministvoices.com/helen-flanders-dunbar/.

39. Anya Seton Bound Journals, July 20 and August 3, 1948.
40. Anya Seton Bound Journals, December 15, 1948.
41. Anya Seton Bound Journals, December 21, 1948.
42. Anya Seton, "Childhood Memories," ASC for HFD (Helen Flanders Dunbar), September 21, 1948, ASP, series 1 (Biographical and Personal Material), box 1, folder 3.
43. Anya Seton Bound Journals, February 11, 1949.
44. Anya Seton Bound Journals, May 24, 1943.
45. The story was told by Charles's son, also Charles Chase, to Anya's daughter Pamela long after their parents' deaths. Pamela was very surprised, since everyone assumed that the plot for *Foxfire*, the novel begun shortly after the Chases were all together in Arizona, was fictional, while its undercurrents had to do mostly with Anya and Chan's relationship.
46. Anya Seton Bound Journals, February 11, 1949.

8. Where to Go from Here?

1. Anya Seton Bound Journals, May 1, 1949.
2. Anya Seton Bound Journals, June 28, 1949.
3. Anya Seton Bound Journals, July 27 1949.
4. Anya Seton Bound Journals, March 2, 1949.
5. Anya Seton Bound Journals, March 9, 1949.
6. Anya Seton Bound Journals, August 10, 1949.
7. Anya Seton Bound Journals, December 15, 1949.
8. Anya Seton Bound Journals, December 15, 1949.
9. Anya Seton Bound Journals, June 2, 1950.
10. Seton, *Foxfire*, 36.
11. Anya Seton Bound Journals, June 30, 1950.
12. Anya Seton Bound Journals, February 26, 1950.
13. Anya Seton Bound Journals, April 18, 1950.
14. Anya Seton Bound Journals, May 5, 1950.
15. Anya Seton Bound Journals, May 5, 1950.
16. Anya Seton Bound Journals, June 2, 1950.
17. Anya Seton Bound Journals, January 22, 1951.
18. Anya Seton Bound Journals, February 10, 1951.
19. Anya Seton Bound Journals, January 25, 1950.
20. Anya Seton Bound Journals, March 2, 1951.
21. Anya Seton Bound Journals, July 28, 1953.
22. Anya Seton Bound Journals, July 30, 1956.
23. Anya Seton, "For the Atlanta Constitution by Anya Seton" (typescript), n.d., FTPC.

24. Anya Seton Bound Journals, December 15, 1949.

25. Seton, *Foxfire*, 6.

26. Seton, 305.

27. Book Jacket, Anya Seton, *Foxfire* (Boston: Houghton Mifflin Riverside Press edition, 1951).

28. Book Jacket, Seton, *Foxfire*.

29. Anderson, *The Chief*, 178.

30. Anya Seton Bound Journals, November 12, 1946.

31. Seton, *Foxfire*, 19.

32. Seton, 88.

33. E. Seton, *Gospel of the Red Man*, 3. When ETS used the term "Red Man," "Redman," or "Indian," he did not in any conscious or explicit sense intend the derogatory meanings now associated with them. He was generally guided in his usage by his friend and fellow activist Charles Eastman. "Redman," for him, meant a title coequal to and in a positive way opposite from "White Man."

34. Seton, *Foxfire*, 178.

35. Seton, 180.

36. G. Seton, *Poison Arrows*, 126–27.

37. Seton, *Foxfire*, 180.

38. Seton, 185.

39. Seton, 342.

9. Midway

1. Anya Seton Bound Journals, May 12, 1950.

2. Anya Seton, "Childhood Memories," September 21, 1948, 7.

3. Anya Seton Bound Journals, March 20, 1951.

4. Anya Seton Bound Journals, November 16, 1951.

5. Anya Seton Bound Journals, November 7, 1950.

6. Anya Seton Bound Journals, November 7, 1950.

7. Anya Seton Bound Journals, May 24,1951, and January 7, 1953.

8. Anya Seton Bound Journals, June 7 and November 7, 1950.

9. Anya Seton Bound Journals, November 7, 1950.

10. Anya Seton Bound Journals, November 26, 1950.

11. Anya Seton Bound Journals, November 26, 1950.

12. Anya Seton Bound Journals, January 2, 1951.

13. Anya Seton Bound Journals, June 5, 1951.

14. Anya Seton Bound Journals, March 2, 1951.

15. Anya Seton Bound Journals, April 27 and August 14, 1951.

16. Anya Seton Bound Journals, August 29, 1951.

17. Anya Seton Bound Journals, August 14, 1951.

18. Anya Seton Bound Journals, October 24, 1951.

19. Anya Seton Bound Journals, October 24 and November 16, 1951.

20. Anya Seton Bound Journals, November 16, 1951.

21. Anya Seton Bound Journals, November 22, 1951.

22. Anya Seton Bound Journals, January 7, 1952.

23. Anya Seton Bound Journals, February 1, 1952.

24. Anya Seton Bound Journals, February 6, 1952

25. Anya Seton Bound Journals, February 6, 1952.

26. Anya Seton Bound Journals, February 20, 1952.

27. Anya Seton Bound Journals, March 20, 1952.

28. Anya Seton Bound Journals, June 12, 1951, and February 6, 1952.

29. Doyle-Jones, foreword, *A Summer to Be*, 3.

30. Anya Seton Bound Journals, June 12, 1952.

31. Anya Seton Bound Journals, August 14, 1952.

32. Anya Seton Bound Journals, August 29, 1952.

33. Anya Seton Bound Journals, September 8, 1952.

34. Anya Seton Bound Journals, September 15, 1952.

35. Anya Seton Bound Journals, September 15, 1952.

36. Anya Seton Bound Journals, September 17, 1952.

37. Anya Seton Bound Journals, September 17, 1952.

38. Anya Seton Bound Journals, September 25, 1952.

39. Anya Seton Bound Journals, September 25, 1952.

40. Anya Seton Bound Journals, October 2, 1952

41. Anya Seton Bound Journals, October 2 & 15, 1952.

42. Anya Seton Bound Journals, October 11, 1952.

43. Anya Seton Bound Journals, October 31 and November 17, 1952.

44. Anya Seton Bound Journals, November 17, 1952.

45. Anya Seton Bound Journals, November 27, 1952.

46. Anya Seton Bound Journals, January 15, 1953.

47. Anya Seton Bound Journals, January 7, 1953.

48. Anya Seton Bound Journals, February 13, 1953.

49. Anya Seton Bound Journals, March 11, 1953.

50. Anya Seton Bound Journals, March 11, 1953.

51. Anya Seton Bound Journals, March 26, 1953.

52. Anya Seton Bound Journals, May 5 & 11, 1953.

53. Anya Seton Bound Journals, May 20, 1953.

54. Anya Seton Bound Journals, June 19, 1953.
55. Anya Seton Bound Journals, July 10, 1953.

10. Herstories

1. Anya Seton Bound Journals, October 9, 1953.
2. Alison Weir writes that the movie idea was shelved because of "the moral climate of 1950s America," which made it impossible to show the adulterous duke and duchess "enjoying a happy ending without incurring any penalties for their immorality." Weir, *Mistress of the Monarchy*, 309.
3. Anya Seton Bound Journals, November 5, 1953.
4. Anya Seton Bound Journals, October 9, 1953.
5. Anya Seton Bound Journals, September 14, 1953.
6. Anya Seton Bound Journals, June 11, 1954.
7. Anya Seton Bound Journals, June 20, 1954.
8. Anya Seton Bound Journals, July 8, 1954.
9. Anya Seton Bound Journals, July 24, 1954.
10. Anya Seton Bound Journals, September 27, 1954.
11. Anya Seton Bound Journals, September 28, 1954.
12. Anya Seton Bound Journals, October 3, 1954.
13. Anya Seton Bound Journals, October 3, 1954.
14. Anya Seton Bound Journals, October 24, 1954.
15. Anya Seton Bound Journals, October 3, 1954.
16. Anya Seton Bound Journals, September 23, 1953.
17. Anya Seton Bound Journals, October 9, 1953.
18. Anya Seton Bound Journals, October 9, 1953.
19. Anya Seton Bound Journals, August 21, 1954.
20. Anya Seton Bound Journals, August 21, 1953.
21. Anya Seton Bound Journals, July 1, 1954.
22. Seton, "For the Atlanta Constitution."
23. In an appendix to her exhaustively research biography *Mistress of the Monarchy*, Alison Weir provides an especially helpful assessment of Anya Seton's "vision" of *Katherine* (although her date for Anya's birth is in error; Seton was born in 1904). Weir stresses that *Katherine* was fiction, and as such was "of its own time," by which she means the time in which Anya wrote it, with the sources that were available to her and with the cultural biases of the 1950s. She also makes the case that the novel is "as much about Anya Seton as it is about Katherine Swynford." using as her source my online biography of the Setons ("The Setons at Home," www.nhc.rtp.nc.us:8080). Weir, *Mistress of the Monarchy*, 307–309.

24. Seton, *Katherine*, 298.
25. Seton, 544, 555–556.
26. Anya Seton Bound Journals, June 19, 1953.
27. Anya Seton Bound Journals, March 13, 1946.
28. Anya Seton to Frank Taylor, October 2, 1957, ASP, series 3.2 (General Correspondence), box 19, folder 103.
29. Anya Seton Bound Journals, July 12, 1954.
30. Seton, *Mistletoe and Sword*, 7.
31. Seton, 42, 46.
32. Seton, 76.
33. Anya Seton, "Radio Interview" (typescript), n.d., noted in Anya Seton Bound Journals, January 22, 1951.
34. Anya Seton Bound Journals, July 1, 1954.
35. Anya Seton Bound Journals, September 20, 1954
36. Anya Seton Bound Journals, December 27, 1954, and January 9, 1955.
37. Anya Seton Bound Journals, January 9, 1955.
38. Anya Seton Bound Journals, January 18 and March 2, 1955.
39. Anya Seton Bound Journals, March 2 & 4, 1955.
40. Anya Seton Bound Journals, March 10, 1955.
41. Anya Seton Bound Journals, April 1 and July 17, 1955.
42. Anya Seton Bound Journals, July 17, 1955.
43. Seton, *Mistletoe and Sword*, 252.
44. Anya Seton Bound Journals, March 20, 1952.

11. Dichotomies

1. Anya Seton Bound Journals, August 26, 1954.
2. Anya Seton Bound Journals, August 24, 1954.
3. Anya Seton Bound Journals, August 16, 1957.
4. Anya Seton Bound Journals, August 4, 1955.
5. Anya Seton Bound Journals, April 1 and June 8, 1955.
6. Anya Seton Bound Journals, April 1, 1955.
7. Anya Seton Bound Journals, April 8, 1955.
8. Anya Seton Bound Journals, April 1, 1955.
9. Anya Seton Bound Journals, June 23, 1955.
10. Anya Seton Bound Journals, August 4, 1955.
11. Anya Seton Bound Journals, August 15, 1955.
12. Anya Seton Bound Journals, August 16, 1957.
13. Anya Seton Bound Journals, July 31, 1955.

14. Anya Seton Bound Journals, September 2, 1955.

15. Anya Seton Bound Journals, September 25, 1955.

16. Anya Seton Bound Journals, September 26, 1955.

17. Anya Seton Bound Journals, October 22, 1955.

18. Anya Seton Bound Journals, October 25, 1955.

19. Anya Seton Bound Journals, November 4, 1955.

20. Anya Seton Bound Journals, November 4, 1955.

21. Anya Seton Bound Journals, November 28, 1955.

22. Anya Seton Bound Journals, December 12, 1955.

23. Anya Seton Bound Journals, December 21, 1955.

24. Anya Seton Bound Journals, January 2, 1956.

25. Anya Seton Bound Journals, February 11 & 23, 1956.

26. Anya Seton Bound Journals, April 10 & 21, 1956.

27. Anya Seton Bound Journals, May 31, 1956.

28. Anya Seton Bound Journals, June 25, 1956.

29. Anya Seton Bound Journals, July 1, 1956.

30. Anya Seton Bound Journals, July 1 & 17, 1956.

31. Anya Seton Bound Journals, July 22, 1956.

32. Anya Seton Bound Journals, August 3, 1956.

33. Anya Seton Bound Journals, August 3, 1956.

34. Anya Seton Bound Journals, November 7, 1956.

35. Anya Seton Bound Journals, December 31, 1956.

36. Anya Seton Bound Journals, February 18, 1957.

37. Anya Seton Bound Journals, February 25, 1957.

38. Anya Seton Bound Journals, June 10, 1957.

39. Anya Seton Bound Journals, June 14, 1957.

40. Anya Seton Bound Journals, June 10, 1957.

41. Anya Seton Bound Journals, June 14 and July 4, 1957.

42. Anya Seton Bound Journals, July 4, 1957.

43. Anya Seton Bound Journals, July 4, 1957.

44. Anya Seton Bound Journals, July 18, 1957.

45. Anya Seton Bound Journals, July 18 and August 4, 1957.

46. Anya Seton Bound Journals, August 16, 1957.

47. Anya Seton Bound Journals, August 16, 1957.

48. Anya Seton Bound Journals, August 16, 1957.

49. Anya Seton Bound Journals, August 16, 1957.

50. Anya Seton Bound Journals, August 26, 1957.

51. Anya Seton Bound Journals, September 5, 1957.

52. Anya Seton Bound Journals, September 5 & 9, 1957.

53. Anya Seton Bound Journals, September 14, 1957.

54. Anya Seton Bound Journals, September 23, 1957.

55. Anya Seton Bound Journals, August 16, 1957.

56. Anya Seton Bound Journals, September 14, 1957.

57. Anya Seton Bound Journals, September 23, 1957.

58. Anya Seton Bound Journals, November 28, 1957.

59. Anya Seton Bound Journals, January 23, 1957.

12. The Glass Crutch

1. Anya Seton Bound Journals, November 16, 1958.

2. Anya Seton Bound Journals, September 14, 1957.

3. Anya Seton Bound Journals, September 23, 1957.

4. Anya Seton Bound Journals, December 6, 1957.

5. Anya Seton Bound Journals, January 27, 1958.

6. Anya Seton Bound Journals, November 26, 1958.

7. Anya Seton Bound Journals, May 1, 1959.

8. Anya Seton Bound Journals, November 3, 1959.

9. Anya Seton Bound Journals, February 15, 1958.

10. Anya Seton Bound Journals, January 7, 1958.

11. Anya Seton Bound Journals, December 16, 1957.

12. Anya Seton Bound Journals, May 1, 1958.

13. Anya Seton Bound Journals, May 5, 1958.

14. Anya Seton Bound Journals, June 19, 1958.

15. Anya Seton Bound Journals, July 11, 1958.

16. Anya Seton Bound Journals, July 23, 1958.

17. Anya Seton Bound Journals, November 4, 1958.

18. Anya Seton Bound Journals, November 9, 1958.

19. Anya Seton Bound Journals, November 9, 1958.

20. Anya Seton Bound Journals, November 14, 1958.

21. Anya Seton Bound Journals, November 19, 1958

22. Anya Seton Bound Journals, November 26,1958.

23. Anya Seton Bound Journals, December 10, 1958.

24. Anya Seton Bound Journals, December 31, 1958.

25. Anya Seton Bound Journals, January 24, 1959.

26. Anya Seton Bound Journals, January 24, 1959.

27. Anya Seton Bound Journals, March 11, 1959.

28. Anya Seton Bound Journals, February 24, 1959.

29. Anya Seton Bound Journals, February 16, 1959.
30. Anya Seton Bound Journals, March 25, 1959.
31. Anya Seton Bound Journals, May 16, 1959.
32. Anya Seton Bound Journals, June 19, 1959.
33. Anya Seton Bound Journals, August 11, 1959.
34. Anya Seton Bound Journals, August 3, 1959.
35. Anya Seton Bound Journals, August 30, 1959.
36. Anya Seton Bound Journals, September 10, 1959.
37. Anya Seton Bound Journals, September 10, 1959.
38. Anya Seton Bound Journals, November 15, 1959.
39. Anya Seton Bound Journals, January 1, 1960.
40. Anya Seton Bound Journals, January 15, 1960.
41. Anya Seton Bound Journals, April 24, 1960.
42. Anya Seton Bound Journals, April 24, 1960.
43. Anya Seton Bound Journals, April 24, 1960.
44. Anya Seton Bound Journals, June 24, 1960.
45. Anya Seton Bound Journals, August 21, 1960.
46. Anya Seton Bound Journals, August 21, 1960.
47. Anya Seton Bound Journals, October 3, 1960.
48. Anya Seton Bound Journals, October 13, 1960.
49. Anya Seton Bound Journals, February 13 & 22, 1961.
50. Anya Seton Bound Journals, March 19, 1961.
51. Paul Brooks to Anya Seton, April 17, 1961, HMP.
52. Anya Seton to Paul Brooks, April 21, 1961, HMP.
53. Anya Seton Bound Journals, April 21 & 24, 1961.
54. Anya Seton Bound Journals, October 10, 1960.
55. Anya Seton Bound Journals, March 12, 1961.

13. There Is No Avalon

1. Anya Seton Bound Journals, May 9 & 15, 1961.
2. Anya Seton Bound Journals, May 15, 1961.
3. Anya Seton Bound Journals, May 24, 1961.
4. Anya Seton Bound Journals, May 16, 1961.
5. Anya Seton Bound Journals, June 8, 1961.
6. Anya Seton Bound Journals, July 7, 1961.
7. Anya Seton Bound Journals, June 25, 1961.
8. Anya Seton Bound Journals, July 1, 1961.
9. Anya Seton Bound Journals, August 7, 1961.

10. Anya Seton Bound Journals, August 11, 1961.
11. Anya Seton Bound Journals, September 30, 1961.
12. Anya Seton Bound Journals, November 16, 1961.
13. Anya Seton Bound Journals, February 2, 1962.
14. Anya Seton Bound Journals, February 10, 1962.
15. Anya Seton Bound Journals, February 2, 1962.
16. Anya Seton Bound Journals, March 12, 1962.
17. Anya Seton Bound Journals, February 22, 1962.
18. Scholes, "Jenny's Noble and Peasant Blood."
19. Anya Seton Bound Journals, November 15, 1959.
20. Seton, *Devil Water*, 117.
21. Anya Seton to Paul Brooks, April 21, 1961, HMP.
22. Anya Seton Bound Journals, March 19, 1962.
23. Anya Seton Bound Journals, July 14, 1961.
24. Anya Seton Bound Journals, August 8, 1962.
25. Anya Seton Bound Journals, March 12, 1962.
26. Anya Seton Bound Journals, April 16 & 18, 1962.
27. Anya Seton Bound Journals, May 3, 1962.
28. Anya Seton Bound Journals, May 17, 1962.
29. Anya Seton Bound Journals, May 25, 1962.
30. Anya Seton Bound Journals, July 30, 1962.
31. Anya Seton Bound Journals, August 1, 1962.
32. Anya Seton Bound Journals, September 22, 1962.
33. Anya Seton Bound Journals, November 19, 1962.
34. Anya Seton Bound Journals, October 23, 1962.
35. Anya Seton Bound Journals, October 26, 1962.
36. Anya Seton Bound Journals, November 25, 1963.
37. Anya Seton Bound Journals, November 30, 1963.
38. Anya Seton Bound Journals, December 8, 1962.
39. Anya Seton Bound Journals, July 31, 1963.
40. Anya Seton Bound Journals, December 5, 1962.
41. Anya Seton Bound Journals, January 5 & January 11, 1963.
42. Anya Seton Bound Journals, January 29, 1963.
43. Scholes, "Jenny's Noble and Peasant Blood."
44. Anya Seton Bound Journals, September 16 & 19, 1963.
45. Anya Seton Bound Journals, March 12 & 20, May 1, and July 20, 1963.
46. Anya Seton Bound Journals, July 13, 1964.
47. Anya Seton Bound Journals, August 16 & 30, 1964.

48. Anya Seton Bound Journals, December 15, 1964.
49. Anya Seton Bound Journals, January 2, 1965.
50. Anya Seton Bound Journals, April 26, 1965.
51. Paul Brooks to Anya Seton, April 12, 1965, HMP.
52. Brooks to Seton, April 12, 1965.
53. Anya Seton to Paul Hodder, May 7, 1965, FTPC.
54. Anya Seton to Graham Wilson, July 19, 1963, FTPC.
55. Anne Barrett to Paul Brooks, April 27, 1965, FTPC.
56. Anya Seton Bound Journals, April 26, 1965.
57. Anya Seton Bound Journals, May 19, 1965.
58. Anya Seton Bound Journals, June 3, 1965.
59. Anya Seton Bound Journals, September 15, 1965.
60. Anya Seton Bound Journals, September 15, 1965.
61. Seton, *Avalon*, 416.
62. Anya Seton Bound Journals, September 19, 1963.
63. Seton, *Avalon*, 427.
64. Anya Seton Bound Journals, October 23 and November 11, 1965.
65. Seton, afterword, *Avalon*, 439.

14. Into Green Darkness

1. Anya Seton Bound Journals, November 11, 1965.
2. Anya Seton Bound Journals, November 22, 1967.
3. Anya Seton Bound Journals, December 5, 1967.
4. Anya Seton Bound Journals, November 22, 1967.
5. Anya Seton Bound Journals, April 10, 1968.
6. Anya Seton Bound Journals, January 23, 1968.
7. Anya Seton Bound Journals, April 18, 1968.
8. Anya Seton Bound Journals, April 25, 1968.
9. Anya Seton Bound Journals, April 10, 1968.
10. Harriet Stix, "Successful Novelist," *New York Herald Tribune*, February 26, 1962, clipping, FTPC.
11. Anya Seton Bound Journals, April 18, 1968.
12. Anya Seton Bound Journals, April 25, 1968.
13. Anya Seton Bound Journals, August 24, 1968.
14. Anya Seton Bound Journals, August 24, 1968.
15. Anya Seton Bound Journals, January 2, 1967.
16. Anya Seton Bound Journals, October 27, 1966.
17. Anya Seton Bound Journals, October 27, 1966.

18. Anya Seton Bound Journals, May 25, 1973.
19. Anya Seton Bound Journals, April 25, 1968.
20. Anya Seton Bound Journals, October 10, 1968.
21. Anya Seton Bound Journals, April 18, 1968.
22. Anya Seton Bound Journals, October 10, 1968.
23. Anya Seton Bound Journals, January 31 and October 26, 1968.
24. Anya Seton Bound Journals, April 18, 1968.
25. Anya Seton Bound Journals, April 25, 1968.
26. Anya Seton Bound Journals, August 24, 1968.
27. Anya Seton Bound Journals, January 31, 1969.
28. Anya Seton Bound Journals, February 5, 1969.
29. Anya Seton Bound Journals, March 21, 1969.
30. Anya Seton Bound Journals, April 28, 1969.
31. Anya Seton Bound Journals, April 11 & 14, 1970.
32. Anya Seton Bound Journals, May 1, 1970.
33. Anya Seton Bound Journals, August 7, 1970.
34. Anya Seton Bound Journals, August 7, 1970.
35. Seton, *Green Darkness*, 577.
36. Seton, 33.
37. Anya Seton Bound Journals, August 21, 1970.
38. Anya Seton Bound Journals, January 4, 1971.
39. Anya Seton Bound Journals, March 21, 1971.
40. Anya Seton Bound Journals, January 22, 1972.
41. Anya Seton Bound Journals, January 22 and February 15, 1972.
42. Anya Seton Bound Journals, February 15, 1972.
43. Anya Seton to "Paul" (Brooks) and "Anne" (Barrett), February 15, 1972, ASP, series 5.12 (*Green Darkness*), box 40, folder 276.
44. Anne Barrett to Paul Brooks, February 22, 1972, HMP.
45. Seton, *Green Darkness*, 4.
46. Seton, 5.
47. Seton, 4.
48. Seton, preface, *Green Darkness*, x.
49. Seton, *Green Darkness*, 434.
50. Seton, preface, *Green Darkness*, x.
51. Anne Barrett, memorandum to Paul Brooks, February 22, 1972, HMP.
52. Barrett, memorandum to Brooks, February 22, 1972.
53. Anya Seton Bound Journals, April 18, 1973.
54. "Live Bombs and Dud People," *New York Times*, November 5, 1972.

55. Anya Seton Bound Journals, February 15, 1972.
56. Anya Seton Bound Journals, April 17 & 23, 1972.
57. Anya Seton Bound Journals, April 23, 1972.
58. Anya Seton Bound Journals, June 29, 1972.
59. Anya Seton Bound Journals, July 29, 1972.
60. Anya Seton Bound Journals, December 21, 1972.
61. Anya Seton Bound Journals, January 14, 1973.
62. Anya Seton Bound Journals, January 25, 1973.
63. Anya Seton Bound Journals, February 16, 1973.
64. Anya Seton Bound Journals, June 2 & 8, 1973.

15. The Source and She Were One

1. Anya Seton Bound Journals, April 28, 1969.
2. Anya Seton Bound Journals, December 21, 1972.
3. Anya Seton Bound Journals, June 8, 1973.
4. Brooks, *Two Park Street*, 132.
5. Brooks, 49.
6. Brooks, 48–50.
7. Anya Seton Bound Journals, September 28, 1972.
8. Anya Seton Bound Journals, February 16, 1973.
9. Anya Seton Bound Journals, February 23, 1973.
10. Anya Seton Bound Journals, April 18, 1973.
11. Pamela Forcey to Seton and Zizi, July 16, 1973, FTPC.
12. Anya Seton Bound Journals, June 8, 1973.
13. Anya Seton to Janet Chenery, August 1, 1973, ASP, series 5.2 (*Smouldering Fires*), box 26, folder 160.
14. Seton to Chenery, August 1, 1973.
15. Seton to Chenery, August 1, 1973.
16. Seton to Chenery, August 1, 1973.
17. Seton to Chenery, August 1, 1973.
18. Seton, preface, *Smouldering Fires*, 7.
19. Anya Seton, preface to *Smouldering Fires* (draft typescript), n.d., ASP, series 5.2 (*Smouldering Fires*), box 26, folder 162.
20. Janet Chenery to Anya Seton, November 21, 1974, ASP, series 5.2 (*Smouldering Fires*), box 26, folder 162.
21. Chenery to Seton, November 21, 1974.
22. Chenery to Seton, November 21, 1974.
23. Seton, *Smouldering Fires*, 117.

24. Seton, 155–56.
25. Seton, preface to *Smouldering Fires* (draft typescript).
26. Anya Seton, "Greenwich: A Personal Memoir," *Village Gazette*, October 16, 1980, clipping, FTPC.
27. Austin Olney to Anya Seton, January 3, 1980, HMP.
28. Lucinda MacKethan, interview with Blythe Forcey Toussaint, June 10, 2019.
29. Dorothy Friedman, "Anya Seton Shares New Novel Set in Greenwich," *Greenwich Time*, December 22, 1975, FTPC.
30. Friedman, "Anya Seton Shares New Novel."
31. Friedman, "Anya Seton Shares New Novel."

SELECTED
BIBLIOGRAPHY

"This thing is a means of watching life, but I never seem to get permanent conclusions."
—Anya Seton Bound Journals, July 22, 1963

Anya Seton Journals

Ann Seton Diary: Ann Seton started what she called her "little book," made up of dated entries, beginning in the summer of 1921, when she was seventeen. She continued writing these entries intermittently in notebooks until her marriage in 1923. These writings are housed in the Anya Seton Papers at the Greenwich Historical Society (ASP), series 1 (Biographical and Personal Material, 1904–1992), box 4.

Ann Cottier Diary: Ann Cottier began keeping another set of dated entries, what she called a "journal," in 1924, a year after her marriage while she and Hamilton lived in Oxford, England. She continued her entries when they returned to Princeton, New Jersey, in 1925 and kept them going after she left Hamilton in November 1929 to move to Reno, Nevada. She continued this set until her divorce was finalized and she married Hamilton Chase in February 1930. These writings are housed in the Anya Seton Papers at the Greenwich Historical Society (ASP), series 1 (Biographical and Personal Material, 1904–1992), box 4.

Anya Seton Bound Journals: On August 6, 1932, Ann began her first entry in a leather-bound, three-hundred-page journal that looked much more, physically, like a real "book." She recorded on page one that "this volume was bought in O'Reilley's Stationary, Kinston, N.Y." The nine volumes of these journals, all similar physically, will be housed in the GHS and are referenced in this work as Anya Seton Bound Journals. A tenth book disappeared during the last years of her life.

I have made no changes in the wording of the journals and changed punctuation marks in only a few instances, for clarity.

Other Archival Sources

This bibliography does not list the specific letters, newspaper clippings, biographical musings, diaries, or other archival documents bearing on Anya Seton's life. Those materials and the archives in which they are housed have been cited in the individual chapter notes using the following abbreviations.

ASP: Anya Seton Papers. Library & Archives at Greenwich Historical Society, Greenwich, CT.

FTPC: Forcey-Toussaint Private Collection. Longmont, CO.

HMP: Houghton Mifflin Papers. MS Am 2105 (225). Houghton Library, Harvard University.

RIHU: Papers of Grace Gallatin Seton-Thompson. Schlesinger Library. Radcliffe Institute, Harvard University. Series 1.

Published Works of Anya Seton

My Theodosia. Boston: Houghton Mifflin, 1941.

Dragonwyck. Boston: Houghton Mifflin, 1944

The Turquoise. Boston: Houghton Mifflin, 1946.

The Hearth and Eagle. Boston: Houghton Mifflin, 1948.

Foxfire. Boston: Houghton Mifflin, 1951.

Katherine. Boston: Houghton Mifflin,1954.

The Mistletoe and Sword: A Story of Roman Britain. New York: Doubleday, 1955.

The Winthrop Woman. Boston: Houghton Mifflin,1958.

Washington Irving. Boston: Houghton Mifflin, 1960.

Devil Water. Boston: Houghton Mifflin, 1962.

Avalon. Boston: Houghton Mifflin, 1965.

Green Darkness. Boston: Houghton Mifflin, 1973.

Smouldering Fires. New York: Doubleday, 1975.

Non-archival Secondary Sources

Anderson, H. Allen. *The Chief: Ernest Thompson Seton and the Changing West.* College Station: Texas A&M University, 1986.

Atta, John Van. "Ernest Thompson Seton and the Woodcraft Indians in Greenwich." *Greenwich History* 7 (2002): 9–27.

Bolt, Penny. "Seton's Indians." Oral history interview with Leonard S. Clark. Greenwich, CT: Friends of Greenwich Library, 1976.

Brizendine, Bodie. "Words shared at the 2016 Alumnae Luncheon, 'An Intellectual and Moral Adventure.'" Spence School, April 25, 2016. https://www.spenceschool .org/2017---bodies-vantage-points-news-detail?pk=849666.

Brooks, Paul. *Two Park Street: A Publishing Memoir.* Boston: Houghton Mifflin, 1986.

Côté, Richard. *Theodosia Burr Alston: Portrait of a Prodigy.* Mt. Pleasant, SC: Corinthian Books, 2003.

Doyle-Jones, Victoria. Forward to *A Summer to Be: A Memoir by the Daughter of Hamlin Garland,* by Isabel Garland Lord, 1–16. Edited by Keith Newlin. Lincoln: University of Nebraska Press, 2010.

Finz, Stacy. "Governor's Mansion Empty in Sacramento." *SFGate,* October 24, 2010. https://www.sfgate.com/homeandgarden/article/Governor-s-mansion-empty-in -Sacramento-3248686.php. September 21, 2019.

Forcey, Pamela. "Grace Gallatin Seton." *The Historical Society of the Town of Greenwich Newsletter,* Winter 1994: 1–5.

Garland, Hamlin. *Companions on the Trail.* New York: MacMillan, 1931.

Keller, Betty. *Black Wolf: The Biography of Ernest Thompson Seton.* Vancouver: Douglas and McIntyre, 1986.

MacKethan, Lucinda H. "Profile of Grace Gallatin Seton." *Legacy: A Journal of American Women Writers* 27, no. 1 (2010): 177–194.

New York Times. "Edmund Wilson Dies." June 13, 1972.

———. "Live Bombs and Dud People." November 5, 1972.

———. "Lee Barker Dead, Doubleday Aide." July 3, 1973.

Newark (OH) Daily Advocate. "Alonzo E. Cottier Gets Divorce." February 22, 1896. https://newspaperarchive.com/newark-daily-advocate-feb-22-1896-p-1/.

Roberts, Charles G. D. "The Home of a Naturalist." *Country Life in America,* December 1903.

Scholes, Robert. "Jenny's Noble and Peasant Blood." *New York Times,* February 25, 1962.

Seton, Ernest Thompson. *Wild Animals I Have Known.* New York: C. Scribner's Sons, 1898.

———. *Trail of an Artist-Naturalist: The Autobiography of Ernest Thompson Seton.* New York: C. Scribner's Sons, 1940.

———. *The Gospel of the Red Man: An Indian Bible,* 2nd ed. Santa Fe: Seton Village Press, 1948.

Seton, Grace Gallatin. *Poison Arrows: Strange Journey with an Opium Dreamer. Annam, Cambodia, Siam, and the Lotos Isle of Bali.* London: Travel Book Club, 1938.

Seton, Grace Thompson. *A Woman Tenderfoot in the Rockies.* New York: Doubleday, Page, 1900.

SELECTED BIBLIOGRAPHY | 279

——. *Nimrod's Wife.* New York: Doubleday, Page, 1907.

——. *A Woman Tenderfoot in Egypt.* New York: Dodd Mead, 1923.

——. *Chinese Lanterns.* New York: Dodd Mead, 1924.

——. *Yes, Lady Saheb.* New York: Harper and Brothers, 1925.

——. *Log of the Look-See.* London: Hurst and Blockett, 1932.

Seton, Julia. *By a Thousand Fires.* New York: Doubleday, 1967.

Stanton, Elizabeth Cady, et al. *The History of Women's Suffrage.* Rochester, NY: Charles Mann Press, 1922.

Steffens, Lincoln. *The Autobiography of Lincoln Steffens.* New York: Harcourt, 1931.

Ueland, Brenda. *If You Want to Write: A Book about Art, Independence and Spirit.* New York: Putnam's, 1938.

Uzzell, Thomas. *Narrative Technique: A Practical Course in Literary Psychology.* New York: Harcourt Brace, 1934.

Weir, Alison. *Mistress of the Monarchy: The Life of Katherine Swynford, Duchess of Lancaster.* New York: Ballantine, 2009.

Whitelock, William. "Ernest Seton-Thompson at Home. His Home in New York and a Conversation with Him There." *New York Times Saturday Review of Books and Art,* August 3, 1901.

Wilson, Edmund. "Ambushing a Best Seller." *New Yorker,* February 2, 1946. Reprinted in *Classics and Commercials: A Literary Chronicle of the 1940s.* New York: Farrar Strauss, 1950, 311–318.

——. "Portrait: Christian Gauss." *American Scholar* 21, no. 3 (Summer 1952): 345–355.

Witt, David. *Ernest Thompson Seton: The Life and Legacy of an Artist and Conservationist.* Layton, UT: Gibbs Smith, 2010.

INDEX